MICHAEL HAMBURGER

CONTRARIES
Studies in
German Literature

E. P. DUTTON & CO., INC. NEW YORK 1970

Published simultaneously in Canada by
Clarke, Irwin & Company Limited, Toronto and Vancouver

Library of Congress Catalog Card Number: 70-119479

SBN   0-525-08520-3

FIRST EDITION

Contents

Preface

Most of the studies presented here were written some fifteen years ago or more and collected in the volume *Reason and Energy* (1957), which has long been out of print. From their inception they were addressed less to specialists in German literature than to what, at that time, one still liked to think of as the general reader, a person interested in literature and ideas simply because they are interesting. In revising the early studies I have made no concessions to the specialists. Even factual information that will be familiar to them, and therefore redundant, has been retained in the hope that its usefulness to nonspecialists will outweigh its redundancy for them. The biographical sections, in any case, are as brief as possible, and they can easily be skipped.

As for interpretation, although my assumptions and attitudes have changed, very little could be done about that. A few judgments have been qualified or reformulated, but anyone who is rash enough to involve himself in judgments at all, to commit himself to the inescapable subjectivity of criticism, as distinct from pure scholarship, must also bear the consequences, including the embarrassment of being confronted with his outgrown selves. If an exception has been made in the case of Gottfried Benn, it is because I now find my earlier conclusions about his work not only opinionated but positively wrong. The polemical character of the whole study had to do with the circumstance that I was engaged with a living writer whom I found at once admirable and exasperating. The general character of that study, too, could not be changed; but since I had come to see that my quarrel with Benn's ideas had led me to misjudge and misread some of his later poems, my original conclusions had to be revised.

To the studies in *Reason and Energy* I have added a later essay on Hölderlin and Milton—more overtly comparative than the other studies, though all are comparative in perspective— partly to make up for the excised sections of the original Hölderlin chapter. These excised sections were an interpretation of a single long poem, an interpretation invalidated for me not so much by what other people have written about the poem as by my later concern with the question of the kind of truth that poetry such as Hölderlin's may be expected to embody and enact. I have also added the Nietzsche and Thomas Mann sections of a later book, *From Prophecy to Exorcism* (1965), because of their relevance to the dominant theme of the earlier pieces.

MICHAEL HAMBURGER

London
July, 1969

Without Contraries is no progression. Attraction and Repulsion, Reason and Energy, Love and Hate, are necessary to Human existence.

WILLIAM BLAKE

An absolute urge towards perfection and completeness is a kind of disease, as soon as it adopts a destructive and hostile attitude towards the imperfect, the incomplete.

NOVALIS

Part I

Part I

I

HÖLDERLIN

The gnomic grandeur of Hölderlin's late poetry, his prophetic and visionary hymns, is of a kind that must strike an unprepared reader as not only strange and perplexing, but as anachronistic. These hymns have no parallel in any modern literature, either of Hölderlin's time or later. Yet, unique and esoteric as they are, the hymns become clearer in the light of Hölderlin's earlier work and even of general trends perceptible in the German literature of Hölderlin's time. Such background features, it goes without saying, can no more explain its unique qualities than the climate and soil of its setting explain the shape, color, or scent of a plant; their only function here is to make Hölderlin's late poetry more accessible to readers who might otherwise be repelled by its oddity. It is well known that these hymns are the work of a poet who had suffered at least one serious mental breakdown and was about to succumb to incurable madness; but the fact is irrelevant. The hymns show no slackening of intellectual control. What makes them difficult throughout, ambiguous and obscure in parts, is the heightened concentration of all the poet's faculties on a single task. They are incoherent only where they are fragmentary; and, unlike the poems of Hölderlin's madness proper, they are never inane. Hölderlin's mature poetry was the product of so intense a development, compressed into a period of time so incredibly short, that one could easily be misled into treating it as a single poetic sequence, rather than a series of poetic sequences whose only unity is that of growth. The whole body of his mature work can be divided into three principal phases: the idealistic, the tragic, and the prophetic. These phases, as one would expect, are not wholly distinct; but they are sufficiently so to provide rough boundary lines that help one to find one's way. But since growth is a cyclic process, it is important to treat these phases as concentric circles; few poets have been as conscious as Hölderlin that the "course of life" is circular, its end linked to its beginning. A few of the poems that Hölderlin wrote in his late adolescence, such as the powerful "Die Bücher der Zeiten," [1] are closer to his tragic and prophetic phases than to the idealistic phase that followed these early attempts.

Hölderlin's idealistic phase was coeval with the "classical" phase of the German literary renaissance, which was instituted by Goethe and Schiller as a deliberate campaign against forces that they themselves had once invoked. It was the eruption of these forces, the chthonic powers, in the seventeen-seventies that made modern German literature different from any other. After releasing the chthonic powers in *Werther* and in his early dithyrambic verse, Goethe spent the rest of his life in the strenuous and multiple endeavor to put them back in their place. In the seventeen-nineties, after his own period of *Sturm und Drang*, Schiller applied his very different gifts to the same task; and Hölderlin, who began as Schiller's disciple and protégé, dedicated his early poetry to the same didactic, enlightening and educational function, that of a secular priest who expounds not scripture, but philosophy. Yet from the start, Hölderlin had grave doubts about this function. Schiller found it difficult enough to cope with the philosophy of Kant; but Hölderlin had to come to terms with the teaching of Kant's successors, espe-

[1] *Works* (Grosse Stuttgarter Ausgabe) I (i), 69–74.

cially with that of Fichte, whose lectures he attended in 1794 and 1795. Hölderlin's novel *Hyperion* shows how deeply and dangerously Fichte's ideas affected him.

Just because German classicism was so much of a hothouse growth, carefully and lovingly fostered in the shelter of little Weimar in defiance of the tempests raging outside, Goethe could not afford to be generous to younger writers, like Hölderlin and Kleist, whom he could not fit into his civilizing scheme. Just because his own balance was so precarious, Goethe grew intolerant of all that was morbid, one-sided or self-destructive. Hence his horror of the tragic in later life, the incongruous redemption of his Faust in Part II, his fear of music. (The "spirit of music," which Nietzsche was to relate to tragedy, became a powerful influence on the Romantics; because Goethe was so susceptible to its vague incitements, but felt it to be an anticlassical force, he made a point of learning to use his eyes, of studying concrete phenomena and counting out hexameters on his mistress' back.[2] Yet Goethe's all-embracing philosophy, his morphological view of nature, history, and art, resembled the thought of Hölderlin and Novalis in being syncretic; it could only attain the cohesion of a system by continually breaking down the barriers of orthodoxy, both theological and scientific, by resolving long-accepted antinomies and by applying an almost mystical vision to the most diverse empirical disciplines.) This achievement, made possible only by his genius and by that wisdom to which T. S. Eliot paid tribute,[3] is unprecedented and inimitable; and so, in its different way, is Hölderlin's, though Hölderlin begged in vain to be admitted to the shelter of Weimar or Jena, struggled heroically with all the daemons of the age and transcended tragedy by approving his own destruction.

The transition from Hölderlin's idealistic phase to the tragic was gradual. Many of his early odes in classical meters—those written before 1799—uphold the ideals of Hölderlin's youth against experiences and forces that threaten them. Thus in his ode "Der Mensch," [4] of 1798, his idealistic vision of man con-

[2] See Goethe's *Römische Elegien.*
[3] In *Goethe as the Sage* (Hamburg, 1955).
[4] *Works* (Grosse Stuttgarter Ausgabe) I (i), 263. English rendering in my *Hölderlin: Poems and Fragments* (London and Ann Arbor, Michigan, 1967), p. 75.

flicts with a tragic one. Man is the most highly gifted and blessed of all living creatures. Like the rest of creation, he is the child of Earth, the material principle, and of Helios, the spiritual; but, unlike his fellow creatures, he has an irresistible urge to better himself, to explore, to advance, to idealize, "to sacrifice a certain present for something uncertain, different, better and still better," as Hölderlin explained in another context.[5] The tension of the poem arises from Hölderlin's dual view of the human condition. Considered idealistically, Man's urge to improve himself accounts for human progress, in which Hölderlin the philosopher continued to believe long after Hölderlin the poet had begun to contradict him; considered tragically, it is the *hubris* that estranges men from Nature, offends the gods and involves the offender in endless conflict and suffering. Hölderlin does his best to reconcile the two views, by that progression through contraries so characteristic of his poetry; but "Der Mensch" is one of the few poems of this period in which his tragic vision predominates.

Hölderlin's dualism—the dualism of a poet whose whole work, at the time, was directed toward pantheistic communion with "all that lives," whose principal doctrine was the ἕν και πάν, One and All, of antiquity—would be difficult to understand but for his prose works of that period, *Hyperion*, the letters and the philosophical fragments. As we can see in *Hyperion*, with its cycles of exaltation and dejection, Hölderlin's desire to be at one with the cosmos continually came up against his philosophical awareness of complete isolation from the rest of the created world. This awareness, confirmed by the solipsistic idealism of Fichte and its development by Hölderlin's own friends, Hegel and Schelling, accounts for those moments in *Hyperion* that shock the reader by their unexpected cynicism, by their nihilistic despair. *Hyperion,* in fact, is pervaded by the same dualism.

"Man is a god when he dreams, a beggar when he reflects" [6] Hyperion writes. Dreaming here means the state of mind that permits communion with Nature; reflection, the self-consciousness that cuts off the individual from the rest of creation. It is

<hr/>

[5] Letter to his half-brother, June, 1799. *Works* (G.S.A.) VI (i), 327.
[6] *Works* (Zinkernagel) II, 14.

the alternation of these states of mind, with infinite variations and a gradual progression toward synthesis, that gives *Hyperion* its peculiar structure, an almost musical structure that suggests sonata form. The two themes are elaborated in another passage: "There is an oblivion of all existence, a silencing of all individual being, in which it seems as if we had found all things.

"There is a silencing, an oblivion of all existence, in which it seems as if we had lost all things, a night of the soul, in which not the faintest gleam of a star, not even the phosphorescence of rotten wood can reach us." [7]

The difference between these states of mind is that between being and existence. The positive state is that in which we forget ourselves because we feel at one with the world; the negative state is that in which we forget the world and are conscious only of ourselves. When Hyperion is plunged into this negative state of mind, what had been "all" before suddenly turns into nothing; he becomes like one of those persons whom he pities for being "in the grip of that Nothing which rules over us, who are thoroughly conscious that we are born for Nothing, that we love a Nothing, believe in a Nothing, work ourselves to the bone for Nothing, until we gradually dissolve into Nothing . . ." [8]

It is clear enough from these extracts that Hölderlin's pantheistic faith had a reverse side of unmitigated pessimism. This dichotomy goes back to Rousseau's doctrine that what is natural is good, all evil is due to the corrupting influence of civilization. The German adaptation of this doctrine was to identify evil with consciousness itself, to deify Energy and discredit Reason. Schiller had contributed to this adaptation by his distinction between "naïve" and "sentimental" literature, for the "naïve" embraced all that is natural and spontaneous, the "sentimental" all that is the result of reflection. Kleist was to make the antithesis even more extreme; and it has been developed by German writers ever since.[9]

[7] *Ibid.*, 57.
[8] *Ibid.*, 61.
[9] See p. 141; and compare Thomas Mann's antithesis between "intellect" and "life" (*Geist* and *Leben*). D. H. Lawrence presents an English parallel.

In a letter of 1797 [10] Hölderlin characterized the evils of his time in terms of the following antinomies: "Culture and crudity . . . Unreasoning cleverness, unclever reason. Mindless sensibility, insensitive mind . . . Energy without principles, principles without energy." The remedy, he proposed in the same letter, was a marriage of the "childlike heart" to the "virile mind."

Hölderlin's work entered its tragic phase when he could no longer accept any of the philosophical explanations of evil current in his time. Though he was reluctant to revert to any doctrine that reminded him of his theological studies, his view of the human condition—even in the comparatively early poem "Der Mensch"—does presuppose something not unlike original sin. There is an obvious connection between the knowledge of good and evil in Genesis and the foreknowledge of death that distinguishes Hölderlin's Man from his fellow creatures. Hölderlin's pantheism, in essence, was the aspiration to return to the state that preceded the Fall of Man. Now this pantheism was gradually modified by Hölderlin's recognition that evil is inherent in Nature and in Man; and that there is a gulf between the human and the divine, a gulf that men ignore at their peril.

In his letters of this transitional period, Hölderlin still clung to the philosophic humanism of his youth. As late as 1799 he assured his half-brother of the "salutary effect of philosophic and political literature on the education of our country." Because the Germans, by nature, are *"glebae addicti* and in one way or another, literally or metaphorically, most of them are bound to their little plots"; because they lack "elasticity" and breadth, "Kant is the Moses of our nation, who leads them out of their Egyptian inertia into the free and open desert of his speculations, and who brings down the rigorous law from the holy mountain." [11] Yet in the course of the same month Hölderlin confessed to his mother that all his philosophical studies —undertaken against his inclinations out of the fear that his poetry would be condemned as "empty"—left him not only unsatisfied, but restless and unpleasantly excited: and that he al-

---

[10] To. J. G. Ebel. *Works* (G.S.A.) VI (i), 229. English version of Christopher Middleton in *The Poet's Vocation* (Austin, Texas, 1967), p. 13.

[11] *Works* (G.S.A.), VI, 303–304.

ways longed to return to his "dear occupation," poetry, much as "a conscripted Swiss shepherd longs for his valley and his flock." [12] The matter was not as simple as that. Hölderlin remained a truly philosophical poet; but the philosophy to which he felt drawn as a poet was not that of contemporary Germany, but that of pre-Socratic Greece; a philosophy close to religious experience and to myth: a philosophy of nature unencumbered with modern subjectivity. It was not only because of his legendary suicide that Hölderlin made Empedocles the protagonist of an unfinished tragedy.

Hölderlin's last attempt to become a *praeceptor Germaniae* in the humanistic tradition of Goethe and Schiller was his plan to edit a journal, *Iduna,* in 1799. Its purpose, as he defined it in a letter to a publisher interested in the scheme, was as follows: "The unification and reconciliation of the sciences with life, of art and good taste with genius, of the heart with the head, of the real with the ideal, of the civilized (in the widest sense of the word) with nature—this will be the general character, the spirit of the journal." [13] In a later letter to Schelling, whom he asked for a contribution, Hölderlin very aptly described it as a "humanistic journal," but was careful to distinguish his own humanism from the so-called humanism of others.[14]

The failure of this project, and Schiller's failure to find Hölderlin a congenial post as an alternative to the project, which he advised Hölderlin to abandon, was a decisive turning point. It meant that Hölderlin must give up hope, once and for all, of having any influence on the public of his time; and, since it deprived him of his last possibility of economic independence, it meant that he was faced once more with the drudgery and humiliation of being a private tutor, just when he was ready to write his greatest poetry and when his nerves could no longer bear the strain of petty frustrations and irritations. To read his subsequent letters is a harrowing experience. Even before his enforced separation from Susette Gontard he had felt that his fate would be a tragic one; but he had resisted this feeling. While he was at Homburg, where he would have remained if

[12] *Ibid.,* 311.
[13] *Ibid.,* 335.
[14] *Ibid.,* 346.

the journal had materialized, he was still able to communicate with Susette and to meet her, though only rarely and furtively. Now he was to lose his last support against the sense of personal tragedy. As he had foretold in 1798, all that remained was his art and the quite impersonal faith that sustained his art; he had come to the end of that respite for which he begged the Fates in 1798:

> Nur Einen Sommer gönnt, ihr Gewaltigen!
>> Und einen Herbst zu reifem Gesange mir,
>>> Dass williger mein Herz, vom süssen
>>>> Spiele gesättiget, dann mir sterbe.

> Die Seele, der im Leben ihr göttlich Recht
>> Nicht ward, sie ruht auch drunten im Orkus nicht;
>>> Doch ist mir einst das Heil'ge, das am
>>>> Herzen mir liegt, das Gedicht gelungen,

> Willkommen dann, o Stille der Schattenwelt!
>> Zufrieden bin ich, wenn auch mein Saitenspiel
>>> Mich nicht hinabgeleitet; Einmal
>>>> Lebt' ich, wie Götter, und mehr bedarfs nicht.

> One summer only grant me, you powerful Fates,
>> And one more autumn only for mellow song,
>>> So that more willingly, replete with
>>>> Music's late sweetness, my heart may die then.

> The soul in life denied its god-given right
>> Down there in Orcus also will find no peace;
>>> Yet when what's holy, dear to me, the
>>>> Poem's accomplished, my art perfected,

> Then welcome silence, welcome cold world of shades!
>> I'll be content, though here I must leave my lyre
>>> And songless travel down; for *once* I
>>>> Lived like the gods, and no more is needed.

What Hölderlin did not know when he wrote this poem is that long after his heart had indeed died, as he says, his "mellow song" would continue; that the music of his strings *would* escort him down. And, whereas in 1798 he spoke of being denied the "divine" rights that were due to him, later he was to regard the death of his heart as a just punishment. The question as to the immediate cause of his mental breakdown in 1802 seems almost pointless when one reads the terrible letters of the two preceding years. By 1800 Hölderlin had given himself up. In thanking his sister for writing to remind him of their family bond, he tells her that "this sustains my heart, which in the end too often loses its voice in a loneliness all too complete and withdraws from our very selves." [15] If these words seem strange, so is the state of mind which they convey. Hölderlin's feelings were withdrawing from his own self and from all those who had once been close to him. The poetry of his tragic and prophetic phases became more and more impersonal, till they were more like oracles than the utterances of a man; and he came to accept his own self-estrangement as a punishment for overreaching himself, for having lived once as the gods live. This is what he implies in one of his last intelligible letters, written after his return from Bordeaux, when he tells his friend that "as one relates of heroes, I can well say that Apollo has struck me." [16] Hölderlin was probably thinking of the mythical poet Linos, who was killed by Apollo—or, according to a different legend, brained with his own lyre by Hercules—for the sin of presumption, of *hubris*. The exact nature of the sin that Hölderlin imputed to himself is specified in his *Empedocles* fragments and in several of the late hymns.

Hölderlin's plans for an Empedocles tragedy go back to his Frankfort period, to 1797. Earlier still, he had intended to write a *Death of Socrates;* significantly, his subject had been closer to modern times and to his own philosophical preoccupations in his idealistic phase. Socrates—very much like Hyperion—would have been represented as a kind of martyr to the materialism, narrow-mindedness, and corruption of his age, the victim of a reactionary ruling class and a hypocritical priesthood. Even when Empedocles took the place of Socrates, much of this conception survived. Hölderlin's three successive drafts show how he gradually abandoned this modern conception of the hero as martyr. In the last version of all, Empedo-

[15] *Ibid.,* 402–403.
[16] *Ibid.,* 432.

cles is no longer hounded to his death by the Archon, the Chief Priest and an irresponsible mob, but, from the start, looks upon his death as the necessary expiation of his own guilt. Hölderlin has substituted a truly tragic conception, derived from his insights into Greek tragedy and from his own immediate experience.

While he was at work on *Empedocles,* Hölderlin wrote down his reflections on the differences between epic, lyric, and tragic poetry. A lyric poem, he says, is "the continuous metaphor of a feeling." A tragic poem, on the other hand, is the "metaphor of an intellectual point of view"; and this intellectual point of view "can be none other than the awareness of being at one with all that lives." [17] To this definition one should add a considerably later one, part of Hölderlin's commentary on his translation of *Oedipus Rex,* published in 1804: "The representation of the tragic is mainly based on this: that what is monstrous and terrible in the coupling of god and man, in the total fusion of the power of Nature with the inmost depth of the man, so that they are one at the moment of wrath, should be made intelligible by showing how this total fusion into one is purged by their total separation." [18] This statement is almost as cryptic and mysterious as the poems that Hölderlin wrote in his last, oracular phase; for that very reason, it is highly relevant not only to the last *Empedocles* fragment, but to many of his odes, elegies and hymns. Hölderlin himself recognized such a genre as the "tragic ode"; and much of his later poetry, according to his own definitions, is not lyrical at all, but tragic, precisely because it hinges on the mystery to which this statement points.

Empedocles is in conflict with the rulers and priesthood of Agrigentum because he has received the direct inspiration of the mystic and visionary; because he has been aware of "being at one with all that lives" and experienced a "total fusion" with the divine. This privilege might have been forgiven him if he had not also tried to convey this inspiration to the community

---

[17] *Works* (Zinkernagel) II, 368–371. See also Meta Corssen's excellent applications of these definitions to Hölderlin's poetic practice in *Hölderlin-Jahrbuch* (Tübingen) for 1948/9 and 1951.

[18] *Works* (G.S.A.) V, 201.

at large, thus traducing them from established religion and morality, as well as being guilty of profaning a mystery. In the first version, Hölderlin's sympathy with the protagonist blurs the tragic issue; for it causes him to put too much stress on the external conflict and to weigh the scales too heavily in Empedocles' favor, at the expense of the Archon and the Chief Priest. In the second, but more fragmentary, version, he allows the Priest to utter the crucial accusation, which Empedocles himself admits and confirms:

Verderblicher denn Schwerd und Feuer ist
Der Menschengeist, der götterähnliche,
Wenn er nicht schweigen kann, und sein Geheimniss
Unaufgedekt bewahren. Bleibt er still
In seiner Tiefe ruhn, und giebt, was noth ist,
Wohlthätig ist er dann; ein fressend Feuer,
Wenn er aus seiner Fessel bricht.
Hinweg mit ihm, der seine Seele blos
Und ihre Götter giebt, verwegen
Unauszusprechendes aussprechen will
Und sein gefährlich Gut, als wär es Wasser,
Verschüttet und vergeudet; schlimmer ists,
Wie Mord, und du, du redest für diesen? [19]

More ruinous than sword or raging fire
Is human spirit, though akin to gods,
If it can not keep silent and contain
Its secret unexposed. If in its depth
It lies at rest and proffers what is needed,
Wholesome it is; a wild devouring flame
As soon as from its fetters it breaks loose.
Away with that man who lays bare his soul
And, with it, his soul's gods, recklessly seeks
To utter the unutterable, wasting
His dangerous wealth like water lightly spilt.
That folly is worse than murder; and can you,
Can you, of all men, plead on his behalf?

The idealism and the unqualified pantheism of Hölderlin's youth had been beyond good and evil; but now his profound re-

[19] *Works* (G.S.A.) IV (i), 97.

flections on the nature of tragedy taught him that the desire to "be at one with all that lives" was a Titanic urge, rebellious, chaotic, and destructive. As Arthur Häny has already demonstrated in convincing detail,[20] after *Empedocles* the Titanic nature of the desire for "boundless," unlimited being became increasingly clear to Hölderlin, and allusions to the Titan myth itself assumed a new significance in his works. I shall have more to say of it in connection with the hymns. At this point I should like to note that already in *Hyperion* there are important allusions to the Titans; but, as Häny observes, Hölderlin is still inclined to see the Titanic urge as something wholly positive, in the manner of Goethe's *Prometheus* and the *Sturm und Drang* in general.

In the preceding version of *Empedocles,* the protagonist had chosen to die mainly because he was the "vessel" of divine Nature, and such vessels must be broken before they can be profaned by being put to a merely human use. In the later version Empedocles accuses himself of having presumptuously risen above his own nature and profaned divine mysteries. His blasphemy, which he repeats ironically to his disciple Pausanias,[21] was nothing less than the nihilistic skepticism already present in *Hyperion* as the reverse side of the pantheistic urge. It is the Fichtean solipsism that transforms a holy cosmos into the meaningless creation of the individual mind, All into Nothing: and it is a form of *hubris* that has beset a whole succession of modern poets not necessarily burdened with Hölderlin's philosophical tasks, to reconcile natural religion with the extreme forms of German idealistic philosophy. (Walt Whitman, in all seriousness, asks the same question: ". . . [for without me what were all? what were God?] . . .")

The death of the heart, both in *Empedocles* and in Hölderlin's more personal odes and elegies, has a particular significance. Pantheism is a religion of the heart,[22] as distinct from a religion of the *logos;* the human heart is that "vessel" into which the gods pour the divine frenzy that moves the poet and

[20] *Hölderlins Titanenmythos* (Zürich, 1948).
[21] Quoted below (p. 63 of *The Sublime Art.*)
[22] Cf. the chapter on Hölderlin in Hermann Boeschenstein, *Deutsche Gefühlskultur* (Berne, 1954), 189–220.

seer to celebrate them. Even in his late poems, right up to "Patmos"—in which he came as near as was possible for him to a religion of the *logos*—Hölderlin continued to expound the doctrine that the gods need men in order to realize their being; and the particular service that men render the gods is to "feel" on their behalf:

> . . . Denn weil
> Die Seeligsten nichts fühlen von selbst,
> Muss wohl, wenn solches zu sagen
> Erlaubt ist, in der Götter Nahmen
> Theilnehmend fühlen ein Andrer,
> Den brauchen sie.[23]

> . . . For since
> The most Blessed in themselves feel nothing,
> Another, if to say such a thing is
> Permitted, must, I suppose,
> Vicariously feel in the name of the gods,
> And him they need.

It is this anthropomorphic, or at least anthropocentric, conception of the divine that links Hölderlin to Novalis, Rilke, and the existentialism of Heidegger;[24] its corollary is the religious function of the poet and seer, who becomes no mere guardian of the word, but the indispensable mediator between gods and men, literally creating the world anew so that the divine may realize itself in the human, just as the human realizes itself in the divine. But since the feeling heart of men is the means by which this necessary interchange takes place, it follows that when the poet's or seer's heart becomes incapable of feeling, he is not only cut off personally from communion with the divine, but rendered incapable of fulfilling his religious duty toward the gods. This gives a terrible and cruel twist to his punishment by the death of the heart; for the punishment in turn implicates him in an offense no less serious than his original *hubris*. Hölderlin did his utmost to break out of this vicious circle. Though

[23] *Der Rhein* (1801). *Works* (G.S.A.) II (i), 145.
[24] See Martin Heidegger, *Erläuterungen zu Hölderlins Dichtung* (Frankfurt am Main, 1951).

he almost collapsed under the burden of his dual guilt, he succeeded in resolving the dilemma. The way in which he did so was to interpret his punishment as a sacrifice; and gradually to modify his anthropocentric conception of the divine, together with his view of the poet's function. This modification is already implied in the passage quoted above, by the doubt he expresses as to whether his anthropomorphic attribution is permissible. In many of his later poems two fundamentally different religious conceptions run parallel: an anthropocentric one, according to which the gods are transient and mutable, because they are partly dependent on the capacity of their worshipers to "endure" the searing intensity of divine revelation; and a theocentric one of the *logos*. For above the hierarchy of transient gods, demigods, and heroes, Hölderlin recognized the immutable divine Spirit, the "God of gods." [25]

The transition from Hölderlin's tragic phase to the prophetic, again, is not one that can be neatly dated. "Wie wenn am Feiertage . . . ," the earliest of his hymns and the only one in which he attempted to reproduce the strict Pindaric structure, was written as early as 1799; but it remained unfinished, not so much, perhaps, because of the difficult form—Hölderlin had already mastered forms quite as refractory—as because Hölderlin was still overwhelmed by his personal affliction, and knew that Pindar's public ode form could not be adapted for the expression of a private grief. Where the public theme breaks off, Hölderlin's prose draft continues with an agonized confession of his own guilt. This passage not only clashes violently with the oracular character of the foregoing strophes, but seems to contradict what they say about the poet's religious function.

> Doch weh mir! wenn von
> [selbgeschlagener Wunde das Herz mir blutet, und tiefver-
> loren
> der Frieden ist, u. freibescheidenes Genügen,
> Und die Unruh, und der Mangel mich treibt zum
> Überfluss des Göttertisches, wenn rings um mich]

[25] "Der Götter Gott." In *Versöhnender . . . Works* (G.S.A.) II (i), 132.

Weh mir!

[Und sag ich gleich, ich wär genaht, die Himmli(schen zu)
schauen, sie selbst sie werfen mich tief unter die Lebenden
alle, den falschen Priester hinab, dass ich, aus Nächten herauf,
das warnend ängstige Lied den Unerfahrenen singe.[26]]

But woe is me! when from
[a self-inflicted wound my heart is bleeding, and deeply lost
are peace and the contentment of true modesty,
And when unrest and lack drive me towards
The superfluity of the gods' own table, when round about me]

Woe is me!

[And let me say at once: that I approached to look
upon the heavenly beings, they cast me down themselves,
far down beneath all the living
cast the false priest, so that now from the depth of nights
I should sing for the inexperienced my awed and warning
                                                    song.]

This gruesome self-exposure—with its allusion to the Tantalus
myth, which identifies Hölderlin's sin with the *hubris* of
Empedocles—is certainly out of place in his oracular hymn;
but it does not really contradict what he has just said about the
poet's function:

Doch uns gebührt es, unter Gottes Gewittern,
Ihr Dichter! mit entblösstem Haupte zu stehen,
Des Vaters Stral, ihn selbst, mit eigner Hand
Zu fassen und dem Volk ins Lied
Gehüllt die himmlische Gaabe zu reichen.
Denn sind nur reinen Herzens,
Wie Kinder, wir, sind schuldlos unsere Hände,
Des Vaters Stral, der reine versengt es nicht . . .

Yet, fellow poets, us it behooves to stand
Bare-headed beneath God's thunderstorms,
To grasp the Father's ray, no less, with our own two hands
And, wrapping in song the beautiful gift,

[26] *Ibid.*, 120; and II (ii), 669–670.

> To offer it to the people.
> For if only we are pure in heart,
> Like children, and our hands are guiltless,
> The Father's ray, the pure, will not sear our hearts . . .

What Hölderlin is making clear is the difference between the humility of the true priest and the arrogance of the false one; this is also the essential difference between his own idealistic phase and his prophetic one. In his idealistic phase he had been moved by the Titanic urge to violate the divine mysteries, instead of waiting patiently for the moment of revelation. God's lightning had seared his heart precisely because it was impure, filled with Titanic impatience.

This tragic impulse is not confined to heroes, poets, and seers; it can affect not only individuals, but whole peoples, as Hölderlin relates in his tragic ode of 1801, the second version of "Stimme des Volkes" ("Voice of the People"):

> Du seiest Gottes Stimme, so glaubt' ich sonst
> In heil'ger Jugend; ja, und ich sag' es noch!
>   Um unsre Weisheit unbekümmert
>   Rauschen die Ströme doch auch, und dennoch,
>
> Wer liebt sie nicht? und immer bewegen sie
> Das Herz mir, hör' ich ferne die Schwindenden,
>   Die Ahnungsvollen meine Bahn nicht
>   Aber gewisser ins Meer hin eilen.
>
> Denn selbstvergessen, allzubereit den Wunsch
> Der Götter zu erfüllen, ergreift zu gern
>   Was sterblich ist, wenn offnen Augs auf
>   Eigenen Pfaden es einmal wandelt,
>
> Ins All zurük die kürzeste Bahn; so stürzt
> Der Strom hinab, er suchet die Ruh, es reisst,
>   Es ziehet wider Willen ihn, von
>   Klippe zu Klippe den Steuerlosen
>
> Das wunderbare Sehnen dem Abgrund zu;
> Das Ungebundene reizet, und Völker auch
>   Ergreift die Todeslust und kühne
>   Städte, nachdem sie versucht das Beste,
>
> Von Jahr zu Jahr forttreibend das Werk, sie hat
> Ein heilig Ende troffen; die Erde grünt

    Und stille vor den Sternen liegt, den
        Betenden gleich, in den Sand geworfen,

Freiwillig überwunden die lange Kunst
    Vor jenen Unnachahmbaren da; er selbst,
        Der Mensch, mit eigner Hand zerbrach, die
            Hohen zu ehren, sein Werk der Künstler . . .

The voice of God I called you and thought you once,
    In holy youth; and still I do not recant!
        No less indifferent to our wisdom
            Likewise the rivers rush on, but who does

Not love them? Always too my own heart is moved
    When far away I hear those foreknowing ones,
        The fleeting, by a route not mine but
            Surer than mine, and more swift, roar seaward,

For once they travel down their allotted paths
    With open eyes, self-oblivious, too ready to
        Comply with what the gods have wished them,
            Only too gladly will mortal beings

Speed back into the All by the shortest way;
    So rivers plunge—not movement but rest they seek—
        Drawn on, pulled down against their will from
            Boulder to boulder—abandoned, helmless—

By that mysterious yearning toward the chasm;
    Chaotic deeps attract, and whole peoples too
        May come to long for death, and valiant
            Towns that have striven to do the best thing,

Year in, year out pursuing their task—these too
    A holy end has stricken; the earth grows green,
        And there beneath the stars, like mortals
            Deep in their prayers, quite still, prostrated

On sand, outgrown, and willingly, lies long art
    Flung down before the Matchless; and he himself,
        The man, the artist with his own two
            Hands broke his work for their sake, in homage.[27]

------

[27] *Works* (G.S.A.) II (i), 51–53. English rendering of the whole poem
in *Hölderlin, Poems*, 231–235.

In the opening lines Hölderlin suggests that there is a difference between his youthful belief in the truth of *vox populi, vox dei* and his present, modified acceptance of it; but he does not say in what that difference consists. Coleridge's comment on the same dictum is illuminating: "I never said that the *vox populi* was of course the *vox Dei*. It may be; but it may be, and with equal probability, *a priori, vox Diaboli*. That the voice of ten millions of men calling for the same thing, is a spirit, I believe; but whether that be a spirit of Heaven or Hell, I can only know by trying the thing called for by the prescript of reason and God's will." [28] Hölderlin, by 1801, was well aware of this ethical aspect of the tragic, self-destructive urge; and his awareness of it may well account for the reticent opening lines. If he never explicitly condemns the urge in this poem—except insofar as he disassociates himself from the river's impetuosity— but treats it under the aspect of sacrifice, it is mainly because the function of chronicler, which is Hölderlin's here, demands a perspective different from the prophet's and moralist's; but the tragic mystery remained present in his poetry throughout his prophetic phase. On the one hand, his understanding of tragic *hubris* brought him closer to a Christian view of good and evil; Lucifer is closely related to Prometheus and the Titans. On the other, it caused him to treat even the death of Christ as a tragic sacrifice, in a sense much more Greek than Christian.

Hölderlin's great elegies, written between 1799 and 1801, form a transition from the tragic to the prophetic mode. *Menons Klagen um Diotima,* written in 1800, still alternates between the tragic mode and the idealistic; although in the last section Hölderlin turns to the future, his prediction is not prophetic in the larger sense of the hymns. But *Brod und Wein,* begun later in the same year, *Der Archipelagus* and *Heimkunft* complete the transition.

The relation between the different modes is particularly striking in another ode of 1801, the second version of "Ermunterung" ("Exhortation"), with its sudden modulation from personal lament to impersonal prophecy:

[28] *Table Talk* (Ashe, 1888), 160.

Echo des Himmels! heiliges Herz! warum,
  Warum verstummst du unter den Lebenden,
    Schläfst, freies! von den Götterlosen
      Ewig hinab in die Nacht verwiesen?

Wacht denn, wie vormals, nimmer des Aethers Licht?
  Und blüht die alte Mutter, die Erde nicht?
    Und übt der Geist nicht da und dort, nicht
      Lächelnd die Liebe das Recht noch immer?

Nur du nicht mehr! doch mahnen die Himmlischen,
  Und stillebildend weht, wie ein kahl Gefild,
    Der Othem der Natur dich an, der
      Alleserheiternde, seelenvolle.

O Hoffnung! bald, bald singen die Haine nicht
  Des Lebens Lob allein, denn es ist die Zeit,
    Dass aus der Menschen Munde sie, die
      Schönere Seele sich neuverkündet,

Dann liebender im Bunde mit Sterblichen
  Das Element sich bildet, und dann erst reich,
    Bei frommer Kinder Dank, der Erde
      Brust, die unendliche, sich entfaltet

Und unsre Tage wieder, wie Blumen, sind,
  Wo sie, des Himmels Sonne sich ausgetheilt
    Im stillen Wechsel sieht und wieder
      Froh in den Frohen das Licht sich findet,

Und er, der sprachlos waltet und unbekannt
  Zukünftiges bereitet, der Gott, der Geist
    Im Menschenwort, am schönen Tage
      Kommenden Jahren, wie einst, sich ausspricht.

Echo of heaven, heart that are hallowed, why,
  Why do you now fall silent, though living still,
    And sleep, you free one, by the godless
      Banished for ever to Night's deep dungeons?

Does not the light of Aether, as always, wake?
  And Earth, our ancient mother, still thrive and flower?
    And here and there does not the spirit
      Love with a smile wield her laws as ever?

You only fail! Yet heavenly powers exhort,
   And silently at work like a stubble field,
      The breath of Nature blows upon you,
         She the all-brightening, soul-inspiring.

O hope! now soon, now soon not the groves alone
   Shall sing life's praise, for almost the time is come
      When through the mouths of mortals this, the
         Lovelier soul will make known her coming.

Allied with men more lovingly then once more
   The element will form and, not rich or full
      But when her pious children thank her
         Endless the breast of our Earth unfolds then,

And once again like blossoms our days will be
   Where heavenly Helios sees his own light shared out
      In quiet alternation, finding
         Joy in the joy of those mortal mirrors,

And He who silent rules and in secret plans
   Things yet to come, the Godhead, the Spirit housed
      In human words, once more, at noontide,
         Clearly will speak to the future ages.

The inception of this poem goes back to 1799; since Hölderlin blames his godless persecutors, rather than his own tragic offense, for the apathy of his heart, it may well have been written before the last version of *Empedocles,* during the crisis that he characterized in retrospect as a loss of faith in "eternal Love":

I was now to fall into the terribly superstitious belief in that which is certainly a sign of the soul and of Love but, misunderstood in this way, is the death of both. Believe me, dearest brother, I had struggled to the point of deadly exhaustion to fix my faith and my vision upon that which is highest in life; indeed, I had struggled amidst sufferings which—to judge by all the evidence of which I know—were more overwhelming than anything that men are capable of enduring, though they exert their utmost strength.—I am not telling you this without good reason.—At last, when my heart was torn on more sides than one, and yet held fast, I must also be induced to embroil my thoughts in those evil doubts, that question so

easily solved if only one's eyes are clear, namely: what is
more important, the eternal source of all life or the temporal.
Only too complete a contempt for all that is necessary was
capable of leading me into that greater error of gazing too
intently, with a truly superstitious earnestness, at everything
external, that is, at everything outside the realm of the heart,
so as to make it my own. But I continued to struggle until I
found out the truth . . . There is only one quarrel in this
world: which is more important, the whole or the individual
part. And that quarrel, in every instance and application, is
proved invalid in action, because the man who acts truly out
of a sense of the whole, for that very reason, is more dedicated to peace and more disposed to honor every individual
person and thing, since his sense of humanity, just what is
most individual to him, will sooner permit him to fall into
egoism, or whatever you choose to call it, than into pure generality.

   A Deo principium. Whoever understands this and acts accord-
ingly . . . that man is free and strong and joyful . . .[29]

This account of his Homburg crisis—and, more important still,
of the renewed faith that followed the crisis—helps to explain
why Hölderlin could now dispense with the progression through
contraries of his earlier odes. Only the third strophe of "Ermunterung" serves as a transition from the personal theme to the
prophetic; and it makes the transition by implying that the
poet's immediate state of mind, the apathy of his heart, does
not have the absolute significance that he would once have attributed to it. The full frenzy of inspiration is withheld from
him, but even that lack has its purpose in the divine order, just
as winter has its place in the natural order of the year. Hölderlin can turn to prophecy because he has resolved the dilemma
of his idealistic phase, with its tension between the particular
and the general, between the ego conscious of its isolation and
the holy cosmos with which it longs to unite. As the imagery of
his early poetry shows, Hölderlin had once been apt to "fall
into pure generality"; for his idealism had hinged on the modern distinction between subjective and objective reality. Like
his new faith, the poetry of his prophetic phase was to reconcile

[29] Letter to his half-brother (1801). *Works* (G.S.A.) VI (i), 418–419.

the timeless with the temporal, the whole with the part, the individual phenomenon with the Platonic Idea. The change, once
again, is most apparent in his imagery: the visionary landscapes
of the hymns are both concrete and symbolic, specific and general, just as the figures in those landscapes are both historical
and mythical, individual and allegorical.

It is essential, therefore, to interpret Hölderlin's prophecies
without too pedantic a concern with their temporal aspect. To
complain that one of these prophecies has not yet come true is
as foolish as to complain that Hölderlin's vision of ancient
Greece does not accord with all the historical and archeological
facts. The analogy is not irrelevant; for, in one respect at least,
Hölderlin's visionary exploration of the past corresponds exactly to his visionary exploration of the future. The purpose of
both journeys was to embody spiritual truths in a wholly poetic
manner, that is, in a manner that bridges the gulf between the
ideal and the actual without recourse to the language of philosophy. More than one of the hymns explores both the past and
the future; and the present moment too receives its due, in the
light that past and future shed on it to reveal both its temporal
and its timeless significance.

I cannot deal here with all the manifold aspects of Hölderlin's concern with the past and the future, or with the complex
relation between his Greek and "Hesperian" visions. To do so,
I should have to analyze all those poems in which he turned
from one to the other, sometimes to connect them, sometimes
to take leave of ancient Greece because he was no longer permitted to converse with the dead:

> Nicht sie, die Seeligen, die erschienen sind,
> Die Götterbilder in dem alten Lande,
> Sie darf ich ja nicht rufen mehr, wenn aber
> Ihr heimatlichen Wasser! jezt mit euch
> Des Herzens Liebe klagt, was will es anders,
> Das Heiligtrauernde? Denn voll Erwartung liegt
> Das Land und als in heissen Tagen
> Herabgesenkt, umschattet heut
> Ihr Sehnenden! uns ahnungsvoll ein Himmel.
> Voll ist er von Verheissungen und scheint
> Mir drohend auch, doch will ich bei ihm bleiben.

Und rükwärts soll die Seele mir nicht fliehn
Zu euch, Vergangene! die zu lieb mir sind.
Denn euer schönes Angesicht zu sehn,
Als wärs, wie sonst, ich fürcht' es, tödtlich ists
Und kaum erlaubt, Gestorbene zu wecken.

Entflohene Götter! auch ihr, ihr gegenwärtigen, damals
Wahrhaftiger, ihr hattet euere Zeiten!
Nichts läugnen will ich hier und nichts erbitten.
Denn wenn es aus ist, und der Tag erloschen
Wohl trifts den Priester erst, doch liebend folgt
Der Tempel und das Bild ihm auch und seine Sitte
Zum dunkeln Land und keines mag noch scheinen.
Nur als von Grabesflammen, ziehet dann
Ein goldner Rauch, die Sage drob hinüber,
Und dämmert jezt uns Zweifelnden um das Haupt,
Und keiner weiss, wie ihm geschieht . . .[30]

Not them, the blessed, who once appeared,
The images of gods in the ancient land,
Them, it is true, I may not now invoke, but if,
You waters of my homeland, now with you
The love of my heart laments, what else does it want, in
Its hallowed sadness? For full of expectations lies
The country, and as though it had been lowered
In sultry dog-days, on us a heaven today,
You yearning rivers, casts prophetic shade.
With promises it is fraught, and to me
Seems threatening too, yet I will stay with it,
And backward now my soul shall not escape
To you, the vanished, whom I love too much.
To look upon your beautiful brows, as though
They were unchanged, I am afraid, for deadly
And scarcely permitted it is to awaken the dead.

Gods who are fled! And you also, present still,
But once more real, you had your time, your ages!
No, nothing here I'll deny and ask no favours.
For when it's over, and Day's light gone out,
The priest is the first to be struck, but lovingly
The temple and the image and the cult

---

[30] "Germanien" (1801 or 1802). *Works* (G. S. A.) II (i), 149.

Follow him down into darkness, and none of them now may
                                                      shine.
Only as from a funeral pyre henceforth
A golden smoke, the legend of it, drifts
And glimmers on around our doubting heads
And no one knows what's happening to him . . .

Even this, perhaps the most impassioned of all Hölderlin's
leave-takings from ancient Greece, is far from being unambi-
guous. The main reason that the poet must no longer invoke the
Greek gods in this poem is that he loves them too much; for
this excessive love, only because it is excessive, would prevent
him from observing the moderation, or "measure" as he calls it,
which Hölderlin now thought incumbent on the poet-seer.
Hölderlin's duty now is to strike the right balance between
past, present, and future. If he were wholly preoccupied with
the Greek gods, he would be unable to respond to those "promises" and "forebodings" that the present landscape conveys to
him; but those promises and forebodings are of a new epiphany
of the gods in which the Greek gods, too, will take part. The
leave-taking, therefore, cannot be isolated from the prediction
that follows it. Nor is it permissible to assume that Hölderlin
took leave of the Greek gods in order to transfer his devotion to
Christ; before *Patmos* at any rate, his work provides no basis
for that assumption. In the first draft of his hymn "Der Einzige"
("The Only One") of 1802, he condemns his attachment to Christ
for the very same reason—because it threatens to become exclusive:

> . . . Ich weiss es aber, eigene Schuld
> Ists! Denn zu sehr,
> O Christus, häng' ich an dir . . .
>
> And yet I know, it is my
> Own fault. For too greatly,
> O Christ, I'm attached to you . . .

and he attributes this fault to the immoderation of his heart:

Es hänget aber an Einem
Die Liebe. Diesesmal
Ist nemlich vom eigenen Herzen
Zu sehr gegangen der Gesang,
Gut machen will ich den Fehl
Wenn ich noch andere singe.
Nie treff ich, wie ich wünsche,
Das Maas.[31]

To One alone, however
Love clings. For this time too much
From my own heart the song
Has come; if other songs follow
I'll make amends for the fault.
Much though I wish to, never
I strike the right measure.

As Hölderlin himself implies here, his statements in one hymn are qualified by his statements in another; and one would need to be quite certain about their exact chronology to attempt a general account of his relation to the Greek gods and to Christ in his prophetic phase.

The leave-taking in "Germanien" raises another important issue. This particular hymn is dedicated to Germany; and—as Hölderlin told Princess Auguste von Homburg in his dedication to her of his translations from Sophocles—"apart from these, if time permits, I will sing (in praise of) the parents of our princes, their seats and the angels of our holy country." [32] Yet one must beware of misinterpreting and misapplying these words. To begin with, they are more likely to refer to those hymns that Hölderlin was planning to write immediately before his final breakdown than to those that he was able to complete; and even his last fragmentary hymns bear such titles as "To Our Lady," "The Vatican," and "Columbus," as well as "The Titans" and "Greece." Others are devoted to German subjects; but even these "national" fragments preclude too narrow an interpretation of the words "the parents of our princes." As for

[31] *Works* (G. S. A.) II (i), 154, 155.

[32] *Ibid.* V, 119–120. The Princess, incidentally, was secretly in love with Hölderlin. See Werner Kirchner, *Das "Testament" der Prinzessin Auguste von Hessen-Homburg. Hölderlin-Jahrbuch* (1951), 68–120.

the "angels of our holy country" (or "fatherland"), Hölderlin used the word "angels" as an equivalent for the tutelary spirits, the *genii loci, lares,* and *penates* of the ancients; in the last of his elegies, *Die Heimkunft,* he addresses the "angels of our house," once again lending a peculiar extension of meaning to the word "house," which stands for a whole region or country, but country in a different sense from nation. In the same way, the words "holy country" could well denote not Germany— which, in any case, was not a nation at the time—but the whole of modern Europe, as distinct from ancient Greece.

The "waters of home," with which Hölderlin now contents himself, are filled with a yearning for other places. The reason that Hölderlin desires nothing but those waters is that he has already satisfied his yearning for what was foreign to him, by his past explorations of ancient Greece. He is therefore ready to return home, to "go to the source" as he says elsewhere, and face the most difficult task of all, that of learning "what is proper to oneself." "What is proper to oneself must be learnt just as much as what is foreign," he wrote to his friend Böhlendorff. "That is why the Greeks are indispensable to us. Only we shall never equal them in those very qualities which are proper, native to us and national, because, as I have said, the free use of what is proper to one is the most difficult thing of all." [33] What was proper to the Greeks, the same letter explains, was their "holy pathos"; for that very reason they became masters of the descriptive and narrative arts, ever since Homer was "spirited enough to acquire occidental Junonian sobriety for his Apollonian realm."

Hölderlin's hymns, then, aim at a fusion of the ancient and the modern, a fusion already indicated by their formal structure, a free adaptation of the Pindaric ode. Their diction, too, combines the "holy pathos" of the Greeks with the "occidental" sobriety proper to the Germans; it has the directness of popular speech, but a directness that can be more evasive than the most intricate of euphuisms. Hölderlin had learnt the lesson of his Empedocles. The doctrine of his hymns may be no less heterodox than the pantheistic teaching of his Empedocles, but we

---

[33] Letter of December 4, 1801. *Works* (G.S.A.) VI (i), 426.

can never be absolutely sure what that doctrine is. Hölderlin constantly alludes to mysteries known to no other poet, but he is careful not to give them away or to explain them in other but mysterious terms. His hymns are direct and ambiguous, in the manner of oracles; and their ambiguity is due not to confusion —though wherever Christ is in question, even in the last version of *Patmos,* Hölderlin is apt to be overwhelmed by conflicting emotions, so that his balance is threatened—but to the discreet suppression of the logical and syntactical links between one image or idea and another. These logical gaps are the stylistic counterpart of the mysteries to which the hymns allude, but only to "circumscribe" them, as Hölderlin says in "Germanien":

> . . . Denn Sterblichen geziemet die Schaam,
> Und so zu reden die meiste Zeit,
> Ist weise auch von Göttern.
> Wo aber überflüssiger, denn lautere Quellen
> Das Gold und ernst geworden ist der Zorn an dem Himmel,
> Muss zwischen Tag und Nacht
> Einsmals ein Wahres erscheinen.
> Dreifach umschreibe du es,
> Doch ungesprochen auch, wie es da ist,
> Unschuldige, muss es bleiben.

> For shame behooves us mortals,
> And most of the time to speak thus
> Of gods indeed is wise.
> But where more superabundant than purest wellsprings
> The gold has become and the anger in heaven earnest,
> For once between Day and Night must
> A truth be made manifest.
> Now threefold circumscribe it,
> Yet unuttered also, just as you found it,
> Innocent virgin, let it remain.

Hölderlin knew exactly what the hymns must reveal and what they must conceal; and the commentator, too, proves only his folly if he tries to fill all the gaps that Hölderlin so carefully left unfilled, corresponding, as they do, to the void that holds the mystery. Writing of *Patmos* as long ago as 1935, Edwin

Muir drew attention to this peculiarity of Hölderlin's hymns: "This omission of connecting links is characteristic of the poem, and I think of the kind of poetry to which it belongs, where mystery is not a thing to be explained, but a constant and permitted presence." [34] Too many of Hölderlin's commentators have disregarded the warning contained in that penetrating observation. The very mysteriousness of these poems invites exegesis of a kind that violates the mystery by resolving ambiguities.

Strangely enough, this difficulty has never been more apparent than at the present time. The work of few poets has received the concentrated and expert attention that Hölderlin's work has received in the past half century; but the more the experts know about his work, the more they are made aware of what they do not and cannot know. For a few brief years it may have seemed as if all the crucial problems had been, or were being, solved; but this state of truce was shattered by the discovery in June, 1954, of a lost hymn by Hölderlin, his "Friedensfeier," and by the violent controversy to which its publication gave rise.

The voluminous controversy over the interpretation of "Friedensfeier" cannot be summarized here. Hölderlin's little preface to the poem attests that he was well aware of its difficulty: "All I ask is that the reader be kindly disposed toward these pages. In that case he will certainly not find them incomprehensible, far less objectionable. But if, nonetheless, some should think such a language too unconventional, I must confess to them: I cannot help it. On a fine day—they should consider—almost every mode of song makes itself heard; and Nature, whence it originates, also receives it again.

"The author intends to offer the public an entire collection of such pieces, and this one should be regarded as a kind of sample."

This preface has the dual importance of being one of Hölderlin's very few comments on his later poetry and of being the only one addressed to its potential readers. Not only does it re-

[34] "Hölderlin's *Patmos," The European Quarterly,* Vol. I, No. 4 (February, 1935); and in Edwin Muir, *Essays on Literature and Society* (London, 1949), 90–102.

veal his intention to publish "Friedensfeier" and other poems of the same kind—in fact only one of his late hymns, "Die Wanderung," was published before his mental breakdown—but it offers a laconic apology for a "language" that Hölderlin knew to be without parallel in his time. Even in this late phase of his development he appealed to the authority of Nature, not to any supernatural privilege that might be due to the seer or prophet. If this distinction implies an antagonism between the natural and the spiritual that remained alien to Hölderlin even when Christ had become the "jewel" of his pantheon, the analogy with birdsong is still a modest one. (In another poem of this phase it is "beginners" who "learn from nightingales.") Nature remained the starting point of Hölderlin's poetry, as the movement of "Friedensfeier" itself bears out, since Nature dominates its opening and closing triads. Nature, too, justified the poet's idiosyncracies of style and structure, because those idiosyncracies were as natural to him as any bird's peculiar song is to that bird. This points to a quality of Hölderlin's genius that distinguishes him from many lesser and more self-conscious poets who have assumed the prophet's function. As another great visionary poet, William Blake, affirmed, "no bird soars too high, if he soars with his own wings." Because Hölderlin soared so high it was wise of him to disarm his potential reader's mistrust by modestly stating that his wings were his own—as indeed they were, despite his debt to Pindar.

"Difficulty," in T. S. Eliot's words, "may be caused by the reader's having been told, or having suggested to himself, that the poem is going to prove difficult. The ordinary reader, when warned against the obscurity of a poem, is apt to be thrown into a state of consternation very unfavorable to poetic receptivity . . . The more seasoned reader, he who has reached, in this matter, a state of greater *purity,* does not bother about understanding; not, at least, at first." Hölderlin's appeal to Nature is also an appeal for the reader's trust, since that trust is conducive to an open mind, to the receptivity of which Eliot speaks; and the most effective means of winning the reader's trust is to assure him of the inevitability of the difficulties he is invited to face. These difficulties, too, are "natural," as distinct from the willful and affected obscurities that ingenuous readers distrust.

As Hölderlin wrote to the publisher who failed to produce
"Friedensfeier" and other hymns, "it is a pleasure to sacrifice
oneself to the reader and, with him, to confine oneself to the
narrow bounds of our as yet childlike culture." [35] Yet Hölderlin's magnificent integrity did not permit him to make any real
concessions to his public; his "sacrifice" took the form of the
purest and most selfless love, a love that was never recipro-
cated.

This love, communicated in utter solitude, can be sensed behind the impersonal pronouncements of "Friedensfeier"; for the
desire to communicate with a public remote from him in space
and in time helped him to discover that timeless and spaceless
dimension in which his late poetry moves. This spaceless and
timeless dimension is not to be identified with the past or the
future; but Hölderlin's exploration of past and future served to
strip the immediate moment of its merely phenomenal significance. "Friedensfeier" begins with a definite historical moment,
the Peace of Lunéville concluded in February, 1801, and goes
on to illuminate that moment by looking forward and back for
its full significance. The prophetic glance, as Edwin Muir observed in his essay on *Patmos,* is not different in kind from the
backward glance:

> To divine the workings of God in history is what we gener-
> ally call prophecy. The prophet in the narrower sense foresees
> these workings in the future: Hölderlin saw them in the past,
> in the universal history of mankind. Yet the prophetic gift, if
> we are to allow it all, consists rather in that perception than in
> the uses for which it is employed, and it is that perception
> which gives the prophetic part of Hölderlin's poetry its unique
> intonation, its loneliness as of a single voice speaking to the
> gods amidst vast spaces. His utterance at its most intense is
> like that of a man accounting to himself for things which he
> cannot tell to others. The impression of vastness given by his
> poetry is partly caused, I think, by the fact that the past with
> all its powers—gods, heroes, emanations—seemed to be as
> real to Hölderlin as the present. It was not something that
> could be thrown into contrast, or paralleled, with the present,

[35] Letter to Friedrich Wilmans, December, 1803. *Works* (G.S.A.) VI
(i), 436.

as in the poetry of Mr. Eliot and Mr. Pound. It entered into and incalculably widened the present; and this expansion gives us a feeling not of a strictly demarcated period in some ways like and in some unlike other periods, but of a vast and indivisible whole, a universal dispensation which is the life of mankind from beginning to end. As all prophecy looks to the fulfilment of time, this vastness is a constant element in prophetic literature, whether it is written by Isaiah or Blake or Hölderlin, and is at the source of its shadowiness and its grandeur.

"Friedensfeier," too, is not merely a prophetic poem, but a chiliastic one; for it looks to the fulfillment of time, in this case, to the reconciliation of all the gods at the "Evening of Time."

The opening triad is devoted to the temporal occasion that called forth the poem. Characteristically, Hölderlin sets the scene by a description both concrete and symbolic of the banqueting hall, conveyed in a long opening period that serves to create suspense. For the banqueting hall, of course, is capable of indefinite extension in space and time, being the immediate site of a historical event, a landscape that is "familiar" —so that one thinks of a region close to the poet's home or to one's own—and an anagoge of Nature itself, for Nature is familiar to all men. The ambiguity and the suspension prepare us for the appearance of persons and powers of more than temporal import, of the guests already announced at the end of the opening strophe.

If mystery, suspense, and ambiguity are of the essence of that opening evocation of the banqueting hall—and Hölderlin wrote a theoretical justification of the syntactical inversions, suspensions, and ellipses that are their structural enactment—the same is true of those personages whose identity was the main bone of contention in the war of the "Friedensfeier" exegetes. The very next strophe, the antistrophe of the first triad, opens with a syntactical ambiguity:

Und dämmernden Auges denk' ich schon
Vom ernsten Tagwerk lächelnd,
Ihn selbst zu sehen, den Fürsten des Fests.

> And already with eyes dusk-dim,
> With solemn day-labour smiling
> I think that I see him in person, the prince of the feast day.

Here both "with eyes dusk-dim" and "with solemn day-labour smiling" should be attributes of the "I," not of the prince of the feastday, according to the strict rules of grammar. The first attribution makes sense however we apply it. The second seems to apply primarily to the prince, because of the peculiar significance given to "Tagwerk," day-labor, throughout the whole poem. Yet unless we believe that Hölderlin was no longer capable of simple grammatical construction—in which case much of the exegesis lavished on this and other late poems would be a waste of time—the important thing to be apprehended here is that Hölderlin does employ ambiguity, just as he takes care not to name or particularize the identity of the prince. Neither the prince nor Christ, who is celebrated in the second triad as the chief guest to be invited to the feast, is ever named in the poem —a notable instance of Hölderlin's resort to circumlocution in these late poems. If Hölderlin was in command of his intellectual faculties at this point—and I am convinced that he was—a proper reading of his late poems demands that we do not attach names to those figures and presences that he chose to leave unnamed. Within the context of each poem, the nameless Christ of "Friedensfeier" is not identical with the named Christ of "Der Einzige."

In the epode of the second triad of "Friedensfeier," Hölderlin records that even in the age of "wilderness"—the period which began with the death of Christ—men enjoyed the use of divine gifts, but without being aware of it. During the age of wilderness the gods are only distantly and vicariously present in the affairs of men. Their presence is perceptible in the forces of Nature and in the stars, from which men learn something about the divine mystery, though without that direct communication that would permit names. In one of Hölderlin's late mythological odes, "Chiron," these lines occur:

> Und bei der Sterne Kühle lernt' ich,
> Aber das Nennbare nur.

And in the cool of stars I learned, but
Only the namable.

Paracelsus writes: "And mark well this point, that all natural
art and wisdom are given to men by the stars, and that nothing
is excepted; that all things are given to us by the stars, and we
are the students of the stars, and the stars are our teacher." [36]
But this is only the case at times when there is no wisdom other
than natural wisdom, when there is no direct revelation of
God's will. And in "Friedensfeier," Hölderlin turns to the new
revelation about to be granted. God the Father—the source of
all life—has granted a sign; and Christ, too, has been recognized as a living power, though this power was concealed during the preceding age. In *Patmos,* Hölderlin was to write:

> Still ist sein Zeichen
> Am donnernden Himmel. Und Einer steht darunter
> Sein Leben lang. Denn noch lebt Christus.

> Now silent is
> His sign on thundering heaven. And there is one who stands
> Beneath it his whole life long. For Christ lives yet.

But in "Friedensfeier" Christ is not recognized until God the
Father gives that sign. The "Geist der Welt" is another circumlocution for the Father, this time as the mind that directs, and
lends significance to, history. Once again Hölderlin may have
been thinking of St. John 4: "God is a Spirit"; but the influence
on Hölderlin's thought of his friendship with Hegel and of Hegel's early writings may also be relevant here.[37]

Another ambiguity occurs in the opening of the third triad of
"Friedensfeier." There the subject could be either Christ or
God the Father. From the evidence of Hölderlin's other poetry
—but this evidence is not conclusive—the opening strophe
would seem to refer to God the Father, who, during the period
of "wilderness," became too great to rule temporally and

---

[36] Paracelsus, *Schriften* (Kayser) (Leipzig, 1924), 328.
[37] See B. Allemann, *Hölderlin's "Friedensfeier"* (Pfullingen, 1955), 40–
41; and his reference to Kant's *Zum ewigen Frieden,* 30.

"averted His face from mankind" (*Brod und Wein*). In "Der Einzige," too, Hölderlin writes:

> Denn nimmer herrscht er allein

> For never He reigns alone

and, in a draft of the same poem, elaborates this statement as follows: "Immer stehet irgend/ Eins zwischen Menschen und ihm./ Und treppenweise steiget/ Der Himmlische nieder." ("One or another always/ Stands between men and Him./ And step by step/ The Heavenly One descends.") Yet the supreme God Himself may choose to participate actively in the affairs of men; by sharing "all manner of fate," like mortals, and revealing His will in history; "Tagwerk," daily labor, stands for the historical, temporal activities of men. At this point Hölderlin asserts his belief in a kind of free will: although God's active participation in history creates a new, communal fate, the individual's will is not suspended; the new communal spirit does not suppress individual differences, but blends them into harmony. That is why Hölderlin can now express his personal hopes for the new era. His own belief, as formulated in a letter to his brother of 1801, was that the Peace "will bring about much that many hope for, but it will also bring about what few expect. Not that any one form, any one conviction or opinion will prevail, . . . but that egoism in all its forms will yield to the holy dominion of Love and Goodness, that the communal spirit will reign supreme, and that in such a climate the German heart, amidst the blessings of this new peace, will only begin to unfold and, silently, like burgeoning Nature, develop its secret, far-reaching powers . . ." [38] Two later letters, written after the conclusion of the Peace of Lunéville, confirm these hopes; [39] but Hölderlin emphasizes their nonpolitical nature.

The antistrophe of the second triad relates these hopes to the past and the future. One of the characteristics of the past era was that men were isolated, "each man forged to his labour, only his own, and in the workshop's uproar hears only

[38] *Works* (G.S.A.) VI (i), 407.
[39] *Ibid.*, 413, 416–417.

himself".[40] During this era men had exchanged their differences—they had been a "discourse"—but had lacked the divine directive that transforms this discordant discourse into harmonious song. Hölderlin's hymn reaches its climax at this point, a climax rendered by the overflowing of the antistrophe into the epode. The feast day now is not only the occasion where men are reconciled to one another, or where men are reconciled to the gods, but where all the gods are reconciled among themselves: it is no longer the "evening of the age," but "the Evening of Time." The new epiphany of the gods is a spiritual one, manifested not in miracles or in the thunderstorm which was Hölderlin's favorite "sign" [41] for God's presence in Nature, but in the symbolic banquet itself and in the choir of communion. Christ remains the principal guest, no longer concealed from the poet by the gods of classical antiquity, as in "Der Einzige," where they hide "des Hausses Kleinod," "the jewel of the house," but freely recognized as such by the other gods themselves. In a single sweeping sentence Hölderlin links the chiliastic theme of his hymn to its temporal starting point: Napoleon's victory and the peace that follow it represent the beginning of a new era, but only by virtue of Christ's presence at the banquet. That is why the poet has invited the most loved of gods to join the prince of the feast day. The concluding lines of the triad, perhaps, convey the impetuosity of hope, rather than the calm of fulfillment; but a calmer note would be out of place at the end of this triad. Hölderlin strikes it in the next.

This last triad observes another law of Hölderlin's late poetry, that of "progression" and "regression." [42] After the climactic third triad, this one not only reverts to the "naïve tone" of the first, but descends again to the more limited sphere of Nature and ordinary human life. The smoking valley and subsiding thunder recall the apocalyptic imagery of the first triad; but whereas there it served to prepare us for the wider implications of the cessation of war, now its direction is reversed, since it leads back from these implications to the historical moment

[40] *Der Archipelagus,* lines 242–244.
[41] See his letters of December 4, 1801 and 1802 to Böhlendorff. *Works* (G.S.A.) VI (i), 427, 433.
[42] Cf. B. Allemann, *op. cit.,* 35–38.

as such. This backward direction of the first strophe is beautifully realized in the humbly idyllic image of mother and child, sitting in front of a house that one takes to be of very modest proportions; the contrast is especially marked because in the epode of the preceding triad—in the very last line—Hölderlin had used the same word "house" in his special, extended sense, as the place where one has one's being. Heidegger uses the word "Ort," place or location, in a similar sense. The restricted use of the same word here serves to realize Hölderlin's vision on the most immediate and familiar level, and so, psychologically, does the naïve conceit at the end of the strophe, the momentary suspension of death. The hymn now completes that arc that is the characteristic form of Hölderlin's poetry: "Nature, whence it originates, will also receive it again," One of Hölderlin's constant aspirations was to reconcile Nature with Art, as both Goethe and Schiller had also endeavored to do; and Art, to Hölderlin, meant civilization itself. As he had written as early as 1794, "there are two ideal forms of existence: a state of extreme ingenuousness, in which our needs themselves are in harmony both with our abilities and with everything related to us, solely through the organization of Nature, without our interference; and a state of highest culture, where the same harmony would be attained with infinitely multiplied, varied, and strengthened needs and abilities, through the organization that we are able to give to ourselves." [43] Hölderlin attained this second "ideal state," the state of Art or culture, by basing the very structure of his poetry on natural patterns and processes, the cyclic movement of the year, growth and decline, progression and regression, systole and diastole. "A living, harmoniously changing whole," is how he described the perfect work of art in a letter to Schelling of 1799; [44] and in his ode "Der Frieden," begun in the same year, he described the seasons as "melodiously changing," contrasting their cyclic progression with the wavering, chaotic desires of men.[45] Even when his inspiration had become supernatural as much as natural, this conception of his own art and of Art itself as "the bloom and perfection of

---

[43] *Thalia* fragment of *Hyperion. Works* (Zinkernagel) II, 213.
[44] *Works* (G.S.A.) VI (i), 348.
[45] *Ibid.,* II (i), 6.

Nature" [46] continued to influence the formal composition of his poems. That is one reason that Nature is present in the first and last strophes of "Friedensfeier."

Another is the fact, already intimated, that the whole hymn constantly hints at a vision of evil, which Hölderlin chose not to make explicit. "Friedensfeier" performs the dual function of prophecy, not only pointing to a better future, but warning the community of what will happen if this direction is not followed; but Hölderlin's vision of past, present, and future was a poetic one, more imaginative than moralistic. Evil, therefore, could only enter it in a guise more general than specific, in the form of myth; and Hölderlin was always especially reluctant to "name" evil. In his later poetry, as I have mentioned, Nature is no longer wholly innocent or wholly harmonious. If, in the epode, she is said to have "buried" as much as she has "built," it is because she herself has fostered the insolent and barbaric powers that threaten her peace. Now, Napoleon himself—and in the poem "Buonaparte" of 1797 Hölderlin had referred to him as "the spirit of Nature"—had once been an agent of destruction. There is clearly a link between Napoleon's destructive rôle during the era of "wilderness" and the "enemy" whom Nature is accused of having tended. What that link is, the last cryptic lines suggest; for they allude to the "untimely growth" which, according to a late fragmentary hymn, is a characteristic of the Titanic powers active in Nature and in human life. In this fragmentary hymn, "Wenn aber die Himmlischen . . . ," Hölderlin wrote:

> Denn es hasset
> Der sinnende Gott
> Unzeitiges Wachstum.[47]

> For the pensive God
> Hates
> Untimely growth.

To be "fearfully active" is an aspect of "untimely growth"; the Titans act out of fear, filled with "ever-anxious arrogance" [48]

[46] *Works* (Zinkernagel) II, 381.
[47] *Works* (G.S.A.) II (i), 225.
[48] "Der Mensch." *Works* (G.S.A.) I (i), 264.

because they are conscious of transgressing the divine order, the "bounds" and the "measure" of their own nature. This last allusion to the Titans, then, sums up the hidden warning contained in "Friedensfeier." The whole poem—and especially the poet's appeal to Christ to preside spiritually over the feast day —has a poignancy that derives in part from the fear lurking behind the poet's hopes.

If this fear and this warning are understood, it becomes irrelevant, as well as boorish, to object that the era of "wilderness" did not, in fact, end with the Treaty of Lunéville. The objection is boorish in any case, just as it would be boorish to complain that no golden age began at the moment when Vergil wrote his fourth Eclogue. Among other things, prophecy is the "objective correlative" of hope, that is, the rendering of hope in terms of poetry; and Hölderlin is the last poet who can be accused of facile optimism, at least as far as his post-idealistic phases are concerned. His prophetic hopes were wrested from an anguish of heart and spirit, which it is neither necessary nor possible to describe; they survived the ruin of his personal life and the very disintegration of his mind. The mythological odes and fragments that followed the completed hymns show how desperately he struggled to preserve all that was most precious to him from the contagion of his own decline; and the same selfless purity—now relieved of the tension that made it admirable— gives certain poems of his madness a value quite distinct from their pathological interest.

The formal and stylistic innovations of Hölderlin—of which I shall have more to say in a different context [49]—are less puzzling to a modern reader than the peculiar vision that caused Hölderlin to make those innovations. The music of poetry— and music itself, for that matter—only seems self-sufficient, unrelated to anything outside itself, because we don't know how to interpret it in terms of another medium, the medium of expository prose; both poetry and music are symbolic media, governed by a logic different from that which governs prose argument—but a logic nonetheless. An infringement of that logic can offend us even if we know little about the art in ques-

[49] See pp. 267–271.

tion, less about what the artist wished to "communicate." The beauty of a work of art is inseparable from its peculiar logic; and the closer we get to understanding the difficult logic of a poem like "Friedensfeier"—and by logic I don't mean its literal argument, but the law that rules its music as much as its sense—the closer we are to appreciating its beauty. It is easy to fall into the error of supposing that anything that a work of art communicates must be reducible to the logic of expository prose; and, where it obviously is not, that the work has no "matter" at all or that such "matter" is negligible.

That brings me to another possible stumbling block, the question of Hölderlin's beliefs. The "suspension of disbelief" that we experience in reading great poetry is nothing other than our perception of its peculiar logic. Disbelief occurs only where the artist himself offends against the logic of his art, often because he is momentarily misled into a logic alien to it, which may well be closer to our own. A single momentary lapse of that kind can sever the thread that suspends our disbelief, so that it comes crashing down with a vengeance. To some extent, of course, the reader's response to a particular work of literature, however great, will depend on his own opinions and beliefs, and on the degree of balance or bias with which he holds them; yet the very fact that two persons of sound judgment, but entirely different opinions and beliefs, can agree about the merit of certain works of literature, shows that opinion and belief are not the decisive criteria. Such agreement has certainly been reached in the case of Hölderlin.

In *Goethe as the Sage* T. S. Eliot returned to this question of poetry and belief; and he qualified his earlier answer to it by making a valuable distinction "between the *philosophy* of a poet and his *wisdom.*" The philosophy we can quarrel with; but the wisdom is "the same for all men everywhere." On those grounds, Eliot was able to make his peace with Goethe; and to recognize him as a "great European poet." Of Wordsworth and Hölderlin Eliot said in the same address: "Wordsworth was surely a great poet, if the term has any meaning at all; at his best, his flight was much higher than that of Byron, and as high as that of Goethe. His influence was, moreover, decisive for English poetry at a certain moment: his name marks an epoch.

Yet he will never mean to Europeans of other nationality, what he means to his compatriots; nor can he mean to his own compatriots what Goethe means to them. Similarly—but here I speak with becoming diffidence—it seems to me possible to maintain that Hölderlin was at moments more inspired than Goethe: yet he also, can never be to the same degree a European figure." [50]

Hölderlin lacked the universal range of Goethe's wisdom, a range as wide as it was deep; and he lacked Goethe's patient concern with the minutiae of nature—a concern that only the greatest poets can pursue without becoming trivial themselves. But Hölderlin's wisdom extended to heights and depths that few poets have had the strength to endure; and by wisdom here I mean neither knowledge nor experience, but the sense of "measure" that is rarer than these. His influence, too, was as decisive for German poetry as Wordsworth's was for English poetry, though his moment did not come till long after his death: and it now seems that even his most difficult work has come to mean a great deal to Europeans—and even non-Europeans—of other nationality than his own.

[50] *Ibid.*, 55.

II

THE SUBLIME ART

Notes on Milton and Hölderlin

All the rules of criticism seem to forbid a comparison between two poets as incommensurable in kind, period, nationality, and personal temper as Milton and Hölderlin, who were not even linked by an immediate influence, far less by borrowings that would provide a solid and respectable basis for the attempt. The differences between Milton and Hölderlin are blatantly obvious. Their affinities are real, but so impalpable as to resist formulation in terms that are more than vague generalities. A common tradition can be sensed behind the work of the two poets; but to establish the exact nature of their common ground would call not only for elaborate delvings into the minutiae of Milton and Hölderlin scholarship but an encyclopedic knowledge of theology and classical literature too forbidding to outline. If the gulf that divides the two poets can be bridged at all, however flimsily, these notes may challenge others to apply the necessary equipment. Meanwhile it may prove of some value merely to survey and measure the gulf, to establish the extent of the differences and indicate where those real but impalpable affinities lie.

A start was made by L. S. Salzberger in her monograph on Hölderlin,[1] in which she traced the "typical Renaissance view of the *poeta theologus* or *sacer vates*," and concluded: "Hölderlin was himself one of the poets who embodied the Renaissance ideal. His spiritual forbears were Vida, Tasso, Ronsard, and Sidney, as well as Milton and Klopstock. All these poets belong to the period that began with the Renaissance and ended some time after the French Revolution." Hölderlin owed his participation in the Renaissance tradition to the German writers who influenced him in his youth, especially Klopstock and Herder, but also to his education at Denkendorf, Maulbronn, and Tübingen, with their emphasis on the harmonious blending of theological and classical studies. As Dr. Salzberger mentions, the inner gate of the Protestant Seminary at Tübingen bore the inscription *Aedes Deo et Musis Sacrae*. So much for spiritual genealogy. To enter into the peculiarities of Swabian theology, or Hölderlin's possible debt to the millenarian and mystical doctrines of Bengel or Oetinger would be to plunge into the gulf with little hope of ever emerging; but even here certain interesting genealogical convergences and divergences with Milton might well be revealed. Essentially, the Swabian tradition insists that the glory of God is manifested in nature.[2]

If Hölderlin had been born some twenty years earlier than he was, Milton would almost certainly have been one of his masters. Kant's admiration for Milton is well known; even Goethe, born twenty-five years after Kant and twenty-one years before Hölderlin, had read Milton by the time he was seventeen, in 1766. The first three books of *Paradise Lost* had been translated into German as early as 1678; the Latin translation by Hog followed in 1690. But it was in the half century between

[1] L. S. Salzberger, *Hölderlin* (Cambridge, 1952), 8–12.
[2] Hölderlin's debt to the Swabian theologians has been investigated by Herbert Wocke, *Hölderlins Christliches Erbe* (1949). Robert Minder has written a brilliant summary of a tradition which he traces not only to Hölderlin, but to Hegel and Karl Marx. See his " '*Herrlichkeit*' *chez Hegel ou Le Monde des Pères Souabes*," *Etudes Germaniques* (July–December, 1951), 225–290.

1720 and 1770, the year of Hölderlin's birth, that Milton's example was of crucial importance to Germany. The advocacy of French classicism as the chief exemplar for German writers was effectively opposed from three directions: that of classical antiquity, that of bardic or folk poetry, and that of modern English literature. To Gottsched's emphasis on discursive logic, correct usage, and pedantic good sense, the two Swiss critics Bodmer and Breitinger opposed the view that "a well-cultivated imagination distinguishes the good poet from the vulgar versifier because it is the rich, modulating poetry, which derives its life and character from the imagination alone, that chiefly distinguishes poetry from prose." This "rich modulating poetry" was none other than Milton's. From 1724 to 1754 Bodmer worked at three consecutive translations of *Paradise Lost,* all of them in prose but designed to approximate more and more closely to Milton's poetry. In 1741 Bodmer published a defense of Milton, *On the Marvellous in Poetry,* closely related to Breitinger's earlier treatise on the peculiar logic of poetry, which proceeds by "images of sensible objects."

Bodmer and Breitinger liberated German poetry much as Lessing liberated German drama; and Milton was their battle cry, as Shakespeare and the Greek dramatists were Lessing's. Bodmer's translation of *Paradise Lost* inspired Klopstock with the ambition to write his *Messias.* "To judge by this fragment, Milton's spirit rests upon the poet," was Bodmer's comment on the early prose version of the first three cantos that Klopstock submitted to him. Bodmer's enthusiasm was such that he invited Klopstock to be his guest in Switzerland. Because of the wide acceptance of Bodmer's and Klopstock's own belief that he had done for Germany what Milton had done for England, it was Klopstock's, not Milton's, epic that Hölderlin read and imitated in his formative years, in the seventeen-eighties. One other translation of *Paradise Lost* had appeared in 1760; but this German rendering by Zachariä in the modified classical hexameters which Klopstock chose for the final version of his *Messias* was the last to appear before Milton's replacement by Klopstock in Germany.[3] The complete *Messias* was published

[3] A few allusions in Hölderlin's early poems suggest that he may have read, or at least glanced at, Zachariä's translation, as Professor Paul

in 1773. Milton continued to be read by Germans of the older generation, or by those with a special interest in English literature, but his general influence rapidly declined.

It will be impossible here to trace the development that divides Klopstock from Milton; the reduction of cosmology to inwardness, the substitution of enthusiasm for Milton's vast range of learned allusion, scientific as well as theological and mythological. Once again it is convenient to take refuge in "the Renaissance ideal." From his adolescence onward, Hölderlin aimed at a synthesis characteristic of this ideal. At Tübingen he wrote an essay on the parallels between the Proverbs of Solomon and Hesiod's *Works and Days*. Milton's account of his aspirations in the Preface to Book II of *The Reason of Church Government* applies almost equally to Hölderlin's: "That what the greatest, choicest wits of Athens, Rome, or modern Italy, and those Hebrews of old did for their country, I, in my proportion, with this over and above, of being a Christian, might do for mine." So does his comparison of himself in the same Preface with Jeremiah and Tiresias; but the closest analogy of all occurs in the following passage: "The Scripture also affords us a divine pastoral drama in the Song of Solomon, consisting of two persons, and a double chorus, as Origen rightly judges. And the Apocalypse of St. John is the majestic image of a high and stately tragedy, shutting up and intermingling her solemn scenes and acts with a sevenfold chorus of hallelujahs and harping symphonies . . . Or if occasion shall lead, to imitate those magnific odes and hymns, wherein Pindarus and Callimachus are in most things most worthy . . ." The Apocalypse and Pindar's odes are the very two works that Hölderlin emulated in his prophetic "hymns."

Because of his syncretism, it could be said of Hölderlin, as of Milton, that "he had his thoughts constantly fixed on the contemplation of Hebrew theocracy, and of a perfect commonwealth," though it was the theocracy of an idealized Greece that Hölderlin much more frequently invoked; and, as Hazlitt also observed of Milton, "his religious zeal infused its character into his imagination, so that he devotes himself with the same

Böckmann has pointed out to me; but no evidence for this assumption has yet been published.

sense of duty to the cultivation of his genius, as he did to the
exercise of virtue, or the good of his country." To these attributes of the *sacer vates* we can add the religious radicalism that
prevented both men from making a profession of their vocation, though both were intended for the Church; both were
mainly deterred by "a conscience that would retch," though
their more specific reasons for preferring "a blameless silence"
were far from identical. Milton at one time chose to be "de-
graded to a schoolmaster," as Johnson put it; and for the
greater part of his active life Hölderlin was reduced to the
drudgery and servitude of a private tutor, although, at least in
youth, he also shared Milton's political radicalism.

The *sacer vates,* as such, is intransigent and incorruptible. If
he tends toward one sin or excess, that sin or excess is pride,
—a pride as far removed from mere social or moral convention
as his egregious ambition. Milton and Hölderlin are personally
incommensurable because Hölderlin's vocational pride conflicted with the humility and tenderness of his nature. Indeed,
his late poetry is pervaded by the anguish that sprang from the
recognition of this pride as the sin of *hubris.* Because Milton
does not appear to have suffered any such conflict or recognition, he remains personally aloof from us moderns, if not personally loathsome, monstrous, "inhuman"—and this despite the
egotism on which Coleridge remarked, adding that "the egotism
of such a man is a revelation of the spirit." We can understand
Hölderlin's strength and forgive his pride because he was aware
of his weakness, and this awareness entered into his work. I
shall have more to say of this difference, which is not one of
personality alone.

Hölderlin's brief poetic career was a perpetual crisis, a perpetual revision of the premises and functions of the *sacer vates.*
For that reason, his work cannot be classified as a whole. He
began by being "not a picturesque, but a musical poet," as
Coleridge said of Milton, with the musical poet's leaning toward generality and abstraction. The distinction of course is
one of degree rather than of kind; one doubts whether it would
have occurred to any reader of Milton who was not familiar
with Shakespeare. Hazlitt denied its relevance to Milton, but
T. S. Eliot's essays took it up again with a vengeance. Within a

few years Hölderlin's poetry underwent a complete transformation; the visual sense became increasingly important to him; and, with it, the particular image.[4] From being at least as abstract a poet as his immediate exemplars, Klopstock and Schiller, Hölderlin became one of the most concrete and sensuous by the time of his mental breakdown and the pure imagism of "Hälfte des Lebens." To understand this development it would be necessary to refer once more to the mystical realism of the Swabian theological tradition. Whatever its causes, it is this development, as well as the difference in kind between *Paradise Lost* and Hölderlin's predominantly lyrical and choric poetry, that makes it impossible to compare the two poets' work as a whole. Only Milton's *Samson* and Hölderlin's *Empedocles* are sufficiently close to each other in kind to permit a valid comparison; and one would expect even this comparison to illumine little more than the vicissitudes and decline of the *sacer vates* in "an age of dearth." [5]

A few preliminary observations must be made. In his history of Hölderlin criticism,[6] Professor Alessandro Pellegrini summed up the crucial difference between Hölderlin and his predecessors—Milton, Dante, Sophocles, and Pindar are those whom he mentions—by observing that "Hölderlin's world was one in which he alone believed." Whereas for Milton "poetic vision was a symbol of theological reality and the testimony of a communal faith, of an 'Ecclesia' and the spiritual unity of a people," Hölderlin "spoke to a chorus that could not respond to him, because it did not exist." There is a good deal of truth in this historical view; but I sometimes suspect that we exaggerate the isolation of poets close to us in time, and invent a mythical state of community for poets more remote. It has always been in the nature of a prophet to be without honor not only in his own country, but in his own time. Milton's personal, and even

---

[4] The various drafts of his ode "Des Morgens" (1799) show how "the leaves of the trees" becomes "the poplar bends," then "the birch-tree bends," finally "the beech-tree bends."

[5] Hölderlin, *Brod und Wein*, VII ". . . wozu Dichter in dürftiger Zeit?"

[6] Alessandro Pellegrini, *Hölderlin: Storia della Critica* (1956), 414–415.

literary, isolation in his later years was hardly less extreme than Hölderlin's before his madness; and his "Ecclesia," like Hölderlin's, was largely invisible. Neither Milton nor Hölderlin could become wholly identified with any political or sectarian cause; and for much the same reasons.

Without going as far as Denis Saurat, who speaks of Milton's pantheistic ideas[7] and discovers a host of heterodox beliefs that were certainly Hölderlin's, if they were not Milton's, one cannot help being struck by certain basic assumptions common to the two poets. One of these can be summed up by Saurat's statement about Milton that "the early days before the Fall will become for him the normal state of a man." [8] This is the "concord and law of nature" of *Paradise Lost* (Book xii, 29), the peace whose loss Hölderlin laments in his ode "Der Frieden," ending with the prayer:

> Komm du nun, du der heiligen Musen all,
> Und der Gestirne Liebling, verjüngender
> Ersehnter Friede, komm' und gieb ein
> Bleiben in Leben, ein Herz uns wieder.

> Now come, best loved by all the nine Muses and
> The circling constellations, you long desired
> Rejuvenator, Peace, and give us
> Back a firm foothold in life, a centre.

It is true that Milton's Michael says a little later in the same speech:

> Tyrannie must be,
> Though to the Tyrant thereby no excuse
> (Bk. xii, ll. 95—96)

of realization of the necessity of evil that also runs through Hölderlin's later poems; but it remains equally true that the

---

[7] Denis Saurat, *Milton: Man and Thinker* (1944), 13—14, and *passim*.
[8] *Ibid.*, 56.
But the statement is a half-truth at the most. Surely the turning-point of *Paradise Lost,* on the human level at least, is Adam's change of heart in Book x, when he ceases to blame Eve and accepts the consequences of the Fall.

sacer vates can approve nothing but perfection. "Milton," Saurat also comments,[9] "will think that the best government is that which governs least"; and, after his disillusionment with the revolutionary cause, in a letter of 1801, Hölderlin wrote: "In the end it is still true, that the less men discover and know about the State, whatever its form, the freer they are."

In his early *Tractate of Education* Milton professed that "the end of learning is to repair the ruin of our first parents . . ." To Hölderlin, writing after Rousseau and Herder, the problem presented itself not in terms of sin and redemption, but of nature and art—art in its wider Renaissance sense which embraced all that we now call culture and civilization; granted his greater emphasis on this antinomy, which worried Goethe and Schiller also, his aspirations were akin to Milton's. "There are two ideals of our existence," Hölderlin wrote in 1794, "a state of extreme ingenuousness, in which our needs themselves are in concord, both with our abilities and with everything related to us, solely through the organization of nature, without our interference; and a state of extreme culture, where the same would take place with infinitely mutiplied, varied and intensified needs and abilities, through the organization which we are able to give to ourselves." [10]

Like Hölderlin, though not as constantly or emphatically, Milton vindicated the "faultless proprieties of nature," "the faultless innocence of nature"; and the most "artificial" of English poets wrote in *The Apology for Smectymnuus:* "For doubtless that according to art is most eloquent, which turns and approaches nearest to nature from whence it came; and they express nature best, who in themselves least wander from her safe leading, which may be called regenerate reason." To Hölderlin art was "the bloom and perfection of nature." [11] In his short Preface to the hymn "Friedensfeier" he apologized as follows for the unconventional and difficult manner of his late poems: "On a fine day almost every mode of song makes itself heard; and nature, whence it originates, also receives it again."

These affinities must be noted, though they are tenuous with-

[9] *Op. cit.*, 53.
[10] Hölderlin, Preface to the *Hyperion* fragment of 1794.
[11] Hölderlin, *Grund zum Empedokles.*

out an account of the theological and philosophical premises that divide the two poets, but especially the polytheism and pantheism of Hölderlin's earlier work. One must distinguish between a purely artistic insight in Milton, related to his famous (and usually misquoted) dictum that poetry is "more simple, sensuous and passionate" than rhetoric, and Hölderlin's fervent faith in the regenerative power of nature. Here Milton is "naïve" and Hölderlin "sentimental," according to Schiller's distinction. The modern feeling for nature, Schiller pointed out, "is not that which the ancients had; rather it is similar to that which we have for the ancients." It is only when Paradise is lost that Adam invokes its scenery in the pathetic mode of Hölderlin's odes and elegies:

> O Woods, O Fountains, Hillocks, Dales and Bowrs,
> With other echo late I taught your Shades
> To answer, and resound farr other Song.
> (Bk. x, ll. 860–862)

The same is true of the great pantheistic climax of Hölderlin's novel, *Hyperion,* with its resolution of every conflict and division in the One and All of nature: "Men drop from you like rotten fruit, oh, let them perish, and to your root they shall return, and I, O Tree of Life, let me grow verdant again with you and waft around your crests with all your burgeoning twigs! Peaceful and closely akin, for all of us grew up out of the golden seed-grain." It is not till the loss of Eden that Adam and Eve will be consoled by the thought of their unity with the maternal substance, which in Hölderlin is not separated from the male principle, "spirit," "ether," and "light," and Milton's Michael does not take the sting out of death when he touches on this corporeal return, because it is far from being spiritual redemption:

> So mayst thou live, till like ripe Fruit thou drop
> Into thy Mothers lap, or be with ease
> Gatherd, not harshly pluckt, for death mature . . .
> (Bk. x, ll. 535–537)

Saurat writes of Milton that "for him the body and soul came to be one." [12] But even Hölderlin found it increasingly difficult to maintain this premise, crucial though it is to his earlier work.

Nor is there any real and immediate connection between the doctrine of "retraction," which Saurat (incorrectly, some say) attributes to Milton, and Hölderlin's belief in the alternation of "day" and "night," divine revelation and divine absence. The dazzling brightness that in Milton is the timeless quality of both the Father and the Son, even when their full blaze is diffused through a cloud (*P.L.* Bk. iii, 372–389), is subject to a cyclic process in Hölderlin, depending on the capacity of mortals to endure the light of revelation. The only possible parallel occurs in Book xii, when Michael forecasts an era of utter retraction:

> Thus will the latter, as the former World
> Still tend from bad to worse, till God at last
> Wearied with thir iniquities, withdraw
> His presence from among them, and avert
> His holy Eyes;
>
> (ll. 105–109)

But this era is not the one to which Hölderlin alludes in his elegy *Brod und Wein,* viii, when "the Father averted His face from mankind, and all over the earth sorrowing, rightly, began." Hölderlin means the era between the decline of Hellas and the birth of Christ; and he sees his own age as a similar era of darkness that will end only with the joint epiphany of Christ and the ancient gods. Before his late hymns, Hölderlin's cosmological vision recalls the pre-Socratic philosophers, and particularly Empedocles, because it derives from the cycles of nature, not from history in the Christian sense. The precise relation between Christ and the gods of Greece will be the subject of his later prophetic hymns; and it is only gradually that Christ becomes more than the "genius" of *Brod und Wein,* more than one of many mediators—including the demigods, prophets, and poets of antiquity—between mortals and "the God of gods," the supreme and timeless deity.

Even Hölderlin's chiliasm rests on a tradition, though a tra-

[12] *Op. cit.,* 49.

dition more esoteric than that on which Milton mainly drew. Neither, intrinsically, was a popular poet. If *Paradise Lost* found its way into thousands of English nonconformist homes, Hölderlin's poems, by a rather different posthumous development, found their way into the packs of thousands of German soldiers in World War II. A special "field selection" was issued for this purpose in 1943, the centenary year of Hölderlin's death. But what an irony! It is as though British soldiers had been provided with copies of Milton's *Areopagitica* so that they could read: "What does He do then but reveal Himself to His servants, and as His manner is, first to His Englishmen?" Milton's messianic patriotism is related to that which inspired a number of Hölderlin's late hymns dedicated to Swabia, the Rhine, and Germany respectively. These three prophetic hymns were duly included in the "field selection." But what were Hitler's soldiers to make of the conclusion of "Germania"?

> . . . Germania, wo du Priesterin bist
> Und wehrlos Rat giebst rings
> Den Königen und den Völkern.

> . . . Germania, where you are priestess and
> Defenceless proffer all round
> Advice to the kings and the peoples.

In view of such historical realities, it is not the isolation of the modern *sacer vates,* but his fame, that seems anomalous. If we add that Hölderlin had to contend with the secular philosophy of his time, the subjective, if not solipsistic idealism of Kant's successors, we can appreciate the difference between the dilemmas of Milton's Samson and Hölderlin's Empedocles. It is a triple estrangement, from the gods, from society, and from himself, that defeats the protagonist of Hölderlin's unfinished tragedy.

The two works are commensurable only because both derive from what Milton called "Attic tragedies of stateliest and most regal argument." Hölderlin, it is true, was less concerned with stateliness, the classical decorum that had been replaced in his time and country by the starkness of unadorned emotion; he anticipated Nietzsche in recognizing the "Dionysian" character of the ancient Greeks, in seeing them dialectically as acquiring "Junonian sobriety" just because, innately, they inclined to "holy drunkenness" or "holy pathos." The modern "occidental" poet, who is colder and more sober by nature, must reverse this dialectic process. What is tragic in modern times is "that we leave the realm of the living quite calmly, packed into a container, not that devoured by flames we atone for the flame which we could not master." [13]

I have already quoted Hölderlin's definition of ancient tragedy from his later commentary on his translation of *Oedipus Rex,* published in 1804, but it is so crucial that it must be repeated here: "The representation of the tragic is mainly based on this: that what is monstrous and terrible in the coupling of god and man, in the total fusion of the power of nature with the inmost depth of the man, so that they are one at the moment of wrath, should be made intelligible by showing how this fusion into one is purged by their total separation." Both Milton and Hölderlin rendered much of the outer form and structure of Greek tragedy; but Milton, who in any case modeled himself on Euripides, not on Sophocles, appears to have emulated its gravity and morality rather than the mystery of which Hölderlin wrote. Yet Goethe said to Eckermann (January 31, 1830) that *Samson Agonistes* is "closer to the spirit of the ancients than any other play by any modern poet whatever."

Goethe also mentioned that "Milton's own blindness proved a great advantage to him in rendering Samson's condition with such verisimilitude." In fact it is the rare degree to which both Milton's Samson and Hölderlin's Empedocles are identified with their authors, so that these works can be interpreted either as tragedies or as elaborate *personae,* that casts so much light on my present theme. Like Coleridge, both Goethe and Schiller were also acutely aware of Milton's personality in *Paradise Lost.* Just as Coleridge stressed the subjectivity of *Paradise Lost,* remarking that "in all modern poetry in Christendom there is an under-consciousness of a sinful nature, a fleeting

---

[13] Hölderlin, Letter to Böhlendorff, December, 1801.

away of external things, the mind or subject greater than the object, the reflective character predominant," Schiller wrote to Goethe: "In this poem too, as with all modern works of art, it is really the individual manifested in it that arouses our interest. The topic is abominable, outwardly plausible, but inwardly worm-eaten and hollow . . . But certainly it is an interesting man who speaks . . . Indeed, the strange, unique case that, as a revolutionary come to grief, he (Milton) is better able to assume the rôle of the devil than that of the angel, has a great influence upon the characterization and structure of the poem, as the circumstance of the author's blindness has upon its tone and colouring." [14] But Milton criticism in the late eighteenth and nineteenth centuries shows how each writer projects his own subjectivity, and his own beliefs, into Milton's poem; with *Samson* we are on slightly firmer ground.

The very choice of their respective heroes reveals the gulf between Milton and Hölderlin. We know what Milton thought of Hölderlin's hero, because he placed him in the Paradise of Fools:

> . . . he who to be deemd
> A God, leap'd fondly into *Aetna* flames
> *Empedocles* . . .

in the company of

> Embryoes and Idiots, Eremits and Friers
> White, Black and Grey, with all thir trumperie.
> (*P.L.* Bk. iii, ll. 469–475)

Doubtless Milton would have thought as little of Hölderlin's Empedocles, with his modern sensibility and tenderness added to pagan heresies, as he did of the historical Empedocles. Hölderlin, on the other, might have thought Milton's hero just a little bit smug, a little bit priggish even, and more than a little barbaric. The short chorus in praise of Samson's temperance

[14] Schiller to Goethe, July 31, 1799; he goes on to criticize Milton's preoccupation with free will. Goethe's reply (August 3) is also critical of the poem, on different grounds, and also concludes that Milton remains "an excellent, and in every way an interesting man."

(ll. 541–546) would have struck him as wholly contrary to the spirit of Greek tragedy, if not as ludicrous as Milton thought Empedocles; and he would scarcely have sympathized with the manner in which Samson justifies "the ways of God to men," not only because here "the moment of wrath" is also the moment of indiscriminate slaughter—and Hölderlin's sensibility was Christian, even when his beliefs were not—but because it might have seemed to him that Samson's *hubris* is not sufficiently purged by "total separation" from his God. Samson's outward pride remains unbroken, as the scene with Dalila shows; and so does his immense egotism, the "alcohol of egotism" that Coleridge discovered in Milton's Satan and "all the mighty hunters of mankind from Nimrod to Napoleon," these "great men as they are called." But Hölderlin would have been less interested in these relatively superficial aspects than in Milton's treatment of the tragic crux; and this he would undoubtedly have approved and admired.

Milton's Samson and Hölderlin's Empedocles have this in common, that—like the *sacer vates* himself—they are the elect of God, called and chosen for a unique mission. In the pantheistic terms that were Hölderlin's at the time, this means not so much an identification with the will of God, as the "awareness of being at one with all that lives," the "intellectual point of view" of which a tragic poem is the "metaphor." [15] Samson's physical prowess has its counterpart in Empedocles' political power and influence over the people of Agrigentum, though this power is far less important to him than its source, the divine favors bestowed on him. What the Philistines are to Samson, the rulers of his own State are to Empedocles, though this external opposition, too, ceases to be of great account in the late version, since Empedocles has condemned himself even more rigorously than his enemies condemn him. In Hölderlin's original plan for the tragedy, drafted in 1797, there is no mention of Empedocles' guilt at all, only of his "hatred for culture" —culture as opposed to nature—his "contempt for any very definite occupation" and for "any interest directed toward diverse ends," rather than "the great harmony with all that lives."

[15] Hölderlin, *Über den Unterschied zwischen lyrischer, epischer und tragischer Dichtung. Works* (Zinkernagel) II, 368–376.

Pride is implied, but not censured. According to this early plan, Empedocles was also to be provoked by the sarcasms of his wife into leaving Agrigentum and seeking solitude near Etna—a detail of the plot that would have appealed to Milton, but never carried out by Hölderlin. The earliest fragment of the play stresses the conflict between Empedocles and the representatives of the religious and political status quo. The citizens of Agrigentum even offer to make Empedocles their king, but with the noble scorn of the *sacer vates* for anything less than Heaven on earth, the divine republic, he declines the honor. "The time of kings is past," he says, and tells them to be ashamed of themselves for wanting a king.

But in 1799 Hölderlin attempted a second version of *The Death of Empedocles;* though very much more fragmentary than the first, this conforms to his deeper insights into the nature of tragedy. The last of the three fragmentary versions is a magnificent poem, but hardly a dramatic one; written in 1800, it belongs to Hölderlin's prophetic phase and has an impersonal grandeur that transcends tragedy. Empedocles, in fact, has become a seer as far above political conflict as above personal guilt. It is the second fragment, therefore, that concerns me here.

Unlike the earlier plan and the first version, the second opens with the hero's "separation," like Milton's tragedy, though Empedocles' external downfall has not yet been brought about by Hermocrates, the priest, and Mecades, the archon, who plot it in the first scene. In this way Hölderlin at once establishes a tragic irony not unlike that in *Samson,* for Empedocles is beyond them, as Samson is beyond Dalila, Harapha, and even Manoah—only more so. Samson has his chorus instead to give him moral solace and support. A chorus of Agrigentines was part of Hölderlin's scheme, but it is significant that he failed to make use of it in any of the fragments. In the first version of *The Death of Empedocles* the function of the chorus has to be taken over by the archon's daughter, Panthea, who comments, chorus-like, on Empedocles' death. At the beginning of the second version we read "Chorus of Agrigentines in the distance," but that is all. The reason, of course, is not that Hölderlin was incapable of writing choric verse—the greater part of the third fragment is more choric than dramatic in character—but that Empedocles is not sustained by a community, as Samson is. Yet Empedocles' tragic offense, the offense with which Hermocrates rightly charges him and for which he is punished by "separation," is precisely that he seeks this community, that "he loves mortals too well" and has betrayed divine mysteries to the populace, as Samson has to a woman.

The close affinity of the two tragedies becomes clear as soon as we look not at the superficial aspects of Samson's offense, of Samson's strength, and of Samson's vengeance or vindication, but at what they symbolize. Both works hinge on the betrayal of a mystery and a consequent loss of the power that is divine grace; and the betrayal in both cases is expiated by a form of suicide, which, at the same time, represents a return to grace. To object that the form of Empedocles' death is also symbolic of his return to nature, a fusion with nature at its darkest, most elemental and most inchoate, merely brings us back to the doctrinal difference and Hölderlin's reasons for choosing this particular hero; we need not consider them at this point, any more than we need to stress Samson's much greater concern with outward reputation and honor, the social face of pride:

> . . . tell me Friends,
> Am I not sung and proverbd for a Fool
> In every street?
>
> (ll. 202–204)

This outward pride, in any case, is criticized by Manoah, who relates it to Samson's more essential and deep-rooted *hubris,* when he reproaches his son for preferring death to compromise:

> . . . perhaps
> God will relent, and quit thee all his debt;
> Who evermore approves and more accepts
> (Best pleas'd with humble and filial submission)
> Him who imploring mercy sues for life,
> Than who self-rigorous chooses death as due;
> Which argues over-just, and self-displeas'd
> For self-offence, more than for God offended.
>
> (ll. 508–515)

Empedocles' disciple Pausanias pleads with him in a similar strain, though his arguments are less cogent, because he does not understand the offense that Empedocles is determined to expiate. Empedocles' isolation is indeed absolute, as the comparison with Samson shows. But what is more important is Samson's own repeated allusions to the nature of his offense:

> . . . who have profan'd
> The mystery of God giv'n me under pledge
> Of vow . . .
>
> (ll. 377–379)

> But I
> Gods counsel have not kept, his holy secret
> Presumptuously have publisht, impiously
> Weakly at least, and shamefully . . .
>
> (ll. 496–499)

> . . . while I preserv'd these locks unshorn,
> The pledge of my unviolated vow.
>
> (ll. 1143–1144)

Empedocles' strength, too, flows from his divine inspiration, as the Chief Priest says:

> Das hat zu mächtig ihn
> Gemacht, dass er vertraut
> Mit Göttern worden ist.

(What has made him too mighty is that he became familiar with gods). And this is also the source of his weakness; Empedocles is the spoiled child of the gods, and, as such, becomes guilty of *hubris,* a *hubris* that takes the form of exuberance, indiscretion, and excessive love:

> Der sie versteht,
> Ist stärker, denn die Starken.
> Und wohlbekannt ist diese Seltne mir.
> Wirkend über der Erde
> Ihm ist von Anbeginn

> Der eigne Sinn verwöhnt, dass ihn
> Geringes irrt; er wird es büssen,
> Dass er zu sehr geliebt die Sterblichen.

> Stronger than strong men
> Are those who understand them.
> And this egregious one is known to me.
> Too happily he grew up;
> Well I could hear you
> His will was pampered, so
> That little things confuse him; he will pay
> For having loved mere mortal men too much.

Samson was equally privileged, and equally tempted:

> I was his nursling once and choice delight,
> His destind from the womb,
> Promis'd by Heavenly message twice descending.
> (ll. 633–635)

> . . . like a petty God
> I walkd about admir'd of all and dreaded
> On hostile ground . . .
> (ll. 529–531)

In both tragedies there is the same "coupling of god and man" and the same "total separation." Samson speaks of his "sense of Heaven's desertion"; and it is no accident that the Chorus, however briefly and negatively, consider the notion of atheism:

> Unless there be who think not God at all,
> If any be, they walk obscure;
> For of such Doctrin never was there School,
> But the heart of the Fool,
> And no man therein Doctor but himself.
> (ll. 295–299)

In this, as throughout the play, they faithfully respond to Samson's state of mind. Empedocles, as I have mentioned, has no chorus to support him, only his faithful but uncomprehending disciple Pausanias, who lacks all comparable assurance. Empedocles' separation, therefore, is unrelieved; and so are his doubts, which cannot be dismissed as atheism is dismissed by Samson's chorus. This greater isolation can be explained historically or biographically, in terms of Hölderlin's philosophical and religious views, his situation as a belated *sacer vates,* even of his approaching madness. Corresponding to Samson's great outcry:

> O dark, dark, dark, amid the blaze of noon,
> Irrecoverably dark, total Eclipse
> Without all hope of day!
>
> (ll. 80–82)

there is Empedocles' opening lamentation:

> Weh! einsam! einsam! einsam!
> Und nimmer find' ich
> Euch, meine Götter,
> Und nimmer kehr'ich
> Zu deinen Leben, Natur!
>
> Ah, lonely, lonely, lonely!
> And nevermore
> I shall find you,
> My gods, and nevermore
> Nature, return to your life!

It is easy enough to account for the parallel and the divergence by pointing out that whereas Milton was blind, Hölderlin succumbed to the impenetrable isolation of schizophrenia; but in the context of the two tragedies the darkness of Samson has exactly the same meaning as the loneliness of Empedocles. In other passages of this very monologue Empedocles also renders his separation by metaphors of light and darkness, vision and blindness:

> In meine Stille kamst du leisewandelnd,
> Fandst drinnen in der Halle Dunkel mich aus,
> Du Freundlicher! du kamst nicht unverhofft,

Und fernher wirken über der Erde vernahm
Ich wohl dein Wiederkehren, schöner Tag! . . .

. . . Vertrauert? bin ich ganz allein?
Und ist es Nacht hier aussen auch am Tage?
Der höher, denn ein sterblich Auge, sah,
Der Blindgeschlagne tastet nun umher . . .

Your movement hushed, you came into my stillness
Deep in the gloomy hall you sought me out
You kindly light; and not unhoped for came,
But from afar, at work above the earth
Well I would hear you come again, bright Day!

All saddened? Am I quite alone?
And is it night out here in daytime too?
He who saw higher things than ever did mortal eye
Now struck with blindness faltering picks his way.

Clearly, Goethe and Schiller missed something through caring more for Milton's personality than for Samson's tragic separation—though Goethe must have been aware of both when, much later, he said that the play is closer to the spirit of the ancients than any other modern work. The two interpretations are not mutually exclusive, though the less literal interpretation of Samson's darkness, not as Milton's, but as the loss of divine grace, is very much more to the point. One could pursue the personal parallel also and go on to speculate whether Milton, toward the end of his life, experienced doubts concerning his function as *sacer vates,* if not a crisis comparable to that which Hölderlin's tragedy undoubtedly marked. Hölderlin's *Empedocles,* among other things, is a self-condemnation, a condemnation also of the pride inseparable from the vocation of *sacer vates* and a *reductio ad absurdum* of pure pantheism; but here we must return for a moment to the philosophical aspects of the work.

In *Samson Agonistes* atheism is dismissed by the chorus, and mainly because there is no tradition that warrants such a creed. The philosophic idealism of Hölderlin's time was an attempt to meet the challenge of a frequently atheistic rationalism, and meet it on its own ground. The pantheism which Hölderlin shared with Schelling, and to a lesser extent with another of his coseminarists, Hegel, was one such attempt. The first act of the second version of *The Death of Empedocles* breaks off before the end of the "separation," and shortly after a speech by Empedocles distinguished by a razor-edged irony as untypical of this hero as of Hölderlin; and the irony is directed at Empedocles himself. Pausanias has tried to comfort him by reminding him of his intimacy with the powers of nature and his ability to rule them as he pleases. Empedocles replies:

Recht! Alles weiss ich, alles kann ich meistern;
Wie meiner Hände Werk, erkenn' ich es
Durchaus und lenke, wie ich will,
Ein Herr der Geister, das Lebendige.
Mein ist die Welt und unterthan und dienstbar
Sind alle Kräfte mir, ...
. . . . zur Magd ist mir
Die herrnbedürftige Natur geworden,
Und hat sie Ehre noch, so ists von mir.
Was wäre denn der Himmel und das Meer
Und Inseln und Gestirn' und was vor Augen
Den Menschen alles liegt, was wär' es auch,
Diss todte Saitenspiel, gäb' ich ihm Ton
Und Sprach' und Seele nicht? was sind
Die Götter und ihr Geist, wenn ich sie nicht
Verkündige. Nun! Sage, wer bin ich?

Quite true, I know all things, can master all.
Like my own handiwork thoroughly I control it
And as I please, a lord of spirits, rule,
Manipulate, make use of all that lives.
Mine is the world, submissive and subservient
To me are all its powers,
                    Nature herself,
Unfit, as well you know, to have her way,
Is now my servant girl; such honour
As men accord her still, she owes to me.
And what indeed would Heaven be and Ocean
And islands and the stars, and all that meets
The eyes of men, what would it mean or be,
This dead stringed instrument, did I not lend it

A resonance, a language and a soul?
What are the gods, and what their spirit, if I
Do not proclaim them? Tell me now, who am I?

This ironic reversion to his *hubris,* which at the same time reads like a reflection on modern science, but is rather a devastating exposure of the subjective basis of modern pantheism, and of philosophic idealism generally, may well indicate what kind of barrier it was that prevented Hölderlin from completing the tragedy. Hölderlin's subsequent development bears out the conjecture. The pure, virtually unmediated, pantheism of his Empedocles' creed—which alone made his tragic offense possible—is gradually modified in Hölderlin's prophetic poetry of the next few years; and the third Empedocles fragment transcends tragedy because the hero has become as selfless as an oracle.

There is no reason to assume that Milton had to suffer a religious crisis of this order before he could write *Samson Agonistes,* or that only his blindness enabled him to give such noble and moving expression to the inner blindness of Samson. To do so, is to fall into the error of making Milton more "human," more like ourselves, than he was, or of seeing him through post-Romantic spectacles, as Saurat did. What we can say is that the diction of *Samson Agonistes* combines starkness with stateliness, the colloquial phrase with the formal inversion [16] in a way that has analogies in *Paradise Regained,* but not in *Paradise Lost,* and that does suggest a possible change in Milton's conception of the *sacer vates;* and this is another reason that *Samson Agonistes* is less remote from Hölderlin, whose diction shows the same alternation of directness and obliqueness, conciseness and involution.

Because the later *sacer vates,* by his very nature, can hardly avoid a tragic phase, Hölderlin's failure to finish any of the three successive versions of *Empedocles* was not an absolute defeat; the tragic spirit was carried over into his last odes and

[16] What I have in mind are lines like the following: "Whom have I to complain of but myself?" (46), "And I shall shortly be with them that rest" (598); "Rise therefore with all speed and come along" (1316), balanced against even one-line inversions like "Should *Israel* from *Philistian* yoke deliver" (39).

elegies, the prophetic spirit into his "hymns." What it did mean was that tragedy as such is too essentially public an art form to be cultivated by poets whose vision could no longer be anything but esoteric. Lyrical poetry has the added advantage of brevity and compression, a consideration that is not irrelevant if we remember that the modern *sacer vates* is continually threatened by something much worse than the boos and catcalls of his audience, or than the lack of one, namely by the "circus animals' desertion," the reduction of all his visions to "the foul rag-and-bone shop of the heart." The very speed of Hölderlin's development, so hectic that in the six months' interval between the second and last *Empedocles* he passed from his tragic into his prophetic phase, points not only to his almost incredible efforts and achievements, but to the instability of the age. In its conception, Hölderlin's second *Empedocles* fragment is comparable to *Samson Agonistes;* but Milton's tragedy remains the last, and only, work of its kind.

III

NOVALIS

If the name of Novalis is often linked with Hölderlin's name, it is not because these two poets were born within two years of each other, or yet because both wrote poems in free verse that are usually known as "hymns." There is no evidence that either was influenced by, or even knew, the other's work; and Hölderlin's late "hymns" bear only the most superficial resemblance to certain of the *Hymnen an die Nacht* of Novalis, for their freedom rests on formal laws that Novalis did not observe. Rather it is because both men were ruled by a sense of dedication so single-minded and so intense that their works seem as inseparable from their lives as a flame seems inseparable from the fuel on which it feeds. "The artist," Novalis wrote "belongs to his work, not the work to the artist." [1] It can also be said that, like Hölderlin, Novalis pursued his mission to the point of no return; but Novalis' early death was not tragic in the sense that Hölderlin's madness was truly so. Novalis was committed to death by a pledge more decisive than the later resolutions by

[1] *Works* (Tieck; Schlegel. Paris, 1837), 320.

which he willed himself to live. Since he acknowledged no guilt, such as Hölderlin believed himself to have incurred, and expected no punishment, his early death was a consummation, not a catastrophe. "All that we call chance," he noted in his diary, "comes from God"; [2] but as I shall try to show, both "chance" and "God" in that context have a meaning peculiar to Novalis, who was conscious of a mission but not of a fate. Hölderlin's later poetry has this awareness of fate to a degree almost unique in modern literature; it affirms life by resolving conflict and sacrifice into tragic joy—by turning the utmost cruelty of fate into glory. All Novalis' later works are oriented toward death, but none of them is tragic. His treatment of death—and that is where his originality lies—was idyllic.

In spite of this radical difference between the idyllic mode and the tragic, Novalis had more in common with Hölderlin than is generally recognized; but because Novalis belonged to the Romantic School and because his vision appears to owe as much to the Christian Middle Ages as Hölderlin's owes to ancient Greece, it is easy to forget their common starting point, just as it is easy to forget that Novalis' dream of a united Christian Europe and his cult of the Virgin Mary were those of a Protestant. Novalis too began with the secular humanism and neoclassicism of Goethe and Schiller. Even after the spiritual experience that estranged him from these masters, it was only by a long detour through ancient Greece that he arrived at his ultimate acceptance of the Christian revelation; and this acceptance remained both eccentric and incomplete. If we inquire not into the nature, but into the origin, of either man's vision, it is the similarities that strike us rather than the overt differences. Both Hölderlin and Novalis were thinkers as much as poets; and their different visions could not have arisen but for a common predicament, the tyranny of philosophical and scientific systems based on the opposition between world and mind, between outward and inward reality. Both Hölderlin and Novalis were deeply and dangerously affected by the extreme intensification of this opposition in their own time; by Fichte's solipsism on the one hand, purely mechanistic interpretations of nature on the other. Both eagerly availed themselves of Schelling's

[2] *Works* (Minor) II, 102; entry of July, 1800.

doctrine of the identity of world and mind, for it offered a way out of this predicament; but neither found it adequate. Novalis continually reverted to Fichte's solipsism, with the result that his poetry is exceptionally poor in concrete imagery derived from the observation of nature. Hölderlin's poetry became more and more concrete, but he went out of his mind.

The wholeness which Hölderlin looked for in ancient Greece and later struggled to widen till it could embrace the person and the historical mission of Christ—this wholeness was not basically different from that which Novalis looked for in medieval Christendom and extended till it could embrace all the discoveries of modern science, the heritage of classical antiquity, and the political institutions of his own time. There is a little grain of truth in Heine's remark that the first Romantics "acted out of a pantheistic impulse of which they themselves were not aware. The feeling which they believed to be a nostalgia for the Catholic Mother Church was of deeper origin than they guessed, and their reverence and preference for the heritage of the Middle Ages, for the popular beliefs, diabolism, magical practices, and witchcraft of that era . . . all this was a suddenly reawakened but unrecognized leaning toward the pantheism of the ancient Germans." [3] Like Hölderlin's, Novalis' vision was a syncretic one; and he resembled Hölderlin in his attempt to reconcile pantheism with the worship of Christ.[4] On the religion of the Greeks and Romans Novalis remarked that "in a certain sense it was already what our religion must become—practical poetry." [5] Both men regarded poetry as a means—perhaps the only means still available—of healing the wounds inflicted by modern philosophy and modern science, of opposing that trend toward specialization to which they attributed the decline of Europe. Their ultimate aspiration, therefore, was not the exclusiveness of orthodoxy—which they thought no longer possible or even desirable—but a fusion of the heterodox elements of European culture into a new and splendid synthesis. The alternative, they both believed, was something more hateful than

[3] Heine, *Salon II* (1852), 250–251.
[4] See the passage on monotheism and pantheism, *Blütenstaub* No. 74. *Schriften* (Minor) II, 126–128.
[5] *Works* (Minor) III, 35.

heresy: a society disintegrating into cells of isolated activity; a world no longer inhabitable by the human mind.

Politically, Novalis differed from Hölderlin in being critical from the start of the French Revolution; but, as Hölderlin's own development bears out, a crucial shift of perspective took place between 1790, when Hölderlin was reading Rousseau and Schiller, and 1797, when Novalis began to write his characteristic works and praised Edmund Burke for writing "a revolutionary book against the Revolution." [6] Hölderlin's later political views are close to those of Novalis; he would have endorsed most of the reflections on monarchy and republicanism in Novalis' *Glauben und Liebe,* even the paradox that "the true King will be a republic, the true republic a King," [7] an aphorism that becomes clear in the light of Novalis' doctrine of correspondences, in this case of the correspondence between an exemplary monarch and the character of his subjects.

Some two years before Hölderlin wrote his "Friedensfeier," Novalis responded to the same political reality, the Napoleonic wars, with hopes and fears remarkably similar. His unfinished essay "Die Christenheit oder Europa" opens with an evocation of the unity of medieval Christendom and continues with a horrifying account of the same secularizing and disrupting process that Hölderlin had described in his novel *Hyperion.* Novalis attributes it to the Reformation and to the secular philosophies that grew out of it. "Hatred of religion . . . ," he continues, "turns the unending creative music of the cosmos into the monotonous rattling of a monstrous great mill, driven by the current of chance and itself drifting on this current, a mill per se, without builder or miller, in truth a genuine *perpetuum mobile,* a mill that grinds itself." Like Hölderlin, Novalis believed that a new religious revelation was at hand; for "true anarchy is the native element of religion. Out of the destruction of all that is positive Religion rears her glorious head, to endow a new world." "Still we have only signs, incoherent and crude, but to the historic eye they reveal a universal individuality, a new phase of history, a new humanity, the sweetest embrace of a Church surprised and of a loving God, and the fervent concep-

---

[6] *Blütenstaub. Works* (Minor) II, 136.
[7] *Ibid.,* II, 152.

tion of a new Messiah in all her thousand limbs." Novalis expresses the same high hopes for the coming of peace, and in words and images sometimes identical with those used by Hölderlin in the "Friedensfeier"; "Who knows whether there has been enough of war, but war will never cease until we grasp the palm tree branch which a spiritual power alone can proffer. Blood will flow over Europe until the nations recognise the dreadful madness that drives them round in circles. Until, struck and soothed by sacred music, they approach forsaken altars, a many-coloured company, undertake works of peace and, amidst hot tears, institute a great love-feast on the smoking battle-field, in celebration of peace." In the concluding passage of his short essay, Novalis speaks of Europeans united by a common religion who "will gladly forgather and intune holy choruses." [8]

It is not so much these chiliastic hopes themselves as the words in which he chose to express them that seem to indicate an unexpected affinity between Novalis and the Hölderlin of "Friedensfeier." But other German writers and philosophers of the time entertained such hopes; and some of their common vocabulary even could probably be traced back to the religious and secular literature that both men read in their youth. Also, Novalis differed from Hölderlin in directing his energies toward a philosophical synthesis of the most ambitious kind. Whereas Hölderlin had little use for modern philosophy once his poetry had become capable of conveying his peculiar vision, Novalis desired nothing less than to master the whole of modern science and philosophy in order to "poeticize" them, to integrate them into his own ideal of wholeness. Here he had more in common with Goethe than with Hölderlin; and Goethe was more favorably disposed toward Novalis than to Hölderlin, although Novalis' highly subjective approach to the natural sciences, his magical short cuts, could not fail to displease Goethe. As a poet, Novalis does not bear comparison with either Goethe or Hölderlin.

The name that Novalis gave to his projected synthesis was

[8] "Die Christenheit oder Europa." *Works* (Minor) II, 33, 38–39, 43–45.

Totalwissenschaft, total science or knowledge; [9] one might also describe it as comparative science, if that name did not suggest an austere academic discipline. "With the sciences," he remarked "it has been as with human beings: in order to work upon them and shape them more easily, they have been divided into separate sciences (and States); and the basis for this division, in either case, was fortuitous and inapt." [10] Novalis set out to remedy this false division; in what spirit, one can see at once from his daring juxtaposition of disparate orders in this dictum.

If one looks to the English poets and thinkers contemporary with Novalis for a man of comparable aspirations, only one name immediately comes to mind; the name of Coleridge. "My system," Coleridge told his nephew, "if I may venture to give it so fine a name, is the only attempt I know, ever made to reduce all knowledges to harmony. It opposes no other system, but shows what was true in each; and how that which was true in the particular, in each of them became error, because it was only half the truth. I have endeavoured to unite the insulated fragments of truth, and therewith to frame a perfect mirror . . ." [11] Those words are very much in the spirit of Novalis; but Coleridge's qualification of his "system"—"if I may venture to give it so fine a name"—at once establishes a difference not so much personal, as national. Coleridge's thought, however daring at times, could lean not only on past traditions, but on present institutions; just as his imagination, which could be more daring still than his thought, was held in check by the habit of good sense. Novalis' thought had no perch to rest on in the present; it was compelled to fly incessantly, pursued by an imagination that knew no bounds whatever.

Had he lived longer, Novalis would have attempted to incorporate all his diverse observations, reflections, and speculations into a single work; as it is, he left only aphorisms (or *Fragments* as he called them) and sketches. These *Fragments* con-

[9] Coleridge's "Universal Science" presents an exact and significant parallel.
[10] *Works* (Minor) III, 93.
[11] *Table Talk* (Ashe, 1888), 138–139.

tain enough substance for any number of philosophical treatises; but it is the fragmentary form that best conveys the
wholeness of Novalis' vision. For his philosophy, his "magic
idealism," [12] rests on the correspondence between mind and
matter, between the particular and the universal, between microcosm and macrocosm; any systematic exposition of his
thoughts would almost certainly have upset their delicate balance, limited their suggestiveness, and destroyed the very
"magic" that distinguishes them from the thoughts of professional philosophers. The strength and the weakness of Novalis'
thought is that it is the thought of a poet; not, as is commonly
said, the thought of a mystic, though the distinction in this case
is so fine as to be almost inexplicable.

His own word "magical" much more aptly describes his
thinking. It is by magical substitution that his dead fiancée, Sophie von Kühn, gradually became identified with the Virgin
Mary, his own longing for union with her was transformed into
a longing for Night and for union with God beyond the grave.
This capacity for magical substitution is a peculiarity of the poetic mode of thought; the mystic may employ imagery almost
indistinguishable from the poet's, but his images do not become
a substitute for the quality, person, or process that they serve to
embody. Novalis' true affinities as a thinker are not with the
Christian mystics proper, but with Gnostics, theosophists, and
alchemists, the seekers of magical correspondences between
matter and spirit, nature and the divine.

Because of this very capacity for magical substitution, a brief
biographical summary may be called for at this point. Friedrich
von Hardenberg, who wrote under the name of Novalis, was
born on May 2, 1772 on the family estate near Mansfeld in
Saxony. He was the eldest of eleven children. Both his father,
an ex-officer and director of a Saxon salt mine, and his mother
belonged to the pietistic sect of Moravians, or *Herrenhuter*.
After studying law at Jena, Leipzig, and Wittenberg, Novalis
went to Arnstadt in Thuringia to learn the practical duties of a
public administrator; his teacher, Kreisamtsmann Just, became
an admired friend and one of his early biographers. During his

12 *Works* (Minor) III, 107.

university studies Novalis had made the acquaintance of Friedrich Schlegel, the leading literary theorist of the German Romantic Movement, and of Fichte, its leading philosopher. At Arnstadt he met Sophie von Kühn, then a girl of thirteen, and spent most of the spring and summer of 1794 at Grüningen, Sophie's home; they became secretly engaged in the autumn of that year. Soon after, Sophie fell ill. In 1795 Novalis moved to Weissenfels, to work as an accountant in his father's department. He visited Sophie in the spring of 1796 and found her health improved; but the visit was cut short by the illness of his favorite brother, Erasmus. In the summer Sophie was moved to Jena for an operation on her liver; after a second operation, Novalis joined her there. In December Sophie wished to return home. Erasmus acted as her escort, but was seriously ill himself by January 1797. On March 19 Sophie died, two days after her fifteenth birthday. The death of Erasmus followed a few weeks later, on April 14.

At this period Novalis began to write his characteristic works. The experience of Sophie's death, recorded in a diary begun four days after the death of Erasmus, led to the following resolution: "My death shall be the proof of my feeling for what is highest, true immolation—not an escape—not a last resort." [13] In the same year he prepared his first collection of philosophical fragments, *Blütenstaub* (Pollen) and *Glauben und Liebe* (Faith and Love) both of which were published by Schlegel in the following year; conceived the *Hymnen an die Nacht* (Hymns to Night), published in 1800; and worked at his unfinished novel, *Die Lehrlinge zu Sais* (The Disciples at Sais) which, like most of his later writings, remained unpublished till after his death.

The remainder of his life was devoted to a course in geology and engineering at the Mining Academy in Freiberg, his duties as an administrator of the Saxon salt mines, his scientific, literary, and philosophic studies and the writing of his last works. These included many philosophical fragments and sketches, the final version of the *Hymnen an die Nacht,* the *Geistliche Lieder* (Spiritual Songs)—a sequence of poems that were to form a new hymnbook—and the unfinished novel, *Heinrich von Ofter-*

[13] *Works* (Minor) II, 88.

dingen. Less and less consciously Novalis was also preparing for his death. "Life," he wrote in *Blütenstaub,* "is the beginning of death. Life exists only for the sake of death. Death is both the end and the beginning, both the parting and the closer union of selves . . ." [14] In the second part of *Heinrich von Ofterdingen* he returns to this theme when he says of the Pilgrim that "death seemed to him like a higher revelation of life, and he contemplated his own brief existence with childlike, cheerful, emotion." In the *Fragments* he goes so far as to propose that "the true philosophical act is suicide; this is the real beginning of all philosophy, in that direction all the needs of the philosophical apprentice tend, and only this act corresponds to all the conditions and characteristics of transcendental action." [15] The German word *Selbsttötung* could perhaps have a different meaning also; this might be rendered as "egocide" or "unselfing"; more probably the aphorism relates to Novalis' own pledge to seek reunion with Sophie in death, thereby proving that the creative imagination and will are stronger than the physical forces that resist them. Yet in the last two years of his life Novalis did everything in his power to preserve his ties with this world; and already soon after Sophie's death he was able to perform all his duties with cheerfulness and enthusiasm, making it a rule continually to widen the scope of his activities. The following is a late entry in his *Studienhefte,* philosophical notebooks in which he put down his thoughts and plans for future use: "If I should fall ill, the order of the day demands edifying tracts, novels etc.; chemical experiments, drawing, music, guitar, copying and making excerpts, cooking, examining charts, visiting workmen, turnery, woodcarving etc; inspecting offices, observation of the illness, acoustic experiments, descriptions of fossils, meteorological observation etc.; visits, movement, rest, gymnastics and language studies, patience. (Morality and religion in illness and as many different occupations as possible.) (Even the blind and deaf man still has a large sphere of activity.)" [16] In the same notebooks Novalis reminds himself

[14] *Ibid.,* 113.
[15] *Ibid.,* 178.
[16] *Ibid.,* III, 388. Cf. Coleridge: "I should not think of devoting less than twenty years to an Epic Poem. Ten, to collect materials and warm

to "make anatomical observations when eating and carving meat." [17]

Already in 1798 Novalis became engaged once more, to Julie von Charpentier. In the following year he spent much time at Jena with the Romantic writers A. W. Schlegel and Ludwig Tieck, also making the acquaintance of G. F. J. Schelling; and in the same year he formed new friendships with two very different types of men, von Thielmann and von Funk, both of whom later became generals. He planned to marry Julie in August 1800, but shortly before that time began to show symptoms of consumption. In November the sudden death of a younger brother precipitated a serious hemorrhage. Novalis wished to convalesce in Austria, but was advised to remain at Dresden with his parents and his fiancée. At the end of January 1801 he returned to his professional duties at Weissenfels and continued his literary work. Two months later, on March 25, he died. He would have been twenty-nine years old on his next birthday.

Most of Novalis' major works were left unfinished when he died. But it is hard to imagine how any of them could have been completed. "Die Christenheit oder Europa," written in 1799, does not call for elaboration at all; and, like his notes toward a vast, encyclopedic treatise, his plans for the continuation of *Heinrich von Ofterdingen,* as recorded by Tieck, are so ambitious as to seem impracticable even for a writer of Novalis' energy and insight. Both the completed novel and the philosophical treatise would have been more than microcosms; the first an all-embracing allegory of human life, the second a syncretic and "syncritical" [18] exposition of human science and thought. For reasons already stated it is the microcosms that concern me here: a few of the ideas contained in the *Fragments* and a single sequence of poems, the *Hymns to Night.*

my mind with universal science. I would be a tolerable mathematician. I would thoroughly know Mechanics, Hydrostatics, Optics, all Astronomy, Botany, Metallurgy, Fossilism, Chemistry, Geology, Anatomy, Medicine—then the *mind of man,* then the *minds of men*—in all Travels, Voyages and Histories." S. T. Coleridge, Letter to Joseph Cottle, Spring, 1797. *Works* (Nonesuch, 1933), 573.

[17] *Ibid.,* 189.

[18] The word is Novalis' own. See *Works* (Minor) III, 307.

In spite of its fragmentary character Novalis' thought is remarkably consistent. Since his philosophy is a dynamic one, a philosophy of becoming, we must allow for a certain measure of development; but though his later thoughts may add to the earlier ones, they rarely contradict them. "To philosophize," Novalis wrote, "is to dephlegmatize, to vivify"; [19] and that is what his own thinking was designed to do. For that very reason, it is very difficult to give a summary of his thought; all I can do is to pick out a few representative ideas and indicate the spirit in which the reader himself should enlarge them to cover all the related spheres.

Novalis began with the extremely subjective idealism of Fichte on the one hand, the no less subjective religious emphasis of the *Herrenhuter* on the other; to this must be added the literary and personal influence of Friedrich Schlegel, with his theory of "romantic irony" and his analytical finesse (which derives in part from the French school of aphorists, from La Rochefoucauld to Chamfort in Schlegel's own time). The subjective tendency of Novalis' thinking was confirmed by Schlegel's literary program for the Romantic School, his emphasis on fantasy, free association, and deliberately contrived illusion (which could be shattered by romantic irony or by other sophisticated devices). Other thinkers whose influence on Novalis is apparent in the *Fragments* include Plotinus, Jacob Boehme, Spinoza, Hemsterhuys, Lavater, Zinzendorf—the founder of the Herrenhut communion—Schleiermacher, and Schelling. Novalis' debt to Goethe, especially to his *Wilhelm Meister,* which he both admired and condemned as a "pilgrimage to the patent of nobility," is clearly acknowledged in the *Fragments.*

Novalis set out to "philosophize" literature and to "poeticize" philosophy. "The world must be romanticized. Only in that way can one rediscover its original significance. Romanticization is nothing other than qualitative potentialization. The baser self is identified with the better self in this operation . . . By giving a lofty sense to what is vulgar, a mysterious aspect to what is commonplace, the dignity of the unknown to what is familiar, an infinite extension to what is finite, I romanticize them. This operation is reversed for what is sublime, unknown,

19 *Works* (Tieck; Schlegel), 256.

mystical, infinite—these are turned into logarithms by the connection—they are expressed in familiar terms. (Romantic philosophy. *Lingua romana.* Reciprocal elevation and debasement.)" [20]

The subjective basis of Novalis' thought can be seen in an early aphorism: "Inwards leads the mysterious way. Within us, or nowhere, is eternity with all its worlds, the past and the future. The external world is the world of shadows, it casts its shadows into the realm of light." [21] Novalis' individual contribution to philosophy was to concentrate on the relation between these two worlds of light and shadow. By taking subjectivity even further than mere philosophers had dared to do, he arrived at the point where subject and object are indistinguishable. "The proof of realism is idealism, and vice versa," [22] a later aphorism asserts; and again: "The world is a universal trope of the mind, a symbolic image of the same." [23] The word "trope" is the operative one; for, like Rilke after him, Novalis evolved a philosophy based on the poetic process itself, on the freedom of the individual mind to re-create the world in its own image. The relation between world and mind becomes reciprocal; long before Rilke claimed that it is the business of men to transform the outward and visible world by the act of creative contemplation, Novalis wrote: "We are on a mission, our calling to fashion the earth." [24] It is in the light of the same creative philosophy that we must interpret Novalis' maxim that "to become a human being is an art." [25] But Novalis' doctrine is more extreme than Rilke's; his whole philosophy and literary practice are based on the belief that the perfectly developed man can turn thoughts into things and things into thoughts.

Rilke, too, was long regarded as a mystic. Perhaps one ought to distinguish the ascetic tradition in mysticism from the aesthetic or pantheistic. If an ascetic mystic denies the reality of the outward world, it is in favor of a reality that transcends the capacity of his senses. Novalis and Rilke, on the other hand,

[20] *Works* (Minor) III, 46.
[21] *Ibid.,* II, 114.
[22] *Ibid.,* III, 332.
[23] *Ibid.,* II, 118.
[24] *Ibid.,* III, 55.
[25] *Ibid.,* 70.

endow the senses with the power, if not to create, to re-create and to transform the outward world; their vision is the "unmediated vision" [26] of modern poets, not the mediated vision of the traditional religious poet, who employs a symbolism that can be interpreted in terms of dogma. Where Novalis differs from Rilke is in directing his unmediated vision toward the plane of revealed religion; his magical philosophy was intended to open a new approach to Christian doctrine. For that reason, Novalis was careful to make a clear distinction between natural and revealed religion. His magical synthesis applied only to the natural sphere; but since he accepted the superiority of revealed religion to natural religion, there would come a point where "God must be separated from Nature. God has nothing to do with Nature. He is the aim of Nature; that with which Nature must one day harmonize. Nature must become moral . . . The moral God is far superior to the magical God . . ." [27] But this point could be reached only when rational, scientific, and natural knowledge cease to conflict with the truths of revealed religion. That is why Novalis chose the way of a magical synthesis: "We must endeavour to become magicians in order to become truly moral. The more moral we are, the more God-like, the more closely united and in harmony with God. Only through the moral sense does God become perceptible to us." [28] This vital distinction should be borne in mind by readers of Novalis; for in practice he never reached the point where "God is separated from Nature." All his work remained magical and animistic, even where it was dedicated to the "moral God" of Christianity. Novalis foreshadowed the three categories of Kierkegaard—aesthetic, ethical, and religious—when he wrote: "Every mathematical science aspires to become philosophical once more, to be animated or rationalized; then to become poetic; then ethical; lastly religious." [29] But it is to the poetic or aesthetic category that nearly all his work belongs.

Like Rilke, again, Novalis endowed inanimate objects with a life lent to them by the beholder's eye; in *Heinrich von Ofter-*

[26] I borrow this term from Geoffrey H. Hartman, *The Unmediated Vision* (Yale, 1954); for his definition of the term see 127–173.

[27] *Works* (Minor) III, 296.

[28] *Ibid.*, II, 288.

[29] *Works* (Tieck; Schlegel), 308.

dingen he speaks of the happy relationship that once existed between household utensils and their owners; and in the fragmentary second part of the novel he writes of his hero's father: "His eye stirred with the desire to become a true eye, a creative instrument." [30] Although he is rarely mentioned by name, the invisible hero of this novel, and of all Novalis' work is Orpheus,[31] with whom Rilke also identified himself. The myth of Orpheus is implicit in the first of the *Märchen* interpolated into *Heinrich von Ofterdingen,* the story of a poor bard who wins a princess and a kingdom through the power of his art. Other allusions to the myth occur in Novalis' earlier prose parable *The Disciples at Sais:* "Is it not true," one of the disciples asks, "that stones and forests obey music and, tamed by it, submit to every will like domestic animals?" And the enigmatic Teacher is described in these words:

. . . He watched the stars and imitated their courses and positions in the sand. Into the ocean of the air he gazed incessantly; and never tired of observing its clearness, its movements, its clouds, its illumination. He collected stones, flowers, beetles of every kind and arranged them in various patterns in front of him. To men and animals he gave his attention, on the shores of the sea he sat and looked for shells. To his own heart and thoughts he listened intently. He did not know where his longing would lead him. When he had grown up, he wandered about, viewed other countries, other seas, other atmospheres, stones that were strange to him, unknown plants, animals, men; descended into caves, saw how the earth has been built up in shelves and many-coloured layers, and pressed clay into curious rock formations. Now he discovered familiar patterns everywhere, only weirdly mingled and combined, and in this way often the strangest objects fell into order in his mind. Soon he looked for analogies in all things, conjunctures, correspondences; till he could no longer see anything in isolation.—All the perceptions of his sense crowded into great variegated images: he heard, saw, touched and thought at the same moment. He loved to bring strangers together. Now stars

[30] *Ibid.,* 136.
[31] Cf. Walter Rehm, *Orpheus: Der Dichter und die Toten* (Duneldorf, 1950); and Elizabeth Sewell, *The Orphic Voice* (London, 1961), 202–209.

were men to him, now men were stars, stones were animals, clouds were plants; he played with the powers and phenomena, he knew just where and how to find this shape and the other, to make them appear; and thus he himself drew tones and passages from the strings." [32]

The unexpected musical metaphor at the end evokes Orpheus once more; for Orpheus does not merely play music he has learned, but creates music that transforms the natural world. The whole passage is an apotheosis of the poetic process, written in the spirit of that magical tradition that revived in the late Middle Ages to inspire the medical practices of Paracelsus and the symbolic experiments of the alchemists.

"The idea of the microcosm," Novalis writes in one of the *Fragments,* "is the very highest to which men can attain." [33] How crucial it was to his own thought appears from another: ". . . A man possesses what one could call certain physical zones. His body is the nearest, his immediate surroundings come next, his town and province are the third; and so it continues as far as the sun and its system . . ." [34] If we add to this that every physical process has its parallel in the spiritual sphere we hold the clue to the whole of Novalis' philosophy. Thus he comments on the "symbolism of the human body" and points out that "thinking is a kind of galvanism"; [35] on the basis of this analogy he remarks elsewhere that "poets are both insulators and conductors of the poetic current," [36] so that an aesthetic process is related to a physical phenomenon and its mental counterpart. In the same way he takes up the current medical theories of Dr. John Brown on sthenia and asthenia, but extends their relevance from the nervous system to the whole psyche and even to the inanimate world. Novalis was planning nothing less than a "scientific Bible, the paragon, both real and ideal, and the germ of all other books." [37] The scheme of this book demanded that all the frontiers between the differ-

[32] *Ibid.,* 221.
[33] *Works* (Minor) III, 51.
[34] *Ibid.,* 86.
[35] *Ibid.,* 51.
[36] *Works* (Tieck; Schlegel), 321.
[37] *Works* (Minor) III, 332.

ent arts and sciences should be demolished—sometimes by empirical means, more often by magic. Mathematics is the key to all arts and sciences; and "true mathematics," Novalis writes, "is the proper element of the magician. In music, mathematics takes the form of revelation, of creative idealism . . . pure mathematics is religion." [38] And again: "Metaphysics and astronomy are one science. The sun is to astronomy what God is to metaphysics; freedom and immortality will one day become the basis of spiritual physics, even as the sun, light and temperature are the basis of material physics." [39] Just as science becomes a part of religion, religion itself becomes "experimental." Novalis himself refers to his system as *Experimental-religion.*[40]

In reading Novalis we have to try to clear our minds of certain deep-rooted prejudices; for instance of the prejudice that to understand the psychological mechanism by which we attain any particular state of mind detracts from the validity or the value of that state of mind. Novalis does not rate empirical knowledge lower than spiritual knowledge, for he does not accept the division. His psychological observations can be devastating; but he does not mean to disparage philosophy when he reduces it to a subjective craving, remarking that it is "really nostalgia, the urge to be at home everywhere." [41] This psychological aperçu must be related to the very different one in *Heinrich von Ofterdingen:* "Where, then, are we going? Always to our home." Nor must we be too much disturbed by the positively Freudian penetration of his remark on the cult of Nature: "The reason why people are so attached to Nature is probably that, being spoilt children, they are afraid of the father and take refuge with the mother." [42] Novalis himself was deeply attached to nature and studied it with indefatigable zest; for nature, to him, was also "an encyclopedic, systematic index or plan of our minds. Why content ourselves with a mere inventory of our treasures? Let us look at them ourselves, use them and work

[38] *Works* (Tieck, Schlegel), 276.
[39] *Ibid.,* 306.
[40] *Works* (Minor) III, 285.
[41] *Works* (Tieck; Schlegel), 258.
[42] *Works* (Minor) II, 186.

upon them in manifold ways." [43] His analytical inquiries are all part of his great scheme; there could be no "syncretism" without "syncriticism." It was only by giving scope to his skepticism that Novalis attained certainty in his faith. In the *Fragments* he asks: "How does one avoid tediousness in representing perfection? The contemplation of God seems too monotonous as a means of religious enquiry; one has only to think of perfect characters in plays, of the dryness of genuine, pure, philosophical or mathematical systems etc. Thus even the contemplation of Jesus is wearying. Sermons should be pantheistic; they should contain individual religion, individualised theology." [44] Novalis himself intended to write a series of sermons on this principle, as a complement to the hymns of his *Spiritual Songs*.

Although some of them did in fact find their way into a hymnbook, the *Spiritual Songs* are no less magical in origin than the rest of Novalis' work. It is the same process of magical substitution that enabled Novalis to translate his love for Sophie into poems devoted to the praise of the Virgin Mary. Novalis believed that the love between men and women could transcend its natural bounds, that *eros* could turn into *agape*. "By absolute willpower," he noted, "love can be gradually transmuted into religion. Of the highest being we become worthy only through death. (Expiatory death)." [45] This belief, again, is familiar to readers of Rilke, with his cult of young lovers who exhausted the possibilities of human passion and looked to death or religion for its consummation. In the case of Novalis the belief derives from the central experience of his own life. In the context of his scientific speculations in the notebooks, he wrote of his dead fiancée: "What I feel for Sophie is religion— not love." Indeed Novalis could not conceive of a true love between man and woman that was not "a union formed also for death." [46] Heinrich von Ofterdingen says of his beloved, Mathilde: "She will dissolve me into music. She will become my inmost soul, the guardian of my sacred flame"; and he says to

[43] *Ibid.*, 198.
[44] *Ibid.*, 295.
[45] *Ibid.*, 299.
[46] *Ibid.*, 295.

Mathilde herself: "You are the saint who conveys my wishes to God, through whom He reveals Himself to me, by whom He manifests to me the plenitude of His love." And again: "Who knows but that one day our love will turn into pinions of fire that will lift us up and bear us to our heavenly home before old age or death can reach us." In the allegorical *Märchen* that concludes the first part of the novel—an invention so free that one understands why the French Surréalistes were interested in Novalis—the same conception of love is personified in the Hagia Sophia, Divine Wisdom, whose traditional significance Novalis discovered in the works of Jacob Boehme.[47]

If we choose to remember its subjective origin in the case of Novalis, it is easy to condemn such love as "morbid"; but we should at least consider that Novalis would not have been unduly abashed by that word. He himself remarked that "Love is essentially an illness; hence the miraculous significance of Christianity." [48] Illness too, both mental and physical had its place in his system; in fact he speculated whether "illness could not be a means to a higher synthesis" and went so far as to claim that "illness is one of our human pleasures, like death." True to the spirit of Paracelsus (and not unlike the more advanced medical theorists of our time), Novalis devoted special attention to the relation between physical and spiritual or mental disorders. He stressed the importance of dreams to the psychologist; [49] but here had the precedent of a brilliant German aphorist of the pre-Romantic era, Georg Christian Lichtenberg, whose works he knew. Of organic illnesses he remarked that they should "be considered in part as physical madness or, to be more precise, as *idées fixes* of the body." [50]

[47] Jacob Boehme derived his knowledge of Sophia from the Gnostics, whose teaching in turn derives from ancient Babylonian, Persian, and Egyptian sources. According to Valentinus the Gnostic, Sophia was one of the Aeons who together constituted the Pleroma—the totality of God's attributes; but Sophia fell and, by her fall, caused this lower world to be created by the Demiurge, Sophia's son, an unintentionally evil being sometimes identified with Jehovah. The breaking up of the Pleroma occasioned by Sophia's fall can only be repaired by the superior Aeon, Christ, the Savior and Redeemer who comes down to rescue the fallen Sophia and take her back to her true home.

[48] *Works* (Tieck; Schlegel), 288.

[49] *Works* (Minor) III, 83.

[50] *Ibid.*, II, 25.

He would have laughed at the idea that the morbid origin of a state of mind makes it incompatible with true spirituality; for illness is as much a part of our condition as any ideal norm of health that we may oppose to it. "It is their illnesses that distinguish men from animals and plants. Man is born in order to suffer. The more helpless a man, the more receptive he is to morality and religion." [51] Against this necessary condition Novalis prescribed the "panacea of prayer," by which one "attains all things."

The importance of dreams is equally relevant to Novalis' practice as a poet and to his theories about art. As I have tried to show, his whole magical and syncretic philosophy is an attempt to reconcile traditional beliefs with a mode of vision that is poetic rather than religious. The main distinction between the traditional religious artist and the modern artist lies in their different conceptions of artistic creation. The traditional religious artist assumes that the world has been created once and for all: his only freedom, therefore, can be one of rearrangement. The modern artist, on the other hand, accepts no such restriction; whether he is aware of it or not, his practice rests on the assumption that art, quite literally, is a creative process and that the product of this process is not subject to whatever laws may govern the universe as a whole.

Since these two views are not, in fact, compatible, it was almost inevitable that Novalis should come to consider the question of poetic creation. Very significantly, he concluded that "the poet borrows all his materials, with the exception of his imagery," [52] for it is the gradual liberation of the poetic image from its traditional functions and associations that characterizes the progress of modern poetry.

The state in which we create images most freely, without need to borrow more than the rawest of material from the created world, is the state of dreaming. It can be argued that the mind, including that part of it which generates images in the dream state, is also a part of the created world; and that, as such, it is subject to universal laws of one kind or another. But

[51] *Works* (Tieck; Schlegel), 287.
[52] *Works* (Minor) III, 14.

one may still doubt that even the most devout of dreamers has ever succeeded in imposing the strictest orthodoxy in his dreams; and it is the issue of orthodoxy, not of religious belief in the widest sense, that divides the modern poet from the traditional religious poet.

Novalis believed that literature should aspire to the dream state. All his imaginative works tend toward a magical equilibrium in which "Die Welt wird Traum, der Traum wird Welt" [53] (World becomes dream, dream becomes world). "Poetry is what is truly and absolutely real," Novalis wrote; "this is the kernel of my philosophy. The more poetic, the more true." [54] It is clear from this statement alone that poetry, to Novalis, meant something quite different from the literary productions for which we commonly reserve that name. What Novalis meant by poetry is the magical mode of vision that some, but by no means all, of these literary productions embody. "Poetry" was a synonym for the creative imagination, that faculty which he described as an "extramechanical power" [55]—a power exempt from the physical laws that govern the universe. This power he identified with the principle of freedom itself; for it enables us to fulfill his demand that "life should not be a romance given to us, but a romance that we have made." [56]

On that basis, we can understand all Novalis' exorbitant claims for poetry and for poets; it is always in his own special sense of the words that he makes these claims. If poetry becomes "the basis of Society, as virtue is the basis of the State," and the poet becomes a "transcendental physician," [57] we must not refer these statements to any poet other than Orpheus. Novalis' interest in the actual craft of verse was no greater than his interest in any other human skill; nor did he particularly like professional writers as such. "Writers are as one-sided as all artists in any particular medium, only still more stiff-necked. Indeed, among professional writers one finds few persons of large and liberal disposition, especially where such persons are

[53] *Astralis. Works* (Minor) IV, 215.
[54] *Ibid.*, III, 11.
[55] *Ibid.*, 384.
[56] *Ibid.*, 73.
[57] *Ibid.*, 177.

wholly dependent on writing for their livelihood." [58] This criticism is more than an aristocrat's comment on the professional classes; it comes from the heart of Novalis' philosophy. For genius, to Novalis, was "the capacity to deal with imagined objects as with real ones, and to accord them the same kind of treatment." This gift is not confined to artists and writers; in fact there are many good writers who have only "the talent to present something, to observe it exactly and to give a fitting account of the thing observed," a talent that Novalis thought "different from genius"; [59] although he concedes that literary genius cannot do without it, Novalis' true concern was with genius itself, whether manifested in the arts or in any other field of activity.

For the talent itself, mere realism or verisimilitude, he had so little respect that in *Heinrich von Ofterdingen* he grants a long sequence of important dialogue to a kind of composite character or chorus whom he calls "the merchants"—and this in the most mundane part of the narrative. Heinrich himself and Mathilde have little more personality. Yet this lack of individual characterization does not strike one as more than faintly grotesque; for one knows from the start that, even where it deals with waking life, the logic of *Heinrich von Ofterdingen* is the logic of dreams. The highest form of art, in Novalis' system, is the *Märchen* or supernatural tale, a genre which in the classical era had been regarded as fit only for children and peasants. But of all literary genres, the *Märchen* permits the closest approximation to the dream state; and Novalis, like other Romantic writers, so greatly extended its traditional freedom that it became the one medium in which the creative imagination is very nearly autonomous. *Heinrich von Ofterdingen* progresses by logical stages to the *Märchen* that concludes Part I, a tale so freely imaginative that no traditional symbolism quite exhausts its meaning. It is supernatural to the point of surrealism.

Novalis' imaginative works are most original and most successful where they come closest to his ideal of creative autonomy; they are often commonplace where this ideal conflicted

---

[58] *Works* (Tieck; Schlegel), 301.
[59] *Works* (Minor) II, 114–115.

with his religious faith. The difference, again, lies in his choice of poetic media, but especially in his use of imagery. His proper medium was the prose poem or fantasy, like the un-rhymed parts of the *Hymnen an die Nacht,* the whole of *Die Lehrlinge zu Sais* and the *Märchen* woven into the narrative of *Heinrich von Ofterdingen.* With few exceptions—the truly magical "Lied der Toten" written for Part II of the same novel is a splendid one—regular verse forms had the effect of inhibiting his imagination and of making his imagery both incongruous and bizarre. One reason, perhaps, is the very simple one that Novalis never lived to perfect his art; and that even in his lifetime the actual writing of poetry occupied only a small space in his larger "poeticizing" activities. But a more deep-rooted reason is that Novalis' magical practices conflicted with his theological commitment; and this commitment is much more apparent in his poems written in regular meters—poems that were intended to rise from the aesthetic plane to the strictly ethical or religious—than in his free verse and poetic prose. The "Lied der Toten" again, is an exception, because it is not a devotional poem but an imaginative and idyllic account of domestic life among the dead. But the disparity is very striking in the *Hymnen an die Nacht,* a single sequence that combines poems in free verse, in rhythmical prose, and in regular stanza form.

When these *Hymns* were first published in Novalis' lifetime, all the free verse passages were printed as prose; more than a century later, in 1901, the discovery of a manuscript version [60] showed that most of these passages had originally been composed in the form of free, dithyrambic verse.[61] The extracts

[60] In 1930 an even earlier, uncorrected manuscript version of the *Hymns* was published, H. Ritter, *Novalis' "Hymnen an die Nacht" ihre Deutung nach Inhalt und Aufbau auf textkritischer Grundlage* (Heidelberg, 1930).

[61] The free verse dithyramb had been well established in German literature since Goethe's *Wanderers Sturmlied* of 1771, written in imitation of what was wrongly believed to be the freedom of Pindar's odes, whose complex metrical structure was not generally recognized at that time. The misunderstanding was a fruitful one; it gave rise to some of the best poems of Goethe, Novalis, Heine, and Nietzsche, to mention only a few of the poets who availed themselves of a freedom wholly appropriate to the needs of German poetry, though alien to the practice of Greek poets.

that follow are taken from the printed version, which incorporates revisions so vital as to change the very tenor of the *Hymns;* but in the case of passages written out in verse form before their final transformation into prose, the English rendering was done in two stages, the first keeping as close as possible to the rhythmic structure of the original verse draft. Sections I and II of the *Hymns* were composed in the form of free verse; Section III in the form of prose. Section IV partly in prose, partly in free verse, partly in rhymed verse; Section V partly in free verse, partly in various forms of regular verse; Section VI in regular verse throughout.

The first extract comprises the end of Section II, the whole of Section III and the beginning of Section IV; it includes the poet's account of the central experience—a personal experience —that gave rise to all the *Hymns.* He leads up to this account with a passage in praise of Light as a cosmic principle that is "like the inmost soul of life itself" and animates the whole of creation; yet the poet turns away to "holy unspeakable, mysterious Night," which at first he had treated as a negative power, since all his senses were still attached to Light. Gradually Night reveals her true significance as "Queen of the Universe, the exalted herald of holy worlds, the nurse and guardian of blissful love." The language of the first section is close to the language of Christian mysticism; one thinks of the "dark night of the soul" of St. John of the Cross. But Night, so far has become only the means by which the poet may consummate his "bridal night" with his dead beloved; this consummation is a spiritual one, but it is not yet a religious one in the Christian sense, since there is no allusion to any mediator other than Night herself. The Creator is addressed in terms that imply a belief very much like Hölderlin's belief in the cyclic recurrence of divine revelation, alternating with periods of "Night" or of divine absence; and like Hölderlin,[62] Novalis associates Light or Day with the era of the Olympian gods, Night with the Christian era. (Friedrich Schlegel characterized Christianity as the "religion of death.") Section II is devoted to the praise of Night and sleep. "To Light its time was allotted, but timeless and space-

[62] In *Brod und Wein.* The symbolism of night and day is very nearly reversed in "Friedensfeier."

less is Night's dominion." Day has become a mere interruption of Night, and one in which "unhallowed activity" prevails.

. . . Heiliger Schlaf—beglücke zu selten nicht der Nacht Geweihte in diesem irdischen Tagewerk. Nur die Toren verkennen dich und wissen von keinem Schlafe, als dem Schatten, den du in jener Dämmerung der wahrhaften Nacht mitleidig auf uns wirst. Sie fühlen dich nicht in der goldnen Flut der Trauben—in des Mandelbaums Wunderöl, und dem braunen Safte des Mohns. Sie wissen nicht, dass du es bist, der des zarten Mädchens Busen umschwebt und zum Himmel den Schoss macht—ahnden nicht, dass aus alten Geschichten du himmelöffnend entgegentrittst und den Schlüssel trägst zu den Wohnungen der Seligen, unendlicher Geheimnisse schweigender Bote.

III

Einst da ich bittre Tränen vergoss, da in Schmerz aufgelöst meine Hoffnung zerrann, und ich einsam stand am dürren Hügel, der in engen, dunkeln Raum die Gestalt meines Lebens barg—einsam, wie noch kein Einsamer war, von unsäglicher Angst getrieben—kraftlos, nur ein Gedanken des Elends noch. —Wie ich da nach Hülfe umherschaute, vorwärts nicht konnte und rückwärts nicht, und am fliehenden, verlöschten Leben mit unendlicher Sehnsucht hing:—da kam aus blauen Fernen—von den Höhen meiner alten Seligkeit ein Dämmerungsschauer—und mit einem Male riss das Band der Geburt—des Lichtes Fessel. Hin floh die irdische Herrlichkeit und meine Trauer mit ihr—zusammen floss die Wehmut in eine neue, unergründliche Welt—du Nachtbegeisterung, Schlummer des Himmels kamst über mich—die Gegend hob sich sacht empor; über der Gegend schwebte mein entbundner, neugeborener Geist. Zur Staubwolke wurde der Hügel— durch die Wolke sah ich die verklärten Züge der Geliebten. In ihren Augen ruhte die Ewigkeit—ich fasste ihre Hände, und die Tränen wurden ein funkelndes, unzerreissliches Band. Jahrtausende zogen abwärts in die Ferne, wie Ungewitter. An ihrem Halse weint ich dem neuen Leben entzückende Tränen. —Es war der erste, einzige Traum—und erst seitdem fühl ich ewigen, unwandelbaren Glauben an den Himmel der Nacht und sein Licht die Geliebte.

IV

Nun weiss ich, wenn der letzte Morgen sein wird—wenn
das Licht nicht mehr die Nacht und die Liebe scheucht—
wenn der Schlummer ewig und nur Ein unerschöpflicher
Traum sein wird. Himmlische Müdigkeit fühl ich in mir.—
Weit und ermüdend ward mir die Wallfahrt zum heiligen
Grabe, drückend das Kreuz. Die kristallene Woge, die gemein-
en Sinnen unvernehmlich, in des Hügels dunkeln Schoss
quillt, an dessen Fuss die irdische Flut bricht, wer sie gekostet,
wer oben stand auf dem Grenzgebirge der Welt, und hin-
übersah in das neue Land, in der Nacht Wohnsitz—wahrlich der
kehrt nicht in das Treiben der Welt zurück, in das Land, wo
das Licht in ewiger Unruh hauset.

Oben baut er sich Hütten, Hütten des Friedens, sehnt sich
und liebt, schaut hinüber, bis die willkommenste aller Stunden
hinunter ihn in den Brunnen der Quelle zieht—dash Irdische
schwimmt oben auf, wird von Stürmen zurückgeführt, aber
was heilig durch der Liebe Berührung ward, rinnt aufgelöst
in verborgenen Gängen auf das jenseitige Gebiet, wo es, wie
Düfte, sich mit entschlummerten Lieben mischt.

. . . Holy sleep—not too rarely make glad those who to
Night are dedicated in this earthly day-labor. Only fools do
not honor you nor know of any sleep but the shadow which in
the dusk of true night out of pity you cast on us. They do not
feel your presence in the golden flood of grapes—in the almond tree's miraculous oil and the poppy's brown juice. They
do not know it is you that airily surround the breast of the
delicate girl and of her lap make a heaven—nor ever guess
that it is you that, unlocking heavens, meet us in ancient lore,
bearing the key to the dwelling-place of the blessed, the silent
guardian of infinite mysteries.

III

Once, when I shed bitter tears—when dissolved in sorrow
my hopes flowed away and lonely I stood by the arid hill
which in a narrow dark vault entombed the image of my life
—lonely as never a lonely man has been, compelled by unspeakable fear—enfeebled, no more than a single thought concentrated on misery.—When thus I looked out for help, could
move neither forward nor back—and clung to my fleeing, ex-

tinguishing life with an infinite longing:—then, from the pale
distance—from the heights of my former bliss there came a
thrill of twilight—and all at once I had broken the bond of
birth—the fetters of light. Gone was the glory of Earth and
my sadness with it—all my griefs converged to flow into a
new, unfathomable world—rapture of Night, heavenly sleep
possessed me—The landscape gently rose; and above the landscape there hovered my newborn, newly delivered spirit. Into
a cloud of dust the hill was transformed and through the cloud
I glimpsed the beloved's transfigured face. In her eyes eternity
rested—I seized her hands and my tears turned into a spar-
kling, unbreakable chain. Millennia vanished away in the distance, like thunderstorms. In her arms I wept enrapturing tears
for the new life.—This was the first, the only dream—and
only that dream confirmed my lasting, unalterable faith in the
heaven of Night and its luminary, the beloved.

IV

Now I know when the last of mornings will come—when
Light no longer drives Night and love away—when sleep is
endless and all is a single, inexhaustible dream. Heavenly weariness I feel within me.—Far and wearying was the way to the
Holy Sepulchre, and the Cross a painful burden. He whose lips
have once tasted the crystal wave which, imperceptible to our
cruder senses, wells from the dark interior of that hill at whose
foot the earthly current breaks, he who has stood on the bordering mountain range of the world and looked across into the
other land, the domain of Night—that man truly will never
return to the bustle and din of this world, to the land in which
Light dwells in eternal unrest.

Above he will build himself tabernacles, tabernacles of
peace, will yearn and love, will gaze across, until the most
welcome of hours draws him down to the source of the spring
—what is earthly will float to the top, to be swept back by the
tempests, but what was hallowed by the touch of love will flow
dissolved through hidden channels into the realm beyond,
where, like scented vapors, it will mingle with loved ones de-
parted . . .

Here the symbols of Holy Sepulchre and Cross, which form a
transition from the poet's personal experiences to the later,
more strictly religious, sections of the *Hymns,* do not conflict

with the images of wine, oil, and opium or even with the erotic imagery of Section II; yet these latter images, even in their larger context, are firmly anchored in aesthetic or natural experience. In the same way, the conclusion of Section II, with its allusion to "ancient lore" or stories, makes one think of popular legends, myths or other receptacles of magical mysteries, which are more likely to be pagan than Christian. There is no need to apply theological criteria to the first four *Hymns*. They can be read as poetry, as they were meant to be read, or even as autobiography; in either case they are beyond dispute.

Section IV continues on the plane of personal experience; the poet addresses Light once more, affirming his own resolution—also recorded in his journal and letters—to give Light its due as long as he remains alive: "Gladly I will bestir my busy hands, look about me everywhere to see where you have need of me—praise the full splendor of your effulgence—unreluctant pursue the fine cohesion of your artifice—gladly contemplate the meaningful workings of your mighty luminous clock—lay bare the symmetry of powers and the rules that govern the marvelous interplay of immeasurable spaces and the aeons of time . . ." But "there will come a moment when your clock will strike the end of Time, when you will become like one of us, when full of longing and ardor you will extinguish and die." Once again, Light is associated with classical antiquity, but also with the revival of secular science and philosophy that culminated in the eighteenth century—the age of enlightenment; to these Novalis opposes a different humanism: "Indestructible, proof against fire, stands the Cross—proclaiming the victory of our kind." (Even the later of the two manuscript versions corresponding to this passage contains no reference to the Cross or to any other Christian symbol: from this, and other instances, it is clear that the Christian symbolism was added only when Novalis revised the *Hymns* in the light of his later beliefs, in 1799.) The fourth *Hymn* concludes with a passage in rhymed, but rhythmically irregular verse—still on the plane of personal experience. An extract must suffice:

| Hinüber wall ich, | A pilgrim I cross to |
| Und jede Pein | The realm of Night |

Wird einst ein Stachel	Where all my pains will
Der Wollust sein.	Be pangs of delight.
Noch wenig Zeiten	A little time longer
So bin ich los,	And freely I'll move
Und liege trunken	Till drunken I lie in
Der Lieb' im Schoss.	The lap of Love.
Ich fühle des Todes	I feel Death's mighty
Verjüngende Flut,	Renewing flood
Zu Balsam und Äther	Which to balm and aether
Verwandelt mein Blut—	Has transmuted my blood—
Ich lebe bei Tage	Full of faith and courage
Voll Glauben und Mut	I live by day
Und sterbe die Nächte	And each night in pure fire
In heiliger Glut.	Death melts me away.

The fifth *Hymn* is a historical and eschatological summary of the relation between men and gods from premythical antiquity to the present and the future. In the pre-Olympian age men were ruled by an "iron fate, a dark and heavy bond blindfolded their anxious spirits"; but with the triumph of the Olympians and the defeat of the Titans a happier age began. The Olympian age proper—only briefly touched on by Novalis— was succeeded by the hedonistic age, "when wine tasted sweeter, vouchsafed by the visible profusion of youth—a god in the grapes—a loving, maternal goddess growing in the full golden sheaves—the sacred frenzy of love a sweet service of the loveliest woman among the gods—an endlessly varied feast for the children of heaven and the inhabitants of Earth . . ." This feast was interrupted by Death, whose coming terrified and scattered the guests. There followed an age of dearth and desolation. "The gods and their retinue vanished.—Lonely and lifeless nature lay prone, fettered with an iron chain, strict measure and the arid number prevailed. As into dust and winds, into dark words the immeasurable flower of life disintegrated. Gone was the faith that conjures up spirits, gone the all-transmuting, all-unifying handmaid of Heaven, Imagination." This is the age of late antiquity, when rational philosophy and empirical science took the place of religion; and it also corresponds to the "classical" period in Germany against which Novalis was in reaction, though he made use of its achievements for his own magical, vivifying, imaginative synthesis. As in Hölderlin's system, this phase is the beginning of Night; and the birth of Christ, which illuminates the Night, is also a new epiphany of the Greek gods.

The birth of Christ is related as follows: "Among that people who, more despised than any other, had matured precociously and, stubborn in defiance, had grown estranged from the innocence of youth, the new world revealed a face never yet beheld —in the poetic hovel of poverty—Son of the first Virgin Mother . . ." This curious reference to the Jews of the Old Testament is the only one accorded to them in the *Hymns*. Novalis' account continues with the birth, death, and resurrection of Christ; but he interpolates the story of a bard "born under the unclouded sky of Hellas," who came to Palestine to worship Christ and moved on to Hindustan—"his heart drunken with sweet love: and poured it out in fiery songs under that gentle sky, so that a thousand hearts received its riches and the glad tidings took root, to rise in a thousand branches." Perhaps this bard can be identified as one of "certain Greeks" mentioned by St. John; but his function in the *Hymn* is that of linking Greece to Christendom in a more than geographical sense. The short poem that he addresses to Christ connects Novalis' account of classical antiquity with the central theme of the *Hymns,* but especially with the celebration of death in Christ that concludes them. This is the poem in question:

> Der Jüngling bist du, der seit langer Zeit
> Auf unsern Gräbern steht in tiefem Sinnen;
> Ein tröstlich Zeichen in der Dunkelheit—
> Der höhern Menschheit freudiges Beginnen.
> Was uns gesenkt in tiefe Traurigkeit,
> Zieht uns mit süsser Sehnsucht nun von hinnen.
> Im Tode ward das ewge Leben kund,
> Du bist der Tod und machst uns erst gesund.

> You are that youth who long in meditation
> Upon our graves has kept his face inclined;
> A token in the dark, our consolation,

Joyful beginning of a new mankind.
The very power that wrought our sad prostration
Now moves our hearts to leave that gloom behind.
In death eternal life was first revealed,
That youth is death, by him our ills are healed.

The poem which concludes the fifth hymn and the whole of the
sixth hymn (which bears a separate title, "Longing for Death"
and is sometimes regarded as a mere epilogue to the *Hymns*
proper) are devoted to the significance of Death in the new era,
the significance lent to it by the passion and resurrection of
Christ. The erotic imagery of the earlier sections recurs, but it
is now combined with an unambiguously religious symbolism.
Death—already identified with Christ in the poem cited above
—calls the redeemed to their "nuptials," which are both a reunion with those whom they loved on earth and a union with
the Virgin Mary, Christ, and God the Father. As in the *Geistliche Lieder* also, the Virgin Mary becomes more than an in-
tercessor; Novalis associates her both with his own Sophie and
with the Hagia Sophia, Divine Wisdom, whom he praises in
Heinrich von Ofterdingen as "for ever the Priestess of our
hearts."

I shall not cite these concluding poems, because I regard
them as poetically inferior to the preceding parts; indeed, they
take liberties with the reader's sensibility that are not defensi-
ble on any grounds. However conscious of the difficulties of
rendering spiritual experience in the language of sensuous
experience—and there is no other language to draw on—one
must object emphatically when Novalis characterizes the "night
of bliss" that precedes union with God as an "everlasting
poem":

> Nur eine Nacht der Wonne—
> Ein ewiges Gedicht—
> Und unser aller Sonne
> Ist Gottes Angesicht.

This is the conclusion of the fifth *Hymn;* the sixth concludes
with these lines:

Ein Traum bricht unsre Banden los,
Und senkt uns in des Vaters Schoss.

The significance of dream in Novalis' aesthetic philosophy does not justify its introduction at this climactic point of the *Hymns;* like the word "poem" in the other context, it can only serve to call in doubt the reality of what it is meant to render. Dream and poetry take us back to the realm of imagination, which is that of every poet *qua* poet; but at this point we grow aware of its bounds. That there are such bounds Novalis himself admitted when he acknowledged the superiority of the "moral God" to the "magical God." Yet in practice his conversion to the "moral God" was not complete even at the time when he prepared the final draft of the *Hymns.* It is either foolish or dishonest to compare Novalis' *Hymns* to the work of poets who succeeded in extending their vision beyond the magical sphere. As far as the initial experience is concerned, it may be permissible to compare Novalis' transfiguration of Sophie with Dante's of Beatrice; but when critics go on to compare the *Hymns* with the *Divina Commedia,* as they frequently do, they discredit both Novalis and themselves. Dante wisely parted with Vergil at a crucial stage of his journey. But Orpheus remained Novalis' guide well beyond the point where even Orpheus loses his power; the myth itself relates how the underworld defeated him.

The one major contradiction in Novalis' thought and practice will by now be obvious enough to every reader; but I shall try to recapitulate my main arguments. The contradiction to which I refer is that between Novalis' belief in the unlimited power of the creative imagination—as summed up in his aphorism: "Life should not be a romance given to us, but one that we have invented"—and his statement: "All that we call chance comes from God." If the very course and import of our lives can be determined by an act of creative choice, neither chance nor Providence can have any true significance; and the qualities of God Himself become subject to the requirements of the imagination. To a certain degree, this contradiction is inherent in idealism itself, at least in modern idealism from Descartes and

Berkeley onward; but there is a vital difference between the *cogito, ergo sum* of Descartes and the *imaginor, ergo est* that is constantly implied by Novalis. It is only with Fichte that modern idealism reaches its logical and absurd conclusion; and Novalis, being inhibited neither by logic nor by the *logos* itself, was able to improve on Fichte's absurdities.

The former of the two aphorisms I have just quoted is part of the fragment that begins as follows: "Whoever looks upon life as anything but an illusion that destroys itself, is himself still caught up in life." This is the kind of statement to which Novalis owes his reputation as a mystic; and it might indeed be a mystical statement but for the corollary cited above, and a host of other statements that contradict it. No true mystic could have asserted, as Novalis did, that "when our intelligence and our world are in harmony, we are like God." [63] It is clear enough from Novalis' writings that this very harmony between mind and world can be attained by allowing full play to the creative imagination; and the creative imagination usurps the place of God.

Novalis' philosophy, then, is not mystical, but utopian. That is why his imaginative works are almost wholly lacking in conflict. They are a perpetual idyll, an idyll in which evil does not exist and death is a rare sort of pleasure. The true religious mystic may reach conclusions not unlike those of Novalis: but he does not reach them so easily. Novalis' mysticism is a shortcut from the aesthetic plane to the religious; it leaves out the ethical, which is the plane of conflict. Thus Novalis asserts: "To the truly religious, nothing is sinful." [64] But the truly religious man, to Novalis, is the truly imaginative man; the only sense in which his assertion is true is that the imagination is harmless as long as it functions *in vacuo*. His assertion becomes not only inept but dangerously misleading as soon as we extend its relevance from art to life. The imagination intrinsically may be harmless, but it is not innocent. Novalis' own imagination was no exception, as we can see when he passes on from his favorite idyllic themes to the bloody cannibalistic fantasies in No.

---

[63] *Works* (Minor) III, 102.
[64] *Ibid.*, III, 111.

XV of the *Geistliche Lieder;* his answer, in the same sequence, was that the coming of Christ caused sin to disappear:

> Da kam ein Heiland, ein Befreier . . .
> . . . Seitdem verschwand bei uns die Sünde.

> Then came a savior, a redeemer . . .
> Sin vanished from among us then.

The same poem dismisses sin as an "ancient burdensome delusion":

> Ein alter schwerer Wahn von Sünde
> War fest an unser Herz gebannt.[65]

It was only by denying the existence of evil that Novalis was able to create his perpetual idyll; and to claim that "all absolute sensation is religious."

Novalis had no use for the whole range of experience that lies between pure sensation and universal truth; for the imagination deals in archetypes, not in particular phenomena or individual persons. Just as he leaps straight from the aesthetic plane to the religious, in the historical summary of the fifth *Hymn to Night* he leaps straight from classical antiquity to the Christian revelation, leaving out the ethical heritage of the Old Testament. The Old Testament era, perhaps, is intended to correspond to that phase of antiquity in which "strict measure and the arid number prevailed," the "flower of life disintegrated into dark words" and—most important of all—Imagination withdrew; his characterization of the Old Testament Jews as a people who "had grown estranged from the blessèd innocence of youth" would suggest as much. The "blessèd innocence of youth" is apt to be lost when a person or a people reaches moral maturity; but there is a different, much rarer, innocence that outlasts experience. This is not to be found in Novalis' works. The Romantic cult of innocence is the sentimental one of the very sophisticated; it is an escape from experience, not a renewal of innocence by the acceptance of experience and of

[65] *Geistliche Lieder I. Works* (Minor) I, 63.

guilt. Novalis' idealization of childhood—"Where there are children, there is a golden age," he wrote [66]—is connected with his denial of sin; and the golden age of childhood corresponds to early antiquity in his historical vision. That vision itself is utopian, being directed only at an idealized past and an ideal future.

One of the fragments provides a comment on his vision of classical antiquity in the *Hymns to Night* and of medieval Christendom in the essay "Die Christenheit oder Europa": "Absolute abstraction, annihilation of the present, apotheosis of the future, that essential and better world: this is at the root of the injunctions of Christianity, and at this point Christianity links up with the religion of the antiquaries, the divinity of the ancient religion, the institution of antiquity as the second main wing; these two wings together bear up the universe, the Angel's body, in an eternal state of hovering suspense, in the eternal enjoyment of space and time." [67] In his imaginative works, Novalis far exceeds the bounds of even this highly synthetic interpretation of history; for the autonomous imagination has as little respect for historical restrictions as for ethical or physical ones. His projected continuation of *Heinrich von Ofterdingen* not only includes parts to be set in ancient Greece and the Orient, with corresponding excursions into Greek and Indian mythology, but culminates in a purely utopian realm in which "the Christian religion is reconciled with the pagan. The legends of Orpheus, Psyche, will be sung." Even this is not enough; the idyll is not complete, since even this realm is still subject to certain physical laws of the created universe. The seasons, therefore, must be abolished: "Heinrich destroys the dominion of the sun." [68]

The triumph of the imagination over matter—and over the *logos*—can hardly go further than that. But in justice to Novalis it must be added that its apotheosis in Part II of *Ofterdingen* was to be followed by six other novels that would have em-

[66] *Works* (Minor) II, 135.
[67] *Ibid.*, 295.
[68] *Works* (Tieck; Schlegel), 154–155.

bodied his views on physics, social life, action, history, politics, and love. *Ofterdingen* itself is concerned with the development of a poet; more than one of the projected novels would have required a very different sort of treatment. Novalis would have attempted to fill the gaps between desire and its fulfillment, just as he planned to fill these gaps in his projected philosophical work. In the case of a writer so ambitious as Novalis, one must consider the intention, as well as the achievement. This ambition itself one may censure as a form of *hubris,* a *hubris* more extreme than that of which Hölderlin thought himself guilty, though Novalis' gentle nature and undisturbed piety seemed to appeal against such a judgment. As it stands, Novalis' work is rich in fragments that do not call for considerations of so general a kind; of visionary prose and verse that may take us well beyond our own experience, without trespassing on any truth that our own experience or beliefs may oppose to them. And perhaps Novalis was right in claiming that reality is indivisible, the quarrel between world and mind a mere historical misunderstanding. If so, the creative imagination itself may yet find its place in an order not of its creation.

IV

HEINRICH VON KLEIST

If we wish to understand the second, tragic phase of the German literary renaissance, no writer's life and work are as illuminating as those of Heinrich von Kleist. Like Hölderlin and Novalis, he began with a set of ideals inherited from his humanistic predecessors, such as Schiller's ideals of liberty, friendship, classical beauty, and the ethical sublime; but just as Hölderlin's juvenile rhapsodies on his favorite abstractions gave place to his mature odes, elegies, and hymns—lyrical poems that are tragedies in miniature, moving from thesis and antithesis to synthesis on the plane of tragic joy, of a joy purged by conflict and suffering—and just as Novalis turned his back on the present, even on life itself, to seek fulfillment in the past, the future, and the timeless world beyond the grave, so Kleist's most vital energies were not released until he experienced the so-called Kant crisis of 1801; a crisis which, at the age of twenty-three, left him bewildered, aimless, disillusioned, and desperate —at the mercy of Energy divorced from Reason. To say that his early phase of enlightened idealism had been unproductive is an understatement; his desire to believe in the panacea of Reason, with its concomitant benefits of Truth, Virtue, and Happiness, had prevented him from even beginning to discover his true gifts and his true vocation. Another few months went by before —to his own astonishment—he found himself at work on his first tragedy. In the meantime he had considered almost every possible profession open to a man of his rank and supposed talents; imaginative literature was not one of them.

Even now, and till the very end of his life, Kleist persisted in regarding himself as a man of action and never quite succeeded in shedding the conviction that "it is better to act than to think." What he did not know was that his proper field of action was literature; and that only literature could liberate him from the false antinomy between action and thought. This lack of self-knowledge and of wisdom, a lack that has caused more than one critic to brand Kleist as a case of "infantilism," accounts for the long sequence of resolutions, ambitions, and "life plans" by which Kleist endeavored to exorcise his daemon, and their invariable failure: his broken engagement to Wilhelmine von Zenge; his abortive attempts to settle down as a teacher, farmer, civil servant, soldier, publisher, and editor; his wanderings around Germany, Austria, France, Switzerland, and Italy; his fantastic plan to take part in Napoleon's projected invasion of England in order to die an honorable death; and, soon after, his threat to assassinate Napoleon in the cause of German nationalism. As he grew older, his plans to act became not less, but more impracticable, until he could think of only one act that was both possible and sufficiently decisive to qualify as a "great deed": this act was the act of suicide.

Hölderlin too considered himself doomed to destruction; but because he felt himself to be a mere "vessel" for divine truths and because such vessels must be broken once they have served their purpose.[1] Kleist, being neither priest nor seer, was even denied the comfort of immolation; all he knew was that the plane of action permitted no realization of his ambitions, passions, and fantasies. His life was a long sequence of ironic contradictions. He resigned his commission in the army to devote

[1] See p. 14.

all his time to scientific and philosophic studies; soon after, he put away his textbooks in disgust and never attained prominence as a scholar or scientist. At the time when he was expected to serve his country in a military or administrative capacity, he spent his time abroad and described himself as "a man who has no political opinions at all"; when his country adopted a policy of appeasement toward Napoleon, he flared up into a patriotism so extreme as to embarrass the Prussian government, who suppressed his newspaper and so deprived him of his livelihood.

Like Hölderlin again, Kleist became one of the legendary heroes of literature long before his works were widely or fully appreciated. In 1827, sixteen years after Kleist's death, so well-informed a critic of German literature as Carlyle could mention him in passing as "a noble-minded and ill-fated man of genius, whom the mismanagement of a too impetuous and feeling heart has since driven to suicide, before the world has sufficiently reaped the bright promise of his early years." [2] This brief obituary suggests little more than another addition to that line of unhappy geniuses who, ever since Chatterton, had been invested with the function of stimulating the imagination and jolting the conscience of the contemporary public, not by the quality of their works, but by the wretchedness of their lives. We have learned to despise this incidental function of the artist; but though largely irrelevant to literary criticism, it satisfied a genuine public need, which has existed since ancient times and will probably continue to exist in one form or another. (It is highly questionable whether the modern cult of success—as personified in record-breakers, film stars, best-selling authors and multi-millionnaires—has in fact superseded the cult of the tragic hero; rather it would seem to satisfy a different, more rational but less vital, need. Murderers and gangsters are the true popular successors of the tragic hero.)

Even later critics of Kleist, from Grillparzer and Hebbel in the nineteenth century to Friedrich Gundolf in the twentieth, did not succeed in disengaging Kleist's great qualities as a writer from their own reactions to his person; but there is little

[2] *Friedrich de la Motte-Fouqué,* in *German Romance: Critical and Miscellaneous Essays* (London, 1857), Vol. I, 312.

point in tracing all the misunderstandings that constitute the progress of a writer's reputation, especially as such histories always imply that error and prejudice have at last been miraculously dispelled. Perhaps it is more useful to say that Kleist has come to be recognized as a writer of the first rank; and that a French adaptation of his last drama, *Friedrich Prinz von Homburg,* proved that his work can be highly appreciated outside Germany. A French critic [3] has also paid him the fashionable compliment of considering the same play in the light of existential philosophy. As we shall see, this means little more than that Kleist was one of the many writers of past centuries who at one time in their lives reached the point at which Existentialism proper begins, the point at which "the strange institution that is this world"—to use Kleist's words—ceases to tally with any of the systems that have been designed to explain it.

The seven completed plays and eight long stories of Kleist need little support from his biography; but it is useful nevertheless to know what he was up against in his lifetime, for he was not altogether mistaken in believing that he was born at the wrong time, at the wrong place and into the worst possible circumstances. Absolutely, such a belief must always be wrong; but, given the basic error, Kleist was relatively right. As it will be impossible here to investigate all the causes—ideological, political, and social—that gave a tragic turn to the second phase of the German literary renaissance, these will have to be inferred from the facts of Kleist's life. In giving a brief account of his personal dilemma, I do not wish to imply that this was the immediate "subject" of his works; on the contrary, Kleist's outstanding gift as a writer was the powerful imagination that made it unnecessary for him to draw on his immediate experiences and circumstances. At the same time, as adverse critics from Goethe onward were the first to discover, Kleist's own problems and obsessions are always perceptible beneath the surface of his dialogue and narrative, like the figured bass in a musical composition. The analogy is Kleist's own. A few months before his death he wrote of his intention to put aside

[3] A. Schlagdenhauffen, *L'Univers Existentiel de Kleist dans "Le Prince de Hombourg"* (1953).

his literary work and devote himself to two earlier pursuits, to science and music. Of the latter he writes:

> I regard this art as the root or rather—to put it more scientifically—as the algebraic formula of all the other arts; and just as we already have a writer [4]—with whom, incidentally, I don't wish to compare myself—who has based all his ideas about his art on colours, so I, from early youth, have based all my general ideas about the art of literature on tones. I believe that the figured bass holds implications of the utmost importance and relevance to the art of literature.[5]

In Kleist's own case—and what critical generalizations by an imaginative writer are not, in fact, insights into his own practice, or deductions made from such insights?—the figured bass corresponds to the irrational obsessions to which we can trace the genesis of all his works. On these constant figures—supplied to him, because outside the scope of his intellect and his will—all his comic and tragic inventions are based. While it is more rewarding in the long run to concentrate on the skill with which Kleist developed and varied the given scheme, it is impossible to do justice to this skill without undertaking detailed analyses of more than one of his works. In the present study, intended as an introduction and a general interpretation, all I can hope to do is to shed a little light on Kleist's premises and compulsions, the figured bass of his work.

Bernd Wilhelm Heinrich von Kleist was born at Frankfort on the Oder on October 18, 1777. His noble birth—both parents belonged to the minor aristocracy of Prussia—was the first of his disadvantages. The Kleist family was expected to produce army officers of distinction, with such possible variants as the officer-poet Christian Ewald von Kleist, who had died in the service of his king, and the amateur scientist Ewald Georg von Kleist, the inventor of an electric accumulator known as the Kleistian flask. Heinrich always remained proud of his fam-

[4] Goethe?

[5] Letter of May, 1811, to Marie von Kleist. *Works,* ed. H. Sembdner (Munich, 1953) II, 895.

ily, but his family soon ceased to be proud of him; and he inherited all the obligations and restrictions of his class without the wealth that would have enabled him to break away.

Kleist lost both his parents at an early age; his father, the commander of a battalion, died in 1788, his mother in 1793. For a time he was educated by a Lutheran clergyman; then, at the age of fourteen, he became an officer-cadet in the Prussian Royal Guards and saw active service in the following year. After the death of his mother a maternal aunt became his guardian. Of his six brothers and sisters, it was his half-sister Ulrike, three years older than himself, to whom he remained most closely attached for the rest of his life; even if she did not "wholly understand him," as he thought at one time, she never turned against him and never failed to help him in every possible way.

Soon after becoming a lieutenant in 1797, Kleist began to devote most of his leisure to the study of mathematics, logic, and Latin. A year later he took the dangerous step of resigning his commission so as to be able to continue his studies at the university, where he planned to take up theology, philosophy, higher mathematics, and physics; a dangerous step because he was risking the King's disfavor, and even civilian appointments open to a man of Kleist's rank were subject to the King's approval. Kleist took the risk. For one thing, as he wrote to a friend, "the greatest marvels of military discipline, which were an object of admiration to all the experts, became the object of my most heart-felt contempt; I began to regard the officers as so many drill sergeants, the men as so many slaves; and when the whole regiment was exhibiting its skill I could still see it only as a living monument to tyranny." [6] For another, he wished to be happy, and "there is no better incentive to virtue than the close prospect of happiness, nor is it possible to conceive of a finer or nobler means to happiness than the way of virtue." [7]

Yet he admitted that he did not really know what he meant by virtue; it seemed to him only an "exalted, sublime, ineffable

[6] Letter of March 19, 1799, to C. E. Martini. *Works* II, 477.
[7] *Ibid.*, 472.

something." [8] It is clear that the two moral codes that he had been brought up to accept—the Protestant's reliance on his own conscience and the Prussian officer's unquestioning loyalty to a secular authority—had begun to clash in his mind. Kleist never ceased to waver between the two. An essay of this year on "The Sure Way to Find Happiness and to Enjoy it even Under the Greatest Stresses of Life" [9]—Kleist's first literary work except for a few juvenile verses—is an unsuccessful attempt to arrive at a more precise definition both of happiness and of virtue. Many of his later works hinge on the insoluble conflict between different moral codes; this conflict could lead either to the complete defiance of secular authority on the part of an individual conscious of being in the right—as in his longest story, *Michael Kohlhaas*—or, conversely, to the complete subordination of the individual's conscience to a national cause, as in his patriotic drama *Die Hermannsschlacht*. Virtue, in the age of German idealist philosophy, was an abstraction invoked to take the place of a consistent morality. It was so vague a concept that it could be used to justify almost any action; and the vaguer it grew, the greater its potency as an intoxicant.

Kleist's later experiences were to teach him that in the Prussian State there was no place for any virtues but the military and administrative ones; and even Goethe—comparatively civilized as the Court of Weimar was—could hardly avoid tragedy when, in *Tasso*, he came to deal with a poet's relationship with his patrons and rulers. The difference between German and English literature of this period can hardly be understood without considering that the German writers as such had simply no status in society; this is one reason why many of them strike us as so curiously modern. For a time, Kleist took refuge in a generous cosmopolitanism not unlike Goethe's; but Kleist's cosmopolitanism proved a poor substitute for the sense of security enjoyed by those who feel that they belong to a powerful, or at least to an independent, nation; and it did not stand up to the test that Goethe's alone was able to pass: the defeat and invasion of his country by a foreign power. Kleist's sense of isola-

[8] *Ibid.,* 472.
[9] *Ibid.,* 305–321.

tion and insecurity within the Prussian State eventually brought about a complete reversal of his former attitude: it caused him to seek compensation in extreme nationalism. Unlike Goethe, whose all-embracing philosophy of permanence within change was proof against every form of fanaticism, Kleist became a reactionary.

While a student at the university of his native town, Kleist attempted to draw up what he called a "life plan." He was afraid that even after his drastic assertion of independence his future life would still be "determined by chance," that he would remain a "puppet on the wires of Fate"—a condition he thought so contemptible that "even death was preferable to it." [10] His letters on this subject reveal the same confusion; for what he meant was neither chance nor fate, but the pressure of circumstances, and particularly of social conformity, on his mind. Kleist now decided that Reason alone was holy and that he must concentrate all his energies on the acquisition of knowledge. A letter to Wilhelmine von Zenge, to whom he became engaged at this time, contains a list of all the different professions for which he could now prepare; he mentions law, diplomacy, finance, only to dismiss them as unworthy of his ambition. Of the two he considers favorably, only economics would be compatible with government service; the other, an academic career, he pronounces unfit for a "citizen of the State," though most desirable for a "citizen of the world." [11] In his present rationalistic and humanistic phase he wanted nothing so much as to be a citizen of the world, responsible only to his own ideals and his own conscience.

Kleist went on to ask his fiancée which of these courses she preferred; but in view of the later developments of their relationship and Kleist's peculiar attitude to women, one must infer that he had no intention of taking her advice. Rather his question was the first of many designed to test Wilhelmine's intelligence, her feelings toward him, and her fitness to become his wife. It must be mentioned that Wilhelmine was three years younger than Kleist and that—as the daughter of a Prussian general—she was associated in his mind with his own family

[10] Letter of May, 1799, to Ulrike von Kleist. *Works* II, 485–492.
[11] Letter of 1800. *Works* II, 504.

background and with all the prejudices that he was now trying hard to overcome. This helps to explain why his later letters to her often took the form of lengthy questionnaires— examination papers, in fact—which had the dual purpose of exacting confessions from Wilhelmine and of allowing Kleist to educate her by correcting her answers. They also include such general conundrums as "What is better, to *be* good or to do good deeds?" [12]—a theological question that Kleist was really putting to himself, but never succeeded in finally answering.

There is no reason to doubt the sincerity or intensity of Kleist's love for Wilhelmine; but incapable as he was of coming to terms with his own impulses, he was wholly unable to cope with any relationship that involved an adjustment to the feelings or opinions of another person. Up to his very last works he could not conceive of a relationship between the sexes that was anything but a conflict of wills, a protracted struggle that must end with the total submission of one combatant to the other. True, this very submission could assume heroic proportions, as in *Käthchen von Heilbronn,* the most popular and least plausible of Kleist's dramas; but there was no question of anything like a partnership between man and woman, far less of a spiritual union achieved by the merging of two wills. Kleist admitted to Wilhelmine that his interest in girls was mainly educational: "However perfect a girl may be, once she is formed, she is no good to me. I myself must mould and educate her to my needs, otherwise it will be with her as with the reed of my clarinet: one can buy dozens of them at the fair, but when one comes to use them every note is impure." [13] Kleist prefers to cut his own reed. He does not seem to be aware that the comparison is hardly flattering, even to a girl brought up to respect the supremacy of the male. His real motive, of course, was the same fear that urged him to draw up a "life plan"; his independence was so precarious that he could not afford to make any concessions to others, neither to society nor even to the woman he loved. Marriage was only one of the many modes of life with which his imagination experimented, but to none of which he would ever commit himself. This is evident enough from two

[12] Letter of spring, 1800. *Works* II, 509.
[13] Letter of September 5, 1800. *Works* II, 554.

letters to Wilhelmine of the following year, fantasies of married life so various that they cancel one another out, so idyllic that they discourage every attempt to realize them.[14]

As Kleist told Wilhelmine, he had a rare capacity for day-dreaming: "When I shut my eyes I can imagine anything I please." Yet in the same letter [15] he writes of "the peculiar talent of poets, who do not live in Arcady any more than we do, but can discover what is Arcadian or simply interesting about the commonest objects around us." Kleist had not yet begun to cultivate this other faculty and even when, a year and a half later, he suddenly found himself in the throes of his first major work, he remained painfully conscious of a discrepancy between the realm of fantasy and the realm of facts. It is highly significant that Kleist's first imaginative experiences were neither visual nor literary, but musical; and that these experiences took the form of hallucinations. This is how he described them in a letter to Wilhelmine:

> At times—I don't know whether you're fortunate enough ever to have experienced anything similar and, consequently, whether you can believe this to be true—but at times, when at dusk I am walking alone with the wafting breath of the West wind in my face, and especially if I then close my eyes, I hear a whole concert, complete with all the instruments from the tender flute to the roaring double bass. Thus I recall a particular occasion, when as a boy of 14 I was facing both the Rhine and the evening breeze and was thus surrounded with the combined sounds of the wind and the water; then I heard a melting adagio, with all the magic of music, with all the modulations of melody and all the accompanying harmony. It was like the effect of an orchestra, like a complete Vauxhall, indeed I believe that all that the wise men of Greece have said about the music of the spheres was not sweeter, lovelier or more heavenly than this strange reverie.[16]

In one of his last stories, *Die heilige Cäcilie oder die Gewalt der Musik,* Kleist described the effect of religious music on four fanatical anti-Papists, who are not only converted to Ca-

---

[14] Letters of August 16 and September 3, 1800. *Ibid.,* 518, 549.
[15] Letter of September 20, 1800. *Ibid.,* 581–583.
[16] Letter of September 19, 1800. *Works* II, 579.

tholicism in the course of the very service which they intended to break up, but left in a state of religious mania after hearing a *gloria in excelsis* performed. This performance, if not a hallucination, is a miracle; for St. Cecilia herself has come to the rescue of her convent by conducting the work.

In the summer of 1800 Kleist went to Berlin to prepare for a government post; he had suddenly announced his decision to leave Frankfort, borrowed a sum of money from his half-sister, and burst into tears when asked for an explanation. In August, even more unexpectedly, he left Berlin for a long journey whose object has remained as obscure as he wished it to be. Together with an older companion, carefully chosen for the purpose, he set out for a destination of which only two other persons, Ulrike and Wilhelmine, were to be informed. Kleist's letters disclose the following facts: that he undertook the journey for Wilhelmine's sake, after coming to the conclusion that he was "unworthy of her"; that he expected Wilhelmine to be grateful to him, for he had "risked *his life*" for her sake; that at Würzburg, his destination, Kleist visited a hospital for nervous and mental diseases and himself received some kind of medical treatment at his lodgings; and that he was grateful to Wilhelmine for *saving* his life by her support. Back in Berlin he was calm and happy "after an affliction of 24 years"—that is, from birth.

His letters written during the journey are full of vivid descriptions of the landscape and architecture of southern Germany, revealing a receptivity to visual impressions that his fiction may often seem to contradict. The reason is that the hectic tempo of his narrative rarely permits any amplification of visual details, far less any indulgence in "atmospheric" description; only the slow movements of his stories, such as the lull after the earthquake in *Das Erdbeben in Chili,* left him free to exercise this particular talent. From the same letters we learn that marriage and self-education were still Kleist's immediate ambitions; that it is every individual's duty to think about this life, rather than the next, so as to discover how he may best perform his proper function; that this is more difficult for men than for women, since women are spared the rival claims of Nature and the State; and that the first duty of women is to serve Nature by bearing children. Kleist also expresses his antipathy to the ritual and influence of the Roman Catholic Church, as observed at Würzburg, mainly on the grounds that "all ceremonies stifle feeling." [17] About half a year later he very nearly became a convert.

In October, 1800, he had returned to Berlin. His latest resolution was to accept no official post but to oppose the demands of convention and earn a humble living by coaching occasional pupils. He now wrote of the opportunities offered by the literary profession, but was still thinking of scientific or academic treatises, not of drama or fiction. He proposed that he and Wilhelmine should marry at once and settle in France or Switzerland, where their reduced social status would matter less than at home. Meanwhile he continued to educate Wilhelmine, for instance by expounding the proper use of metaphor and simile —an interesting point, for Kleist himself was to become a master of this art. Kleist's characteristic concentration and economy of style owe much to his ingenious use of imagery. Not only by the careful placing of significant images, but—more important still—by the rigid avoidance of insignificant ones, he learned to compress into a single sentence what other writers would have spread over whole paragraphs of analysis or exposition.

Kleist's wish to marry at once—without the wealth or security still considered indispensable for marriage—was motivated by the usual fear of his own instability, this time by the fear that he would cease to love his fiancée. In January, 1801, he told her of his apprehension that "the precious stone which he had wrought upon with all his soul should prove not to be precious at all"; and in the same month concluded a long eulogy of Ludwig von Brockes, his traveling companion of the previous year, with more than a hint that Wilhelmine's character would not stand comparison with his friend's. Kleist was already approaching another crisis, the most shattering of them all. It was Brockes whose example had convinced him that "it is better to act than to think" [18]—another of those false antitheses that were to torment Kleist for the rest of his life. In February, still undecided about his future, he complained to Ulrike about

[17] Letter of September 11, 1800. *Works* II, 561.
[18] Letter to Ulrike von Kleist of February 5, 1801. *Works* II, 645.

"that sad clarity . . . which shows me the thought behind every expression, the sense behind every word, the motive behind every action; it shows me all things around me, and even myself, in all their pitiable bareness, and in the end I feel nauseated by this nakedness." [19] This clarity was to become one of Kleist's greatest virtues as a writer; but few great writers have needed to try out so many blind alleys before beginning to know where to apply their talents. In the same letter Kleist complained of his morbid shyness—undoubtedly an aftereffect of his adolescence as a Prussian cadet—and ascribed it to a physical cause; if, as is probable, he was thinking of his stammer, he was confusing cause and effect. His moral dilemma obsessed him more than ever: "Gladly I would always do what is right, but what is one to do if one doesn't know in what right consists?" [20] His head, he wrote, was like a container of lottery tickets, with a thousand blanks and only one chance of a prize. Worst of all, "one science has come to mean as much to me as another." [21] Clearly he was only waiting for the blow that would absolve him from choosing between them.

This blow came a fortnight later. In two letters, March 22 and 23, 1801, he informed Wilhelmine and Ulrike that his reading of Kant's works had convinced him of the futility of all his scientific studies, since there was no such thing as absolute truth and "what in this life we call truth is known by a different name after death." [22] Kleist had discovered the metaphysical basis of his moral and emotional dilemma; and though he did not know it, his misinterpretation of Kant was the most important stage in his progress toward self-knowledge. It was not so much Kant as Kleist's own daemon that precipitated his present crisis; for only the crust of a shallow rationalism had prevented his daemon from breaking through. "My *unique* and *highest* aim has sunk, I now have none at all," [23] he wrote to Ulrike, and told her that his textbooks had come to disgust him, that he could do no work and spent his time in coffeehouses, theatres,

[19] *Ibid.*, 644–645.
[20] *Ibid.*, 642.
[21] *Ibid.*, 646.
[22] Letters of March 22 and 23. *Ibid.*, 651–652, 654–655.
[23] *Ibid.*

and concert halls; his only hope was that he might find a new aim by traveling. "At home I could only lay my hands on my lap and think; so I may as well move about and think. I shall turn back as soon as I know what to do." [24]

Kleist never turned back; and it was not thinking that led him to his true vocation, one of the few he had omitted from all his calculations. In April he left with Ulrike for Paris; at Dresden, on the way, he almost became a Catholic convert,[25] but, as usual, could not commit himself. All he wanted, he wrote to Wilhelmine, was peace; and a few days later summed up his ambitions as "a wife, a house of my own and independence." [26] By August he had changed the order to "independence, a house of my own and a wife." [27] Although he continued to inform his fiancée of his various projects—"Is it possible that so many contradictions can find room in the same heart?" he exclaimed —he also began to write to other women, acquaintances of his military years to whom he sent nostalgic reminiscences of that period. Wilhelmine's sister Luise was another woman to whom he addressed one of his minor works in letter form, a treatise on the virtues and vices of the French. He praised their wit and soundness of judgment, but censured them for frivolously pursuing their pleasures after the damage done by Napoleon. "But a whole nation never blushes. It divides its guilt by 30,000,000, so that only a tiny share falls to each individual, and this every Frenchman can easily bear." [28] Kleist's own debt to French lucidity is very great; not only his adaptation of Molière's *Amphytrion,* one of Kleist's very finest works, but all his later writings profited by his familiarity with French literature of the classical period; without its help he would hardly have attained the sobriety and restraint which, just because they were foreign to his nature, became indispensable to his art. In spite of his condemnation of French frivolity, Kleist's own morality was soon to prove no less ambiguous, frivolously so in his comedies, all too solemnly in his weaker dramas. The crisis that had

[24] *Ibid.*
[25] Through the effect on him of liturgical music. Letter of May 21, 1800. *Ibid.,* 671.
[26] Letter of April 14, 1801. *Ibid.,* 666.
[27] Letter to Wilhelmine v. Zenge of August 15, 1801. *Ibid.,* 707.
[28] Letter to Adolphine von Werdeck of July 28, 1801. *Ibid.,* 698.

destroyed his belief in absolute truth had also destroyed his belief in the absolutes of good and evil. Absolute evil, he wrote to Wilhelmine from Paris, does not exist, since evil actions may lead to good results in a world "where all things are linked and tangled a thousandfold and every deed gives birth to millions of others." [29] This moral confusion of ends and means, cause and effect, became as essential a premise for Kleist's works as his metaphysical disorientation. Yet even now, and at every time of his life, his one desire was "to do something *good:*" he promised Wilhelmine never again to act precipitately: "If I do so once more, it will be for the last time, since it will make me despise either my soul or this earth, and I shall separate them." [30] He was aware that he had disappointed the expectations of all his relatives and friends, having accomplished nothing by defying the conventions. They looked upon him as "a genius come to grief," [31] a judgment with which he agreed for other reasons than theirs: because he despised the knowledge which they considered his only asset, yet had wasted years in acquiring it. What he did not mention to anyone is that he had already written the first draft of a tragedy, *Die Familie Thierrez,* later renamed *Die Familie Schroffenstein* and wisely transferred to a German setting.

Once again, on October 10, 1801, he formulated three ambitions—"to cultivate a field, to plant a tree and to engender a child," an entirely different complex of possibilities that shows the influence of Rousseau (whom earlier on he had fervently recommended to Wilhelmine). If Wilhelmine was to be the mother of this child, her role had ceased to be important enough for inclusion in the new triad. In November Kleist parted company with Ulrike, sending her back alone while he stopped in the Rhineland before moving to Switzerland in December. He had informed Wilhelmine that he intended to settle in Switzerland as a simple peasant, but also that he intended to earn his living by writing books; Wilhelmine was to join him as soon as possible. She replied that she objected to becoming a farmer's wife, that her constitution was not strong enough and

[29] Letter of August 15, 1801. *Ibid.,* 707.
[30] *Ibid.,* 708.
[31] Letter to Wilhelmine v. Zenge of October 10, 1801. *Ibid.,* 718.

that she suffered from headaches in the sun. Kleist assured her that she would have two or three maids to help her with the work; but his letters grew shorter and fewer until, in May, 1802, he told her that most probably he would never return to Germany—not, at least, until he could fulfill the expectations of those whom he had "foolishly provoked by a great number of boastful actions"; [32] and that his present venture, to buy land and farming equipment in Switzerland, would cost him the whole of his small fortune and probably leave him destitute by the following year. He concluded: "Dear girl, don't write to me any more. I have no other wish than to die soon." [33]

In actual fact Kleist had already dropped his plan to buy land; ostensibly because his "new fatherland," as he had called Switzerland in December, was in danger of being annexed by Napoleon; but really because his vocation had caught up with him at last. In February he had rented a small house on a lake island near Thun, quickly completed his first tragedy *Die Familie Schroffenstein,* and soon started work on another. Shortly before his farewell letter to Wilhelmine, in which there is no mention of his new occupation, he wrote to Ulrike telling her of his fear that he might die before completing the second work; yet he has no other wish than to die as soon as he has attained three objects, "a child, a fine poem and a great deed." [34] What is strange is that Kleist seems to have attached no value at all to *Schroffenstein,* which he published anonymously in 1803; for all its gruesome crudities—reminiscent of some of the minor Jacobean dramatists—this tragedy has most of the stylistic qualities of Kleist's later works. With its peculiar syntax, colloquialisms, frequent enjambment, and sudden changes of tempo, the blank verse is essentially dramatic and unmistakably Kleistian. Underneath the somewhat unoriginal plot—a barbarous variation on the *Romeo and Juliet* theme—the play reveals that obsession with the question of truth and error which remained the pivot of all Kleist's works.

The "fine poem" of Kleist's letter is not *Schroffenstein* but *Robert Guiskard,* his second tragedy, part of which he read to

[32] Letter of May 20, 1802. *Ibid.,* 750.
[33] *Ibid.,* 751.
[34] Letter of May 1, 1802. *Ibid.,* 749.

C. M. Wieland at Weimar in December, 1802. Kleist's fear that he might die before completing it was irrational but not unfounded; for in the summer, in the course of struggling to finish the play, he succumbed to the first of the serious illnesses that were to recur throughout his life, whenever his mental stress became more than he could bear. These illnesses affected his stomach and induced fevers, delirium, and morbid terror. After recovering at Berne, Kleist moved to Weimar, then to Ossmannstedt, where he was Wieland's guest for some months. Wieland's daughter Luise was one attraction; and Wieland's enthusiastic response to *Guiskard*—the only encouragement Kleist ever received from an old and distinguished writer—gave Kleist what he later called the proudest moment of his life.

In March, 1803, Kleist moved on to Leipzig, where he took lessons in elocution and declamation, practicing on his own play. Later that summer, at Dresden, he wrote the greater part of his first comedy, *Der Zerbrochene Krug*. There, too, he met a number of old friends, his former fellow officers Friedrich de la Motte Fouqué, August Rühle von Lilienstern and Ernst von Pfuel, with the last of whom he set out on another journey to Switzerland, Northern Italy, and France. Ulrike offered her company once more, but had to be content to finance her brother's journey.

Even Kleist's literary works were not safe from his fits of heroic despair. From Geneva he wrote to Ulrike about *Guiskard:* "I have now spent half a thousand consecutive days—the nights of most included—on the attempt to add one more wreath to the many already won by our family; now our tutelary goddess calls out to me that I have done enough." He attributes his failure to the fact that "this northern strip of sky" —meaning either Prussia or contemporary Europe in general —is not ready to bring forth the "necessary link in the chain of human inventions," which his play was to have constituted, so that he must "abdicate" to an artist yet unborn; but he also blames himself: "Hell gave me my half-talents, Heaven gives men a whole one or none at all." [35] A short time later, in Paris, he "read, condemned and burned" all he had written of the

[35] Letter of October 5, 1803. *Ibid.*, 761–762.

play which was to have been his masterpiece and which Wieland compared to the tragedies of Shakespeare. (To judge by the extant fragment, which Kleist rewrote in 1808, what is more striking about *Guiskard* is its approximation to Greek tragedy. The opening scenes convey an extraordinary sense of community between the old warrior and his people; and the plague dominates both like a malevolent manifestation of Fate.) After destroying the play in Paris Kleist wrote again to Ulrike: "Heaven denies me fame, the greatest of earthly possessions; like an obstinate child, I shall throw all the others away." [36] In later years Kleist either lost or destroyed his autobiography and his only full-length novel; his last and greatest drama, *Friedrich Prinz von Homburg,* accidentally survived another holocaust.

In June, 1804, Kleist applied for a government post in Berlin; but he had attempted to keep his promise to throw all his other possessions away by deciding to take part in Napoleon's projected invasion of England and to die in the process. With this end in view, he had traveled to Boulogne, found that there would be no invasion, then moved via Paris to Mainz, where he collapsed and was seriously ill for the next five months. Now, in Berlin, he was forced to excuse his preposterous conduct in France by pleading that he had been out of his mind; but his reception remained cold. He wrote two desperate letters to the King, but received no answer. At last, toward the end of the year, he was admitted to the Department of Finance and, in May 1805, left for a post at Königsberg in East Prussia. Here he put the finishing touches to his first comedy, worked on his second, *Amphytrion,* and started his first two stories, *Die Marquise von O.* and *Das Erdbeben in Chili.* He endured employment for just over a year; then he took advantage of another illness to apply for six months' leave, which he prolonged indefinitely. "My nervous system is ruined," he wrote to Ulrike,[37] who promptly took charge of him at Königsberg.

Die Familie Schroffenstein had been performed at Graz in 1804; but Kleist was still far from being an established writer or dramatist. Of his seven completed plays only three were ever performed in his lifetime. Kleist did not feel that he was any

---

[36] Letter of October 26, 1803. *Ibid.,* 762.
[37] Letter of October 24, 1806. *Ibid.,* 800.

nearer to the fame that was to be his justification for rebelling against the family tradition; and he never forgot his other resolution, to "perform a great deed." When his friend Lilienstern suggested that he and Kleist should not give up hope of being happy one day, Kleist's heroic fury broke out again: "Who would think of being happy in this world! Shame on you, I feel like saying, if that is your hope. What shortsightedness, my noble friend, to strive for anything on this earth where all things end with death. We meet, we love each other for three consecutive springs: and flee from each other a whole eternity. And what is worthy of strife, if love is not? Oh, there must be something other than love, happiness, fame etc., x, y, z, of which our souls are not aware." [38] Kleist was probably alluding to his broken engagement to Wilhelmine, for he met her again at Königsberg, where she lived as the wife of Kant's successor to the chair of philosophy. Kleist still wanted all or nothing: "Come," he wrote to Lilienstern, "let us do something good and die in the process! One of those million deaths we have already died and have yet to die. It's only like walking from one room into the next." [39]

On his way to Dresden in February, 1807, Kleist was arrested by the French authorities—Napoleon had defeated Prussia at Jena in 1806—transported to France and imprisoned there for five months on the erroneous charge of being a spy. If Kleist's account of the hardships he suffered during this period seem strangely dispassionate, it is because for once he did not need to feel responsible for his own misfortune. As for the petty injustice of being treated first as a political offender, then as a prisoner of war, it could no longer outrage "a heart that is intimately familiar with greater things, and with the greatest." [40] Kleist got on with his work while Ulrike came to his rescue as usual, this time by remonstrating with General Clarke in Berlin.

It may seem all the more astonishing that a year later Kleist suddenly turned into the fanatical nationalist who wrote *Die Hermannsschlacht* and the violent diatribes against the French

[38] Letter of August 31, 1806. *Ibid.*, 797.
[39] *Ibid.*, 798.
[40] Letter to Ulrike von Kleist of June 8, 1807. *Ibid.*, 1810.

published in the course of the next few years. In 1802 Kleist had described himself as "one who has no political opinions at all; [41] and three months after his release by the French he was planning to apply for the exclusive German publishing rights of the *Code Napoléon* and other official publications of the French government. The main reason for his change of heart in 1808 has already been touched upon. Another is Kleist's reluctant admission at about this time that "action is not my art"; [42] if he himself could not act, he would at least incite others to action. And there is no doubt that he had long felt personally humiliated by his King's weak policy toward the French, a policy that frustrated his own heroic impulses.

The nature of his interest in Arminius, the German chieftain who defeated the three Roman legions under Varus, is clear from a letter written as early as 1801: "If a young man wishes to take arms bravely against the enemy who threatens his country, he is informed that the King keeps an army which protects the State for money,—How fortunate was Arminius to find the great moment. For what course would be open to him nowadays, unless it were to become a lieutenant in a Prussian regiment?" [43] True, it is difficult at present to read Kleist's *Hermannsschlacht* without the special reactions of one who has seen his barbaric hero and heroine rise again in the flesh; and Kleist's intention to use this play as a means of arousing hostility to the French can be criticized on aesthetic grounds, perhaps even on the moral grounds of Paul Valéry's dictum that "it is infamous to make use of arguments which are not valid in solitude, which are effective only in the presence of a public." [44] But it is important to remember that Kleist's nationalism was wholly sincere; and that in fact the play was neither published nor performed in his lifetime, since nationalism was still in its insurgent phase. As for the morality of *Die Hermannsschlacht,* it doesn't differ radically from that of all but his very last works, certainly not from that of *Penthesilea,* his

[41] Letter to Ulrike von Kleist of January 12, 1802. *Ibid.,* 740.
[42] Letter to Otto August Rühle von Lilienstern of July 15, 1807. *Ibid.,* 819.
[43] Letter to Adolphine von Werdeck of November 29, 1801. *Ibid.,* 724.
[44] *Mélange* (Paris, 1941), 182.

splendid and barbarous tragedy completed shortly before 1808.

After his release from imprisonment, Kleist settled at Dresden, where he founded a publishing firm in collaboration with various friends. In the following year, Goethe produced an adaptation of *Der Zerbrochene Krug* at Weimar—an experiment bound to fail, not only because of the nature of this adaptation, but because the Weimar public could not possibly appreciate either the realism or the allusive metaphysical crux of Kleist's comedy. The comparative success of *Käthchen von Heilbronn,* when performed in Austria and Bavaria in 1810 and 1811, helps to explain the disillusioned bitterness of Kleist's last letters. *Der Zerbrochene Krug* is one of the few great comedies by modern German authors. *Käthchen,* for all its Kleistian qualities, was a compromise with the taste of a public that Kleist despised; and *Penthesilea,* a genuine tragedy weakened neither by a happy ending nor by melodramatic effects borrowed from the Romantic convention, was never performed in Kleist's lifetime, though it was published in 1808.

Earlier in the same year Kleist began to concentrate all his activities on the launching of a literary magazine, *Phoebus,* in which he published some of his own poems, *Die Marquise von O.* and extracts from four of his plays. "On the knees of my heart," [45] he begged Goethe for a contribution to *Phoebus,* but in vain. By April, 1809, the magazine, too, had become impracticable. Exactly ten years earlier, Hölderlin had put all his hopes of economic independence into a similar venture; and had suffered the same rebuff, with consequences no less serious. Kleist's reaction was to leave Dresden with a new friend, the historian Friedrich Dahlmann, asking Ulrike to settle his debts. Their destination was Vienna, for Austria was still resisting Napoleon and Kleist intended to "plunge directly or indirectly into the stream of events." At this time, it was rumored, he planned to assassinate Napoleon; but though the two friends toured the battlefields, they took no active part in the war. In July, after the defeat of the Austrians at Wagram, all Kleist's plans to act directly or indirectly were void once more. He broke down in Prague. After a long and serious illness he

---

[45] The figure of speech derives from the apocryphal *Prayer of Manasses:* "Now therefore I bow the knee of my heart."

went home to Frankfort, set out again for Austria, turned back in southern Germany and arrived in Berlin in January, 1810.

There he founded the first daily newspaper ever to appear in Berlin. In March he wrote a birthday poem for the Queen, who had previously granted him a small yearly pension at the request of his cousin Marie von Kleist; but even this income ceased when the Queen died in July. Kleist's newspaper, *Berliner Abendblätter,* flourished for a time, thanks in part to the brilliance of his own contributions in the form of essays, reports, anecdotes, and political tracts; but the nationalistic fervor of all the contributors was probably the chief attraction. The best of Kleist's journalistic pieces have the same terseness as his admirable short stories, which he now collected for publication in book form; and many of them sprang from Kleist's interest in situations that just fail to cross the borderline of what is credible.

During the last few years Kleist had formed a very close friendship with his cousin Marie. He was also in touch with the Romantic writers, Friedrich von Schlegel, Ludwig Tieck, Achim von Arnim, and Clemens Brentano. He seems to have enjoyed the social life of Berlin, even making occasional appearances in the literary salons; and both his literary and political ambitions were beginning to be fulfilled. For a time it seemed that he would mellow and relax, reconciled both to outward and inward necessity like the hero of his last drama, *Friedrich Prinz von Homburg.* Then, in December, 1810, the Prussian government forbade the publication of independent political articles in his newspaper, offering to supply others representative of official policy; the main issue, of course, was Kleist's hostility to the French. The circulation rapidly declined, while Kleist desperately but vainly applied for the promised compensation for his heavy financial loss. He appealed to the King, to the King's brother, and to the Chancellor, von Hardenberg, even threatening one of the responsible officials with a duel.

At last, in October, 1811, his patience gave out; he thought of returning to Vienna, but could not face yet another attempt to make a new start. "I feel more tired than I can say of always looking in a different place for what—because of my own peculiar disposition—I have never found anywhere," he wrote to Marie; [46] and: "Really, it's strange how everything I undertake at present seems bound to come to nothing; how whenever I decide to take a firm step the ground simply vanishes from under my feet." [47] In November he wrote: "My soul is so sore that— how can I put it?—when I stick my nose out of the window the daylight that shines on it hurts." [48] Soon after, the King offered to renew his military commission; Kleist was to be the King's own adjutant or else a company commander.

This offer came too late. Kleist did not even have enough money to buy his military equipment, as he mentioned in his reply. In November a married woman suffering from cancer, Henriette Vogel, agreed to join him in a suicide pact. In two letters to Marie, Kleist justified his last resolution on the grounds of his King's shameful alliance with Napoleon, the refusal of his own brothers and sisters to regard him as anything but "a useless member of society, no longer worthy of any sympathy" [49] and his readiness for death, "since down here there is nothing left for me to learn or to acquire." [50] In his farewell letter to Marie he describes how "death and love alternate to wreathe these last moments of my life with heavenly and earthly flowers"; [51] he apologizes to Marie for preferring Henriette's love to hers, but reminds her that more than once he had asked *her* to die with him and that she had always refused.[52] Kleist's last literary work is a rhapsodic love poem in free verse, the "Litany of Death" [53] addressed to Henriette Vogel. Finally, in a note to Ulrike dated "on the morning of my death," he thanked her for all her efforts to save him, but concluded: "The truth is that there was no help for me on earth." [54]

On November 21, Kleist shot Henriette and himself on the

[46] *Works* II, 915.
[47] *Ibid.,* 914.
[48] Letter to Marie von Kleist of November 10, 1811. *Ibid.,* 918.
[49] *Ibid.,* 919.
[50] Letter of November 9, 1811. *Ibid.,* 917.
[51] Letter of November 12, 1811. *Ibid.,* 920.
[52] *Ibid.,* 921.
[53] "Für Adolfine Henriette Vogel." *Works* I, 41.
[54] *Works* II, 925.

shore of the Wannsee, near Potsdam. He was just over thirty-four at the time of his death.

The accepted chronology of Kleist's works, to which I have adhered in the foregoing account, has more than once been questioned, as by Professor Hans M. Wolff,[55] who claims that most of Kleist's principal works were in fact drafted long before the completion of his final versions. Professor Wolff not only specifies what he believes to be the dates of the original drafts, but, in the case of two plays and three stories, appends his own reconstructions of these drafts. Professor Wolff's main argument is that most of the works, as we know them, are full of logical inconsistencies; and that these inconsistencies arose when Kleist revised his earlier works in the light of new experience and convictions.

Now, it is well known that Kleist continually revised his works; the extant drafts of his first tragedy, from its inception as *Die Familie Thierrez* to the *Ghonorez* versions and its final removal to a German setting in *Schroffenstein,* show very clearly how Kleist developed and improved his first drafts. It is conceivable, too, that certain of the inconsistencies enumerated by Professor Wolff arose in the process of revision. Yet it is highly unlikely that a writer so intent on correcting and amending his works should spare himself the ordeal of rereading the finished versions; and if he did so, or did reread them but overlooked the inconsistencies, the omission itself would be highly revealing. Professor Wolff, however, was more concerned to remove these inconsistencies by constructing hypothetical versions, than to consider the implications of this extraordinary carelessness on Kleist's part.

According to Professor Wolff, Kleist drafted the following works either in 1800 or 1801: *Das Käthchen von Heilbronn* (whose original title, Professor Wolff suggests, was *Kunigunde von Thurneck*), *Penthesilea, Die Hermannsschlacht, Die Marquise von O., Das Erdbeben in Chili, Die Verlobung in St. Domingo, Die Heilige Cäcilie, Michael Kohlhaas,* and *Der Findling*—not to mention the two tragedies that Kleist is

[55] *Heinrich von Kleist: Die Geschichte seines Schaffens* (Berne, 1954).

known to have begun before 1803. Of all Kleist's major works, only the two comedies are allowed a later date, while *Friedrich Prinz von Homburg* is vaguely traced back to the "critical years between 1801 and 1803." If these dates are correct, Kleist not only began to write before the Kant crisis of 1801, but wrote so much at this period that the strain—rather than the Kant crisis itself—would seem to account for his breakdown of that year.

If it is correct, Professor Wolff's thesis invalidates, or at least contradicts, the present account of Kleist's life and work; but this thesis is largely speculative. It is not so much, therefore, to save my own skin by defending a view of Kleist that appears to have been superseded by Professor Wolff's researches that I must interrupt my own interpretation at this point. My principal reason for discussing his arguments at some length is that they are an attempt to present Kleist as a writer of whom some kind of consistency can reasonably be expected; and this attempt rests on assumptions so false that they cannot be left unchallenged. Professor Wolff's approach is eminently rational; but his reasonableness is of the kind that simply ignores those "raisons que la raison ne connaît point." If any man was guided by reasons not of the head's choosing, that man was Kleist.

Professor Wolff's main error, as I see it, is to divide Kleist's life into clearly differentiated phases of development and to assume that, because a work shows some of the characteristics that he attributes to one of these phases, this work cannot have been written at any other time. Thus he distinguishes an early revolutionary phase of *Sturm und Drang,* during which the influence of Rousseau was predominant, and a later phase during which Kleist transferred his interest from political to psychological motives and made his peace both with the State in general and the aristocracy in particular; but at the time when Professor Wolff supposes him to have been preoccupied with political and social issues, Kleist described himself as a man "who has no political opinions at all." Even such an undoubtedly early work as *Die Familie Schroffenstein* cannot be adequately interpreted in terms of Rousseau's social doctrines, as Professor Wolff attempts to do. The social issues raised by this tragedy are little more than external machinery. Its true mainspring is a tragic sense of inevitable error, not mere social evils that could be remedied by education or reform. Kleist's thinking was never systematic; nor did it progress in a straight line, as Professor Wolff would have it, but followed what Hölderlin called an "eccentric" (or elliptic) course, determined much more by emotional ups and downs than by a steady process of growth or development. Hence the inconsistencies in his works, the only valuable evidence adduced by Professor Wolff. Those of his arguments that rest on biographical evidence—and these occupy the greater part of his book—are farfetched to the point of absurdity.

A few examples will have to suffice. One of Professor Wolff's reasons for attributing the original draft of *Der Findling* to 1800 is that the heroine's name in Elvire; Kleist, therefore, must have been thinking of Mozart's *Don Giovanni* and "the influence of Mozart's libretti very soon disappears" from his works. Kleist must have resumed work on *Michael Kohlhaas* early in 1801 because in a letter from Paris written in that year he deals at some length with two horses that he bought for the journey and was obliged to sell again; and two horses in particular play an important part in *Kohlhaas*. Kleist must have been writing *Die Heilige Cäcilie* in 1801 because one of his letters of that time contains a passage about the effect on him of sacred music he had heard in the Catholic Church at Dresden; and so forth. Professor Wolff's reliance on such data shows a complete misunderstanding of imaginative processes in general and of Kleist's imagination in particular. The same misunderstanding is blatant in the biographical sections of his book.

Thus he devotes much space to a discussion of Kleist's early letter to Martini, which he calls a "systematic exposition of his *Weltanschauung* at the time," a *Weltanschauung* which is that of the Enlightenment: but he neither quotes nor refers to the most significant passage in this letter, that in which Kleist confesses that, although virtue and happiness are now his aims, he has only the vaguest idea of what he is talking about, since virtue, to him, is only "a sublime, exalted, ineffable something." Kleist's exposition of his early *Weltanschauung*—if his momentary state of mind deserves this name—is clear enough; but the *Weltanschauung* itself is not. That is what makes the letter significant. Another of Professor Wolff's errors is to assume that because in 1800 Kleist's letters took on a "poetical coloring," we can assume that he had begun to write his imaginative works. On the contrary, the more deeply a writer is engrossed in imaginative work, the less likely he is to waste any "poetry" on his letters. It would therefore be wiser to conclude that, unlike his later and much less expansive letters, these early ones served as a substitute for imaginative work.[56] Another crucial consideration, which Professor Wolff omits in this context, is that Kleist's imaginative prose is distinguished by an almost total absence of "poetical coloring"—an absence unique in a writer of the Romantic age. Professor Wolff continually disregards such evidence as contradicts his thesis. In the very passage (from Kleist's letter of September 20, 1800) that he cites to prove that Kleist had already begun to regard himself as a poet, Kleist writes of "the peculiar talent of poets, who do not live in Arcady any more than we do, but can discover what is Arcadian or simply interesting about the commonest objects around us." Nothing could be more obvious than the implications of that "we."

Apart from the question of chronology, Professor Wolff everywhere overemphasizes Kleist's development and the systems of belief which he attributes to the various phases; the same applies even to his interpretation of the works. In his insistence on the development that the hero-villain of *Die Marquise von O.* undergoes in the course of the story, he quite loses sight of the moral ambiguity that is his outstanding characteristic. Kleist gives us no reason to suppose that Graf F. is a better man at the end of the story than he was at the beginning; what he does suggest—by means of simile, metaphor, and even allegory, rather than by more direct indications—is that Graf F.'s peculiar virtues are inseparable from the peculiar vice that causes him to commit a criminal offense, his violation of the Marquise. Graf F. is one of those very Kleistian characters who leap before they look; hence his courage, his ardor, and his devotion; and hence the impetuosity with which he satisfies his desire for the Marquise. If Kleist nowhere condemns Graf F., it is because Graf F. is a man of action, rather than reflection;

[56] The "literary" character of these early letters led Kleist to repeat himself almost verbatim in letters addressed to different persons.

and because Kleist's own morality was an ambiguous one. All the imagery of the story tends to illustrate this ambivalence; Graf F. is called bestial and godlike, devilish and angelic. His deepest motive—the desire to sully the purity of the Marquise because he has no other means of asserting his power over her —is conveyed in a seemingly irrelevant passage of sustained allegory, his childhood reminiscence of the swan on his uncle's estate. If this strange morality perplexes us, we have only to read Kleist's essay on the Puppet Theatre [57] to understand the connection between subhuman and superhuman qualities. Both the puppet and the god are free from the self-consciousness that is the mark of the fallen nature of Man. Like Hölderlin in *Hyperion,* Kleist believed that "Man is a god when he dreams, a beggar when he reflects"; but he would have substituted the word "acts" for "dreams," as Hyperion himself does elsewhere, speaking of his wish "to wander around the earth or take part in the first war that may present itself." [58]

Because Professor Wolff dislikes the fanatical nationalism of *Die Hermannsschlacht* he argues that Kleist must have written an earlier version of this play from "a more moral standpoint" influenced by Rousseau. Here, too, he has found support for his argument in a letter of 1801,[59] but the reference could equally well be used to prove that the subject was familiar to Kleist long before he wrote the work—a much more plausible inference. Nor is it valid to argue that "the wild song of hate," which *Die Hermannsschlacht* undoubtedly is in its extant form, was "fundamentally alien to Kleist's tender nature." Kleist was shy and sensitive, but he was also violent; he was tormented by scruples, but most of his actions were inconsiderate and unscrupulous to an outrageous degree.

Most of those contemporaries of Kleist who recorded impressions of his person agreed in finding him inscrutable and incalculable, now almost tongue-tied, now bursting out into vehement, often incoherent eloquence.[60] On the whole he seems to have

[57] "Über das Marionettentheater." *Works* II, 335–342. English version in *Envoy* (Dublin) Vol. 3, No. 10 (September, 1950).

[58] Hölderlin, *Works* (Zinkernagel) II, 32.

[59] Quoted in this study; cf. p. 120.

[60] *Heinrich von Kleists Lebensspuren,* ed. Helmut Sembdner (Bremen, 1957).

been more pitied than loved, more liked than understood. Clemens Brentano's summary of him as "a very curious, good, coarse, narrow-minded, stupid, stubborn person gloriously endowed with a slow consequential talent" is more typical in its ambivalence and faintly patronizing tone than the lone hero-worship of Adam Müller. Yet what is most striking in all the extant accounts of Kleist's person is that it remains shadowy, solitary, not to be understood. Two independent accounts tell of Kleist's sudden passion for Adam Müller's wife and his attempt to kill Müller by throwing him off a bridge. The authenticity of these accounts has been called in question, but they are no more incredible than Kleist's vindictive outbursts against Goethe—"I shall tear the wreath from his brow," Pfuel reports Kleist as saying—or the circumstances of his death, recorded by extant documents in gruesome and grotesque detail. There is one memorable account of Kleist's laughter, when trying to give a reading of his *Schroffenstein* to a circle of friends. Kafka too, according to Max Brod, was afflicted with sinister hilarity when reading his work aloud.

Even the last of all Kleist's actions, his suicide, was preceded by murder; and this after the moderate and humane "philosophy," which all his critics, including Professor Wolff, admire in his last drama, *Friedrich Prinz von Homburg*. There are many good reasons why a critic writing in our time should be more sensitive to the political amorality of *Die Hermannsschlacht* than to kindred excesses on the plane of individual conduct—of which there is no lack in Kleist's other works. One has only to think of Penthesilea's cannibalistic attack on Achilles. But as far as our judgment of Kleist himself is concerned, one form of excess is inseparable from another. If we take up a moralistic attitude to his works, we have little choice but to condemn them, as Goethe did; and if Kleist's works continue to fascinate us, it is best to face up to the nature of that fascination. It is not his tenderness, but his ruthlessness that distinguishes Kleist from other writers of his age.

Some years after Kleist's death, Goethe remarked to Eckermann that Kleist had appalled him "like one afflicted with an incurable disease." This judgment would be merely uncharitable if it were not for Goethe's well-founded horror of the tragic and the morbid; well-founded, because Goethe knew their fascination and their danger for the German writers of his time. What is more, Kleist himself arrived at the same conclusion about himself, though from very different premises; he too concluded that there was "no help for him on earth." Of all the experiments that were his life, only one, his writing, had succeeded; and even this one success had not been confirmed by the few men whose approval might still have mended his self-esteem; nor had his work received the kind of outward response that would have convinced him that it had penetrated from the sphere of "thought" into the sphere of "action." (Kleist was not even aware of the Graz and Bamberg productions of his *Käthchen* toward the end of his life. He never attended a single performance of any of his plays.) Goethe, it is true, had once staged his comedy *Der Zerbrochene Krug* at Weimar; but quite apart from the failure of this performance, Goethe had also informed Kleist of his displeasure at "young men of wit and talent who are waiting for a theatre that is yet to come." Kleist never forgot this snub, to which he replied with a caustic epigram.

The "incurable disease," which Goethe had in mind, was a confusion of all the faculties brought about by disorientation. On the plane of metaphysics, Kleist was a man groping in the dark for the Truth—nothing less than *the* Truth would do, for little truths had no value as long as he did not know where he stood. His moral disorientation followed from the same desire for an absolute, and the same inability to commit himself finally to any one code—to Lutheran or Catholic orthodoxy or to any of such current substitutes as the Prussian gentleman's code of honor, Rousseau's doctrine of natural goodness, or Kant's categorical imperative. In his state of chronic indecision—chronic except when he committed both his imagination and his intellect to a literary work—Kleist could only juggle with these different possibilities, to his own deepening perplexity.

As far as politics are concerned, Kleist's whole life was overshadowed by the Napoleonic wars, in which he took an active part as an adolescent, a vicarious part in his last years, as the author of brilliant, formidable, and fanatical tracts. Here too, he took up every possible attitude in turn; from the conventional patriotism of his early youth, to the nonchalant cosmopolitanism of his young manhood, from the moderate liberalism of the reformers—such as von Hardenberg, who took an active interest in Kleist before and after he became Chancellor, and Kleist's equally influential friend Freiherr von Stein zum Altenstein—to the nationalistic fury of *Die Hermannsschlacht.* During this phase Kleist resorted to the neat division between public and private morality that has been characteristic of so much German political thinking ever since Hegel, Fichte, and Treitschke took advantage of the eclipse of rationalism to establish an idolatrous cult of the State. Until his very last drama, *Friedrich Prinz von Homburg,* absolutism and anarchy were the only fixed points that Kleist could clearly envisage; between them there was only a vague flux of conflicting possibilities.

As for his emotional and erotic instability, we do not need the evidence of his letters to recognize that it amounted to nothing less than a confusion of the male and female principles, a perpetual struggle between his masculine will and a feminine hysteria; the confusion is evident enough in all but his last works. It has often been suggested that Kleist was a homosexual; his contempt for women—other than those who, like Ulrike, had pronounced masculine traits, the masculine traits of his Amazon Penthesilea, and those who were wholly passive like his Käthchen—seems to support the suggestion. It is still more difficult to withhold this conclusion when one reads the following confession—addressed to his friend von Pfuel, who later became a general and Prussian Minister for War: "Often, when at Thun you stepped into the lake in my presence, I contemplated your beautiful body with feelings that were truly girlish" and, in the same letter: "You restored the age of the Greeks in my heart, I could have slept with you, dear boy, so entirely my soul embraced you." [61] But when Kleist concludes: "I shall never marry, so you must be a wife to me, be my chil-

[61] Letter of January 7, 1805. *Works* II, 776. An earlier letter, to Heinrich Lohse of December 23, 1801, is also relevant; but the reader must allow for Kleist's hysteria. Extravagant declarations of friendship, in any case, were common in Germany at this period. Compare Clemens Brentano's letter to Achim von Arnim of February, 1803 (cited by Ralph Tymms, *German Romantic Literature* [London, 1955], 211), in

dren and grandchildren," we know that he has only been indulging in one of his countless imaginative experiments. His momentary aberration has turned into a patent absurdity. Homosexual love, in fact, was no more than one of many possibilities and impossibilities to which Kleist turned in his exasperation. His erotic instability was not the cause, but one of the symptoms, of his general disorientation.

It was this disorientation that gave rise to the emotional possibilities and impossibilities of which I have given examples. Many more examples could be adduced from the works, as well as the letters. From the state of confusion characteristic of Kleist misdirected passions broke loose, only to dash themselves to pieces. Error, and more often than not the very impossibility of discovering the truth, assumes a metaphysical significance in Kleist's works; it is the Purgatory through which all his characters must pass, and from which the tragic ones do not emerge. Already his first play, *Die Familie Schroffenstein,* was a tragedy of errors. Because the truth is concealed from them, the protagonists fall into violent, perverse, and destructive passions. One of them, Sylvester, sums up the dilemma in these words:

> . . . Ich muss mir Licht verschaffen,
> Und sollt' ich's mir auch aus der Hölle holen—

> . . . I must have light,
> Though it be Hell itself I fetch it from—

and he could be speaking for Kleist himself, except that these particular words don't convey Kleist's predilection for Hell, the violent reaction in favor of the monstrous and chaotic that followed his disillusionment with the ideals of the Enlightenment. In *Penthesilea,* there is a clear connection between the heroine's sexual aberration, her extreme love-hatred for Achilles, and her general disorientation in "the strange institution that is this world." After deciding to set her dogs on Achilles, she pronounces this curse on life itself:

which Brentano writes that he loves Arnim as he loves God, cannot live without him, will be his servant, clean his shoes, etc.

. . . Dass der ganze Frühling
Verdorrte! Dass der Stern, auf dem wir atmen,
Geknickt, gleich dieser Rosen einer, läge!
Dass ich den ganzen Kranz der Welten so,
Wie dies Geflecht der Blumen, lösen könnte!

. . . Would that the Spring itself
Would wither! That the star on which we breathe,
Like one of these same roses, lay broken here!
That I might take the weft of all the worlds
And, like this wreath of flowers, rip it to pieces!

If she cannot be revenged on the whole cosmos, she can at least punish Achilles for having excited her desire; this she proceeds to do, by having him torn piecemeal by her dogs. The desire for revenge makes another of Kleist's characters declare: "Ich will nicht selig sein. Ich will in den untersten Grund der Hölle hinabfahren." ("I do not wish to be saved. I wish to descend to the uttermost depth of Hell.") So in his story *Der Findling*.

In comic situations, the sinister enigma of most of Kleist's works may give place to a paradox that can be unraveled by ingenuity; this is the case in *Der Zerbrochene Krug*. Sometimes, as in *Die Marquise von O.*, the events themselves finally offer a solution; in the weaker works that do not end tragically, such as *Käthchen*, a *deus ex machina* is required. There are many variations: *Das Erdbeben in Chili* begins with a *deus ex machina*, the earthquake itself, but this only serves to sharpen the tragic irony of the denouement. In *Amphytrion*, Kleist's admirable adaptation of Molière's comedy, we see the given enigma deepen into a mystery; the error, which was a mere pretext for social comedy in Molière, strikes such deep roots in Alcmene, her perplexity is so greatly intensified by her deeper response to Jupiter's divinity, that the play hangs on the verge of tragedy.

What is constant in all these works is the error itself; and the disorientation of those involved in the error. When error has wholly obscured the truth, they fall into the excessive passions that destroy them. In some cases, as in *Michael Kohlhaas*, the error takes the form of injustice; but injustice is a suppression of the truth on the ethical plane. The resulting disorientation is the same. The righteousness of Kohlhaas turns into destructive and self-destructive fury. If there is no absolute truth, whether metaphysical or ethical, the individual can accept no authority but that of his own impulses; these impulses may proceed from his conscience, from his senses, or from his intellect; but all three are isolated, autonomous and exposed to all the dangers of a conflict with incalculable and merciless powers.

The crowning irony of Kleist's career is that his last play and his last story point to a resolution of the metaphysical, moral, and emotional dilemma to which all his personal failures were due. His literary works were always well ahead of his personal development; for even if he did not know it, they were action as much as thought. Kleist did not live to catch up with *Friedrich Prinz von Homburg* and *Der Zweikampf*. It was not till these last works that he was able to present a love relationship free from confusion and excess. The love between Homburg and Natalie is as far removed from the mixture of sensuality, heroism, and cannibalism that passes for love in *Penthesilea* as from the self-obliterating, abject devotion of Käthchen von Heilbronn (whom Kleist, in one of his rare comments on his own works, described as the minus corresponding to Penthesilea's plus, "the reverse side of Penthesilea, a creature as mighty by virtue of submission as the other by virtue of action").[62] True, it is only the character of Natalie that combines nobility with moderation. When Homburg suffers his existential crisis, he is prepared to renounce not only his honor, but his love:

> Seit ich mein Grab sah, will ich nichts, als leben,
> Und frage nichts mehr, ob es rühmlich sei.
>
> . . . .
>
> Ich gebe jeden Anspruch auf an Glück.
> Nataliens, das vergiss nicht ihm zu melden,
> Begehr ich gar nicht mehr, in meinem Busen
> Ist alle Zärtlichkeit für sie erlöscht.

> I saw my grave, and knew one wish: to live,
> No longer asking whether honourably.

[62] Letter to Heinrich Joseph von Collin of December 8, 1808. *Works* II, 853.

. . . .
All claim to happiness I now give up.
For Natalie—this don't forget to tell him—
Feel not the faintest craving; in my heart
All tenderness for her is quite extinct.

Yet, by having the wisdom and the strength to understand and
forgive this betrayal, Natalie redeems Homburg and the love
between them. She herself echoes Homburg's renunciation of
all but bare life when she says to the Elector:

> Ich will nur, dass er da sei, lieber Onkel,
> Für sich, selbständig, frei und unabhängig,
> Wie eine Blume, die mir wohlgefällt . . .

> Only that he should *be,* I ask, dear uncle,
> Free, by himself, autonomous, uncommitted,
> Like some fine flowering plant that pleases me . . .

The greater maturity of *Homburg* on the erotic plane, as exemplified by Natalie's humane and quite unhysterical attachment,
has an exact parallel in the difference between the "happy ending" of *Käthchen von Heilbronn* and the real transformation
that takes place in *Homburg,* a transcendence of tragedy comparable to that in Shakespeare's later plays. This transformation
is a moral one. A Freudian, of course, would argue that the
moral change proceeds from the erotic, but—in Kleist's case at
least—he would be wrong.

The hero of Kleist's last story, Friedrich von Trota, differs
from Kleist's earlier characters in the quality of his faith; and
this, once more, leads to a difference in the quality of his love.
As in earlier works, everything conspires to undermine the
hero's faith; even the judgment of God seems to be against
him, for it is the guilty man who is absolved in the trial by
combat. This is the most emphatic statement of a theme that recurs throughout Kleist's works. His characters may be virtuous
or even heroic, but their virtues and their heroism have no
place in any order above or outside them. They are hopelessly

disoriented in an incomprehensible world. If they win through, as Trota does in *Der Zweikampf,* it is by a blind faith in their own righteousness that defies all outward appearances and every accepted moral convention.

Kleist was one of the first German writers to face—or at least to suffer—the full implications of those peculiarly modern processes, the isolation of the individual consciousness and the fragmentation of reality into islands of pure subjectivity on the one hand, mere mechanistic phenomena on the other. (These processes, in our time, have culminated in the nihilism of such German writers as G. E. Winckler—who wrote of the "affliction of thinking" ["Unglück des Denkens"] [63]—and Gottfried Benn, with his longing for a form of existence devoid of consciousness and his inability to find any point of contact between the fantasies generated by an isolated ego and a society which is only of statistical interest.) That is why Kleist was inclined to judge his own art in terms of a conflict between reality and imagination—or, in other words, between the individual and his environment. The antinomy between "thought" and "action" is only another variant of the same conflict, the conflict between what Blake called Reason and Energy. The peculiar and admirable tautness of Kleist's blank verse and narrative prose owes much to the tension between them, to Kleist's strenuous endeavors to impose the curb of plausibility on the anarchic products of his imagination. "The truth is," he wrote to a friend, "that I like what I imagine, not what I succeed in putting down on paper. If I were good for anything else, I should take it up with all my heart: my only reason for writing is that I can't help it." [64] And again: "Every first impulse, all that is involuntary, is beautiful; and everything is crooked and cramped as soon as it understands itself." [65] This is the dichotomy that he elaborated in his two important essays, psychologically in the essay "On the Gradual Formation of Thoughts Dur-

[63] Quoted by Hans Egon Holthusen, *Der Unbehauste Mensch* (Munich, 1951); see his essay on Winckler, 99–121.

[64] Letter to Lilienstern of August 31, 1806. *Works* II, 798.

[65] *Ibid.,* 799.

ing Speech," [66] philosophically and theologically in that "On the Puppet Theatre."

Yet the vitalism and antirationalism that these essays propound were counterbalanced by Kleist's inflexible control over his artistic media. Kleist knew very well that spontaneity is not enough. In connection with his projected attempt at a second version of *Robert Guiskard,* he wrote in 1808: "The material —to use the popular terms—is still monstrous; but in art everything depends on form, and everything that has a shape is my province." One of his last letters [67] contains a vivid account of the struggle involved in trying to tame his monstrous fantasies. It is the intensity of this struggle in Kleist's case that justifies the analogy of music, of a mathematical structure raised on a foundation of unreason. Kleist's works are like products of the successful collaboration between a maniac and a mathematician. That is why Kafka could learn from Kleist to illuminate nightmare with a daytime lucidity; not to explain his paradoxes, but to render them; and, however outrageous his visions, to maintain the outward assurance of a somnambulist.

A few instances of Kleist's mastery as an artist will have to suffice for the present. I have already alluded to his ingenious use of metaphor and simile. The entire significance of *Die Marquise von O.* can be shown to hinge on a few words almost casually scattered over the narrative: "god" and "angel" on the one hand, "devil" and "dog" on the other. If, as one might well argue, the introduction of these words was involuntary, the dualism that they convey still remains essential to the story; and it matters very little whether we praise the maniac or the mathematician for finding so subtle a way of conveying it. Since Kleist takes up this dualism in the last sentence, in terms of this very symbolism, it is highly unlikely that he was unaware of its significance; but the "moral" of his story was one so far removed from orthodoxy that he was wise to choose an indirect means of suggesting it to the reader. Kleist was quite capable of

---

[66] "Über die allmähliche Verfertigung der Gedanken beim Reden." *Works* II, 321–327. English version in *German Life and Letters,* Vol. V, No. 1 (October, 1951).

[67] Letter to Marie von Kleist of August, 1811. *Works* II, 910–911.

being inconsistent about such factual details as the number of the Marquise's children; but he was never inconsistent about the significant minutiae of his art.

Although his later letters are disappointingly reticent, Kleist could theorize as lucidly as any critic who knows from his own experience what he is talking about; but he left his theories behind as soon as he started work on a story or a play. Here all his thinking was dramatic, preceded and precipitated by action. However carefully, even painfully, executed, his works created the illusion that he leapt before he looked. In his stories, he plunged straight into the action, skillfully regulating its speed, but rarely stopping to moralize, analyze, or reflect. This is the opening of one of them:

> In M., an important town in Northern Italy, the widowed Marchioness of O., a lady of excellent reputation and the mother of several well-bred children, announced in the newspaper that for reasons unknown to her she found herself in an interesting condition, that the father of the child she was about to bear should present himself and that, out of consideration for her family, she was resolved to marry him.

The long sentence, with its wealth of subsidiary clauses, is typical of Kleist's narrative style, designed to convey as much detailed information as possible without interrupting the flow of action. For the same reason he preferred reported speech, which can be packed into similar sentences, so that the reader is swept on from shock to shock, with no time to formulate his objections.

The dramas demand a little more exposition; but Kleist reduces it to a minimum by avoiding introductory scenes, explanatory soliloquies—still the rule of his time—and all other devices that hold up the action. But his greatest advantage as a dramatist was his extraordinary capacity for reproducing the very processes of thought in his dialogue. Here again his self-knowledge, as recorded in the essay on "Thought and Speech," was invaluable; it showed him that dialogue is only superficially reasonable, that what really matters in conversation is the "electric charge" behind the words and the fluctuations in the power of that charge brought about by communication. We do not need to be told about the state of mind of Kleist's characters. As soon as Homburg speaks, his manner conveys the precise state of almost trancelike distraction that Kleist wished to convey. Both his plays and his stories are singularly lacking in passages of "poetic" abandonment; in the plays there is a single dominant tension, never relaxed by irrelevant emotions, in the stories a single current of action, never broken by intrusions on the author's part. The lyrical moment does not matter; and Kleist's short poems are by far the least distinguished part of his work.

As a dramatist and storyteller, Kleist belonged to no school. His personal contacts with his contemporaries, the Romantics, had little or no effect on his works, though he shared some of their extravagances and some of their ideals, notably nationalism. (And from the point of view of Goethe's humanism, the Romantics, too, were reactionary.) Kleist attributed the decline of European drama to the demands of women for moral and edifying themes, proposing that women should be excluded from theatres as in ancient Greece, or confined to theatres of their own. It is true that Kleist was at his worst when he consciously compromised with the taste of his public, as in the case of *Käthchen;* but his own variety of heroism owes much more to his age and country than he was aware. Though his lack of moral inhibitions and didactic ambitions made it easier for him than for his humanistic predecessors, Lessing, Goethe, and Schiller, to arouse the tragic emotions, he was as far as they were from renewing the religious and cultural function of Greek tragedy. His distinction is that he treated barbarous subjects with a hard precision, which is that of the scientific intellect, disciplined to record phenomena with a steady hand, a cold eye; yet the experiments he recorded were those of passion itself, of passion endured in a social and metaphysical void. His excellence as an artist is unmistakably modern in character: perfect control of the means to an uncontrollable end.

V

HEINRICH HEINE

"No man thinks," says the lizard in one of Heine's early travel books, "only from time to time something occurs to people; these wholly unmerited flashes they call ideas, and the concatenation of these ideas they call thinking . . . No man thinks, no philosopher thinks, neither Hegel nor Schelling thinks; as for their philosophy, it's mere air and water, like the clouds in the sky." A critic about to project his image of Heine has good reason to remember these words. Not only do they reveal the empiricism, the skepticism, and the flippancy which are authentic features of Heine's mind, but they contain a warning against too literal an approach. To take Heine literally is to run the risk of grossly misinterpreting his work, his character, and his function.

But how is one to take Heine? His underlying seriousness is of a kind that defies serious treatment. He is so elusive a writer that every statement about him immediately suggests its exact opposite. After vainly trying to produce a composite image of his work, and a composite image that makes sense, one is tempted to write three separate essays on authors whom one might call Harry, Heinrich, and Henri Heine, as Heine called himself at different stages of his life. Harry, then, would be the Romantic poet of the *Buch der Lieder,* which contains the verse of his first creative phase, the years between 1817 and 1826; Harry, one could assume, drowned himself in the North Sea, as Heine himself might well have done if he had taken his Romantic *Weltschmerz* just a little more seriously than he did. Heinrich would be the vitriolic publicist, deadly to his enemies and dangerous even to his friends, whose activities began in 1826 with the publication of his first travel book, the *Harzreise,* and continued intermittently until 1840, when he published his book on Ludwig Börne. Heinrich, for the sake of convenience, could be said to have been killed in his duel with Salomon Straus on September 7, 1841, as Heine himself could easily have been killed, instead of being only wounded, by the avenger of Börne's sullied reputation. Henri, a much more awkward proposition, would have to include the great prose writer and brilliant critic of the eighteen-forties and eighteen-fifties, the author of the *Romanzero* and last poems, and the *charmant esprit,* as Baudelaire called him, whose influence extended from Gautier, Gérard de Nerval, and Baudelaire himself to Matthew Arnold, Nietzsche, the early Rilke, and countless other writers in every European country; his works would certainly include the late book on France, *Lutezia,* the two ballet scenarios *Der Doktor Faust,* and *Die Götter im Exil,* the private notebooks and the autobiographical works. Yet even these three Heines would not only overlap, but could never be prevented from quarreling with one another. Reluctantly, therefore, one returns to the composite image; but with little hope that it will do justice to every facet.

The difficulty is apparent from the image—projected by Heine himself—which was the subject of Matthew Arnold's essay of 1863:

> I know not if I deserve that a laurel-wreath should one day be placed on my coffin. Poetry, dearly as I have loved it, has always been to me but a divine plaything. I have never attached any great value to poetical fame, and I trouble myself

very little whether people praise my verses or blame them. But lay on my coffin a sword; for I was a brave soldier in the war of liberation of humanity.

To begin with, "brave" is a mistranslation of the German word "brav," which means obedient, reliable, or good, in the sense in which we say that a child is good; and, contrary to Arnold's opinion, Heine was exceptionally brave, both morally and physically, but he was almost totally lacking in the humble virtues he imputed to himself in this passage. The second falsehood in the original is so blatant that Arnold's conscience compelled him to omit it from the translation; after "divine plaything," Heine has "or a consecrated means to heavenly ends." The third falsehood, Heine's pretense of indifference to literary fame, did not take Arnold in any more than the second, but he let it pass because "for his contemporaries, for us, for the Europe of the present century, he (Heine) is significant chiefly for the reasons which he himself in the words just quoted assigns." Heine's significance for Arnold's generation was indeed what Arnold claimed; but even the general tenor of Heine's self-characterization conveys only a little fraction of the truth about his cultural rôle, as I shall attempt to show.

As for another notorious falsehood of a different order, Heine's statement that he was born on the first day of 1800, its primary purpose was not to make himself appear more than two years younger than he was—a kind of vanity inexcusable in a male poet—nor even to permit the witticism that he was *"un des premiers hommes du siècle,"* but to conceal the fact that his parents were not legally married till after his birth. Heine himself does not seem to have been told exactly when he was born; and the social odds against him were so heavy as it was that one can hardly blame him for not offering this particular weapon to his enemies. Yet this factual falsehood has proved as misleading to Heine's biographers as his self-characterizations have proved to his critics and interpreters.

Heine's statements about himself are not always reliable; but the more one studies the works of nineteenth-century writers who had ideas but no philosophy, the more one is prepared to find that it is not their self-characterizations, their confessions, and professions, that reveal their vital preoccupations; not, at least, if taken literally and one by one. Rather, in an age of dialectics—of thesis, antithesis, and, one hopes, of synthesis—it is their self-contradictions. This formula, too, is not generally valid; but it does apply to Heine and to a great many other writers whose minds were melting pots for all the ill-assorted ideas thrown up by the age. In such cases one can be pretty sure that the issues that mattered most to them are those about which they were most apt to contradict themselves.

Heine made ample use of what Baudelaire called "the right to contradict oneself"; but whereas Baudelaire worked hard for a synthesis, ideas in themselves mattered so little to Heine that he was content to let one idea cancel out another. He was prolific of ideas, but he did not respect his wealth. In the very worst sense of the word, he remained a "subjective" writer; not because he made use of the first person singular in his poetry and prose, but because he was more interested in the uniqueness of his person than in its efficiency as a medium. He never learned that a great poet's "I" is a functional, as distinct from a biographical, "I"; that it is an instrument created by the poet for the sake of the poetry, an instrument that may have no value, often indeed no reality, apart from this function. There were times, such as the Middle Ages, when the poetic "I" and the biographical "I" might well happen to be identical; for individuals were no more than embodiments of impersonal virtues and vices, and they were judged by their capacity to perform an appointed rôle. When they spoke for themselves, they spoke for everyone. Modern poets have no such luck; unless they are very naïve or very mad, they have to create their poetic "I," to abstract it from the irrelevances of circumstance. This Heine never succeeded in doing; his many *personae,* like the Quixotic knight-errant, the tragic jester, the romantic lover, and the analyst of love, did not coalesce. The "I" of Heine's poetry—and of his prose, from which it hardly differs—shows all the inconsistencies that are forced upon individuals by changing circumstances, moods, and necessities, and by their changing conceptions of their own personalities. That is why writers on Heine are so apt to produce distorted, simplified, and contradictory images, and why one feels tempted to shirk the labor of a synthesis that Heine himself was too easy-going, too self-indulgent to provide. It is only by balancing one of his statements against another, and balancing every one of them against the facts of his life and works, that one can hope to arrive at anything like the complex truth.

The passage about the laurel wreath and the sword comes from an early prose work of Heine's, the *Journey from Munich to Genoa;* and Heine's early ideas on politics are inseparable from his biography. "By the marching-route of my cradle," as he put it later, he was committed to the political Left, just as he was divided from the start between German sentiment and French *esprit.* His native Rhineland was pervaded by French influences. It was a French writer, Rousseau, who had emancipated his mother from Jewish orthodoxy, and another Frenchman, Napoleon, who had emancipated the Jews of the Rhineland from the ghettoes and—what was more important to Heine—from their confinement to the mercantile trades that he hated and despised. The defeat of Napoleon brought back the old restrictions when Heine was about to enter professional life. Debarred from working as a lawyer or civil servant, he was faced with the choice between a business career under the aegis of his rich uncle Salomon—which he tried and gave up before escaping to the comparative freedom of the universities—and that certificate of baptism which he described as "the ticket of admission to European culture." Heine never really solved this dilemma; he became a Lutheran but made malicious remarks about other distinguished converts not necessarily less sincere than himself, remained partly dependent on his uncle, whom he both admired and hated, and never worked as a lawyer or civil servant. Although he was able to earn his living—or part of it —by his pen, even the freedom of a writer was precarious in an age of strict censorship, frequent political upheavals, and conflicting literary factions.

It was personal, rather than political motives that drove Heine into polemical journalism: above all it was his sense of insecurity, economic pressure, an exuberant delight in controversy, and the spirit of the age itself, which he learned too late to resist. For the intricacies of politics he had no aptitude at all; and though he was vain, he was not ambitious for power. Yet even writers who had no personal grievance comparable to his, found themselves engaged in politics during those years. Gérard de Nerval, the author of a few poems as pure as the medium of words permits, began as the author of political odes; and as late as the Revolution of 1848, when Heine's attitude was one of indifference, even of hostility, Baudelaire acclaimed the event in the columns of *Le Salut Public*.

By conviction, by disposition and, one can almost say, by birth, Heine was a liberal. But liberalism did not exist in Germany; there were revolutionaries and reactionaries, and very little in between. Heine's very first allegiance, that to Napoleon, involved an obvious contradiction; and though he remained faithful to Napoleon's memory—even to the extent of supporting the regime of "Napoléon le Petit"—his awareness of the contradiction forced him into the quibble that he was "not an unqualified Bonapartist: my allegiance is due not to the actions of the man, but only to his genius." A similar ambiguity attaches to Heine's later political associations with the "Young Germans," with the Saint-Simonists and with Karl Marx; and though Heine had no aptitude for either abstract thought or practical politics, he had an almost infallible flair for the practical implications and potentialities of ideas.

Heine's allegiance to Napoleon also involved a conflict with the nationalistic factions, those "Teutomaniacs" against whom he waged a particularly intense campaign. This issue again, was complicated by the connection between nationalism and the German Romantic Movement and by Heine's genuine, though unconventional, patriotism. To the Romantic School he owed his introduction to German literature, the personal encouragement of his teacher A. W. von Schlegel, his interest in medieval literature, history, folklore, and even his love of the *Volkslied,* on which he modeled his own verse: and in spite of his Francophilia, even because of it, he never ceased to feel a very special love for the unawakened, "anonymous" Germany of his youth, a love made more poignant by absence in later years. When Bismarck chose to defend Heine against his anti-Semitic detractors, he did so on the grounds that "Heine was a writer of *Lieder,* second to none but Goethe, and the *Lied,* of all poetic genres, is the one most specifically German." This defense may seem more generous than just, now that Heine's lyrical poetry has been discredited for different reasons. Only a few staunch supporters still deny that his long courtship of the *Lied* was too inhibited by Voltairean *esprit* and Byronic self-consciousness ever to result in an altogether happy marriage; but, curiously enough, the general public seems to have relished this peculiar tension between poem and poet. The enormous popular success of the *Buch der Lieder* continued long after Bismarck's time. It was not until 1926 that a highly fastidious and learned man of letters, Rudolf Borchardt, sounded the alarm by explaining why he found it necessary to reduce Heine's poems to "fragments" in order to include them in his anthology of the best German poetry.[1] Like the Austrian satirist and moralist Karl Kraus, who had also condemned Heine's laxity and impurity of diction, going so far as to imply that Heine's poetry was no more than an imitation of specious Romantic modes,[2] Rudolf Borchardt was of Jewish descent.

Heine's ambivalent attitude to the Romantic tradition in which he wrote his verse needs little explanation. An entry in his private notebooks provides a gloss: "Hatred of the Jews begins only with the Romantic School, with their delight in the Middle Ages (Catholicism, aristocracy), further increased by the Teutomaniacs." And his treatise on the Romantic School, written in 1833 for a French periodical, deals fully with all his objections. But by 1833 he had left Germany for good, settled in Paris, and become involved with the politically active "Young Germany" movement, a group of writers who hoped to launch an international Socialist revolution.

His Romantic—or semi-Romantic—period is the earlier one of his studies at Bonn and Göttingen, his unrequited love for his two Hamburg cousins, his travels in Germany, Poland, Heligoland, England, and Italy.

Even the political and social enthusiasms that are still associated with Heine's name belong to the same early period of his

[1] *Ewiger Vorrat Deutscher Poesie,* edited by Rudolf Borchardt. (Munich, 1926).

[2] Karl Kraus, *Mein Gutachten,* in *Literature and Lüge* (paperback reprint; Munich, 1962), 39–41.

life. These enthusiasms reached their climax in the *Journey from Munich to Genoa,* published in 1828; a second quotation from its rhetorical professions of faith will have to suffice. Heine is writing about the "great task of our time," emancipation. "Not only that of the Irish, Greeks, Frankfort Jews, West Indian negroes and similar oppressed peoples, but the emancipation of the whole world, especially of Europe, which has attained its majority and is now breaking loose from the iron leading-strings of the privileged, the aristocracy. Let a few philosophical renegades of freedom forge the most subtle chains of argument to prove to us that millions of human beings were created to serve as beasts of burden to some thousands of privileged knights; they will never convince us as long as they cannot show us that, in the words of Voltaire, the former were born with saddles on their backs, the latter with spurs on their feet."

Three years after the appearance of this book Heine left Germany, attracted to Paris by the success of the 1830 Revolution. His connection with the "Young Germany" movement and with the Saint-Simonists, formed at that time, seems paradoxical when one considers his writings of the early Paris years; for already in the Postscript of 1833 to his first *Salon* volume he began to recant his republicanism. In Paris he had the opportunity to study revolutionary politics in action, with the result that he wrote in 1833: "It is my most sacred conviction that the Republican form would be unsuitable, unprofitable and uncomfortable for the peoples of Europe, and nothing less than impossible for the Germans." But whereas the *Journey from Munich to Genoa* has circulated freely, and Heine himself had not been arrested, as he half expected to be at the time, his more moderate works of the eighteen-thirties were obstructed by a stiffening of policy. In 1835 a Romantic nationalist and former friend of Heine's, Wolfgang Menzel, attacked the Young Germans and caused their works—including Heine's prose works —to be banned in Prussia, Austria, and most parts of Germany. The same Menzel had previously attacked Goethe for his indifference to the pan-German aspirations of his juniors, his un-Christian morality, and his admiration for Napoleon. Heine, therefore, was in good company; but the Young Germans themselves were working for a united Germany; and most of its members had shared Menzel's disapproval of Goethe, the one prominent survivor from an age when writers were not necessarily committed to a political line. Meanwhile Heine's own position had moved closer to Goethe's than to that of his temporary allies, the Young Germans; and it wasn't long before their leader, Karl Gutzkow, became one of Heine's most implacable enemies.

There were two principal causes for Heine's change of front. The first was his dislike of violent extremes, what I have called his liberalism. This he summed up very neatly in the same Postscript of 1833: "The man who does not go as far as his heart demands and his reason permits is a coward; the man who goes farther than he wished to go is a slave." Above all, Heine feared the effect of revolutionary doctrines on Germany, for reasons already implied in the Postscript and made very clear in a major prose work published soon after it, his *History of German Religion and Philosophy* of 1834. This formidable work, full of brilliant insights and inaccurate generalizations, contains Heine's famous warning to the French to refrain from rousing the Germans from their philosophical meditations, their notorious unworldliness. The Germans, he says, do not hate one another, as the French do, because of injured vanity, because of an epigram, say, or a visiting card not returned. "No, what we hate in our enemies is what is deepest in them, what is essential to them, the idea itself . . . We Gemans hate thoroughly, lastingly; since we are too honest, too clumsy also, to take our revenge by quick perfidy, we hate till our very last breath." The actual prophecy of Germany's awakening takes a form characteristic of Heine's sensitiveness to the potentialities of ideas; for he conjures up a vision of "Kantians who even in the world of phenomena will show no pity of any sort, but mercilessly, with sword and hatchet, will turn up the soil of European life to destroy the very last roots of the past." Then there are "armed Fichteans" who in their fanatical cult of the will, "can be tamed neither by fear or self-interest, since they live on the plane of spirit and defy matter"; and lastly the philosophers of nature who "will form an alliance with the chthonic powers of nature, know how to invoke the daemonic powers of ancient Germanic pantheism and revive that love of battle characteristic of the ancient Germans, which does not fight in order to destroy, nor in order to win, but only for the sake of fighting."

Heine alludes to the second factor in his conversion when he says in the same work that, as a poet and scholar, he himself 'belongs to the sick old world." All his later works, from 1833 to his death in 1856, show the unresolved conflict between two radically different views of life. These he called "sensualism" and "spiritualism." On the one hand he continued to welcome every reform of existing institutions that promised more liberty to the individual; and he even wrote enthusiastically about material innovations like the railway. These were "progress," and they belonged to the order of "sensualism." On the other hand, he doubted the value of such improvements and feared the implications of the philosophy that made them possible; for, as he wrote as early as 1833, "the beginning and end of all things is in God."

Put in those terms, the antinomy sounds simple, familiar, and easy enough to resolve; it is the old conflict between religion and material progress. But Heine made countless subdivisions and subdistinctions that turn his own antinomy between "spiritualism" and "sensualism" into a war between treacherous and undisciplined factions, a civil war that could be neither won nor ended. For "sensualism" too was a religion and it conflicted with the other. The "spiritualistic" principle was that of Judaism and Christianity, which he called the "religion of pain." Opposed to it there was the religion of the heart and senses, the religion of the natural man; and Heine found examples of this "sensualistic" principle in primitive and exotic cults, in pantheism, gnosticism, alchemy, popular lore, and even in certain institutions of the Catholic Church. Where he went wrong was in believing—or rather hoping, for he was never sure enough to believe—that these examples supported his own religion of "light and laughter" that would supersede the religion of pain.

The optimism and hedonism of this pseudoreligion was a product of the Enlightenment, of rationalism, materialism, and Rousseau's sentimentalization of Nature; it had very little to do with natural religions of any kind, for paganism and pantheism rest on a tragic sense of life. Hedonism can temper the observances of most religions, but it can never be a religion in itself. Because they knew only late antiquity, and misinterpreted what they knew of it, a great many eighteenth-century writers came to believe in a paganism without tears, in a Greece and Rome exclusively devoted to the cultivation of beauty and the enjoyment of sensual pleasures. Yet Heine's ironic treatment of the Greek gods—Greek goddesses were a different matter—in his early North Sea poems shows very clearly that he saw more than "light and laughter" in the ancient cults and myths. He had to look elsewhere for a tradition.

For a time he looked to the future and to such contemporary philosophies as that of Saint-Simon. In a poem of his early Paris years he announced the "Third Testament" that was about to replace the Two Testaments of the Bible, and the Church that would be built on this rock. The new God is a "God of Light"—one thinks of Goethe's paganism—but in the last line of the poem this God is said to be "present in our kisses," so that Heine's "theology" is reduced to a trite eroticism. The pagan theme is elaborated in Heine's short novel of that period, *Aus den Memoiren des Herrn von Schnabelewopski*, in which the old religion of pain is contrasted with the realization—brought home to Heine by the paintings of Jan Steen—that "the Holy Spirit is manifested most gloriously in light and laughter." Yet the real hero of the novel is the feeble but plucky little Jew, Simson, who fights a duel "for the existence of God," that is of the "spiritualistic" God of the Old Testament. This symbolic duel—clearly the model for that between Settembrini and Naphta in Thomas Mann's *Magic Mountain*—ends with the death of Simson who has only his faith and his anger to help him in his fight against a much stronger opponent, the good-humored atheist Dirksen; but the pathos of his defeat is sharper than the irony by which Heine tries to deflect it.

With endless variations, Heine returned to this antinomy between "sensualism" and "spiritualism." In the *History of Religion and Philosophy in Germany* he tries to show that "sensualism" is not identical with materialism, or incompatible with "spiritualism." Once his "religion of joy" has been established, "body and soul will be at peace again and will interact in original harmony." Then again he considers the possibility that the quarrel between them, instigated by Christianity is "irreconcilable, mankind predestined to suffer unending misery, the peoples doomed for ever to be trodden down by despots," in which case it is to be hoped that Christianity will maintain its hold. Nietzsche was to develop this idea, and the criticism implied by Heine's earlier description of the Christian era as "a great period of sickness in the history of mankind"; but whereas Heine genuinely doubted the validity of his own substitute, Nietzsche would not rest till he had demolished the very foundations of the Christian "slave morality." Heine was never a modern Prometheus, only a half-hearted Prodigal Son.

This helps to explain the blatant contradictions in the same work. Pantheism, "the secret religion of Germany," as Heine very aptly calls it, is "sensualistic," but not materialistic: yet Heine's praise of Spinoza leads him to assert that "the foremost aim of all our new institutions is the rehabilitation of matter, the restitution of its dignity, its moral acclamation, its religious sanctification, its reconciliation with the spirit." Luther is praised for being "an absolute man in whom spirit and matter were not divided"; but Luther turned against the "Indian-gnostic" element in Christianity, as upheld by the Catholic Church, and brought back the "Judaic-deistic" element, the same element that Heine blames elsewhere for the quarrel between spirit and matter.

Heine's own incurable materialism comes out when he claims that the Catholic Church was prudent enough to form "a concordat between God and the Devil, i.e., between spirit and matter, so that in theory the supremacy of spirit is acknowledged, but in practice matter is enabled to exercise all its annulled rights." Like all materialists, Heine could understand what is meant by the World and the Flesh, but not what is meant by the Devil. He therefore equates the Devil with the Flesh. Although he corrected this gross error in a subsequent treatise, the *Elementargeister,* it reappeared in his late ballet scenario *Der Doktor Faust,* written in 1847 for Her Majesty's Theatre, London, but never, of course, performed there. This would be one of the most profound as well as one of the most imaginative of his works, if only he had not tried to improve on Goethe's *Faust,* and on the legend itself, by turning Mephistopheles into a female character, Mephistophela—thus perpetuating the same confusion between evil and sensuality. Mephistophela, it is true, assumes the power and the glory of a classical witch. But despite Heine's lip service to Astarte, Diana, and Venus Urania, their images even in his last works —from the splendid *Exile of the Gods* to the last love poems written when his body had almost dwindled away—are always obscured by that of a lesser goddess, Venus Pandemos.

To this goddess he remained loyal to his bitter end, throughout his eight years of physical disintegration in the "mattress grave." Yet he was right to pay a last visit to the Venus de Milo, as he claims to have done immediately before retiring to the mattress grave, and to take leave of her for good. He must have guessed that during those same years he might easily enter a final commitment to the "spiritualistic" religion that had transformed the ancient gods and goddesses into daemons. He was only prevented from doing so by another antinomy, the rival claims on himself of Christianity and Judaism. In 1822, before his baptism, Heine had been active in the Berlin Society "For the Culture and Science of Judaism," a group of Jewish scholars who were trying to oppose the rising tide of anti-Semitism by promoting better understanding between Christians and Jews. After this early identification with the Jewish minority —but only with the liberal, emancipated part of it—Heine had tended to treat Judaism and Christianity as branches of the same "spiritualistic" religion. Now he was strongly drawn to Christianity by his own anguish of body and mind; for, as he wrote in his notebooks of those years, "in Christianity one arrives at a consciousness of the spirit through pain—illness spiritualizes, as even animals show." Heine's wife Mathilde was a Roman Catholic and their marriage had been solemnized in a Roman Catholic church. As for Judaism, his attitude to it was complicated by an emotional ambivalence, as well as by his basic resistance to all spiritual religions.

His only early work with a specifically Jewish background and theme, *Der Rabbi von Bacherach,* remained a fragment;

and even that fragment suffers from Heine's divided sympathy. Don Isaak speaks for Heine himself when he says to the Rabbi: "I love your cooking a great deal more than your faith, which lacks the right sauce. As for yourselves, I have never been able really to stomach you. Even at your best times, even under the reign of my ancestor David, who reigned over Judah and Israel, I could not have endured to be one of you but should certainly have escaped early one morning from the Fortress of Zion and emigrated to Phoenicia, or to Babylon, where the love and joy of life effervesced in the temples of the Gods." The myth of the Jews who are turned into dogs, but revert to their true shape on Sabbath day, in Heine's late poem "Die Prinzessin Sabbath," is also relevant to his feeling about the Jews; but by this time it was no longer his "sensualism" that kept him aloof. Apart from little Simson, the only other Jewish characters in Heine's early works are his crude, but lively, comic creations Gumpelino and Hyazinth of *Die Bäder von Lucca*. Here, too, his emotional ambivalence takes the form of vulgar humor, as in this description of Gumpelino: "One could see by his nose that he came of a truly noble line, that he was descended from an ancient family into which God himself had once married without fear of *mésalliance*. Since then, it is true, this family has rather come down in the world, so that since Charlemagne it has had to earn its living mainly by dealing in old trousers and Hamburg lottery tickets, but without ever relinquishing the least part of its family pride or the hope of obtaining back its former property, if only the adequate compensation that is granted to emigrants, when their old legitimate sovereign keeps his promise of a restoration, a promise by which he has been leading them by the nose for the last two thousand years. Is that perhaps why their noses have grown so long? Or are these long noses a kind of uniform by which the Divine Monarch Jehovah recognizes his old lifeguards, even when they have deserted? Gumpelino was such a deserter . . ." But so was Heine, although the same family pride inhibited him from becoming as devout a Christian as Gumpelino. And there was that other difficulty, experienced even by the most ardent Jewish converts to Christianity, of responding emotionally to the message of the Redemption.

In his last years Heine took up the Bible again and resumed

his studies in the history and literature of the Diaspora; these he had put aside together with *Der Rabbi von Bacherach,* for which they had served as a source. The *Hebräische Melodien,* the outcome of these renewed studies, are among the best of Heine's poems; but they are not quite good enough. Once again, it is the notebooks that tell us why. "The history of the modern Jews is tragic, and if one were to write about this tragedy one would be laughed at into the bargain.—That is the most tragic thing of all." Heine could not bear to be laughed at, nor could he keep his own feelings out of his jokes, but, to his dying day, half-hid his face behind a comic mask; and the mask is often that of a rather common clown. Even in reading his last poems one is embarrassed because Heine's own face keeps peering out of the mask, the face of a dying man too vain to be serious, mocking and blaspheming to keep self-pity in check. The *Hebräische Melodien* are the work of a master, but of a master strangely limited even in his range of verse forms, which hardly increased after his early experiments with free verse in the *North Sea* poems. "Bimini" is another late poem that is almost great; but, with less brilliance and profusion of detail, Baudelaire's version of it, "Le Voyage," has a somber grandeur that Heine never attained.

Another of the last poems, "Für die Mouche," reformulates Heine's dilemma in rather different terms. Its unending quarrel between Truth and Beauty is closely related to the one between "spiritualism" and "sensualism," but the difference is important enough to call for separate treatment.

> . . . O dieser Streit wird enden nimmermehr,
> Stets wird die Wahrheit hadern mit dem Schönen,
> Stets wird geschieden sein der Menschheit Heer
> In zwei Partein: Barbaren und Hellenen.

> Oh, never will this battle be decided,
> But Truth fight Beauty still, and neither seek
> To end the strife that keeps mankind divided
> Into two camps: Barbarian versus Greek.

If we ask ourselves to which of these parties or camps Heine belonged as a writer, we come up against another contradiction.

In order to understand it, we have to take up the development of Heine's political views at the point where I dropped it, the critical period of his early Paris years. For the conflict between Truth and Beauty, as far as Heine is concerned, was really one between two different conceptions of the nature and function of art; and even if Truth and Beauty are not intrinsically bound to conflict, those who hold these different views of the function of art have continued to quarrel ever since Heine's poem was written. The fact that Heine describes the two factions as "Greeks" and "barbarians"—a somewhat crude simplification of the issue—seems to betray a bias on Heine's part; but the poem as a whole is impartial, except for the poet's loathing of the conflict itself.

Aestheticism and amorality—the doctrine of "l'art pour l'art"—were the artistic tenets corresponding to the "sensualistic" principle in religion. W. B. Yeats makes the connection when he writes:

> Labour is blossoming or dancing where
> The body is not bruised to pleasure soul.

Heine would have liked to be an out-and-out aesthete once he had ceased to be a "soldier in the war of liberation of humanity." But the same seesaw motion of his mind that kept him divided between "sensualism" and "spiritualism" in religion until his death, made him flit about in a no-man's-land between the warring artistic factions. At one moment he would disclaim all connection with the moralistic barbarians; then again he would express the view that "goodness is superior to beauty"—the more rooted conviction of another post-Hegelian contemporary, Kierkegaard, with whom one doesn't expect Heine to agree about anything.

The question as to the nature and function of art appears early in Heine's writings. Already in the *Salon* of 1831— written before Heine's friendship with Théophile Gautier, who later propagated the doctrine of art for art's sake—he inquired into the relation of truth and beauty in art. Like most of his contemporaries, he thought of truth as verisimilitude; but his conclusion that art is a symbolic process indicates the level on which truth and beauty cease to conflict. "Sounds and words," Heine wrote, "colours and shapes, sensuous phenomena of every kind, are only symbols of an idea, symbols that arise in the artist's mind when it is moved by the holy World Spirit; his works of art are only symbols by which he communicates his own ideas to other minds. The greatest artist is he who uses the fewest and least complex symbols to achieve the utmost significance." By positing a "holy World Spirit" in this context, Heine not only spoils a valuable insight—which even the most recent aestheticians would confirm—but blatantly contradicts himself; for either the ideas communicated by the work of art are the artist's own ideas or they are ideas deriving from the World Spirit—Heine tries to have it both ways. But the "holy World Spirit" is a borrowing from Hegel, and there is a great deal of evidence that Heine did not believe in it. Some years earlier he had made fun of this same philosophical deity in the North Sea poems:

> . . . Die glühende Sonne dort oben
> Ist nur eine rote, betrunkene Nase,
> Die Nase des Weltgeists;
> Und um die rote Weltgeistnase
> Dreht sich die ganze, betrunkene Welt.

> . . . The glowing sun up there
> Is only a red, drunken nose,
> The nose of the world-spirit;
> And around the red world-spirit-nose
> Turns the whole drunken world.[3]

It is not surprising, therefore, that in another passage of the same *Salon* the World Spirit turns into something quite different, into "innate ideas" or, if we prefer, into Jungian archetypes. Heine writes: "In matters of art I am a supernaturalist. I believe that the artist cannot discover all his prototypes in nature, but that the most significant types, as innate symbols of innate ideas, are, as it were, revealed to him within his soul."

Yet in practice Heine's originality lay in his naturalism, his

[3] *Heinrich Heine; The North Sea,* trans. Vernon Watkins (London, 1955).

verisimilitude; he left it to his friends and followers in France, Gérard de Nerval, Gautier, and Baudelaire, to apply these theories and prepare the way for Symbolist art. As Heine points out, all art is symbolic; what Heine failed to do in his poetry was to reduce his material to symbols of "the utmost significance." For he could not be a "supernaturalist" in art without believing in a supernatural order outside it. His honesty got in the way; and it is his honesty that caused the characteristic twist in his lyrical poems, a twist that wrings the neck of his muse. In poetry, if not in life, honesty is not enough; self-knowledge becomes valuable only at the point where the knowledge matters, but the self does not.

Heine, as we have seen, began by thinking of himself as a committed writer, a "soldier in the war of liberation of humanity" whose writings were dedicated to this campaign. Yet he knew very well that his early love poetry did not, and could not, serve any political cause. This awareness brought him up against the antinomy between "truth" and beauty, an antinomy that imposed itself on every important writer of the nineteenth century and is still at the root of most of our literary and aesthetic controversies. It is the quarrel between those who believe that it is the business of artists, and especially of writers, to commit themselves to a cause other than art itself, and those who maintain with the later Auden that:

> Art is not, and cannot be
> A midwife to Society.

The social aspect of this commitment, of course, is only one of several: but in periods when political and social issues are prominent, as they were in Heine's, and in W. H. Auden's, youth, the conflict between "truth" and beauty is apt to present itself as a choice between "social consciousness" and a more or less pure aestheticism. Very few writers of the later nineteenth century were able to rid themselves of the whole antinomy, as Keats did, by denying that it exists; yet, in a sense that is obscured by most of our controversies, Keats was right in affirming that "Beauty is truth; truth Beauty."

Even Heine—as his passage about the symbolic nature of art

suggests—had moments when he guessed that his commitment to "truth" conflicted with beauty only because his particular truth was not true enough, because it was a truth limited by his political preoccupations on the one hand, his preoccupation with his own person on the other. For Heine was a brilliantly intuitive, though sporadic, critic of visual art, music, and literature. The art criticism of his *Salon* served as a model to Baudelaire (whose own critical writings, filled as they are with the same antinomy between truth and beauty, helped both him and later writers to resolve it in practice).

Heine got no farther than those flashes of awareness that were his substitute for hard work. The more he saw of political writers like the Young Germans, Ludwig Börne and Karl Marx, the more the artist in him protested that these were his enemies. By 1840—when he published his vicious attack on Börne, an attack on a dead writer that could serve no other purpose than to ease his own emotional stress—he had decided once and for all that he was no soldier in any war of liberation: "For beauty and for genius there will be no place in the commonwealth of our new Puritans; both will be more grievously insulted and oppressed than under the older dispensations . . . The kings are departing, and, in their train, the last poets."

Börne's accusation against Heine—for which Heine revenged himself by writing this book—was that Heine had "talent, but no character." When Heine's old enemies and former allies could no longer attack him on the grounds that he was a subversive writer, the same accusation became the basis of all their criticisms. Heine's defense was to place talent above character, to proclaim his freedom from every nonaesthetic consideration. Thus, in 1837, he interrupted his account of the French stage to profess his belief in the "autonomy of art," claiming that "art should not serve as a handmaiden to either religion or politics, for its ultimate end is itself, as the world's own ultimate end is the world." If he had acted on this insight as a poet, Heine might have become a true innovator; but its effect on Heine's own work can be studied in his two long poems of the eighteen-forties, *Atta Troll* and *Deutschland, ein Wintermärchen*. The doctrine of the autonomy of art, reformulated in the text of *Atta Troll* itself, meant that Heine could indulge all his personal whims, break off his narrative to aim a quick dart at individuals or institutions he disliked, and commit every manner of inconsequence; for his song, he writes, is "fantastically aimless; aimless like love, like life itself, like the Creator and his Creation, obedient only to its own pleasure."

Heine had Byron's precedent for this particular conception of the poet's freedom; but he had long outgrown Byron's influence and was permitting himself the very vices to which he attributed the decadence of modern art.[4] He was confusing the freedom of poetry with the freedom of poets; and it was this latter freedom that Novalis had in mind when he observed: "The greater the poet, the less freedom he permits himself . . ."[5] Even if poetry is autonomous—and the doctrine itself is questionable—poets certainly are not. It is Heine's application of the doctrine that was pernicious; for a poet as cerebral and self-conscious as Heine can make no progress without some measure of cooperation between creative impulse and critical insight. Where his talent failed him, character might indeed have helped.

It is therefore with very mixed feelings that one reads the notebooks and the *Confessions* of Heine's last years. Politically, he had wholly disengaged himself from the "marching-route of his cradle"; but his professions of conservatism, even his professions of a return to the "spiritualistic" religion, which undoubtedly attracted him at the time, would be more convincing if the cause had been less personal and if his last imaginative works did not refute them. Very few of his last poems show any evidence of the change of heart—and of the corresponding change of style—that one would expect from his notebooks and *Confessions*. The change—as already implied—was genuine, but not complete, and it arose from Heine's fear of a barbarism that he continued to foster even while trying to exorcise it.

In the notebooks Heine does his best to ward off the terrible visions of the future that followed his disillusionment with progressive creeds: "I see the marvels of the past quite clearly," one entry reads. "A veil covers the future, but a rose-coloured

---

[4] See his characterization of modern French literature, *Works* (Tempel-Verlag) Vol. V, 450.

[5] *Works* (Minor) Vol. II, 307.

veil, and through it I glimpse golden pillars and ornaments, and hear sweet sounds." This is an attempt to cheer himself up with aesthetic fantasies, as the vocabulary makes all too clear; but its effect is canceled out by one of his very last prophecies, revealing a very different aspect of what will happen when the "sensualistic" principle has triumphed: "The future smells of Russian hide, of blood, of godlessness and a great many cudgels. I advise our grandsons to be born with a very thick skin to their backs." This prophecy occurs in Heine's last public prose work, *Lutezia.* His *Confessions* of 1854 fill in the biographical background. He had seen socialism turn into Communism, republicanism into a despotic barbarism, which he came to hate and fear more than he had ever hated or feared the old tyrannies. His own denunciations of these creeds, he honestly admits, were inspired by an intuitive antipathy toward their advocates rather than by abstract principle. His revolt was aesthetic before it became ethical, for he did not turn against atheism until it ceased to be the prerogative of a cultured minority and "began to reek very strongly of cheese, brandy and tobacco: then suddenly my eyes were opened, and what I had not grasped by intellect, I perceived through my sense of smell." His personal association with revolutionaries of every shade had taught him to beware of the "fanatical monks of atheism, Grand Inquisitors of unbelief, who would condemn M. de Voltaire to the stake because at heart he was nothing but an obdurate deist." This intolerant materialism, the product of an alliance between atheism and communism, threatened to destroy "our whole modern civilization, the hard-won achievements of so many centuries, the fruit of the noblest endeavours of our predecessors." The same threat accounts for his gloomy jottings in the notebooks about the future of poetry.

"Democratic hatred of poetry," he notes. "Parnassus is to be levelled down, macadamized, and where once the leisured poet had climbed, listening to nightingales, there will soon be a flat road, a railway, where a boiler neighs as it rushes past busy pedestrians." And again: "Democratic rage against love poetry. —Why sing about roses, you aristocrat. Sing of the democratic potato, which keeps the people alive." Most ironic of all is his epitaph for poetry, an epitaph most elegantly and fittingly inscribed—but for his own grave: "Our lyrical poetry is a product of spiritualism, although its material is sensualistic, the longing of the isolated mind to be merged with the world of phenomena, to mingle with nature. As sensualism triumphs, lyrical poetry must end, for there arises a longing for the spiritual: sentimentality, which grows ever thinner and fainter, nihilistic mawkishness, a hollow fog of verbiage, a half-way house between has-been and will-be, tendentious poetry." Many years earlier Heine had observed that "sentimentality is a product of materialism"; and it was Baudelaire who turned the definition against Heine's own work, when he called it "une littérature pourrie de sentimentalisme matérialiste." Heine had never lacked self-knowledge, only the power to act on it. Already in 1834 he had written about "romantic extravagance," due to the predominance of "individuality and skepticism"; and as early as 1829 he had defended himself against the charge of "Byronic dividedness"—by blaming the world: "Oh, dear reader, if you feel like complaining about that 'dividedness,' you should rather complain that the world itself has been torn neatly in half. For since the poet's heart is the centre of the world, it follows that it must now be grievously divided. Whoever claims that his heart has remained whole is only confessing that he has a prosaic, remotely provincial, small-town heart. But through mine the great rift of the world has passed, and for that very reason I know that the mighty gods have granted me high favour above many others and thought me worthy of the martyrdom of poets."

This is Heine the *charmant esprit,* who makes the kind of strictures I have applied to his work sound unduly solemn and heavy-handed; the writer who, as Barker Fairley remarks in his study of Heine's imagery,[6] "had hardly a dull page." Perhaps one should not ask for more than that, though personally I wish that Heine had written a few more dull pages of prose and a few more poems that speak through a single mask, and that mask firmly fixed. My complaint against Heine is not that he was a comic writer, when he ought to have been a serious one, but that his particular brand of tragicomedy was an impure

[6] Barker Fairley, *Heinrich Heine: An Interpretation* (Oxford, 1954).

mixture whose ingredients, after a time, become insipid, because they neutralize one another. The purely comic has a very different effect. Heine's work bears out Novalis' dictum that "the ludicrous is a mixture that amounts to nil." [7] The irony and facetiousness of his manner, though anything but dull in themselves, tend to induce an exasperation that can be more unbearable than dullness.

As Heine himself suggests in a passage on Goethe, this manner may have been imposed on him by an early necessity that turned into second nature: "Those writers who languish under censorship and intellectual restrictions of every kind, and are yet incapable of ever disowning the true convictions of their hearts, are quite especially apt to resort to the ironic or humorous form." [8] But the outward necessity alone does not account for Heine's strange compulsion to let off fireworks of wit at the very moment when the music of his poetry is most intense. Once again Novalis provides an illuminating comment: "In serene souls there is no wit. Wit testifies of a disturbed equilibrium; it is the result of the disturbance and, at the same time, the means of restoring the equilibrium. Passion commands the most violent form of wit . . . The state in which all our relationships break up, that of despair or that of spiritual death, is the most terrifyingly witty of all." [9] Heine was a brave man, but he was afraid of the stark despair that sometimes permeates through the cracks in his verse and prose. He hints at this metaphysical fear when he writes in connection with Kant's arguments for the existence of God: "Only to see the existence of God discussed fills me with such a peculiar terror, such an uncanny anguish, as I once experienced in London, at New Bedlam, when, surrounded only by madmen, I lost sight of my escort. 'God is all that exists'; and to doubt Him is to doubt life itself, it is death." [10] Heine's wit is often of the "terrifying" kind on which Novalis remarks; but it resorts to means unworthy of its function.

[7] Novalis, *Works* (Minor) Vol. II, 302.
[8] Heine, *Works* (Tempel-Verlag) Vol. VI, 172.
[9] Novalis, *op. cit.*, 119.
[10] *Zur Geschichte der Religion und Philosophie in Deutschland. Salon* II (Hamburg, 1852), 211.

The case for Heine the humorist has never been presented more persuasively than by Barker Fairley, in the short study mentioned above. In all but the concluding chapter, that is, in 159 out of 169 pages, he refrains from all qualitative judgment and merely traces the recurrence of certain images and conceits —or "themes and motifs," as he calls them—in Heine's verse and prose. These images and conceits are those of "song within song," "music and dance," "chorus and procession," "theatre and ceremony," "carnival and costume," "animals," and "Heaven and Hell." Almost effortlessly—or so it appears— with admirable deftness and nonchalance, Fairley succeeds not only in establishing the crucial significance of all the references that he groups under these different headings, but in showing that they are closely interrelated. His manner is so unemphatic that the reader is convinced in the process of being entertained. This main body of the book itself is like a show, a procession of pictures, which happen to be lantern slides as well; the reader can enjoy them for their own sake. At one point Fairley writes of Heine's "comic mythology"; this definition very neatly sums up the kind of unity that he has discovered in Heine's writings.

It is only when we come to the brief chapter called *Conclusions,* in which exposition gives way to evaluation, that doubts begin to arise. For the unity that Fairley claims for Heine's work really appertains to his mode of thinking and feeling; it is a quality of his mind. It does not follow that the same unity is present in Heine's works, that his comic vision was constant or that he succeeded in transmuting it into art. Barker Fairley suggests that we should revise our judgment of Heine in the light of the discovery that "after all, there is a certain order in Heine, perhaps a sufficient order, not superimposed intellectually or by reflection, but asserting itself instinctively as what we might call an order of the imagination, and therefore a creative order, an artistic one." But to substantiate this claim, Fairley would have needed to deal not with Heine's work as a whole, represented in this case by a large number of quotations from different works in verse and prose, but with individual works, whether long or short, and to deal with these in their entirety. Strangely enough, Fairley does not agree with Heine's own high estimate of his ballet scenario *Der Doktor Faust,* one of the few longer works by Heine which does possess the imaginative unity that Fairley claims for his work as a whole; and Fairley is severe enough on Heine's most widely read work, the *Buch der Lieder,* of which he writes:

> It is a sobering thought that Heine's most conspicuous success—the greatest hit possible in the history of lyrical poetry —was scored in the one phase of his verse where his richer nature was suppressed. The song form, as he used it, was too slight to release his images freely: he was, in a large measure, reduced to the song image itself, which he then, as we saw, overworked.

The word "success" in this context is ambiguous; it is not quite clear whether Fairley means only the outward success of this collection—by which, incidentally, Heine did not profit financially, since he sold the rights to his publisher for a meager lump sum—or whether he is also implying that Heine made it artistically successful by suppressing "his richer nature." This second possibility is remote, but it is by no means outrageous to propose that Heine might, on occasions, have succeeded better as an artist by doing just that. Even if Fairley did not intend such a *sous-entente,* he does come close to implying that Heine's recourse to "song within song" was a vicarious means of arousing the stock responses associated with song and music; and that, in essence, is what Heine's adverse critics deplore, though it must be added that Heine was almost certainly not conscious of using the device to that end.

Barker Fairley's thesis, then, is double-edged, at least as far as we are asked to regard it as a vindication of Heine as an imaginative artist. Yet the Heine who emerges from Fairley's study is someone who "was fundamentally a social writer, in the broadest sense of the word, an observer, a commentator, not an introvert; and his imagery, we find, was social too. Just as social, in fact, as a variety theatre, a vaudeville, a topical review." This Heine, the brilliant satirist, commentator and wit, is well served by Fairley's book; but the trouble is that Heine was also a serious artist, that Barker Fairley's Heine is no more the whole Heine than Matthew Arnold's chief inheritor of

"Goethe's mantle." Once again, we must content ourselves with an incomplete image; the Heine enigma is not resolved.

The contradiction in Fairley's thesis is that the "high-water marks," as he calls them, in all his different categories of images—such as the chase in *Atta Troll* for "chorus and procession," the dancing of Mlle Laurence for "music and dance," the prose passage on Paganini's playing and the singing in the poem "Jehuda ben Halevy" for music alone—are all episodes, parts of works in which their function may be comparatively insignificant; less significant, that is, than in the general context of Fairley's demonstration. He admits as much in his conclusion, when he writes that "this"—the unity of Heine's work, the work of "one in whom imagination and intellect pull together to make a completed achievement"—"would have been apparent sooner if he had recorded his genius in some work of larger scope like those of his predecessors, Rabelais, Cervantes, Swift." Alas, Heine not only did not do so, but was incapable of doing so; and, much as Barker Fairley tells us about Heine's mind, he cannot expect us to substitute a unity gathered from the "high-water marks" of Heine's verse and prose for the missing unity of that unwritten work of larger scope.

This is not to deny that the high-water marks are significant and memorable; none more so than the dance of Mlle Laurence, the street dancer who made such a deep impression on Heine on the London Embankment. (That, at least, is where he places her in the semifictitious narrative of his *Florentinische Nächte*.) As Fairley indicates, the account of her dancing reveals Heine's awareness of a mystery that cannot be communicated in words; as it happens, the mystery of Mlle Laurence is a tragic one. Her dancing conveys it, but the rest of her conduct—when the narrator becomes better acquainted with her in Paris—denies it. Perhaps it was this incongruity, as much as the nature of dancing itself, that fascinated Heine; and it is no accident that two of his most profound works, *Der Doktor Faust* and *Die Götter im Exil,* were conceived as ballet scenarios or "dance poems," as Heine called them. Few of his purely literary works succeed in conveying the mysterious—except sporadically, as in this very account of Mlle Laurence's dancing:

Dance and dancer demanded my whole attention, almost took it by force. This was no classical dancing, as we find it still in our great ballets in which, as in classical tragedy, only affected unities and artificialities prevail; those were not the danced alexandrines, the declamatory leaps, the antithetical entrechats, the noble passion that performs such whirling pirouettes on one foot, so that you see nothing but Heaven and underwear, nothing but ideal reality and lies . . . Mademoiselle Laurence was no great dancer, her toes were not very flexible, her legs were not practiced in every sort of dislocation, she knew nothing about the art of dancing, as taught by Vestris, but she danced as nature commands human beings to dance: her whole being was in harmony with her steps, not only her feet, but her whole body danced, her face danced . . . sometimes she turned pale, almost deathly pale, she opened her eyes spectrally wide, desire and pain quivered about her lips, and her black hair, which enclosed her temples in smooth ovals, moved like two fluttering raven's wings. This was no classical dancing, again; but neither was it Romantic, in the sense in which a young Frenchman of the school of Renduel would use the word. This dancing had nothing mediaeval about it, nothing Venetian either, nothing macabre, nothing hunch-backed; it contained neither moonlight nor incest . . . It was a kind of dancing that did not seek to amuse by outward motions, but the outward motions seemed like words of a peculiar language that endeavoured to communicate peculiar meanings. But what did this dancing communicate? I could not understand it, passionately as this language expressed itself. Only sometimes I guessed that something gruesomely painful was in question. I, who at other times so easily grasp the signature of all phenomena, could not solve this riddle translated into dance—and perhaps the music too was to blame for my vain groping, for it was surely designed to lead me astray, confuse me cunningly and distract me from the true meaning. Sometimes Monsieur Turlutu's triangle tittered so mockingly! And Madame, the Mother, beat her big drum so angrily that her face peered from the black cloud of her hood like a blood-red northern light.

When the troupe had left, I remained standing in the same place for a long time, wondering what this dance might mean. Was it a national dance of the South of France, or of Spain? Something of the kind was suggested by the impetuosity with which the dancer flung her body to and fro, the savagery with which she sometimes threw back her head, in the wanton and reckless fashion of those Bacchantes whom we observe with amazement on the reliefs of ancient vases. At such times her dancing was somehow drunkenly abandoned, it conveyed something darkly inevitable, something fatalistic; she danced like Fate itself. Or was she dancing fragments of some ancient, obsolete pantomime? Or a personal history? Sometimes the girl bent her head down towards the ground, as if listening for something, as if she could hear a voice that spoke to her from the depths . . . Then she would tremble like an aspen leaf, quickly turned away to another place and there gave herself over to her maddest, wildest leaps, then put her ear to the ground again, listened even more anxiously than before, nodded her head, blushed, blanched, shuddered, stood stiffly upright for a moment, as if transfixed. Finally she made a movement like someone washing his hands. Was it of blood that she cleansed her hands with such protracted care, such horrifying care? While doing this, she cast a sideward glance so supplicating, so imploring, so irresistibly pitiable . . . and this glance happened to fall on me.

The reader, like Heine himself, does not easily forget this dance; but he does easily forget its place and function in the *Florentine Nights,* its connection with the rest of the narrative and even the sequel in Paris that explains it. I have omitted a passage in translating even this brief extract, Heine's account of the first, most powerful impact made on the narrator by Mlle Laurence's dancing; the passage omitted contains a witty observation, but it can only serve to make the reader less receptive to what follows. This is one of many instances where Heine would have been wise to "suppress his richer nature."

When Heine died in Paris on February 17, 1856, his reputation was higher in France than in Germany, though parts of his early *Buch der Lieder* were familiar to a vast body of Germans, educated and uneducated alike, if only because they had been set to music popular to the point of anonymity; and, as lyrics to be sung, rather than read, Heine's early poems are surpassed only by the poems of Eichendorff, who had the advantage of genuine naïveté. During the following decades Heine's fame spread to every European country, to the United States and as far as Japan. By an exclusive emphasis on his "modernity"— that is, on his liberalism, his materialism, and his irreverence —a vast nineteenth-century public, including scientists, politicians, and progressive intellectuals in every field, were able to turn Heine into one of the heroes of their time. As far as his poetry is concerned, Heine's modernity was only skin-deep; he never learned to do without conventional Romantic effects, nor does his imagery show a vital response to the large city in which he spent most of his mature life. It is probably wrong to expect the imagery of modern poetry to be urban, though much of it does reflect the poet's immediate environment; but much of Heine's imagery lacks the immediacy of active observation. With the single exception of the two *North Sea* cycles—whose free verse was by no means unprecedented in German literature, but attained a freedom of a different order—Heine contented himself with variety within an unusually narrow range of verse forms; too often, even in his last and most masterly poems, one feels that the trochaic meters are simply rattling on like some efficient but remorseless machine; and one wishes it would stop for a while, to give the poet a chance to look around.

Heine's prose, on the other hand, was not only modern, but unexcelled in his time. It can be said to have grappled with almost every important issue of the century—or, if not grappled with it, at least toyed with it most pleasantly. Much of his prose remains as stimulating now as it was to all the contemporaries and near-contemporaries who tried to imitate its verve, its wit, and its clarity; and the same qualities keep most of his poetry readable still—which is more than one can say for a great many talented poets writing at the same transitional period, the period when a moribund Romanticism was gradually giving way to Symbolism on the one hand, Naturalism on the other.

In order to overcome the limitations of that period and of his own position in it, Heine would have needed either genius or humility. Both genius and humility are destroyers of circumstance. His younger contemporary Eduard Mörike, a late successor to that "provincial" Swabian school which Heine never tired of ridiculing, proved that even the older tradition of German lyrical verse was still capable of a new and genuine development; but Mörike's way was closed to Heine, for such local roots as Heine had were wrenched out in his youth. This uprootedness was one cause of the sentimentality concealed beneath his wit. To be cosmopolitan is not necessarily to be universal; but Heine's cosmopolitanism could have opened a way that he did not take, a way more vertical than horizontal that leads to universality, since all roots reach down toward the same center. He could have grown deeper roots and become one of the "transplanted" writers whom Remy de Gourmont distinguishes from the "uprooted." [11] A still younger contemporary, Georg Büchner, proved what genius could do in the way of innovation; but Büchner had the ruthlessness of genius and of revolutionaries.

Heine feared nothing so much as to be possessed; this was his dilemma, the dilemma of liberalism in an age of extremes; and he faced it with insight, honesty, and the desperate courage that will not admit defeat. As Nietzsche said, "it can be the sign of a noble mind to make fun of pathetic situations and to respond to them with undignified behaviour." Nietzsche's remark is sound enough psychologically, even if its application to literature is more dubious. If it cannot justify Heine's lapses as a poet, it does help to explain them and to justify him as a man; and such a justification is not irrelevant in the case of a writer whose personality, for good or for ill, is present in all he wrote.

[11] *Les Transplantés,* in *Promenades Littéraires,* 1st. Series (Paris, 1904). 330–347.

VI

GEORG BÜCHNER

Genius is an unfashionable word; and in attributing genius to Büchner, while denying it to Heine whose works exerted a world-wide influence when Büchner's were scarcely read even in his own country, I am aware that the word may call for qualification, if not for a re-definition that I am reluctant to attempt. As often as not, to speak of genius may be the last resort of a critic unequal to his subject, for genius is more easily discovered than analyzed, more easily measured than located, being a sort of phlogiston whose existence in human minds and their products can be neither proved nor disproved by empirical means. The analogy, of course, is only partly apt, like every analogy between the methods of criticism and the methods of scientific research. No work of art can be analyzed or assessed with a degree of accuracy comparable to that obtained in chemical experiments. One critical method may be more "objective" or more rewarding than another, but none is infallible. Unlike the universal ciphers of mathematics, the terminology of literary criticism is capable of no precision other than that which results from an understanding between the critic and his reader.

What is meant by genius here can be best conveyed by stating that even after one has adduced evidence of Büchner's extraordinary talents and accomplishments, as a scientist, political thinker, and imaginative writer, as a moralist, psychologist, and visionary, there remains a residue of the inexplicable. His skill as a dramatist, to cite an example more verifiable than most, seems to have been acquired without the usual process of trial and error; and more generally one can say that Büchner's achievements demanded an incommensurable minimum of experience. Often, in his case, one looks in vain for the cause behind the effect; there is a difference between the mere aggregate of his talents and their totality. For this difference there is no single word but genius.

As German literature suggests all too frequently, genius can exist without the various talents that make it viable; but Büchner's capacity for sheer hard work was no less extraordinary than his genius. He had little of the arrogance of the very gifted, and none of their vanity. Before the end of his short life he had attained a maturity rare enough in artists three times his age. When he died at the age of twenty-three, he was a Doctor of Philosophy and a lecturer in comparative anatomy at the University of Zürich; a former political revolutionary who had been formidable enough to be driven into exile from his native Hessen by the imminent danger of a prison sentence; and the author of those four literary works—three plays and a story— to which he owes his belated fame. The manuscript of a fourth play, *Pietro Aretino,* which his family regarded as his best, was lost or destroyed after his death. He had published a more than competent translation of two dramas by Victor Hugo and written a thesis in French on *le système nerveux du barbeau;* this thesis was followed by a paper on the cranial nerves, the subject of his trial lecture at Zürich. His notes for a projected course of lectures on the history of German philosophy after Descartes and Spinoza, prepared during the last months of his life, include some penetrating and original comments on the subject. It is no exaggeration to say that Büchner excelled at every activity to which he applied himself.

To Büchner's talents and outlook, but not to his genius, his family background is relevant. His father, paternal grandfather, and an uncle on his father's side were medical men; so was his favorite brother Ludwig, the first editor of Georg's posthumous works and himself the author of *Force and Matter, Man and His Place in Nature,* and *Mind in Animals,* important studies in evolution and animal psychology that were popularized in England by Annie Besant. Of Georg's other brothers and sisters, Wilhelm became a research chemist and Reichstag deputy, Alexander a professor of literature in France, Louise a writer in the feminist cause. Although Büchner's father disapproved of Georg's political activities, which were a grave embarrassment to a family enlightened and progressive rather than revolutionary, he was not unsympathetic to the convictions that gave rise to these activities and made his peace with Georg by letter a few months before Georg died in exile. It is also worth noting that the uncle to whom Georg turned when he was in trouble —Eduard Reuss, a brother of Georg's mother—was a Protestant theologian.

It was his meeting with another Protestant theologian, Pastor Weidig, that introduced Büchner to revolutionary politics. After attending school at Darmstadt, Georg Büchner studied the natural sciences—chiefly zoology and comparative anatomy —at Strasbourg, where he became secretly engaged to a pastor's daughter, Wilhelmine Jaegle, who had looked after him when he was ill in her father's house. In October, 1833, at the age of twenty, he moved to the University of Giessen, took up practical medicine at his father's request, but had to return home in the spring after a more serious illness, an attack of meningitis that left him subject to headaches and fevers for the rest of his life. Back in Giessen after his convalescence, he met Pastor Weidig, the leader of the Liberal movement in Hessen. Büchner joined the "Society for the Rights of Man" and, in collaboration with Pastor Weidig, wrote and published an anonymous tract, "Der Hessische Landbote," which called on the peasants to revolt. Büchner contributed facts about the exploitation of the peasants, Weidig the main body of the tract, evangelical exhortations based on quotations from the Bible. In April, 1834, Büchner returned to Strasbourg and announced his engagement to Minna Jaegle. During the Easter vacation he founded a branch of the Society at Darmstadt and, in July, attended a conference of delegates from the various branches; but he had already lost faith in mere Liberal reform, deciding that nothing less than a revolution would prove effective in Germany. On August 1, the stock of the "Landbote" was seized by the government; one of Büchner's associates was arrested and Büchner himself interrogated. For the time being, he continued his studies at home, also giving public lectures on anatomy, but secretly prepared his escape. In order to raise money for his escape, he wrote his first drama, *Dantons Tod,* and undertook the translations from Hugo; Karl Gutzkow, the leader of the "Young Germany" movement, saw to the publication of both books. Soon after getting away to Strasbourg in March, 1835, Büchner was denounced for his part in the authorship of the "Landbote"; in June a warrant was issued for his arrest. *Dantons Tod* and Büchner's letters suggest that he had already grown tired of political action; at Strasbourg he wrote his French thesis, which won him admission to the *Société d'Histoire Naturelle,* his story *Lenz* and his comedy *Leonce und Lena* (which he wrote, but submitted too late, for a competition). In September, 1836, he was granted a Doctor of Philosophy degree by the University of Zürich and, after reading his paper on the cranial nerves, was appointed a lecturer there. Three months later, in February, 1837, he contracted typhus and died in Zürich on February 19.

Dantons Tod was first performed in 1902, *Leonce und Lena* in 1911, *Woyzeck* in 1913. Büchner, in fact, was too "advanced" a dramatist to be acceptable even during the Naturalist eighteen-eighties and eighteen-nineties, when Ibsen, Hauptmann, and Sudermann dominated the German experimental theatres. Gerhart Hauptmann admired Büchner's works, editions of which had been published in 1850 and 1879; but it was not till after the experiments of Strindberg, Wedekind, and the first Expressionists that Büchner's plays established themselves on the stage. This very circumstance serves to confute the arguments of Georg Lukács [1] and other critics of his

[1] Georg Lukács, *Deutsche Realistik des* 19. *Jahrhunderts* (Berlin, 1952).

school,[2] who would like to persuade us that Büchner was an early practitioner of "Social Realism" of an art primarily directed toward social or political ends. For a time, undoubtedly, Büchner's preoccupation with human suffering caused him to seek relief in political action, for tyranny and injustice were two obvious causes of human suffering in his time; but only a very prejudiced reader of his works, from *Dantons Tod* to *Woyzeck,* can fail to see that Büchner's realism goes far deeper than that of the Naturalists and their successors, the Social Realists of this century. Büchner's view of life was a tragic one; his intense pity for the poor, the oppressed and the exploited was never alleviated by the comfortable belief that human suffering is due to no other causes than poverty, oppression, and exploitation. If Büchner had wished to glorify the French Revolution or the ideology behind it, he would have made Robespierre the hero of his play, not the irresolute and dissolute Danton; but Büchner's dominant passion was the passion for truth, for the whole truth; and even if he had taken Robespierre as the hero of his play, it would have been Robespierre at the moment of his fall, the victim of the same inhuman system that had brought about Danton's death. Büchner, in short, was never a party man; he was never purblind, as every party man must be, because he hated ideologies that enslave the minds of men as much as he hated the economic and social orders that enslave men bodily. As a scientist, he knew that body and mind are interdependent; he therefore revolted against the "idealistic" cant that denies or minimizes the extent to which material conditions affect us. Yet his true concern was with mental and spiritual suffering, Danton's vision of vanity and his fear of death, the religious torment of Lenz, the suicidal boredom of Leonce, the physical victimization of Woyzeck that leads to hallucination, paranoia, and murder. Büchner's realism was that of every great writer who seeks the truth about the human situation; a realism that is not incompatible with poetic vision.

I have said elsewhere that, in the age of Hegelian dialectics, it was often the self-contradictions of a writer that revealed his

[2] Hans Mayer is the most outstanding. See his *Georg Büchner und seine Zeit* (Wiesbaden, 1946).

vital preoccupations. Büchner, too, wrote out of a tragic tension between two conflicting views of life. What is so astonishing about his works is their consistency of purpose and achievement. One reason is that Büchner had no use at all for Hegel or for that idealistic German school from which Hegel derived; neither, in fact, had Heine, though he paid lip service to Hegel and concealed the stark pessimism of his last years behind the paraphernalia of a fancy-dress Romanticism. Büchner had no patience with half-measures; like Schopenhauer, whom he resembled in his pessimism and in his pity, he based his thinking not on metaphysical premises, but on the bare condition of man, on the reality of suffering, our participation in suffering not our own and our desire to relieve it. This basic existential preoccupation is at the root of all Büchner's works; but he was divided between a religious view of the human predicament and a cruelly deterministic view, brought home to him by his scientific studies and his reflections on history.

An early letter to his fiancée, written when he was twenty, contains a most poignant account of these conflicting views. The account is especially valuable because of its direct bearing on Büchner's first play, *Dantons Tod*. There can be no better introduction to it than Büchner's own reflections on the events with which it deals:

> I was studying the history of the French Revolution. I felt almost annihilated by the horrible fatalism of history. In human nature I discovered a terrifying sameness, in human institutions an incontrovertible power, granted to all and to none. The individual mere froth on the wave, greatness a mere accident, the sovereignty of genius a mere puppet play, a ludicrous struggle against an inalterable law; to recognize this law our supreme achievement, to control it impossible . . .[3]

It was this experience of determinism that turned Büchner into a revolutionary of the most radical sort, as the same letter shows. It is the extremists of revolutionary politics, the Robespierres rather than the Dantons, who base their policies on the recognition of that "unalterable law." Yet the recognition ran

[3] Letter of November, 1833 (?). *Works* (Leipzig, 1949), 209.

counter to Büchner's nature and convictions, to his Christian sense of the value of the individual and his no less radical belief in free will. Hence the conflicting resolutions that follow:

> . . . Never again shall I feel obliged to bow to the parade horses and corner boys of History. I am accustoming my eyes to the sight of blood. But I am no guillotine blade. The word *must* is one of the curses pronounced at the baptism of men. The dictum: "for it must needs be that offences come; but woe to that man by whom the offence cometh!"—is terrible. What is it in us that lies, murders, steals? I can't bear to pursue this thought any further. But oh! if I could lay this cold and tormented heart on your breast!

The relevance of this passage to *Dantons Tod* would be obvious even if Büchner had not put much of it into Danton's own mouth in Act II of the play.[4] The conflict between Robespierre and St. Just on the one hand, Danton and his friends on the other, is a conflict between two different views of political and historical necessity. Their dramatic conflict would be less convincing if Büchner had not been able to do full justice to both arguments. At one time, there can be no doubt, he would have identified himself with the party of Robespierre and St. Just. Not only Danton expresses thoughts that we know to have been Büchner's; St. Just's great speech in Act II is an apology for the very determinism that Büchner had come close to accepting:

> Nature calmly and irresistibly obeys her own laws; men are annihilated where they come into conflict with those laws. A change in the constitution of the air we breathe, a blazing up of the tellurian fire, a disturbance in the balance in a quantity of water, an epidemic, a volcanic eruption, a flood—each of these can cause the death of thousands. What is the result? An insignificant alteration of physical nature, hardly perceptible in the cosmos as a whole, that would have left no trace to speak of but for the dead bodies left in its wake.
>
> Now I ask you: should mental nature show more consideration in its revolutions than physical nature? Should not an idea have as much right as a physical law to destroy whatever

---

[4] In the scene "Ein Zimmer." *Works,* 43.

opposes it? Indeed, should not any event that will change the entire constitution of moral nature, that is, of humanity, be permitted to attain its end by bloodshed? The World Spirit makes use of our arms in the mental sphere as it makes use of volcanoes and floods in the physical. What difference does it make whether men die of an epidemic or of a revolution? [5]

The appeal to Hegel's "World Spirit" in this context may be an anachronism, but it is a significant one. Büchner was careful to grant both factions their fair share of religious, or pseudoreligious justification. Elsewhere Robespierre compares his mission to that of Christ:

> He redeemed them with his blood, and I redeem them with their own. He made them sin, and I take this sin upon myself . . . And yet . . . Truly, the son of man is crucified in us all, we all sweat blood and writhe in the garden of Gethsemane, but no one redeems another with his wounds.[6]

Dramatically, this passage serves to show that Robespierre too has scruples and affections, for he is moved to express these thoughts by Camille Desmoulins's desertion to Danton's party. Robespierre, who denies his scruples and affections in favor of impersonal ends, is no less deserving of pity than his victim, the individualist. But Büchner takes dramatic impartiality even further by throwing just a little shadow of doubt on the purity of Robespierre's motives, as indeed he suggests several possible explanations for the conduct of Danton himself. That is why *Dantons Tod* is a truly and profoundly tragic play; both Robespierre, who serves a certain ideal necessity, and Danton, who opposes it in the cause of individual freedom, are destroyed by the revolution, though Robespierre first destroys Danton for the Revolution's sake. The Revolution itself assumes a character akin to that of Fate in Greek tragedy; and the voice of the people—*vox populi, vox dei*—expresses a terrible indifference to the virtues and aspirations of both men. Yet amoral and brutish though they are, even the representatives of the people are

---

[5] In the scene "Der Nationalkonvent." *Works,* 47.
[6] Act I, "Ein Zimmer." *Works,* 31–32.

not excluded from the pity that Büchner's play so powerfully evokes.

Danton's disillusionment, too, is Büchner's own. One can follow the process in the few letters and parts of letters by Büchner that have been preserved. In a letter to his family, written when he was nineteen, he defended the use of violence in the revolutionary cause, on the grounds that the so-called laws of the land are nothing more than "a perpetual state of violence" imposed on the suffering people.[7] A year later he could still express his hatred of the aristocracy, or rather of an attitude of mind which he called "aristocratism," describing it "as the most shameful contempt for the Holy Ghost in Man; against this I fight with its own weapons, repaying scorn with scorn, mockery with mockery."[8] The turning-point came when certain of the peasants, for whose sake Büchner was risking imprisonment by his part in the authorship of the "Hessische Landbote," handed over their copies to the police.[9] Büchner was no less critical than before of the bourgeois intellectual reformers, the Young Germans, who did not share his own conviction that "the relation between rich and poor is the only revolutionary factor in the world," as he put it to Karl Gutzkow in 1835; but he had come to fear that the servility of the German working class would frustrate every effort on their behalf. In a later letter to Gutzkow he added a second "revolutionary factor." "With them (the working class), only two levers are effective: material misery and religious fanaticism. Any party that knows how to apply those levers will be victorious." By 1836, Büchner had renounced every kind of political activity; but it must not be supposed that he had made his peace with the existing social order. His quarrel with "the literary party of Gutzkow and Heine" was simply that they were wasting their time and energy in trying to bring about "a total transformation of our religious and social ideas by polemical journalism"; and he was "far from sharing their views on marriage and on the Christian religion."[10] Büchner remained a radical and an extremist; not

[7] Letter of April 5, 1833. *Works,* 204.
[8] Letter of February, 1834. *Works,* 213.
[9] According to August Becher's evidence. *Works,* 281.
[10] Letter to his family of January 1, 1836. *Works,* 239.

because he clung to any rigid political doctrine, but because he believed that "in social matters one must start out with an absolute principle of justice." [11] His own starting point was compassion with the poor; and that is why he stressed the economic basis of injustice in his time. A letter of 1836 to his family ends with a brief account of his visit to a Christmas fair, with its crowds of "ragged, frozen children, who stood gazing with wide eyes and sad faces at all that magnificence, made out of flour and water, gilt paper and muck." [12]

As for our "moribund modern society," he told Gutzkow in 1836 not to waste his talent on literary sallies against it, but to "let it go to the devil" in its own time. "Its whole life only consists in attempts to ward off the most horrible boredom. Let it die out, then, for that's the only new thing it's still capable of experiencing."

Strange, but all Büchner's heroes suffer from different forms of that very boredom—a profound boredom that saps their willpower, sometimes their very desire to live. If this boredom were no more than a late variety of the Romantic *mal du siècle,* we might indeed regard it as the attribute of a single social class of a ruling class in decline, as Büchner's letter seems to imply. The boredom of Leonce could easily pass for the mere languor of enforced idleness; and it is the seemingly innocent, pseudo-Romantic comedy *Leonce und Lena* that contains some of Büchner's most devastating political satire. "My Muse is a Samson in disguise," [13] he wrote to Gutzkow; but of all his works only *Leonce und Lena* makes its revolutionary impact by indirect means, by imitation and parody of current literary conventions. Since Leonce is a Prince, one might argue, and a particularly idle and useless one at that, Büchner used him to satirize the idleness and uselessness of the ruling class; and since boredom results from idleness and uselessness, Büchner saw to it that Leonce should be bored to the point of trying to kill himself. This is the kind of argument put forward by the advo-

---

[11] Letter to Gutzkow, 1836. *Works,* 234–244.
[12] Letter to his family of January, 1836. *Works,* 240.
[13] Letter of March, 1835. *Works,* 225.

cates of Social Realism; like most of their arguments, it is logical, but wholly specious.

Leonce himself is a rebel; his boredom is not the result of idleness and uselessness, but of his awareness that he is idle and useless. This awareness, as we shall see, has deeper implications than the social and political ones. Leonce not only questions his own function in the State—a function which, in any case, he is not prepared to perform—but doubts the value and purpose of human life itself. Romantic languor is the mood evoked at the beginning of his monologue in the first scene of the play; yet this languor soon gives way to reflections that have no place in the Romantic convention:

> The bees cling so drowsily to the flowers, the sun's rays lie so lazily on the ground. A horrible idleness is spreading everywhere. Idleness is the root of every vice.—Just to think of all the things that people do out of boredom! They study out of boredom, they pray out of boredom, they fall in love out of boredom, marry and procreate out of boredom and finally die of it; what's more—and that's what makes the whole thing so funny—they do it all with such a solemn expression on their faces, not knowing why they do it, but attaching all sorts of weighty reasons to their pastimes. All these heroes, geniuses and blockheads, all these saints and sinners and family men are really nothing more than sophisticated idlers.—Why, of all people, do *I* have to know it? Why can't I become important to myself, dress the poor puppet in a morning coat and put an umbrella in its hand, so as to make it very righteous, very useful and very respectable?—[14]

The allusion to a puppet in this passage—the significance of Büchner's obsession with puppets and robots has already been intimated—relates the boredom of Leonce to Büchner's own vision of vanity. Leonce thinks human endeavors vain because they are predetermined; he rebels against this determinism by refusing to marry the Princess for reasons of state, runs away from the kingdom, meets the same Princess without knowing it, falls in love with her and marries her of his own free will. Valerio sums up the grotesque irony of this plot when he presents

[14] Act I, Scene I. *Works,* 112.

the returning prodigals to the Court as "two world-famous automatons":

> Ladies and gentlemen, you have here two persons of either sex, a male and a female, a gentleman and a lady. Nothing but artifice and mechanisms, nothing but cardboard and watch springs! Each of them has a highly sensitive, exceedingly sensitive ruby spring under the nail of the little toe of the right foot; you press it ever so lightly and the machinery runs for no less than fifty years. These persons are of such perfect workmanship that they would be quite indistinguishable from other people if one didn't know that they're only cardboard; they could easily be turned into members of human society. They're very aristocratic too, for they speak with the right accent. They're very moral, for they get up on the stroke of the clock and go to bed on the stroke of the clock; also, they have a good digestion, which proves they've got a clear conscience. They have a fine sense of decency, for the lady has no words for the concept of trousers, and, as for the man, it's quite impossible for him to walk upstairs behind a lady or walk downstairs in front of one. They're highly educated, for the lady sings extracts from all the latest operas and the gentleman wears cuffs.—Attention, ladies and gentlemen, they're now at an interesting stage: the mechanism of love is beginning to function; the gentleman has already once carried the lady's wrap, the lady has already once rolled her eyes and raised them to heaven. Both have whispered more than once: faith, hope and charity! Both already look perfectly synchronized; they need nothing more, but the tiny word "Amen." [15]

For all its whimsical humor, the implications of *Leonce und Lena* are no less terrifying than those of *Woyzeck,* in which a performing horse replaces the automatons of *Leonce und Lena;* both are cruel comments on the illusion of freedom and the pretensions of Homo sapiens. The boredom of Leonce, then, is more than his response to the rottenness of a social system; it is the aftereffect of that experience of the abyss in which all Büchner's principal characters participate.

Danton's boredom has the same origin; but in his case there can be no question of a mere indictment on social or political

[15] Act III, Scene III. *Works,* 138–139.

grounds. To understand his boredom, we should rather consider Baudelaire's "Ennui," which

> ferait volontiers de la terre un débris
> Et dans un bâillement avalerait le monde

and Yeats's bitter comment, true of more than his own time, that

> The best lack all conviction, while the worst
> Are full of passionate intensity.

In the case of Danton, boredom is not the result of idleness, but its cause; and behind this cause there is another, the demoralization induced by his experience of the abyss. In a certain sense one can say of his particular kind of boredom that it afflicts the best, because only those whose moral sense is highly developed are susceptible to demoralization from that cause; but, as Baudelaire knew, the cause does not excuse the effect. Danton is a morally ambiguous character because his boredom—the apathy that springs from despair—is itself a vice and the begetter of other vices.

Danton's apathy is bound up with an almost nihilistic skepticism about human motives. When, in the opening scene, his wife asks him whether he believes in her, he replies: "How can I tell? We know very little about one another. We are pachyderms, we reach out our hands towards others, but it's a wasted effort; all we rub off in that contact is a little of the callous hide;—we are very lonely." And again: "Know one another? Why, we should have to break open the other's cranium and pull his thoughts out of the fibres of his brain." Woyzeck's torment is even more extreme than Danton's; but it is out of the same experience that he says: "Every human being is an abyss; it makes you giddy to look down." [16]

Danton's skepticism extends to his own motives. On the one hand he resists Robespierre's deterministic *"must"* in the cause of individual liberty; on the other, he questions his own free will in a speech that echoes Büchner's letter to his fiancée: "Puppets is what we are, puppets manipulated by unknown

---

[16] In the scene "Mariens Kammer." *Works,* 157.

powers; nothing, nothing at all in ourselves; no more than the swords with which ghosts fight their battles—only one can't see their hands, as in fairy tales . . ." Danton is morally superior to his enemies when he says of himself that he "would sooner be guillotined than condemn another to be guillotined"; but, in his passion for the whole truth, Büchner makes Danton's friend Lacroix say that Danton "would sooner be guillotined than make a speech," thus putting a very different construction on Danton's failure to defend himself and his friends. Both the imputed motives are valid. Danton is morally superior to his opponents insofar as he has experienced the abyss and acts in accordance with that experience; insofar as, having recognized its futility, he refuses to set in motion the murderous revolutionary machine, even to save his own skin. He is morally inferior to Robespierre and St. Just insofar as he lacks all conviction and has fallen into an apathy that takes the form of promiscuous debauchery. Büchner himself doesn't tell us—and doesn't expect us to decide—how far Danton's attitude of laisser faire is due to genuine scruples, to remorse for his former part in the "liquidation" of others and to compassion with the people, who are fobbed off with severed heads and continue to go hungry; and how far it is due only to his *taedium vitae,* weariness and indifference. "I shall show them how to die bravely," he says to Camille; "That's easier than to go on living."

This *taedium vitae* comes out most clearly at the beginning of Act II. Camille tells Danton to hurry, for they can't afford to waste time; to which Danton replies:

> But time wastes us.
> Oh, it's very boring always to put on one's shirt first, and then pull one's trousers over it and go to bed at night and creep out of it in the morning and always be setting one foot before the other; there's simply no telling how this will ever change. It's very sad to think of it, and to think that millions have done it before you and that millions will do it again in exactly the same way, and that, moreover, we consist of two halves, both of which do the same thing, so that everything happens twice over—it's very sad . . .

Camille tells him not to be childish and reminds him that he is ruining not only himself, but his friends as well. Danton refuses to act. He is tired, he says, of being "a wretched instrument, each of whose strings only sounds on one note." He is even prepared to admit that Robespierre, "the dogma of the Revolution," as he calls him, may be indispensable, whereas he, Danton, is not. Danton has ceased to care; his experience of the abyss has stripped him of all but passive virtues and negative desires. "We should sit down one beside the other and have some peace. Something went wrong when we were created; there's something missing in us, I don't know what to call it— but we'll never pull it out of one another's entrails, so why rip open another fellow's belly to find it?"

Here Danton seems to point to something very much like original sin; but, if so, he doesn't recognize its corollary, free will. His tolerance rests on the denial of free will, just as much as Robespierre's intolerance does. The difference is one of emphasis. Robespierre is prepared to sacrifice any number of human beings to an ideal necessity, Danton to sacrifice every ideal to what he regards as the facts of the human condition. Danton's passive resistance to Robespierre's fanaticism would be heroic if Danton believed in heroism; as it is, he can only resist the tyranny of Robespierre's ideal necessity by appealing to a different necessity, based on the inborn corruption of human nature and its dependence on material factors. In the crowd scene of Act I, the citizen who defends an adulteress against her husband's anger speaks in the spirit of Danton: "A knife? True enough, but not for the poor whore. What has she done? It's her hunger that whores and begs . . ." Much more poignantly, Woyzeck resorts to the same argument in defending himself against the Captain's taunts: "As for virtue, sir, I haven't yet got the hang of it. You see, we common people haven't any virtue, we just let nature have its way; but if I was a gentleman and had a hat and a watch and a frock coat and could talk refined, I'd be virtuous in no time. It must be a fine thing—virtue, I mean, sir. But I'm a poor man." [17]

Büchner would hardly have used this argument in two different plays if the moral problem had not concerned him person-

[17] In the scene "Beim Hauptmann." *Works,* 146.

ally; but, because of its very ambiguity, the conflict between Danton and Robespierre is more than a conflict between two political factions, two temperaments, or two views of life. It assumes the inevitability of a tragic dilemma, a dilemma that will recur as long as men disagree as to the relative value of ends and means; and since "there's something missing" in men, as Danton says, and they will always have to choose between one evil and another, *Dantons Tod* will never lose its appeal or its relevance.

It doesn't matter, therefore, that Büchner put his own conflicts, disillusionments, and sufferings into his plays. His magnificent impartiality saves all his works from being mere illustrations of this or that idea. From external evidence it would seem that Büchner would have taken Danton's side against Robespierre, whose fanatical insistence on abstract virtues was repellent to him; but the play both exposes and pardons both men. Büchner's impartiality made all the difference between the didactic realism of the Young Germany group and his own poetic realism. "I shall go my own way," he wrote to Gutzkow in 1836, "and continue to write a kind of drama that has nothing to do with all these controversial issues. I draw my characters in accordance with nature and history, as I see them, and laugh at the people who would like to make me responsible for the morality or immorality of those characters . . ."

This is not the attitude of a Social Realist before his time; nor, on the other hand, does it rest on the same foundations as Heine's arguments in favor of "art for art's sake." Heine took to this doctrine to defend his subjectivity. Büchner stumbled on beauty while he was looking for truth; and by truth he did not mean the writer's moods and caprices, but the facts of life. Being a man of genius, he soon found that the truth of literature includes subjective truth, the head, heart, and imagination of men. In order to present the facts of human nature, he drew on his own experience of life; but always for the sake of impersonal truth, never for the sake of self-expression.

When *Dantons Tod* was attacked for its obscenity, impiety, and subversiveness, Büchner justified himself in a letter to his family:

As regards the so-called immorality of my book, by the way, my answer is as follows: The dramatic poet, as I see it, is nothing but a writer of history, but is superior to the latter for this reason: that he re-creates history for us and, instead of giving us a dry account of it, places us right in the midst of the life of a particular period, gives us characters instead of characteristics and figures instead of descriptions. His supreme task is to get as close as possible to history as it really happened. His book must be neither more moral nor less moral than history itself; but God didn't create history to provide suitable reading matter for young females, and so I mustn't be blamed if my drama is no more suitable for that. How could I turn Danton and the bandits of the Revolutions into paragons of virtue? If I wished to portray their dissoluteness, they had to be dissolute, if I wished to indicate their godlessness, they had to speak like atheists . . . One could now censure me for having chosen such a subject. But this objection was refuted long ago. If one were to accept it, one would have to condemn the greatest masterpieces of literature. The poet is not a teacher of morals; he invents and creates characters, he brings past epochs back to life, and people may then learn from him as they learn from their historical studies and from their observation of all that happens around them in human life . . . If one were then to add that the poet should not represent the world as it is, but as it should be, my answer is that I don't aspire to do better than God, who surely created the world as it should be . . . In short, I think highly of Goethe or Shakespeare, very little of Schiller . . . [18]

If this apology for realism contains much that is generally accepted now, one should remember that Büchner was the contemporary not only of Dickens, but of Richard Wagner; and it is interesting to recall that in 1891 the editor of a Berlin periodical was sentenced to four months' imprisonment for daring to reprint *Dantons Tod*—after more than half a century of liberal reform!

Büchner's passion for realism was such that he based three out of his four extant imaginative works on documentary evidence, much of which is quoted verbatim in his works. *Dantons Tod* was based on histories of the French Revolution by Thiers

[18] Letter of July, 1835. *Works*, 232.

and Mignet, with other borrowings from a German work by Konrad Friedrich; *Lenz* on the diary of Pastor Oberlin, who looked after the poet and dramatist J. M. R. Lenz at the time of his mental breakdown in 1778; *Woyzeck* on reports of the trial and medical examination of a murderer of that name, who was almost reprieved on the grounds of insanity, but finally sentenced to death in 1824. But it would be quite wrong to regard these borrowings as a substitute for invention. What is so remarkable about all these works is their fusion of fact and imagination, verisimilitude, and passion, made possible by Büchner's extraordinary gift of empathy. His Lenz, for instance, expresses a view of art almost identical with Büchner's own when he says:

> Even the poets of whom we say that they reproduce reality have no conception of what reality is, but they're a great deal more bearable than those who wish to transform reality . . . I take it that God made the world as it should be and that we can hardly hope to scrawl or daub anything better; our only aspiration should be to re-create modestly in His manner . . . In all things, I demand life, the possibility of existence, and that's all; nor is it our business to ask whether it's beautiful, whether it's ugly. The feeling that there's life in the thing created is much more important than considerations of beauty and ugliness . . .[19]

But Büchner was also expounding the views of the historical Lenz. He would never have chosen to write about Lenz at all, but for his deep affinity with this unhappy writer of the *Sturm und Drang*. Lenz himself had written: "But since the world has no bridges and we have to content ourselves with the things that are there, we do at least feel an accretion to our existence, happiness, by re-creating its Creation on a small scale." [20] Like Lenz and other writers of the *Sturm und Drang,* Büchner claimed literary descent from Shakespeare; like them too, he was anticlassical and anti-idealistic.[21]

[19] *Works,* 91–92.
[20] J. M. R. Lenz, *Anmerkungen übers Theater.* Quoted by Roy Pascal, *The German Sturm und Drang* (Manchester, 1953), 243.
[21] Goethe, in his *Sturm und Drang* period, put the matter even more forcefully than Lenz, and in terms even closer to Büchner's, as in this

The anti-idealism of Büchner was a philosophical, as well as a literary and political, creed. His caricature of the metaphysical monarch, King Peter in *Leonce und Lena,* makes the connection between idealism in philosophy and the tendency of the Germans to excuse every vicious practice on the grounds of their genuine devotion to abstract ideas. In place of the Divine Right once claimed by absolute rulers, Büchner's nineteenth-century monarch (of a kingdom whose frontiers can be surveyed from the Palace windows!) resorts to Kant's philosophy to justify his absolute power. Not surprisingly, he finds the substitution awkward, as in the scene when his valets are dressing him:

Men must think, and I have to think for my subjects, for they don't think at all.—The substance is the thing in itself, and that's me.

(*He runs around the room, almost naked.*)

Did you get that? *Per se* is the thing in itself, do you understand? Now we need my attributes, modifications, characteristics and accidences: where's my shirt? where are my trousers? —Stop! Shame on it! You've left my free will quite exposed in front. Where's my morality—where are my cuffs? The categories are in a shocking state of confusion: you've done up two buttons too many, you've put my snuff-box in the right-hand pocket: my whole system is ruined.—Ha, what's the meaning of this knot in my handkerchief? Hey there, fellow, what's the meaning of this knot? What was it I wanted to remember? [22]

passage from Goethe's essay on the sculptor Falconet, written in 1776: "What the artist has not loved, does not love, he should not depict. You find the women of Rubens too fleshy? I tell you, they were *his* women, and if he'd peopled Heaven and Hell, air, earth and sea with ideals, he would have been a bad husband, and it would never have become sturdy flesh of his flesh, bone of his bone.

"It is foolish to demand of an artist that he should command every kind of form. Nature too, as we know, often had only one facial type to give to a whole province. The man who wants to be general becomes nothing."

Nach Falconet und über Falconet. Goethes Werke (Hamburg, 1948–1960), Vol. 12, 27.

[22] Act I, Scene II, *Works,* 114.

What King Peter wanted to remember—it turns out after a great deal of questioning and self-examination—is his people!

The identification of clothes with the categories of metaphysics in this passage is characteristic of Büchner. To the muddleheadedness and pretentiousness of King Peter he opposed the realism of "a naked thinking heart that makes no show." The philosophical basis of this realism can't be deduced with certainty from the imaginative works, but a number of indications are common to them all.

All Büchner's major characters resemble him in rejecting every idealistic, a priori explanation of life; and, with the exception only of Robespierre and St. Just, they are no less skeptical of rationalistic and mechanistic interpretations of nature, human and otherwise. This is the crux of Mercier's opposition to Robespierre's faction, and of Danton's too, if only Danton were not too demoralized to believe in his own assertion of the freedom to choose. Mercier says:

> Just pursue your cant for once to the point where it becomes concrete.—Just look around you and say: all this is what we've said; it's a mimed translation of your words. These wretches, their executioners and the guillotine are your speeches come to life. You built your systems as Bajazet built his pyramids, out of human heads.[23]

On the same grounds, but in very cynical terms, Camille Desmoulins mocks Hérault for lapsing into noble rhetoric shortly before their execution:

> From the face he's making one would think it's going to be petrified and excavated by posterity as an ancient work of art.
>
> Go on, then, distort your mouth into pretty shapes, lay on the rouge and talk with a good accent, if you think it's worth the effort. I say we should take off our masks for once: as in a hall of mirrors, we'd see nothing anywhere but the primaeval, toothless, indestructible sheep's head—no more, no less. The distinctions don't really amount to much; we're all of us scoundrels and angels, asses and geniuses, and, what's more,

[23] Act III, "Die Conciergerie. Ein Korridor." *Works*, 54.

we're all these things in one: there's room enough in the same body for all four, they aren't as big as one likes to think. Sleep, digest, conceive children—that's what we all do; as for the other things, they're only variations in different keys on the self-same theme. So there's no need to stand on tip-toe and pull faces, no need to be bashful in company! [24]

What these two speeches have in common is the desire of both speakers to get down to the very rock bottom of human nature; and this, beyond doubt, was also Büchner's desire. The difficulty only comes with the next step. What are the positive convictions that sustained the humanism implicit in all Büchner's works?

An answer is provided in one of his scientific works, his lecture on the cranial nerves. Büchner introduces the subject by making a crucial distinction between two different approaches to the study of natural phenomena; these he calls the "teleological" and the "philosophical." To the teleological view, "every organism is a complex machine, provided with the most ingenious means of preserving itself up to a certain point. It sees the cranium as an artificial vault supported by buttresses, devised to protect its occupant, the brain,—cheeks and lips as an apparatus for masticating and breathing,—the eye as an intricate glass,—the eye-lids and lashes as its curtains;—even tears are only the drops of water that keep the eye moist . . ." Büchner rejects this teleological view, and the scientific methods derived from it, as a vicious circle. His own view, the philosophical, as he calls it for lack of a better word, is that "nature does not act for specific ends, does not use itself up in an endless chain of cause and effect, each of which determines another; but in all its manifestations nature is immediately sufficient to itself. All that is, is for its own sake. To look for the law of this being is the aim of the view opposed to the teleological . . . All that the former sees as a cause, the latter sees as an effect. Where the teleological school is ready with an answer, the question only begins for the philosophical school." [25]

This lecture is a late work; and it may be wrong to suppose that Büchner had reached this philosophical conclusion when

[24] Act IV, "Die Conciergerie." *Works,* 74.
[25] *Works,* 187–188.

he was writing his imaginative works. The existential anguish of his characters would rather seem to be due to their horror of the mechanistic, "teleological" interpretation of life, which they are unable to resist as effectively as Büchner does in this profession of faith. And his "philosophical" view of nature— "ontological" would be a better designation—does amount to a profession of faith. It is a faith that nowadays we should call Existentialist.

But to stick this fashionable label on Büchner's work doesn't mean that one has placed it at all definitely. The existential preoccupation which was certainly Büchner's tells us no more than that he reached the point fixed long ago by Pascal when he faced up to the alternative between God and *le néant,* and made his wager. Büchner's characters are familiar enough with the abyss, and "*abyssus invocat abyssum.*" We also know that Büchner believed his realism, his reverence for the world as it is, to be more compatible with religion than the idealism of those concerned with the world as it ought to be. But the Existentialists themselves have shown that Pascal's wager remains a wager, that one can choose the abyss and base the most weighty philosophies on Nothing.

In Act III of *Dantons Tod,* the imprisoned Girondists discuss religious faith; one of them, Thomas Payne, contributes a speech that runs counter to Büchner's historical sources. We can therefore take it that Büchner had a special reason for interpolating it. Thomas Payne says:

> Do away with all that's imperfect; only then you'll be able to prove the existence of God. Spinoza tried it. You can deny the reality of evil, but not the reality of pain; only reason can prove the existence of God, feeling revolts against it. Take note of this, Anaxagoras: why do I suffer? That is the rock of atheism. The faintest twitch of pain, though it were only within an atom, rends Creation from top to bottom.[26]

It was on this rock that Büchner came to grief when he ceased to believe that political action is a panacea for human suffering. His experience of the abyss came with the discovery that many

[26] *Das Luxembourg.* "Ein Saal mit Gefangenen." *Works,* 50.

of our evils and afflictions are not only irremediable, but—so it seemed to him—inevitable, because they are brought about by forces beyond our control. Hence his horror of the determinism suggested to him by his historical studies. For a time, at any rate, his answer was atheism, but the atheism of revolt, not that of indifference. There is no more extraordinary description of a sudden religious conversion than Büchner's in *Lenz;* and this conversion is a conversion to atheism. It comes as the climax of protracted religious torment, heightened, but not disparaged for that reason, by the incipient madness of Lenz. Its immediate cause is the impotence of compassion, the failure of Lenz's attempt to raise a child from the dead; for in the extremity of his pity for the dead child and his fervent faith in the goodness of God, Lenz thought himself capable of performing this miracle.

. . . Then he rose and clasped the child's hands in his, and said loudly and earnestly: "Arise and walk!" But soberly the walls re-echoed his voice, as though to mock him, and the corpse remained cold. Half mad, he collapsed on the floor; then terror seized him, he rushed out, and away into the mountains.

Clouds were passing swiftly across the moon; now all was in darkness, now the nebulous, vanishing landscape was revealed in the moonlight. He ran up and down. In his breast Hell was rehearsing a song of triumph. The wind sounded like the singing of Titans. He felt capable of clenching an enormous fist, thrusting it up into Heaven, seizing God and dragging Him through His clouds; capable of crunching the world with his teeth and spitting it into the face of the Creator; he swore, he blasphemed. In this way he arrived at the highest point of the mountains, and the uncertain light stretched down towards the white masses of stone, and the heavens were a stupid blue eye, and the moon, quite ludicrous, idiotic, stood in the midst. Lenz had to laugh loudly, and as he laughed, atheism took root in him and possessed him utterly, steadily, calmly, relentlessly. He no longer knew what had moved him so much before, he felt cold; he thought he would like to go to bed now, and went his way through the uncanny darkness, cold and unshakable—all was empty and hollow to him, he was compelled to run home, and went to bed.[27]

[27] *Works,* 99–100.

Woyzeck has the simple religious faith of the peasants in *Lenz;* yet, more than any other of Büchner's characters, he has to accommodate himself to the inevitability of evil. He endures the Captain's taunts of bestiality, the Doctor's experiments on his body, every humiliation, in fact, that society cares to inflict on him, with the patience of one who has accepted his status as an underdog. His faith remains intact. But when Marie deceives him, revealing the abyss of human nature, he is at the mercy of the "voices" that urge him to kill her. These voices are hallucinatory, products of a state of mind bordering on paranoia. Even his last desperate act, therefore, is not an assertion of free will. Woyzeck is a man who obeys orders, even the "supernatural" order to destroy his only source of happiness and himself.

Faith, once again, comes to grief on the rock of suffering, at least as far as most audiences and readers are concerned; but *Woyzeck* is too fragmentary and too complex a play to permit more than conjectures as to Woyzeck's own state of mind at the end. What we can say with certainty is that Woyzeck is a good man, however primitive and unbalanced; and that society—as represented by the Captain, the Doctor, and the Policeman—is not the collective villain of Büchner's play, as some critics would like us to believe. The Captain is a good-natured fool; the Doctor—whose experiments have undermined Woyzeck's health—is a pernicious one; the Policeman's final comment ("A good murder, a genuine murder, a lovely murder!") merely proves that, like everyone else, he takes pride in his work. Suffering is the villain of *Woyzeck;* and society is one of its instruments.

The only direct moral drawn in *Woyzeck* is the Showman's comment when his learned horse relieves itself in the middle of its performance:

> All right then, put the public to shame. You see, ladies and gentlemen, the beast is still nature, unidealized nature. Learn from it! Ask your doctor, he'll tell you it's very harmful to do otherwise. What the horse meant to say was: man, be natural! You were created out of dust, sand and muck. Do you want to be more than dust, sand and muck? [28]

[28] *Buden-Lichten. Volk. Works,* 150.

Why did Büchner introduce a performing horse at all? One reason is that it corresponds to the "automatons" of *Leonce und Lena* and has the function, as the Showman says, of putting the public to shame, of purging us of those pretensions which would act as a barrier between Woyzeck and our sympathy. The parallel between Woyzeck's behavior and that of the horse is obvious; for previously the Doctor had reprimanded Woyzeck for relieving himself in public and depriving him of material for his experiment. On this occasion he had lectured Woyzeck on free will, just as the Captain lectures him on "virtue," and Woyzeck had excused himself by saying that he was dependent on nature. But, being human, Woyzeck experiences nature very differently from the horse. He goes on to ask the Doctor whether he has "ever seen anything of the duality of nature" and tells him of his vision and "voices." The Doctor replies that Woyzeck "has the most lovely specimen of *aberratio mentalis partialis,* of the second order, with beautifully clear symptoms."

Here *Woyzeck* links up with Büchner's profession of faith in his lecture on the cranial nerves. The Doctor is a representative of the "teleological" school, whose intellectual pretensions are a cover for the crudest materialism. The Showman's comment, then, is far from having the nihilistic implications that one might easily read into it. For we have to come to terms with the abyss. We have to strip ourselves of false values before we can even begin to grasp the true ones. This was the basis of Büchner's humanism, of a compassion with the suffering individual that broke down every barrier of circumstance, education, and class. Having broken down these external barriers, Büchner—in *Lenz* and *Woyzeck*—went on to do something still more difficult: he penetrated the inward barrier of madness. In *Lenz* and *Woyzeck* we experience madness from the inside, by an identification made possible by Büchner's gift of compassion.

One other statement of Büchner's must be added here, though it has no place in his work. According to the diary kept by Caroline Schulz—who, together with her husband, Büchner's friend and fellow exile, nursed him during his last illness—Büchner said the following words three days before he died. What is remarkable about them (and no argument against their authenticity, since Caroline Schulz can hardly have known Büchner's dramas well enough to have invented words of such crucial relevance) is that they are so clearly an answer to Thomas Payne's speech on "the rock of atheism" and the Showman's "dust, sand and muck." After an attack of delirium, Büchner said loudly and distinctly:

> We do not suffer too much, we suffer too little, for it's through suffering that we attain union with God.—
> We are death, dust and ashes—how should we have the right to complain?

Büchner's dramatic realism, then, was closely connected with his preference for the "philosophical," as opposed to the "teleological," view of nature; and his rejection of all a priori explanations of the human condition accounts for the impartiality that characterizes his realism. In choosing to write his plays in prose—but a prose highly charged with imagery—Büchner linked his work to the *Sturm und Drang* and took sides in an issue that has divided German literature ever since the seventeen-seventies. Stendhal's names for the two conflicting principles, "Racine et Shakespeare," will do as well as any if we do not interpret them too narrowly in terms of literary schools; and we must not identify the battle cry of "Shakespeare" with the cause of Romanticism, an identification peculiar to France in the eighteen-twenties and eighteen-thirties. As far as Germany is concerned, "Shakespeare" stood for the principle of poetic realism; the German Romantics, philosophically and aesthetically, were idealists.

When the *Sturm und Drang* dramatists resorted to the medium of prose, they did so in order to combine the emotive power and flexibility of Shakespeare's blank verse with the realism of what Diderot called "le tragique domestique et bourgeois," as practiced in Germany by Lessing. If it seems strange that Shakespeare's German disciples should choose to write in prose, one reason is that German blank verse, on the whole, is a medium incomparably more stiff, less capable of rendering delicate modulations of thought and feeling, than its English prototype. When Goethe abandoned dramatic prose in favor of blank verse, he did so for the sake of a classicism closer to Racine than to Shakespeare; and very few German dramatists have followed his example without suffering a loss of expressiveness, if only in the lower registers. Kleist, who chose blank verse from the start, greatly extended its range, even making it capable of assimilating a lower class idiom, but the truly mimetic suppleness of his blank verse was the exception that proves the rule. Very generally speaking, one seems tempted to assert that a "heightened" prose is the German dramatic medium that comes closest to being an equivalent for Shakespeare's blank verse.

The two principles continued to conflict. Schiller followed Goethe's example after his own belated *Sturm und Drang* phase. In Büchner's lifetime, Grillparzer wrote in blank verse or in a trochaic meter adapted from the Spanish dramatists; but Hebbel, who was born in the same year as Büchner, wrote several tragedies in prose before committing himself to the grand manner and blank verse. One cannot help being struck by the curious recurrence of this dichotomy in the works of a long line of outstanding dramatists. As late as the end of the nineteenth century, the two dramatic media (and the two opposing principles they embody) alternated in the work of Gerhart Hauptmann; at the very end of his life, in the nineteen-forties, Hauptmann felt called upon to write a series of blank verse plays on classical subjects. The conflict, it would seem, was not only that between realism and dignity, but a conflict between youth and age. Almost in every case, the direction of the change was from prose to verse; and something of the vigor, as well as the clumsiness, of youth was lost in the process. Yet the example of Hofmannsthal in this century shows that the process can be reversed; Hofmannsthal moved from the "lyrical dramas" of his early youth through blank verse to the poetic prose of his last and greatest tragedy, *Der Turm;* a prose both highly colloquial and highly condensed, like Büchner's prose in *Woyzeck*.

Needless to say, the medium of prose in serious drama and tragedy presents quite as many difficulties as the medium of verse. If the greatest danger of German blank verse is the monotonous sublime, the prose medium is very apt to turn into rhetoric at climactic points, with a corresponding tendency to fall into bathos elsewhere. Very few dramatists, German or otherwise, are fortunate enough to command a variant of the spoken language that strikes us as naturally poetic, such as the idiom of the Aran Islanders—or the adaptation of this idiom —in the plays of John Synge. The *Sturm und Drang* dramatists —and Schiller in his early plays—have a marked tendency to indulge in extravagant and violent trope, only some of which can be traced back to "the very language of men," to make up for the loss of meter. Goethe's prose in *Egmont* avoids this pitfall, but its rhythms at certain climactic points are so marked, so nearly regular, that it becomes a kind of dissimulated verse. Many of the most distinguished of the prose dramatists needed imagery not only to "heighten" their prose when necessary, but to impregnate the whole play with a hidden, unifying significance not easily conveyed in "the very language of men."

The diction of *Dantons Tod* is still close to that of Büchner's predecessors; if it shows little or no discrepancy between colloquialism and rhetoric, this is partly because all the chief characters, in any case, were politicians; partly because it was Büchner's crucial concern to strike just the right balance between public and private utterance. His rhythms, throughout the play, are the rhythms of prose; his imagery, much of which has the *Sturm und Drang* tendency toward extravagant, gruesome, and elaborately sustained trope, also serves to bear the dominant tension of the play, the conflict between determinism and freedom. One or two instances of this symbolism have already emerged in the course of this study (e.g., the puppet and the musical instrument); a detailed analysis cannot be attempted here.

In *Woyzeck,* however, Büchner achieved a fusion of naturalism and intensity both unprecedented and unsurpassed. The play, as we know it, is nothing more than a number of short scenes and fragments of scenes, which Büchner's editors have pieced together in whatever sequence they thought most plausible. That so brief, so fragmentary, and even dubious a work has been acclaimed as a minor masterpiece, and rightly so, is one of the anomalies of modern literature. The plot is that of a vulgar melodrama, mere infidelity and revenge; and the extant scenes leave us in doubt as to its outcome. Yet to see or read

Woyzeck is to gain an experience that no other play affords. Behind its bare diction and commonplace action there is a vision that removes this fragmentary melodrama from all the existing categories. The diction of *Woyzeck* is so perfectly adapted to its dramatic function that it draws the audience or reader into the very vortex of what it serves to express. It is a transparent diction, poetic not in itself, but despite itself, because it reveals what is essentially and timelessly human behind the semi-articulate utterings of vulgar persons, a murderer and a slut.

Woyzeck is the justification of Büchner's "philosophical" view, of his impartiality and compassion. Büchner's principal characters, unlike those of so many German dramatists, especially those that are made to speak in blank verse, do not stand for anything that can be specified with ease or with certainty. Even *Dantons Tod*—condemned as subversive both by the Imperial and the Nazi authorities—can be interpreted as a glorification or as a deadly indictment of the French Revolution. What was really intolerable about it was its refusal to strike any conventional attitude whatever, to worship any hero or do homage to power in any guise. The ruthless realism of Büchner had the effect of stripping human nature down to its constant essentials—to its lowest common denominator, many would say—and it is at this point of exposure that Büchner made his choice: the choice not to hate, despise, or give up this naked humanity at its worst, but to grant it his impartial compassion. The ultimate effect of his work is one of tragic affirmation; not because it contains a cryptoreligious "message," but because it presents the naked truth about men and leaves the ultimate issues open. Büchner's impartiality, in itself, is an act of faith. There is a distinction between the impartiality of the truly imaginative writer, who does justice to all his characters, and that of the merely clever writer—common enough in our time—who does justice to none. If Büchner's realism was poetic, in spite of his medium, it was because his impartiality was of the former, much rarer, kind.

The narrative prose of *Lenz* is no less extraordinary than the dramatic prose of *Woyzeck*. Büchner relates the facts of Lenz's visit to Pastor Oberlin as he found them recorded in Oberlin's diary and in a French biography of Oberlin; but, from the first, he relates them from the point of view of Lenz himself, of a man suffering from religious mania and incipient schizophrenia. This feat of sympathetic penetration called for a new narrative style and technique; Büchner provided both and, in doing so, opened up new possibilities to writers of the twentieth century. The influence of *Lenz* is apparent in Hofmannsthal's prose, particularly in his masterly *Andreas* fragment. The dislocation of syntax in *Lenz* leads straight to the experimental prose of the Expressionists.

Büchner introduces Lenz as he crosses the mountains on foot, on his way to Oberlin's vicarage; he tells us nothing about Lenz or Oberlin, nothing about the purpose of the visit, nothing of what has gone before or is about to happen. He introduces Lenz by making us see the mountain landscape through his eyes:

. . . At first there was an urge, a movement inside him, when the stones and rocks bounded away, when the grey forest shook itself beneath him and the mist now blurred its outlines, now half unveiled the trees' gigantic limbs; there was an urge, a movement inside him, he looked for something, as though for lost dreams, but he found nothing. All seemed so small to him, so near, so wet. He would have liked to put the whole earth to dry behind the stove, he could not understand why so much time was needed to descend a steep slope, to reach a distant point; he thought that a few paces should be enough to cover any distance. Only from time to time, when the storm thrust clouds into the valley, and the mist rose in the forest, when the voices near the rocks awoke, now like thunder subsiding far away, now rushing back towards him as if in their wild rejoicing they desired to sing the praise of Earth, and the clouds like wild neighing horses galloped towards him, and the sunbeams penetrated in between them and came to draw a flashing sword against the snow-covered plains, so that a bright, dazzling light cut across the summits into the valleys; or when the gale drove the clouds downwards and hurled them into a pale-blue lake, and then the wind died down and from the depths of the ravines, from the crests of the pine-trees, drifted upwards, with a humming like that of lullabies and pealing bells, and a soft red hue mingled with the deep azure, and little clouds on silver wings passed across, and everywhere the mountain-tops, sharp and solid, shone and glittered for miles—then he felt a strain in his chest, he stood struggling for breath, heaving, his body bent forward, his eyes and mouth wide open; he thought that he must draw the storm into himself, contain it all within him, he stretched himself out and lay on the earth, dug his way into the All, it was an ecstasy that hurt him—or he rested, and laid his head into the moss and half-closed his eyes, and then it withdrew, away, far away from him, the earth receded from him, became small as a wandering star and dipped down into a roaring stream that moved its clear waters beneath him. But these were only moments; then, soberly, he would rise, resolute, calm, as though a mere phantasmagoria had passed before his eyes—he remembered nothing . . . [29]

Büchner could not have achieved what he did achieve in his short life but for the creed implicit in all his works, a creed that combines an aesthetic doctrine with a new humanism. Lenz formulates this creed in the story:

One must love human nature in order to penetrate into the character of any individual; nobody, however insignificant, however ugly, should be despised; only then one can understand human nature as a whole.[30]

[29] *Works*, 83–84.
[30] *Works*, 92.

Part II

Part II

VII

NIETZSCHE
A Craving for Hell

The misuse of Nietzsche's name by Nazi propagandists, and hence by anti-Nazi propagandists, must have something to do with his eclipse in the English-speaking countries, where, far from profiting by the general acclamation of D. H. Lawrence as a prophet and moral reformer, his work seems to be less widely known and effective now than in the early years of the century. Even if his impact here was never as strong or immediate as his impact on the Continent, a tremor in the atmosphere rather than an earthquake, that tremor can be felt in the works of W. B. Yeats, James Joyce, T. E. Hulme, and Wyndham Lewis, in the circle around A. R. Orage and other groups representative of "advanced" opinion up to the nineteen-thirties.

At least one English writer, Walter Pater,[1] was among that elite whose recognition established Nietzsche as an interna-

---

[1] Though Pater never mentioned Nietzsche, it is generally agreed that his "A Lecture on Dionysus," given at the Midland Institute in 1876 and included in his *Greek Studies* (1895), shows an unacknowledged debt to Nietzsche's earlier writings.

tional figure when he was scarcely read in Germany; and it is important to remember that this recognition in the last years of his active life by Georg Brandes, Strindberg, and Taine meant more to Nietzsche himself than any response his works might have evoked—but did not evoke at the time—in his own country.

Yet in a sense Nietzsche is with us whether we read him or not. It is no exaggeration to say that he anticipated almost every distinct trend in twentieth-century thought, including not only the religions of Art, on the one hand, Life, on the other, but depth psychology, phenomenalism and existentialism, logical positivism and linguistic analysis.[2] Indeed only Nietzsche's demolition of metaphysics marks the place where all these trends originated before their divergence. Nietzsche was delighted when a hostile critic described his work as dynamite. Whatever its part in the explosions of recent decades, we have no reason to assume that it could not have been put to a very different use, or that all its force is now spent.

The precise way in which Nietzsche's works have been exploited, distorted, and deliberately falsified is only now being revealed to the general public in Germany, though it has long been suspected by some, and known to other, specialists. Professor Karl Schlechta, the editor of a new three-volume edition of Nietzsche's selected works and letters,[3] made a start by exposing an astonishing number of plain forgeries by Nietzsche's sister, who was responsible for the early editions of Nietzsche's posthumous works and letters. Only a few details can be given here. According to Schlechta, the letters of Nietzsche to his sister of February 22, March 23, and December 26, 1887 are forgeries by her. The same applies to the letters dated January 25 and March 31, 1888. All these letters serve to put Elisabeth Förster-Nietzsche in a favorable light, to obscure her true relationship with Nietzsche, and to suggest that he regarded her as well qualified to deal with his works. Rudolf Steiner, who gave her private lessons in philosophy from 1896 to 1898, testifies

[2] E.g., in the aphorism (*Morgenröte*, I, 46) headed: "Words get in our way."

[3] Friedrich Nietzsche, *Werke in drei Bänden*, ed. Karl Schlechta (Munich, 1954–56).

that even at that time she showed no true understanding of her brother's works and was incapable of "an independent judgement of his simplest ideas." In one of the forged letters she attributes these words to Nietzsche: "You understand more about me than the others."

The forged letter dated May 3, 1888 serves to falsify Nietzsche's attitude to the Wagnerians and to the Jews. Another, dated End of October, 1888, attributes to him an admiration for the new Kaiser (Wilhelm II), which Nietzsche was far from professing. An attack on the same Kaiser's combination of militarism with Christian piety in the manuscript of Nietzsche's *Der Antichrist* was deliberately obscured by the omission of a word. The true relations between Nietzsche and his sister in October, 1888 are attested by a letter to him in which she wrote that it looked as though he were about to become famous, and added: "A fine lot of scum it will be that believes in *you*."

Schlechta also aroused much controversy by rearranging the aphorisms and fragments known as *The Will to Power* and claiming that this was an arbitrary compilation of material rejected by Nietzsche. Professor Schlechta's editing, in turn, has been severely censured and in part invalidated by several Nietzsche experts, including Dr. Erich F. Podach, the author of admirable Nietzsche studies like *The Madness of Nietzsche* (English version, 1931). Unlike Schlechta, Podach has based his new edition of Nietzsche's late works [4] on the firsthand material at Weimar; and he differs from Schlechta in shifting a good deal of the blame from Nietzsche's sister to her academically trained assistants, coeditors and successors at the original *Nietzsche-Archiv*. This, understandably, was dissolved by the East German authorities after the war; but Podach testifies that all the contents are available once more, even to Western scholars, in the *Goethe-Schiller* Archiv at Weimar.

Schlechta's Nietzsche researches began in the Nazified Archive of the nineteen-thirties and nineteen-forties; and since his experiences there seem to have disgusted him not only with the political exploitation of Nietzsche, but with Nietzsche himself,

[4] Erich F. Podach, *Friedrich Nietzsches Werke des Zusammenbruchs* (Heidelberg, 1961).

it has been suggested that he should never have undertaken an edition of Nietzsche at all. Yet Podach, too, is by no means a wholehearted Nietzschean; and, considering that the whole-hearted Nietzschean is not only a very dubious phenomenon but a contradiction in terms, Schlechta's disenchantment should not be held against him. Nietzsche, after all, did not forbear from writing about Schopenhauer or Wagner when these had become his antagonists. Schlechta's re-editing of the so-called *Will to Power,* and his exclusion of other posthumous works, have rightly been called in question, but his exposure of the sister's forgeries—bearing mainly on Nietzsche's life, his relations with his family and herself especially, but also on his political opinions and the text of several of his works—remains valid, even if we accept Podach's argument that she could not have got away with these forgeries without the collusion of her scholarly friends, some of whom were guilty of even graver offenses against the spirit, if not the letter, of Nietzsche's works. Podach's comment and epilogue are frankly polemical and include a brilliant parody of existentialist obfuscations of Nietzsche *à la* Heidegger, as well as selected quotations from other interpreters of Nietzsche during the Nazi era. Of one of them, Professor F. W. Otto, Podach writes that "he abandoned the study of myths in favour of their fabrication, embellished with pseudo-scholarly frills." The recent controversy may not yet amount to a transvaluation of Nietzsche, but even its asperity is a healthy sign after the pieties of the mythmakers.

There is no doubt at all that Nietzsche planned a work to be called *The Will To Power,* which was to be an attempt "to transvaluate all values." As one of Schlechta's critics, Karl Löwith, points out, Schlechta's pronounced antipathy to this work is largely due to the prominence given to it by the political traducers of Nietzsche, and Löwith cites Nietzsche's own endeavor to forestall such abuse in one of the notes that are part of the projected work:

> *The Will to Power.* A book to *stimulate thought,* no more—it belongs to those who enjoy thinking, no more. . . . That it's written in German is an anachronism, to put it mildly. I wish I had written it in French, so that it could not be used to sup-

port German nationalist aspirations of any kind. The Germans of today have ceased to be thinkers: what they enjoy and what impresses them is something quite different. The will to power as a principle would be understandable enough to them.

True enough, it was the principle of power that was taken up and distorted, Nietzsche's qualifications and warnings that were ignored.

Podach is right, of course, in suggesting that, shocking though many of them are, the sister's forgeries alone neither explain nor made possible the exploitation of Nietzsche for political ends. A complete investigation of how this abuse became possible would have to include a biography of Nietzsche, a study of his relations and friends (as already provided by Podach in earlier books), a cultural history of Germany from Nietzsche's birth in 1844 to about a century later, a survey of the entire body of Nietzsche criticism, and a careful reexamination of all his works and letters on the lines laid down by Podach for the works of the Turin period. Even then a host of ambiguities and contradictions would remain; for it was Nietzsche's peculiarity and distinction to resist the systematization of thought. That is one reason that his works remain uniquely stimulating, inexhaustible—and dangerous.

Needless to say, no such multiple investigation will be attempted here, though a few historical flashbacks will prove indispensable; and in the case of a writer whose thought flowed so directly out of his life, who was consistent only in being unreservedly true to his own nature and his own moods, it is absurd to argue, as Heidegger did, that the biographical approach is outdated and irrelevant. Nietzsche himself claimed that only what is personal remains forever incontrovertible; [5] and he foresaw what might happen if his works were to be taken as impersonal dogma by men incapable of treating him as skeptically as he treated other self-proclaimed leaders of men. A good example of Nietzsche's literary criticism—and he was a re-

[5] E.g., his letter to Lou Andreas-Salomé of September 16, 1882, in which he welcomes the proposed "reduction of philosophical systems to personal documents about their originators" and goes on: "The system is dead and debunked—but the *person* behind it is incontrovertible; the person simply cannot be killed."

markable literary critic among other things—is the following diagnosis of Thomas Carlyle. Typically, it reduces ideas to a personality, or as Nietzsche put it,[6] proceeds from "the deed to the doer, from the ideal to the man who *needs* it, from every way of thinking to the commanding *need* behind it."

I have been reading the life of *Thomas Carlyle,* that farce enacted unwittingly, that heroic-ethical interpretation of dyspeptic states.—Carlyle, a man of strong words and attitudes, a rhetorician by necessity, perpetually agitated by the desire for a strong faith and his sense of being incapable of it (—a typical Romantic in that respect!). The desire for a strong faith is *not* the proof of a strong faith—but rather the opposite. If one *has* a strong faith one can permit oneself the luxury of skepticism: one is sure enough, secure enough, committed enough to be able to afford it. Carlyle deafens something in himself with the *fortissimo* of his hero worship for men of strong faith and his fury against the less simple-minded: he *needs* a loud noise. A constant, passionate *dishonesty* towards himself—that is his hallmark, this makes and keeps him interesting. True, in England he is admired for his very honesty. . . . Well, that is English; and in view of the fact that the English are the nation who have perfected *cant,* it is not only understandable but right. At rock bottom Carlyle is an English atheist who puts all his pride into the claim *not* to be one.

What makes this diagnosis especially interesting and relevant is that Carlyle has been regarded as akin to Nietzsche in this very proclivity toward hero worship![7] The Nietzscheans, of course, have ignored the implications.

Even in the last euphoric and hubristic phase immediately before his mental collapse, Nietzsche could write in a letter: "I decidedly do not wish to appear to men as a prophet, savage beast and moral monster. Even in this respect the book (*Ecce*

[6] In *Die fröhliche Wissenschaft,* No. 370.
[7] See Eric Bentley's book, *A Century of Hero-Worship: A Study of the Idea of Heroism in Carlyle and Nietzsche, with Notes on Wagner, Spengler, Stefan George and D. H. Lawrence* (2nd ed.; Boston, 1957).

Homo) could do some good; it may save me from being confused with my anti-self." [8]

The Nietzschean—that solecism, as Mr. F. A. Lea aptly called him [9]—is any reader of Nietzsche who ignorantly, slavishly, or dishonestly takes Nietzsche's anti-self for the whole man, or its manic utterances for the whole of Nietzsche's doctrine. That Nietzsche quite frequently forgot or perversely disregarded the warning contained in that last letter, claiming an absolute authority for himself and boasting of his ferocious predatory strength, merely testifies to the war between his self and his anti-self. Only a dialectic confrontation of both, which is bound to draw on Nietzsche's biography and letters, can undo the mischief done by his sister, her scholarly abettors and all those Nietzscheans deficient in what Nietzsche himself called the ultimate virtue, the will to honesty. "How much truth can a human mind bear, how much truth does it dare to face?" Nietzsche asked in *Ecce Homo*. His disciples, it seems, could bear very little of the truth about themselves.

Unlike most philosophers, and like most poets, Nietzsche presents experiences, observations, and imaginings to be shared rather than believed. Again and again he cautions his reader not to mistake the one kind of participation for the other, to accept only what his own experience confirms. Even the first book of *Zarathustra,* the least analytical of Nietzsche's works, closes with such a caution:

> You say you believe in Zarathustra? But what does Zarathustra matter? You are my believers: but what do any beliefs matter!
>
> You had not looked for yourselves: then you found me. That is what all believers do: that is why belief is worth so little.
>
> Now I bid you lose me and find yourselves; and not till all of you have denied me will I return to you.

[8] Letter of October 30, 1889. I render *Gegensatz* by the Yeatsian "anti-self" because this best conveys the antithesis Nietzsche had in mind.

[9] F. A. Lea, *The Tragic Philosopher: A Study of Friedrich Nietzsche* (London, 1957).

Even the briefest explanation of the Nietzscheans' victory over Nietzsche would have to go back as far as the year 1882, when at the age of thirty-seven Nietzsche met the one woman who tempted him to renounce his solitude and proposed marriage to Lou Salomé. The intrigues of his sister and mother against Lou and Nietzsche's Jewish friend Paul Rée, who was also in love with Lou but acted as mediator between them, to the point of conveying Nietzsche's proposal to her, helped to bring about Nietzsche's estrangement from both friends and to drive him close to suicide. "I don't like my mother," he wrote in the following year, "and to hear my sister's voice is disagreeable to me; their company has always made me ill." Soon, of course, Nietzsche was to make his peace again with both his mother and sister, whom, with an ambivalence characteristic of all his emotional and intellectual attachments, he at once loved and hated. In 1883 also, Nietzsche's sister became engaged to an extreme German nationalist, Bernhard Förster, who in April, 1881, had addressed a petition to Bismarck demanding restrictive measures against the Jews. "This accursed anti-Semitism is the cause of a drastic rupture between me and my sister," Nietzsche wrote in 1884. Many of the letters forged by Nietzsche's sister served to suppress all hints of such a conflict, even to suggest that Nietzsche admired Förster and approved his views.

The conflicts and reconciliations with his family never wholly ceased until Nietzsche's breakdown on January 3, 1889; and there is no lack of forged documents for these years also, though in 1886 Förster and his wife emigrated to administer a German colony in Paraguay. One of Nietzsche's last gestures before his mental collapse was a declaration of war against the German Reich; and his famous last letter to Jacob Burckhardt of January 5, 1889 includes the laconic communiqué: "Wilhelm Bismarck and all anti-Semites abolished."

Nietzsche's total incapacity from this time until his death on August 25, 1900 to attend to the editing of his still unpublished works meant that some of these—and they make up about one half of his work—could also be tampered with. Thus Podach shows that of the nine poems published by Nietzsche's sister, and subsequent editors, as *Dionysus-Dithyramben,* only seven were included by Nietzsche in this projected work. The poem "Ruhm und Ewigkeit" was intended to conclude *Ecce Homo,* and Podach has restored it to its proper context. The ninth poem, "Von der Armut des Reichsten," was intended to conclude *Nietzsche contra Wagner,* and has been similarly restored in Podach's edition. Schlechta prints both poems as *Dionysus-Dithyramben.* From October, 1889, when Nietzsche was in an asylum at Jena, till February of the following year another extreme nationalist and anti-Semite, Julius Langbehn, attempted to obtain the exclusive control not only of Nietzsche himself, whom he guaranteed to cure, but also of Nietzsche's works and papers. The attempt was frustrated only by Langbehn's rudeness and truculence, which finally alienated Nietzsche's mother and enabled Nietzsche's friends Overbeck and Gast to exert their influence against him. Nietzsche's mother was afraid that Langbehn would take his revenge in a polemic against Nietzsche modeled on Nietzsche's own *The Wagner Case,* just as Langbehn had parodied an early work of Nietzsche's, *Schopenhauer as Educator,* in his notorious book *Rembrandt as Educator.* Apart from an article—not by Langbehn—published in 1888, Nietzsche was not to become a "case" until Schlechta used the title for a book occasioned by the current controversy.[10]

With exemplary devotion, but also with a certain gratification at having her prodigal son restored to her, Nietzsche's mother nursed and guarded him until her death in 1897. This phase has been thoroughly documented by Podach in two earlier books.[11] In September, 1893, Nietzsche's sister returned to Germany—Förster had committed suicide in 1889 because of the failure of his colonial venture—and ordered Peter Gast, who had acted as Nietzsche's literary executor, to break off his edition of Nietzsche's works. Toward the end of 1893 she forced her mother to renounce all rights in Nietzsche's works and soon after founded the *Nietzsche-Archiv* at Weimar, of which she remained the titular head until her death in 1935.

Elisabeth Förster-Nietzsche professed herself a conservative,

[10] Karl Schlechta, *Der Fall Nietzsche* (Munich, 1958).
[11] *Nietzsches Zusammenbruch* (Heidelberg, 1930) and *Der kranke Nietzsche: Briefe seiner Mutter an Overbeck* (Vienna, 1937).

or rather a *Deutsch-Nationale,* as what remained of German conservatism significantly called itself in her time. A few extracts from the recently published diaries of Count Kessler [12] will serve to show how, with her connivance, the Nietzsche Archive came to be taken over by the Nazis even before their rise to power:

Weimar, February 11, 1926
In the afternoon at Frau Förster-Nietzsche's. She burst out with the question, did I know of her latest great friendship— with Mussolini? I said, yes I had heard of it and regretted it; for Mussolini was compromising her brother.

Weimar, October 5, 1927
Called on Frau Förster-Nietzsche. Understandably enough, she was completely preoccupied with the imminent Nietzsche celebration at which Spengler was to give a lecture. . . . She went on to talk of her "dear friend Mussolini," who was the comfort of her old age. . . . In complete contradiction of this passion for Mussolini she professed herself in favour of a "United States of Europe" which her brother had been the first to demand.

October 13, 1927
Unfortunately one feels the petit-bourgeois element, so incompatible with Nietzsche, in everything about her. For instance in her repeated assertion that she is a "Colonial German," (she hasn't been out of Germany for thirty years) and therefore couldn't be anything but "deutsch-national." (When she was in Paraguay, of course, there was no such thing as a "Deutschnationale" Party, and the old Conservatives wanted the whole body of her brother's writings to be pulped; in fact the *Kreuzzeitung* demanded that the police should confiscate copies in private libraries.) It is painful to listen to such nonsense from Nietzsche's sister in the Nietzsche Archives.

October 15, 1927
The hall was packed . . . many had to stand; but Spengler's lecture turned into a debacle. Spengler has actually succeeded in making Nietzsche boring. Only a few funny blunders redeemed the drabness of that hour. In England, he said, philos-

---

[12] Harry Graf Kessler, *Tagebücher 1918–1937* (Frankfurt, 1961).

ophers had never given any thought to the State "because England is not a State!" (Hobbes's *Leviathan,* etc., didn't exist; or more probably Spengler has never heard of Hobbes and his successors). . . . It is a deplorable disgrace to the Nietzsche Archives to have allowed this half-educated charlatan to speak. The lecture was so insipid that even Frau Förster must have had doubts about her Spengler. Perhaps he's the first Nietzsche priest. But God preserve us from that species. . . .

October 22, 1927
Lunched with Frau Förster-Nietzsche. . . . She reminisced about her years in Paraguay and the horrors perpetrated under the dictatorship of Lopez; stories that sounded like something by Hudson or Cunningham-Grahame: the shooting of whole companies who had buried treasures at his orders, so that there would be no survivors to give away the place. . . . Then she told me that she had effected a complete reconciliation with Bayreuth. Last year, during the festival season here for Siegfried Wagner, Countess Gravina had begun by putting out feelers and then the whole Wagner family had paid her a visit; she had given a luncheon for them, at which the reconciliation was solemnly celebrated by a symbolic holding of hands around the table while she read out her brother's "Sternenfreundschaft." . . . So ends the great world-shaking feud between Richard Wagner and Nietzsche, at the coffee-table: prettily and quite in the style of either's disciples.

August 7, 1932
In the afternoon at Frau Förster-Nietzsche's. The Nietzsche Archive, as she herself says, is now "at the centre of politics." As its director they have appointed a Nazi professor, Emge from Jena, a professor of jurisprudence who is even a prospective Nazi Minister in the Thuringian government. In the Archives all, from the Major (her nephew) to the manservant, are Nazis. Only she herself, she says, remains "deutsch-national."

   She told me how Hitler had visited her after the first night of Mussolini's play in the *National-Theater.* While several Italian foreign correspondents were sitting with her, he had had himself announced and entered with an enormous bouquet of flowers, accompanied by his staff. . . . The *Nietzsche-Archiv* at least profits materially by its fascism, since Mussolini, Frau Förster told me, had made it a present of twenty thousand lire towards the end of last year. For next Thursday the "Empress"

Hermine had invited herself to tea with her. . . . To think what's become of Nietzsche and the Nietzsche Archive is enough to make one weep. And that this old woman of 86 is courted by the most powerful man in Germany and the wife of the former Kaiser. The latter is almost grotesque after His Majesty's attitude to Nietzsche before the war! In this connexion she tells me that the officers of the Reichswehr Divisional Staff posted to Weimar are paying her an official visit. How different it was in my youth at Potsdam. When I read Nietzsche with Bernhard Stolberg and my circle, Stolberg's father removed him from Potsdam and locked him up for six months with a parson.

The next phase of Nietzsche's Nazification, after Hitler's rise to power, is outlined by Podach in his Epilogue. In 1934 the ninetieth anniversary of Nietzsche's birth was celebrated at Weimar; the Führer himself was expected, but it was Alfred Rosenberg who formally opened the proceeding when he was received by Frau Förster, her nephew Major Oehler and Professor Emge. Fritz Sauckel presided at an address given by Professor W. F. Otto. One brief extract from it will have to suffice here: "Culture has nothing to do with endeavours to make life more beautiful, comfortable, luxurious or, above all, less dangerous. It has a metaphysical meaning. . . ." Another celebration took place in the following year on the occasion of Frau Förster's death. Hitler himself attended, as well as Baldur von Schirach, Sauckel, and many other representatives of the regime.

In 1935 Oswald Spengler resigned from the Board of the Nietzsche Archive. In a letter of that year he wrote: "Either one cultivates the philosophy of Nietzsche, or that of the Nietzsche Archive, and if these contradict each other as sharply as they do at present it is necessary to decide between them." [13]

The parallel history of Nietzsche literature—editions of his works and letters, critical studies and biographies—is too intricate to permit such summary. Both Schlechta and Podach provide ample information about the deliberate corruption of texts

[13] Letter to Walter Jesinghaus, October 27, 1935. English version in *Oswald Spengler: Letters 1913–1936* (London, 1966), 306.

by omission, juxtaposition, and substitution. Apart from her attribution to Nietzsche of letters or parts of letters, which he did not write or wrote in a different context, the sister's influential introduction and commentaries are full of blatant misrepresentations. Schlechta's biographical table lists countless examples, beginning with the sister's attempts to suppress or distort certain facts about Nietzsche's heredity—like the death of his father at the age of thirty-six of "softening of the brain," the death in infancy of Nietzsche's younger brother, and Nietzsche's own sickly constitution long before his suspected venereal infection or his riding accident on military service. Podach reminds us that Nietzsche himself was quite capable of adapting the facts of his life to the fable, but no sensitive reader of his late works could fail to allow for this even without forewarning. All the biographical evidence merely confirms what the works alone make perfectly clear: that no other great writer has so perfectly exemplified Mr. Edmund Wilson's theory of the wound and the bow. Nietzsche's works are the record of a struggle—unique in its intensity and excess—between self and anti-self.

Podach sums it all up by citing Herr Rudolf Pannwitz's description of Nietzsche's sister as "half Nietzsche, half Naumburg" (their home town after 1850) and pointing out that the description is not wholly inapplicable to Nietzsche himself.[14] Had he been less emotionally dependent on his mother and sister he would have had less need to call himself "the most independent man in Europe," as he did in a letter of 1884, or to become "one of the loneliest men who have ever lived." [15] The more he felt this dependence and recognized how much of Naumburg there was in himself, the more that dependence turned to hatred and self-hatred, and the higher he had to climb to transcend his conditioned self: because to Nietzsche's gentle, compassionate, and overscrupulous nature, pity became "a kind

[14] In his letter of January 6, 1917, to Hans Klöres, Oswald Spengler, too, had remarked: "Every time I read them (i.e., E. Förster-Nietzsche's writings) it gives me a special pleasure, as I can see through the provincialism of her nature, a quality which was shared to a certain extent by her brother." *Ibid.*, 49.

[15] F. A. Lea, *op. cit.*, 104.

of hell," [16] his anti-self glorified hardness and ruthlessness as the liberating virtues. He himself explained it in a letter:

> But till now Schopenhauer's "compassion" has always wrought the worst mischief in my life—and so I have every cause to favour those moralities which include a few other mainsprings in what is morally good and don't try to reduce all our human achievements to "fellow feelings." For this is not only a kind of softness which every large-minded Greek would have laughed at, but a grave practical danger. One should *enforce one's* ideal *of man,* one should impose one's ideal on one's fellow men as on oneself, and so act creatively! But this demands that one keep compassion well under control and also treat whatever is contrary to one's ideal (rabble like L. and R., for instance) as *enemies.*—You see *how* I preach to *myself;* but to arrive at this "wisdom" has almost cost me my life.[17]

It may be that Nietzsche's self-knowledge here, as elsewhere, stopped short at the crucial point—the question why compassion was so dangerous to him, or why the woman to whom he had recently proposed marriage must now be described as "rabble." (A little later he was to admit that he had been at fault in the relationship.) Yet Nietzsche was always ready to expose the experiential and personal roots of his beliefs, and to adduce such self-knowledge as he had where other men would have appealed to principles. No amount of forgeries, therefore, could ever obscure the peculiar processes by which Nietzsche arrived at his beliefs.

Because anti-Semitism was part of Naumburg—Nietzsche's mother professed it too, though as a matter of course, like any other conventional sentiment—Nietzsche's anti-anti-Semitism turned into an obsession, much as Naumburg Christianity turned him into nothing less than the self-proclaimed Anti-Christ,[18] or Naumburg nationalism into the most devastating

---

[16] Letter of December 12, 1882, to Overbeck.

[17] Letter of August, 1883, to Malwida von Meysenburg.

[18] In *Die fröhliche Wissenschaft,* No. 358, he distinguished German Protestantism from the main Christian tradition and even blamed Luther for the modern "intellectual plebeianism." Roman Catholicism is absolved from the critique, clearly because it was not associated with Naumburg and its patriotic Christianity. "The Church," he concludes

critic of all things German. But because Naumburg anti-Semitism had a Christian as well as a racialist basis, and Christian ethics had been drawn into the service of nationalism and its cult of power, Nietzsche's attack was divided between several fronts and threatened with a similar confusion. Heine had taught him to see Judaism and Christianity as a single religion of sickness and suffering, as opposed to a pagan "religion of joy." Nietzsche, therefore, could defend the Jews as a race, but could not exempt them from their part in the responsibility for Naumburg protestantism and the Christian "slave morality." Naumburg was servile; Nietzsche, therefore, must advocate the "will to power," aware though he was that this power might easily be confused with that worshipped by the slaves.

The racialists, of course, were quick to take up his vision of the "innocent conscience of the beast of prey," the "lasciviously prowling blond Germanic beast" in the *Genealogy of Morals,* conveniently ignoring that this was a vision of the past, to which Nietzsche was careful to add this parenthesis "although there is hardly any affinity of concept, let alone of blood, between the ancient Teutons and us Germans"; also that in attributing the dread aroused by Germany's power to memories of the ancient Germanic hordes, Nietzsche was drawing once more on Heine—in this instance on Heine's famous warning to the French to beware of a resurgent German nation. Nietzsche's vision is quite as ambiguous as Heine's, for very similar reasons; but above all because Nietzsche's "Dionysian imperialism," as it has been called, was never identical with the German imperialism of Naumburg and diametrically opposed to the racialism that grew out of it. Nietzsche always insisted on his—very doubtful and remote—Polish ancestry. In connection with his brother-in-law's colonial ventures he wrote to his mother and sister in 1885: "As for enthusiasm for 'German-ness,' I've hardly ever been able to rise to it, far less to the desire to keep this 'glorious' race pure. On the contrary, on the contrary—."

"in all circumstances is a more aristocratic institution than the State." Cf. Søren Kierkegaard "Protestantism is the crudest and most brutal plebeianism," *Journals, 1853–55* (London, 1965), 135. This is one of several extraordinary agreements between the two thinkers. Nietzsche had no knowledge of Kierkegaard's works; but Schopenhauer was one link, Pascal another.

Nietzsche, then, can be absolved of all direct responsibility for what his traducers have made of him by selecting one arc of the circle or failing to recognize that his whole truth lies in his self-contradictions. (Nietzsche explicitly claimed the right to contradict himself in *Human All-Too-Human*.) About the particular danger of being turned into a hero of the German nationalists he could not have been more prescient or more outspoken; and, in his last phase especially, he went to extraordinary lengths to dissociate himself not only from German nationalism but from German philosophy and what he regarded as the German mentality:

> In my case too the Germans will do all they can to make an immense destiny give birth to a mouse. They have compromised themselves in my person until now, and I doubt that they will do any better in the future.—Already my natural readers and listeners are Russians, Scandinavians and Frenchmen—will they always be? The Germans have been inscribed in the history of knowledge with nothing but ambiguous names, they have never produced anything but "unconscious" counterfeiters—Fichte, Schelling, Schopenhauer, Hegel, Schleiermacher deserve this title as much as Kant and Leibnitz; they are all mere veil-makers [literal translation of *Schleiermacher*]. . . . They never went through a seventeenth century of rigorous self-examination like the French—a La Rochefoucauld, a Descartes are a hundred times superior in honesty to the greatest Germans,—they have never had a psychologist to this day. But psychology is almost the measure of a people's cleanliness or uncleanliness. . . . And if one isn't even clean, how could one be deep? With a German, almost as with a woman, one never strikes rock bottom; *he has none:* that is all. (But that doesn't even make him shallow.) What is called "deep" in German is precisely that uncleanliness of instinct in relation to oneself of which I am speaking: they don't want to be clean about themselves.[19]

This, of course, is true of others beside Germans: and, despite his psychological acumen, Nietzsche too was much more

---

[19] *Ecce Homo,* ed. Podach, *op. cit.,* 312–313.

ambiguous than he admits here. The analogy with women is a case in point, because it brings one up against Nietzsche's personal peculiarities—those of a man too inhibited to propose marriage other than by proxy who made up for his deficiencies as a lover with cynical reflections on the inferiority of women, at times with "he-man" fantasies of the whip. In a famous photograph taken in Lucerne on May 13, 1882, it is Lou Salomé who brandishes the whip, while Nietzsche and Rée are harnessed to her cart. The photograph is reproduced in a recent biography of Lou Salomé,[20] "whom Nietzsche fell in love with; who was Rilke's mistress; who knew Wagner, Tolstoy, Strindberg; who became one of the few women admitted to the inner circle of Freud's friends and followers"—to quote the dust cover of Professor Peters's book, which records Lou's career as an intellectual *femme fatale* with frankness and impartiality, though with little distinction of style. Lou's abnormally late development—physical as well as emotional—may help to account for the ruthlessness of the young girl who rejected Nietzsche's proposal of marriage; but Nietzsche was only one of a long succession of men whom she drove to despair, if not suicide, by her insistence that relations between the sexes should be governed by the needs of the moment—and that, invariably, meant *her* needs. It was her needs that imposed those "platonic" cohabitations on Paul Rée and on her husband, and determined the duration of her love affairs with those men, like Rilke, who was lucky enough not to qualify for identification with her father. Strangely enough, not one of Lou's admirers and lovers, not even Nietzsche or Rilke or Wedekind, seems to have matched the ruthlessness of her egoism; that would have called for the superman Nietzsche never was, or even wished to be until his "disciple" Lou had finished with this particular "master." To be a superwoman, it seems, was easier than to be a superman. Lou put hard work into her writings, her intellectual development, and her practice as a psychoanalyst; but all she needed for her conquest of men was the beauty, charm, vitality, perverseness, and invulnerability of the Russian general's

[20] H. F. Peters, *My Sister, My Spouse* (London, 1963).

only daughter. Nietzsche's late fantasies about taking the whip to women were a characteristic reaction of his anti-self for the humiliation suffered by his real self; they were a delayed revenge and compensation for his failure to dominate Lou.

Again, his traducers had only to take up the implied analogy between sexual and national psychology to justify a ruthless manipulation of the "feminine" masses and their deliberate self-delusions. Yet Nietzsche's superman castigates weakness not to manipulate it but to turn it into strength; [21] and his primary concern, in any case, is with his own capacity for self-delusion, his own slavish impulses. As Zarathustra insists, the man who has cured himself of these human foibles is gentle with the sick and generous to the weak.

In the end the intimate connection between Naumburg, Nietzsche, and his sister remains as unmistakable and as inescapable as the young professor's connection with the scholarly and unworldly vicar who was his father. Strangely enough, it is in the last Turin phase, the phase in which Nietzsche exulted in his triumph over the professor he believed himself to have sloughed off forever, that Naumburg asserts itself once more with a vengeance. In his letters of the time he begins to boast of his little social successes, of his mundane appearance and, above all, of his sound digestion and enjoyment of good meals. (In *Ecce Homo,* written at the time, he remarks that "to keep silent is to object, 'swallowing' things necessarily produces a bad character—it upsets one's digestion. All those who keep silent are dyspeptic.") It is striking, pathetic, and somewhat shocking that after his descent from the Alps, the tremendous battles fought out in solitude, and the cosmic visions, Nietzsche should celebrate his victory and relaxation in terms that were so well understood at Naumburg. In his mother's letters also the details of meals eaten assume a prominence only rivaled by considerations of piety and social status. True, in *Ecce Homo* Nietzsche very cogently defends "little things"—"food, place,

---

[21] E.g. in *The Will to Power:* "There is a slavish love that subjects itself and throws itself away: that idealizes and deludes itself—there is a god-like love that despises and loves and transforms, raises up the beloved."

climate, relaxation, the whole casuistry of egotism"—as being "incomparably more serious than everything that people have taken seriously until now," metaphysical concepts that "are not even realities, but mere imaginings, more precisely *lies* proceeding from the bad instincts of sick, in the profoundest sense, pernicious natures," a discovery perfectly consistent with at least one dominant trend in his work; but it is difficult to resist the reflection that this, after all, is what every bourgeois has always practiced, whatever he may have professed, and by no means always with the guilty conscience that Nietzsche posits, because it had been his own.

Nietzsche's self-contradictions cannot be resolved, or can be resolved in so many different ways that one is left only with his bare experience and the pure energy generated by a divided mind. Mr. F. A. Lea was not the first to find evidence in the works of this modern Anti-Christ of a radical primitive Christianity, pointing out that, for all his learning, Nietzsche remained astonishingly ignorant of Christian theology, and that Nietzsche's "positive significance lies in being the first European to rediscover the standpoint of Jesus and Paul and present it in terms of a world view as appropriate to the twentieth century as theirs was to the first." [22] Nietzsche's onslaught was directed less against Christ than against his own Christianity, and hence more against Naumburg protestantism than against the whole Christian tradition. Lea's view of Nietzsche's function is certainly valid; but it is only one of a scarcely limitable number of valid views.

Nor is it altogether surprising to learn from Podach that after handing Nietzsche over to the Nazis, his sister—Bernhard

[22] The same comparison with St. Paul was made by Ernst Bertram in his *Nietzsche* of 1918; and a recent writer, Gerd-Günther Grau, has confirmed Mr. Lea's Christian view of Nietzsche in his study *Christlicher Glaube und intellektuelle Redlichkeit: Eine religionsphilosophische Studie über Nietzsche* (Frankfurt, 1958).

Nietzsche's return to Christian precepts after his mental breakdown is well known, and can be partly accounted for by his mother's influence; but the very title *Ecce Homo,* and the signature *Crucifixus* in several of his last communiques, once again points to the ambivalence of all his concerns. A jotting of his Anti-Christ period confirms it: "Christ on the Cross remains the most sublime of all symbols—even now."

Förster's widow—proceeded to address anti-anti-Semitic appeals to her new masters. Naumburg, too, was a complex phenomenon; and Nietzsche's sister was half in revolt against its conformism. In coming out on the side of the oppressed, she showed once more that she lacked neither her brother's generous courage nor his perversity.

The wheel had come full circle, because dependence and revolt can never break the circle that confines them. Nietzsche suffered "hell" within that circle, and recorded its upward and downward motions with a faithfulness, candor, and lucidity that will always remain admirable and instructive. No wonder that his ultimate "epiphany" was of the eternal recurrence, of the great cosmic wheel forever turning and bringing round again what has passed; or that this very conception was an instance of the eternal recurrence in that it reverted across the millennia to the intuitions of Heraclitus and the poet-philosophers before Socrates—that very Socrates who had been Nietzsche's first antagonist in *The Birth of Tragedy*—so that the Dionysus and Anti-Christ of Nietzsche's last creative phase linked up with the Anti-Socrates of his first. Nietzsche's moral heroism, too, could only affirm and accept the circle, never break it; his *amor fati* embraced the worst, a worst, it may be, never so clearly confronted by a human mind, but made too much of its ability to bear it, to rejoice in it. His *amor fati* was tainted with *Schadenfreude*.

If Nietzsche cannot be blamed for the Nietzscheans, because he cannot be tied down, neither can he be wholly excused for failing to break the circle. Love and hate, reverence and revolt, faith and skepticism interlock with endless variations in his works, but never quite succeed in engendering that third liberating theme. If we grant Nietzsche the privileges of a poet-philosopher, including the right to contradict himself and to remain forever ambiguous, his work must be tested by the standards of poetry for its aesthetic and subliminal effects; and here the combination of analytical thinker and visionary proved even more dubious than on the level of doctrine alone.

Nietzsche's diction, too, shows an obsession with certain primitive relationships, dynamisms, and concepts. Some of these have been brilliantly interpreted by Dr. F. D. Luke,[23] who concentrated on the dynamics of height, metaphors of climbing, flying, leaping, dancing, and the related one of seafaring. As readers of the present chapter may have noticed, a similar study could be made of Nietzsche's animal imagery. His warning that he does not want to be remembered as "a savage beast and moral monster" can be offset by another: "I am a dangerous animal, and don't lend myself well to adulation." [24] Nietzsche's animal imagery is so pervasive and conspicuous that its effect is to suspend all those intellectual and moral reservations, which he undoubtedly wanted his readers to observe. His capacity for self-identification with the animal world in general, not only with predatory animals, is amply attested both in his writings and in his life. That his nickname for his sister was "the llama" may be relatively insignificant: [25] but one of the few physical expressions of affection he is known to have indulged in, and his very last, was toward a cab horse in Turin. An aphorism like the following from *The Dawn of Day* [26] puts the complex in a nutshell: "*Humanity*. We do not regard animals as moral beings. But do you imagine that animals regard us as moral beings?—An animal that could talk once said: 'Humanity is a prejudice, and at least we animals don't suffer from it.' "

As we have seen, Nietzsche was well aware that a doctrine of deliberate brutalism, a kind of ethical Darwinism, could be extracted from his works, as it was to be by the Nazis. Now Nietzsche, as a highly civilized man and a "Good European" (his own phrase), took it for granted that brutality was undesirable, and devoted his therapeutical talents to the vindication of

---

[23] In *Nietzsche and the Imagery of Height,* Publications of the English Goethe Society, Vol. XXVIII (1959).

[24] Letter to his sister of April, 1885.

[25] Podach has published the following note by Nietzsche to his sister, the very last coherent document in his hand to be composed without his mother's help:

"I am glad, my dear beloved Llama—, that according to your letter you, my little animal, are well—with heartfelt greetings—cordialement —your confrère frère.

Friedrich Nietzsche

Naumburg a/Saale 1890"

[26] *Morgenröte*, No. 333.

that part of human nature which civilization had repressed: "The struggle against the brutal instincts is a different one from that against the morbid instincts; indeed, to induce illness can be a means of mastering brutality. In Christianity, psychological treatment often amounts to turning an animal into a sick animal, and thus into a tame one." [27] Nietzsche does not deny that brutal instincts should be held in check, though this was not his business. Yet, subliminally, the effect of his later works is to glorify the predatory beast at the expense of the innocuous or the tame; and it is his metaphors that produce the effect.

It is regrettable, therefore, that *Zarathustra,* the most "poetic" and figurative of Nietzsche's prose works, should have come to be regarded as his *magnum opus,* often as nothing less than the Nietzsche bible. F. D. Luke, too, doubts that "his prose is at its best where it approaches the nature of poetry; he is certainly at his worst when writing verse." The prose poetry of *Zarathustra* is an unhappy amalgam of biblical and Romantic elements, and this in turn rarely blends very happily with the stringencies of Nietzsche's analytical prose. Above all, the metaphors are allowed to proliferate in a manner that shows up Nietzsche's most serious defects both as a thinker and as a poet. "Only very occasionally is Nietzsche able to achieve *poetic* language in which the image or vehicle has become virtually autonomous," Luke remarks; at the same time the imagery comes close enough to autonomy to detract from that clarity and incisiveness for which Nietzsche's analytical prose is justly admired.

The emblematic character of Nietzsche's poetic imagery, to which Luke's stricture alludes, is equally marked in his verse; apart from those obsessive and primitive gestures already mentioned, which also included metaphors connected with eating and swallowing, Nietzsche's poetic diction hardly ever conveys any awareness of the particulars of human or nonhuman nature. Yet the only German imaginative writers of the nineteenth century whom Nietzsche consistently admired were the poetic realists Stifter and Keller, writers who dwelled with loving precision on those "little things" of life that Nietzsche opposed in

[27] *The Will to Power,* 238.

Ecce Homo to the great abstractions. As Schlechta may have had in mind in citing Nietzsche's *Fable* [28] against him, Nietzsche's diction, too, brings us up against that basic contradiction between what he was and what he wanted to be:

> The Don Juan of knowledge: no philosopher or poet has yet discovered him. He is lacking in love for those things which he comes to know, but his intelligence is tickled and gratified by the pursuit and intrigues of knowledge—right up to the highest and farthest stars of knowledge!—until in the end there is nothing left for him to pursue but the absolute hurtfulness of knowledge, like the drunkard who ends up by drinking absinth and *aqua fortis*. So in the end he craves for hell— this being the last knowledge that can *seduce* him. Perhaps hell too will disappoint him, like all that he has known! In that case he would have to remain motionless to all eternity, nailed to his disappointment and himself transformed into the stone guest, longing for a last supper of knowledge of which he will never again partake! —because the whole world hasn't so much as a bite to offer that hungry man.[29]

Because he was lacking in love for particulars, Nietzsche's anti-puritanism never became more than a reflex of his self-hatred and self-dissatisfaction, and found no embodiment in his diction. Like the conventional pedagogues, parsons, and ideologists he despised, Nietzsche could not help holding up an ideal yardstick to individuals; though he remained loyal to a few old friends for friendship's sake, not a single individual of his acquaintance came up to the mark, or could conceivably have done so, since the mark was that of the superman who was Nietzsche's anti-self. As he might have gathered from Pascal, to whom he owed so much, the obverse of that angel is the beast, the obverse of that superman the subman. All his richness, energy, and subtlety cannot make up for the gap in Nietzsche's work, the missing middle register of human experience.

Also Sprach Zarathustra may well come to be regarded not as Nietzsche's masterpiece, but as an aberration and monstrosity, as an instance of that late Romantic inflation that he recog-

---

[28] *Morgenröte*, No. 327.
[29] *Ibid*. Cf. *Die fröhliche Wissenschaft*, No. 338: "that the way to one's own heaven always leads through the delight in one's own hell."

nized in Wagner, as in the German Reich, and hated because he felt its power over himself. Yet if Nietzsche's importance should ever be doubted, we have only to turn to his early polemical works, the *Thoughts out of Season,* in which he was no solitary prophet on the mountaintops—inviting disciples only to scorn and reject them as slaves, needing disciples, but ashamed of his need—to be reassured of his central and seminal relevance to all that has been thought and experienced in the last hundred years. This young classical scholar spoke to men as a member of society, at once involved in it and critical of it, much as Matthew Arnold did in the same years, and about much the same questions; that Nietzsche was more than twenty years younger can only increase one's respect for his incomparable insight, prescience, and daring. Even Nietzsche's discovery of the Dionysian principle, and his self-identification with it, goes back to these early years and *The Birth of Tragedy.*

This is not to deny that he added to his fundamental perceptions in later years, clarifying or enriching them in many cases, but only to suggest that it was precisely his power and range of perception that failed to keep up with the growing tension of his inner conflict. The young professor grappled with a civilization and a culture; the lonely thinker and poet, increasingly, grappled only with himself, yet could not quite accept the prospect of final isolation. Hence the "Dionysian imperialism," the bragging and self-dramatization, the tedious repetitions and overstatements, the self-propelled rhetoric and hyperbole, the strident tone of certain later works and passages. These call for readers truly Nietzschean in their readiness to fight back, to discriminate and deflate; and, more than any other writer of his time, Nietzsche might have served, and can still serve, to create such readers. That the vulgarians seized on his crudities and excesses for their own much cruder and more excessive ends is a reflection not on Nietzsche but on them.

These observations on Nietzsche, too, are intended as premises—not as a critical evaluation of his ideas, but as an attempt to clean the air of the cant and "uncleanliness" to which he himself so consistently objected. When these observations were first published, they elicited violent protests from Professor Walter Kaufmann [30] and from Mr. R. J. Hollingdale, the translator of the Penguin edition of *Also Sprach Zarathustra* and the author of a recent study of Nietzsche.[31] Both Professor Kaufmann and Mr. Hollingdale believe that Nietzsche was "a coherent and consistent philosopher"—to quote Mr. Hollingdale's letter—and that my stress on Nietzsche's self-contradictions and ambiguities detracts from his importance as a philosopher. I was not concerned with Nietzsche's importance as a philosopher, nor am I competent to judge it. Mr. Hollingdale, therefore, is quite right in pointing out that I "stop at the point where commentators on other philosophers begin." That is where I wish to stop; and not because I underrate the importance of Nietzsche's thought—its effect on imaginative literature alone was so decisive as to make it indispensable to the study of all twentieth-century developments, not only in Germany—but because I believe that Nietzsche's later writings cannot be properly understood if they are read only as philosophy; that is, without such adjustments and allowances as my interpretation of Nietzsche's personality proposes. No philosopher before Nietzsche devoted so large a proportion of his writings to self-portrayal, self-confession, and self-projection. Anyone who thinks that this is an accident has not begun to understand Nietzsche or the experiential nature of his thinking.

The political exploitation of Nietzsche's writings is a case in point. Dr. Stern,[32] for instance, quotes the following extract from the drafts formerly known as *The Will to Power: "The 20th Century.* The Abbé Galiani once said: *La prévoyance est la cause des guerres actuelles de l'Europe. Si l'on voulait se donner la peine de ne rien prévoir, tout le monde serait tranquille, et je ne crois pas qu'on serait plus malheureux parce qu'on ne ferait pas la guerre.* Since I am far from sharing the unwarlike views of my friend the late Galiani, I am not afraid to make a prediction or two and so possibly to conjure up a cause of wars." Dr. Stern is arguing that certain "doom-filled prophecies from Heine onwards . . . are not merely prophecies but ex-

---

[30] Printed, and answered, in *Encounter,* Vol. XIX, No. 5 (November, 1962).
[31] *Nietzsche, The Man and His Philosophy* (London, 1965).
[32] J. P. Stern, *Re-Interpretations* (London, 1964), 128.

pressions of intent," and that "Nietzsche at all events knew this well enough." The same dictum could easily be cited as evidence of Nietzsche's support for militarism, but only by a commentator unwilling or unable to make allowances for Nietzsche's self-contradiction on this score and for the self-dramatization—the boosting of Nietzsche's own anti-self—present in all his later utterances about such matters. The dictum, in fact, consists of Nietzsche's endorsement of a general insight—and this may be taken "objectively," as philosophy, if we insist on this rather inappropriate designation in Nietzsche's case—followed by a piece of self-portrayal whose full and right import can be established only in the light of all we know about Nietzsche. If that seems farfetched or sophisticated, it is Nietzsche himself who recommended so personal a mode of judgment; and Nietzsche himself who provided the personal data by which he can and should be judged.

Nietzsche began as a critic of culture, very much as defined by Matthew Arnold in 1869, "Culture being a pursuit of our total perfection by means of getting to know, on all the matters which most concern us, the best which has been thought and said in the world, and, through this knowledge, turning a stream of fresh and free thought upon our stock notions and habits, which we now follow staunchly but mechanically, vainly imagining that there is a virtue in following them staunchly that makes up for the mischief of following them mechanically." [33] Like Arnold, too, Nietzsche rebelled against puritan philistinism, though with a growing vehemence that would have appalled Arnold. What Nietzsche might have said about Arnold is very much what he did say about George Eliot:

> They have got rid of the Christian God and now think they must hold on all the more to Christian morality: that is *English* logic, and we will not quarrel with it in morality-mongering females à la Eliot. In England it is only as an awe-inspiring moral fanatic that one can redeem the disgrace of having emancipated oneself ever so little from theology. . . . For the Englishman morality is not a problem—yet.[34]

---

[33] Matthew Arnold, *Culture and Anarchy* (London, 1869), viii.
[34] *Götzen-Dämmerung: Streifzüge eines Unzeitgemässen,* No. 5.

All Arnold's thinking about culture and society was contained within the framework of an existing society that might be tempered with "sweetness and light," but could be expected to continue substantially unchanged. Nietzsche not only demolished the ethical and metaphysical foundations of the society in which he grew up, but recorded the situation of a mind for whom no such foundation, and ultimately no society at all, could be taken for granted. He also left confused sketches and drafts for a society and a culture that might exist in the future, but that society and culture could only be utopian, since the sketches and drafts were the work of a man less and less capable of getting to grips with realities outside himself. W. B. Yeats said that out of our quarrels with our own selves we make poetry. That Nietzsche's thinking, increasingly, grew out of a quarrel with himself is one reason that I have called him a poet-philosopher. Not only the appeal of his later thoughts, which derives from its experiential urgency and daring, but its limitations and dangers are due to this unprecedented situation.

The quarrel was never resolved. By taking up one side of the argument, certain Nietzscheans could turn Nietzsche into the prophet of German militarism, racialism, and national megalomania. Since they lacked Nietzsche's penetrating and searching honesty, his psychological "cleanliness," they found it easy to ignore what Nietzsche in *Ecce Homo* wrote about Germans like themselves:

It is even part of my ambition to be regarded as the despiser of the Germans *par excellence*. Already at the age of 26 I expressed my *mistrust* of the German character [*Thoughts out of Season,* III, p. 335] —to me the Germans are impossible. When I imagine a kind of person repellent to all my instincts, this person invariably turns into a German. My first test for a human being is to see whether he or she is endowed with a sense of distance, whether he or she perceives differences of rank, grade and order between one person and another, whether he or she *distinguishes:* all this constitutes a *gentleman;* without it one belongs irrevocably to that big-hearted and, oh, so good-natured category, the *canaille.* But the Germans are *canaille*—oh, they are so good-natured. . . . One debases oneself by intercourse with Germans: the German is a *leveller.* . . . Apart from my relations with a few German artists, above all with Richard Wagner, I have not spent a single pleasant hour with Germans. . . . Suppose that the deepest mind of all the millennia were to appear among the Germans, some female saviour of the Capitol would get up and claim that her most unbeautiful soul was quite as good as his. . . . I cannot stand this race with whom one is always in bad company, who have no feeling for *nuances*—it is my misfortune to be a *nuance:*—who have no *esprit* in their feet and can't even walk. . . . In the last resort the Germans have no feet at all, they only have legs. . . . The Germans have no idea how vulgar they are, but that is the extreme of vulgarity—they are not even ashamed to be only Germans. . . . They insist on having a say in everything, they consider themselves decisive; I very much fear that they've decided even over me. . . .

That very criticism, of course, is unbalanced and excessive —excess, in Nietzsche, is also a deliberate stylistic device. But how right Nietzsche was to say that he himself was a *"nuance!"* And how perceptive of him to see that this *nuance* was the one thing that would be smudged and blotted by his coarse disciples and "priests!"

Nietzsche's thought cries out for the kind of psychological scrutiny that he brought to bear on other thinkers and on himself. Even a writer much more competent than I am to judge philosophy as philosophy, Miguel de Unamuno, sums up Nietzsche as follows:

His heart craved the eternal All while his head convinced him of nothingness, and, desperate and mad to defend himself from himself, he cursed that which he most loved. Because he could not be Christ, he blasphemed Christ. Bursting with his own self, he wished himself unending and dreamed his theory of eternal recurrence, a sorry counterfeit of immortality, and full of pity for himself, he abominated all pity. And there are some who say that his is the philosophy of strong men! No, it is not. My health and my strength urge me to perpetuate myself. His is the doctrine of weaklings who aspire to be strong, but not of the strong who are strong.[35]

[35] Miguel de Unamuno, *The Tragic Sense of Life* (London, 1962), 65.

The ultimate criterion by which this kindred spirit condemns Nietzsche's "philosophy"—which his own resembles in its impatience with mere common sense and pedestrian reasonableness—is psychological.

Yet once we have made the necessary psychological adjustment, Nietzsche's work becomes a rich source of stimulating and valuable insights—even into society and culture, though he came to see them from too lonely a vantage point, and into those moral problems that neither Matthew Arnold nor George Eliot, indeed no English writer of his time, had any reason to face. As Nietzsche predicted, some of these moral problems did become urgently relevant wherever traditional moral codes had ceased to be sustained by religious faith. This process had begun long before Nietzsche's time: but it is in our time that its effects have come out into the open, both in public and private life. Nietzsche, therefore, was another of those German writers "distinguished above all by their special combination of the prophetic and the archaic, of the existential and the parochial" —parochial,[36] because for all his brilliance and erudition Nietzsche never succeeded in liberating himself emotionally from the provincialism of Naumburg.

Nietzsche also holds the key to twentieth-century German literature. Ambiguous though his answers were, and various as were the uses to which his ideas were put, his problems were the problems of almost every later writer who matters. If that statement requires statistical proof, the index of a recent German encyclopedia of world literature in the twentieth century [37] provides it: Nietzsche beats such contenders as Ibsen, Joyce, Kafka, Eliot, Proust, and Rilke by achieving more than a hundred references to his name. His contribution to psychology alone—his inquiry into needs and instincts, into the unconscious determinants of behavior and the precariousness of consciously determined attitudes—would have sufficed to make him one of the vital influences on our time.

I have said that Nietzsche's situation was unprecedented, but also that many German writers before Nietzsche were socially

[36] J. P. Stern, *op. cit.*, 1.
[37] *Lexikon der Weltliteratur im 20. Jahrhundert* (Freiburg, 1962).

alienated to a degree without parallel in other European literatures of their time. Half a century before Nietzsche, in 1828
and 1829, Heinrich Heine had summed up some of the national
differences in his *English Fragments:*

> As far as the Germans are concerned, they need neither free-
> dom nor equality. They are a speculative people, ideologists,
> thinkers before and after the event, dreamers who live only in
> the future, never in the present. Englishmen and Frenchmen
> live in the present; for them every day has its struggle and
> counter-struggle, every day has its history. The German has
> nothing to struggle for, and when he began to suspect that
> there might be things worth struggling for and worth possess-
> ing, his philosophers wisely undertook to make him doubt
> their existence. True, the Germans too love freedom, but in a
> different way from other peoples. The Englishman loves free-
> dom like his lawful wife, he possesses it, and even if he doesn't
> treat either with exceptional tenderness, in an emergency he is
> quite capable of standing up for them like a man, and woe to
> the red-coated fellow who forces his way into her sacred bed-
> chamber—whether as a gallant or as an executioner. The
> Frenchman loves Liberty like a sweetheart. He burns for her,
> he blazes, he hurls himself at her feet with the most extrava-
> gant assurances, he fights for her to the death, he commits a
> thousand follies for her sake. The German loves Liberty like
> his old grandmother.

With an urbane detachment and a lucidity that angered those
of his compatriots who preferred metaphysics and mysticism to
psychology, Heine anticipated much of what has been said
about later developments. Stylistically, too he was a forerunner
of Nietzsche the aphorist, as distinct from Nietzsche-Zarathus-
tra the preacher; and many of Heine's most striking perceptions
arose from a quarrel with himself, which was also a quarrel
with Germany. Another passage in the same work goes to the
very root of the difference between the German States of
Heine's time and the England which the Romantic in him
found by no means congenial:

> Despite these contradictory trends in their ways of living and
> thinking, the English people do show a unified outlook which

consists in their very sense of being a nation; their latter-day roundheads and cavaliers may hate and despise one another as much as they like, but they never cease to be Englishmen; as such they are as unified and congenial as plants that have sprung up out of one and the same soil and remain mysteriously rooted in that soil. Hence the secret unanimity of all the English way of life, which at first sight strikes us only as the scene of confusion and contradiction. Excessive wealth and abject misery, orthodoxy and skepticism, freedom and slavery, cruelty and mercy, honesty and knavery—these opposites carried to their craziest extremes, above them the grey, misty sky, on all sides their buzzing machines, figures and accounts, gaslights, chimneys, newspapers, porter jugs, tightly shut mouths —all these hang together in such a way that we cannot imagine one without the other, and a thing that arouses our astonishment or derision on its own seems quite ordinary and serious when combined with the rest.

Nietzsche, however, was active when Germany had not only become a nation, but was on the way to becoming the strongest military and industrial power in Europe, and even a colonial empire, like Britain. Outwardly, Germany was now quite as unified as England had been when Heine visited it in the eighteen-twenties; and indeed in certain respects Nietzsche's quarrel with the Germany of his time was akin to Heine's quarrel with England. Heine had written:

If you talk with the stupidest Englishman about politics, he will still have something sensible to say. As soon as you change the subject to religion, the most intelligent Englishmen will come out with nothing but inanities.

The imprint of John Bull is as deep and sharp as that of a Greek medallion; and wherever you may come across him, whether in London or Calcutta, whether as master or as servant, you will never mistake him. Everywhere he is like a crude fact, very honest, but cold and thoroughly repellent. He has all the solidity of a material substance, and you can never avoid noticing that wherever he may be, in whatever company, John Bull always regards himself as the most important person. . . .

But though John Bull is the coldest of friends, he is the saf-

est of neighbours and the most fair-minded and generous of
enemies; though he guards his own castle like a pasha, he
never tries to force his way into another man's.

Heine had been repelled by all that was un-Romantic in
England and Englishmen as well as by a certain complacency
due to a sense of national superiority, and Nietzsche castigated
the materialism, coarseness and arrogance of the new Germany.
Yet both Heine and Nietzsche were perceptive enough to understand the difference between a complacent self-assurance
and an arrogant aggressiveness. Nietzsche expressly distinguishes the discriminating English gentleman from the "level-
ing" German. The implication is that the new Germany had
succeeded in creating a new State, but not a new society and a
new culture. It is the discrepancy between power and culture
that exasperated Nietzsche; but whereas Heine could still claim
that their philosophers had undertaken to make Germans doubt
the existence of "things worth struggling for and possessing,"
by Nietzsche's time it was the official function of German philosophers to surround the cult of national power with a metaphysical halo. Efficiency had become a notoriously German virtue; and the new religion of Germany was only ostensibly
Christian. The virtue of efficiency was inculcated because it
served the true religion of the new Germany, a religion of the
State.

With a thoroughness that was also German, Nietzsche devoted one part of his work to demolishing this sham religion
and its moral scaffolding; but he was often incapable of distinguishing the new religion and the new virtues from the Christian drapery that served to make them acceptable. Nietzsche
had to become both the anti-Kaiser and the anti-Christ, because
he was taken in by the seeming identity of Christian virtues
with the "slave morality" that was a product of the State. If he
also seemed to become the apologist of the power principle, it
was partly because of his own confusion, partly because his
protestations of strength were useful to his opponents as soon
as they had dropped the Christian mask and decided that a
pagan primitivism was more conducive to their ends.

What was unprecedented about Nietzsche's situation is that

no thinker and no writer before him has presumed to make so clean a sweep of all the values professed by other men, or dared to claim a comparable freedom from all traditional authority, whether divine or human. After Nietzsche this freedom was claimed by many; and a proliferation of prophets broke up whatever appearance of cultural unity had existed in Germany up to Nietzsche's time.

VIII

THOMAS MANN

In 1889, the very year of Nietzsche's breakdown in Turin, Gerhart Hauptmann wrote his play *Vor Sonnenaufgang,* the Naturalist movement began to conquer the German theatres, and its theorists had every reason to believe that their program would succeed in bridging the gulf between literature and modern society. Yet by the early eighteen-nineties a countermovement—variously described as Neo-Romantic, Symbolist, and Neoclassical—had made itself felt in Germany and Austria, and as early as 1907 Oskar Kokoschka's little play *Mörder Hoffnung der Frauen* broke through to a new freedom, a new inwardness that was to be known as Expressionism. The tension between realism and fantasy was greater than ever before: if Naturalism was "scientific" in its rigid documentation of outward realities—Hauptmann's minute stage directions in the early plays go so far as to specify the titles of books on the shelves—the subconscious, too, had become the subject of scientific investigation, and Strindberg had explored the dramatic possibilities of dreams. Naturalism, at best, could establish itself as one of several norms; and not even Gerhart Haupt-mann complied with its demand for consistency, any more than did Arno Holz, who had drafted one of its rigid prescriptions. The so-called poetic realists whom Nietzsche admired had maintained some kind of balance between objective and subjec-tive truth; that balance became more and more precarious in the works of the early Expressionists, and by the time of World War I Gottfried Benn—a scientist by training—could record his conversion to unreality in imaginative prose quite unlike any-thing previously described as fiction.[1]

Despite his early conflicts with the Imperial Establishment, Gerhart Hauptmann was one of the writers who claimed the status of *praeceptor Germaniae*. Almost as ready as Thomas Mann to make public pronouncements on public issues—as Stefan George, for instance, resolutely refused to do, even when such issues had come to concern him as a poet—Hauptmann was notoriously deficient nonetheless in those accomplishments that permit imaginative writers to function as "representative men." For all his spontaneous response to the natural and human world, Hauptmann could not escape the prevalent ten-sion between private and public concerns. Again and again even his Naturalist plays took up the conflict between excep-tional individuals, usually artists, and their social environment, very often in terms of health and sickness, fitness and "degener-ation," terms made familiar both by Nietzsche and by the popu-lar Darwinists. Thomas Mann, Hermann Hesse, and even Rilke, began with the same complex, but kept up with the psy-chological developments that superseded, and largely invali-dated, the rather crudely biological approaches to these matters in the eighteen-eighties and eighteen-nineties. In Hauptmann's poetic drama *Die versunkene Glocke* (1896) the conflict was translated into terms at once more personal and more arche-typal than the Naturalist convention permitted; like Ibsen him-self, and Flaubert before Ibsen, Hauptmann felt the restrictions of the Naturalist medium; and this play was the first of several in which he claimed the license of *Peer Gynt* or *La Tentation de St. Antoine*. One of his later Naturalist plays, *Michael Kra-*

---

[1] In the collection *Gehirne* (Leipzig, 1916).

mer (1900), was delicate enough in its treatment of the artist-bourgeois conflict to win the admiration of Rilke (who, in any case, differed from Stefan George in having no quarrel with Naturalism, even making use of it, where he could, for his own more subjective ends). The same play was one of the two by Hauptmann that a still more devoted and more constant admirer, James Joyce,[2] translated into English.

Yet Hauptmann's early fame declined in the course of his long life; and by no means only because the aged writer allowed himself to be taken over by the "bad" Germany when Thomas Mann had become the almost universally acknowledged spokesman of the "good." Their political positions had once been reversed; and Mann's ascendancy had become decisive during the Weimar Republic, when both men were on the side of democracy and there were even rumors that Hauptmann might become President of the Republic. The more crucial difference between them was that Hauptmann was a naïve writer, in Schiller's sense of the word. As such, Hauptmann was less suitable even than Goethe for the function of *praeceptor Germaniae*. His business was to create characters and enact conflicts, not to comment on them or generalize, philosophize, and ironize his own duality. Hauptmann had taken to Naturalism not because it allowed him to air his ideas and opinions, in the manner of Bernard Shaw, but because it allowed him to refrain from doing so. Even his political, and seemingly revolutionary, play, *Die Weber,* remained extraordinarily ambiguous and impartial as far as ideas and opinions were concerned. The Kaiser and his government need never have been alarmed. Yet the age favored a more sophisticated, more intellectualized kind of writing, and a kind of writer much more conscious than Hauptmann was of what the age demanded. Even a century earlier Schiller, the reflective or "sentimental" writer, had proved much better qualified than Goethe to provide the edification and guidance demanded of a *praeceptor Germaniae*. Hauptmann's old age was more remotely "Olympian" than Goethe's,

[2] As late as 1937 Joyce asked Ezra Pound for an introduction to Hauptmann, who perhaps would do him "the honour and pleasure of signing" the text of *Michael Kramer,* "a play which I still admire greatly." *Letters of James Joyce,* ed. Stuart Gilbert (London, 1957), 398.

with far less justification—if only because Hauptmann's epic poems and mythological tragedies of later years are unthinkable without the example of Goethe's classicizing, which means one further remove from the spring of vision. Hauptmann, in fact, was defeated by the tension of the age; he was not public enough, or private enough to sustain his wrestling with the *Zeitgeist*. What he lacked was not strength, but suppleness and cunning. The public figure and representative German whom the Nazis used—but the Communists continued to respect for his earlier works—was representative only in being helpless and impotent in the face of brutal realities.

One other German writer of the post-Nietzschean era comes close to deserving consideration as a *praeceptor Germaniae*. Like Gerhart Hauptmann and Thomas Mann, Hermann Hesse was a winner of the Nobel Prize; but it is significant that Hesse left Germany as early as 1912 and settled in Switzerland. His works appealed most strongly to young German readers with inner conflicts and disturbances akin to those that he rendered in his semi-autobiographical novels and stories. Until his death in 1962, he continued to act as a guide and confessor to such readers, devoting much of his time to an extensive correspondence with young people who claimed his sympathy and advice. Like Rilke's *Letters to a Young Poet* and *Letters to a Young Woman* quite a number of Hesse's were printed in one form or another, if only for semiprivate circulation among other correspondents. In this way Hesse exerted a real, though limited, influence; but he represented the essentially nonpolitical tradition of German inwardness. Much as Hauptmann's naturalism was imperiled by the early influence of the Silesian mystical tradition, Swabian pietism and Indian mysticism had come together in Hesse's family—his father had worked as a missionary— and Hesse's inner conflict was exacerbated by the revolt of his individualism against their spiritual compulsion. Like André Gide, who recognized the affinity, Hesse was powerfully drawn to a Nietzschean immoralism.

Hesse's quest for spiritual harmony was representative because his peculiar tensions corresponded to the perennial tensions of German intellectual and cultural life, as well as to tensions especially marked in his time and apparent in the works of both Hauptmann and Thomas Mann. Though a pacifist and antinationalist, Hesse rarely felt called upon to take sides in specific issues. As late as 1950, after experiences that might have suggested the need for commitment, Hesse wrote in a letter from Sils Maria (copies of which were sent to various correspondents): "At present, of the two world fronts one is as alien to me as the other: both are militant, both intolerant and unbending, both are basically unimaginative, that is to say, uncreative. Gandhi as a person was worth more than all the American Presidents of the century put together, and all the dogmatists of Communism from Marx to the present day." In the same letter Hesse wrote that "in so far as social conditions at the end of the capitalist era are no longer viable or bearable . . . Truman is fighting as vain a battle as Hitler." This "plague on both your houses" is consistent with Hesse's search for the good life and the good society, the "psychocracy" of his *Morgenlandfahrt* (1932)—and I believe that the utopianism of imaginative writers is far from being pernicious in itself, as long as it is not mistaken for a different kind of political wisdom—but the pronouncement is unlikely to have been of much use to Hesse's correspondent, who had drawn his attention to certain parallels between Communism and primitive Christianity. The comparison between Truman and Hitler is so inept as to be irrelevant to the political situation in 1950, and merely points back to Hesse's spiritual superiority, which makes all politics "alien" to him. His correspondent, clearly, was equally "idealistic," equally reluctant to face the realities of politics and to make the necessary distinctions. The effect on him of Hesse's pronouncement must have been to drive him back to the German intellectual's favorite alibi, the impregnable fortress of his inwardness.

In later years idyllic or utopian allegories were more congenial to Hesse than strictly realistic fiction. Where the modern world seemed to impinge on his fantasies, as in his novel *Der Steppenwolf* (1927), it became a phantasmagorical projection of his inner life. The extraordinary fascination which this and other works by Hesse held for young readers was very apt to fade in the light of more mature experience; and Hesse himself had some doubts about the suitability of books like *Der Step-penwolf* for those readers who were most powerfully attracted to them. In response to a letter by one young reader he wrote that "in exceptional circumstances *Der Steppenwolf* can be read by a very young person without doing him any harm—if the reader is a potential poet or otherwise called." In two privately printed letters, too—*An einen jungen Künstler* (1949) and *Das junge Genie* (1950)—Hesse was very much aware of the differ-ence between the "artistic temperament," identified with genius in the letter, and the discipline of art, going so far as to imply that he himself had partly failed as an artist through an exces-sive preoccupation with personal problems. He became more and more conscious of the need for detachment, until in his last novel, *Das Glasperlenspiel* (1943), he adopted the distancing device that was also to be used by Thomas Mann in *Dr. Faus-tus,* a narrative *persona* not to be identified with the author.

It is Hesse's earlier, more directly confessional works that continue to appeal to young readers not only in the German-speaking countries but—belatedly and surprisingly—in Amer-ica and Great Britain. As far as mature readers are concerned, Thomas Mann alone can be said to have succeeded in carrying out the function of *praeceptor Germaniae* throughout the best part of half a century—for reasons that are more problematical than they seem.

Thomas Mann alone seems to have escaped or transcended the predicament of his German contemporaries, writers at once "prophetic and archaic, existential and parochial," as Hesse un-doubtedly was. Thomas Mann alone was seen as a novelist in the main European tradition, firmly rooted in nineteenth-cen-tury realism and naturalism, but comparable to Henry James or Marcel Proust in his capacity to refine the material of fiction, to sift it through a sensibility at once highly personal and respon-sive to all the most vital developments of his time. What is more, Thomas Mann alone seems to have been truly represen-tative of the German bourgeoisie as a whole: no other "serious" writer was quite as widely read in his own lifetime or as suc-cessful in bridging the gap between the minority publics availa-ble to other "serious" writters. Only very few of these minority groups rejected Mann before 1933; only very few critics failed to agree that he was the most important, the most distinguished German writer of imaginative prose active during the first half of this century.

I have already suggested that Thomas Mann wrote out of tensions and conflicts not essentially different from those of his major German contemporaries, including Gerhart Hauptmann —whom he admired for being what he was not, and affectionately caricatured as a person in *The Magic Mountain*—and Hermann Hesse. One preoccupation that Mann shared with many German contemporaries was that with the figure of Narcissus. Hermann Hesse's novel or "tale" *Narziss und Goldmund* (1930) is one version of a fable equally important to Thomas Mann and to Rainer Maria Rilke: the autonomous, self-contained personality of the dedicated artist or intellectual (Narcissus) is contrasted with the outward-going and loving. Rilke's obsession with the theme was most marked in the critical years that followed his failure to complete the *Duineser Elegien;* the poems called "Narziss" (1913), "Klage" (1914), "Ausgesetzt auf den Bergen des Herzens" (1914), "Waldteich, weicher, in sich eingekehrter" (1914), and "Wendung" (1914) are variations on it. Professor Peter Szondi [3] has shown that Thomas Mann was equally preoccupied with the problem of narcissism in later works like *Die Vertauschten Köpfe* (*The Transposed Heads,* 1949) and *Der Erwählte* (*The Holy Sinner,* 1951), and that he tended to identify narcissism with intellectual pride. The problem, therefore, hinged on Mann's sense of an irreconcilable conflict between intellect or spirit on the one hand, nature or life on the other. Professor Szondi traces Mann's preoccupation with narcissism to a turning-point in his development that occurred around 1922, but he forgets that the whole complex was prefigured in a story printed [4] in 1906 "Wälsungenblut." In this early story intellectual arrogance and exclusiveness are not only related to self-love, but to the incest theme, which was to recur in *Der Erwählte.* Professor Szondi, therefore, failed to observe that Mann's concern with narcissism is evident in the whole of his work, not least in a

[3] "Thomas Mann's Gnadenmär von Narziss," in Peter Szondi, *Satz und Gegensatz* (Frankfurt, 1964).
[4] But not published until 1921. The early edition was withdrawn.

work published nearly fifty years after the story, the fragmentary *Confessions of Felix Krull* (1954). The close connection with Hermann Hesse's conflict between an ideal of ascetic spirituality and an amoral vitalism is most striking in Mann's Indian legend, *The Transposed Heads;* but the terms in which Mann rendered his dualism are so extreme as to suggest the parallel of Gottfried Benn's "autonomous" and strictly isolated "ego" incapable of any union with another, and longing for dissolution in the sexual act or retrogression to a primitive, preconscious form of existence.

Thomas Mann avoided the more drastic implications of this extreme dualism by adopting an ironic stance and taking great care not to indulge in direct self-confession, as even Hauptmann was inclined to do in his non-naturalist and autobiographical works, not to mention the naked subjectivity of Hesse, Rilke or Benn. Even Hugo von Hofmannsthal once admitted that his relation to society was "a much more nihilistic one than you may assume" [5]—and Hofmannsthal, as an Austrian, was exempt from some of the more violent tensions to which I have alluded. Though real and effectual enough, the representative status of Thomas Mann is one of the strangest phenomena in the strange history of German literature and culture.

"The greatest European Novelist of the twentieth century? Thomas Mann, alas!" This variation, by Mr. D. J. Enright, of a famous judgment on Victor Hugo appears on the blurb of *Essays on Thomas Mann* by Professor Georg Lukács [6]— somewhat surprisingly, since this eminent Marxist critic is far from sharing Mr. Enright's reservations about "all the discursuses and excursuses" of Thomas Mann's novels, and his own rare strictures are of a very different kind. If Professor Lukács has regrets about Mann's greatness, it is not because Mann was prolix or philosophical, but because Mann's critique of a decadent bourgeois order remained ambiguous; even more ambiguous, I am compelled to add, than Professor Lukács is prepared to admit. His three long essays and three shorter pieces on

[5] Hugo von Hofmannsthal, *Poems and Verse Plays* (London, 1961), lv.

[6] Georg Lukács, *Essays on Thomas Mann,* trans. Stanley Mitchell (London, 1964).

Thomas Mann were written between 1909 and 1955; and they are interesting not only for what they tell us about Thomas Mann, but also for what they tell us about the development of Professor Lukács as a critic and thinker during those years.

Reviewing Mann's second novel, *Royal Highness,* in 1909, Lukács made one statement that points forward to his later commitment and goes far toward explaining it:

> For life means being born into a community and fulfilling its duties. Once these are questioned, once their infallibility is called in doubt, once they have to be romanticized to be found beautiful so that one may live by them, then decadence has set in. And each question isolates the questioner, each romanticization separates him from his romanticized object. As soon as the bond snaps between man (or, better, the community of man, the family) and the cause for which he lives, whatever else unites them disintegrates. Man perishes as soon as he has nothing to live by.

This profession of faith, for that is what it amounts to, is unlikely to strike English readers as revolutionary; yet it holds the key to Georg Lukács' quarrel with a "decadent" individualism and, incidentally, to his concern with the works of Thomas Mann. Again and again he quotes Mann's own description of a certain attitude characteristic of German intellectuals as "power-protected inwardness." Since this inwardness also tended to glorify and romanticize power—as Thomas Mann himself did quite unambiguously before his conversion to democracy during the Weimar Republic—Georg Lukács' position makes sense only in the light of peculiarly German phenomena—the *German* bourgeoisie and *German* imperialism, as manifested in German intellectual and cultural life. If Lukács' early profession of faith strikes English readers as conservative rather than revolutionary, it is important to remember that Germany lacked a tradition of conservative thought. The attitude against which Lukács revolted, and which he defines as follows, were not conservative but reactionary:

> the arrogant rejection of economic solutions to social problems as "shallow," touching only the surface of human existence;

the equally arrogant repudiation of all questions and answers based on reason and the understanding; the *a priori* acceptance of the "irrational" as something higher, more fundamental, beyond reason and understanding; above all, the fetish of the *Volk* with all its (then still unconscious) aggressively chauvinistic implications, which still took the "purely intellectual" form of the natural superiority of the Germanic to both East and West, the "purely intellectual" belief in Germany's mission as world saviour.

This excellent summary occurs in the essay on Mann's *Dr. Faustus;* and its relevance to Mann's preoccupations is patent. To Lukács, Mann was "the greatest bourgeois writer of his time" and the last of "the great critical realists." Lukács can approve and admire Mann's work by seeing it as an "objectively" realistic response to the bourgeois world—for this, by his tenets, was bound to include a critique of bourgeois values —and by dissociating it from those "decadent" and "formalist" deviations from realism that he condemns in other major novelists of this century. One instance is Mann's resort to multiple time in *Dr. Faustus.* Lukács has to distinguish this resort to multiple time for strictly objective ends from the "subjective time" of other modern, post-realist novelists like Joyce or Virginia Woolf. These are socially alienated individualists, whereas Mann represented "all that is best in the German bourgeoisie," yet knew that its time was up, that a new order must take its place.

Lukács' loyalty to Mann is admirable and touching; but a great deal of special pleading is needed to maintain this view of Mann. By selective quotation, never supported by detailed analysis of the structure, style, or import of any work as a whole, he is able to find in *Dr. Faustus* the "fullest intellectual and artistic confirmation" of the decree on music issued in 1948 by the Central Committee of the Communist Party in Russia! In the same way, to prove that Zeitblom, the narrator of the same novel, is not a typical intellectual philistine, he quotes Zeitblom's remark that "Bolshevism to my knowledge has never destroyed any works of art"! The very ineptitude of that remark is typical of the unpolitical, politically ineffectual "good" German that Zeitblom is clearly meant to be.

Lukács has an even harder time with Mann's critical writings, for here his reluctant hero openly aligned himself with "decadent" writers of the modern schools, professed his debt to Nietzsche, Wagner, and Freud—and Freud, to Lukács, belongs with Nietzsche, Spengler, and Heidegger to the "intellectual disasters of the imperialist period"—and, above all, betrayed an ambivalence and inconsistency, which raise very serious doubts about Lukács' attempt to see Mann as a writer whose development was crowned by the "merging of these two centres, that of his creative work with that of his philosophical and political struggles." Once again, Professor Lukács does his utmost not to succumb to such doubts, both by claiming that "Mann, the imaginative writer thinks so much more rightly and healthily than Mann, the idea-spinning essayist"—he reads a refutation of Freud into *The Holy Sinner,* a refutation of abstract painting into *The Black Swan*—and by mildly censuring Mann for being prevented by his "organic growth" from keeping up with "the tempestuous development of history."

Yet Lukács is well aware of some of the basic contradictions in Mann's outlook. What prevents him from dwelling on them is that he is fighting on two fronts, not only against Mann's "aberrations" and deficiencies, but against a rigid dogmatism that would utterly condemn his hero. Many of his insights into Mann's works are pertinent and profound, as when he compares Mann's Joseph to his Felix Krull, the confidence man, or observes that "in the world of the dying bourgeoisie only the confidence man can fulfill himself in pleasure."

Professor Lukács is right, too, about the relative merits of "Mann, the imaginative writer" and "Mann, the idea-spinning essayist," but he needs the latter's support and makes what use he can of the latter's interference in the former's business. His fundamental error, in my view, is that he regards Mann as a "naïve" writer, in Schiller's sense, together with Goethe, Balzac and Tolstoy. Lukács' dislike of psychology, whether Freudian, Nietzschean, or pre-Nietzschean, also prevents him from recognizing the degree to which Thomas Mann rendered not objective reality, but subjective conflicts and ambivalences. (The same refusal to consider psychological factors permits Lukács and other Marxists to treat Fascism and National Socialism as phenomena not essentially different from the democratic and pluralistic forms of capitalism, or even as their inevitable consequence. The gospel truth of Marxism must be upheld in the face of any later development that Marx was unable to foresee. Nor is Lukács perturbed by the circumstance—quite evident in *Dr. Faustus*—that Thomas Mann did not accept this Marxist view of the genesis or nature of National Socialism, but saw it as a radical departure from all the social, moral, and cultural standards of "bourgeois capitalism." [7]

Mann, in fact, was much closer to Flaubert than to Balzac or Tolstoy; of his "demonic" and "good" characters alike he could have said, "Leverkühn, c'est moi!," "Zeitblom, c'est moi!"— and did say so repeatedly, if not in those words. Lukács' defense of Mann's "playfulness" is incomplete without those two basic recognitions: that of all the German novelists Mann was the most sophisticated, the least naïve; and that all Mann's quarrels with Germany—the decadent, bourgeois Germany with its "power-protected inwardness"—are quarrels with himself. Realism was a convention that permitted Mann to render these quarrels without giving himself away; and whenever he did give himself away, in critical essays and autobiographical pieces, what emerged was a man with a bad conscience, incapable of wholehearted commitment to either pole of his unresolved antinomies, the artist as illusionist or confidence man.

If that seems an extreme view, Mann's endless vacillations can be followed in a collection of his writings on a single subject, the music of Wagner, posthumously published under the title *Wagner und unsere Zeit*.[8] There is no need to stress that Mann's preoccupation with Wagner, ever since his youth and up to his last years, is inseparable from his obsession with decadence, with the "demonic," and the destructively irrational power of music. Mann's attitude to Wagner shows no progression or development—such as Lukács would like to see in an ever more democratic Mann—but a perpetual pendulum swing

---

[7] This point is made very succinctly by Werner Milch in *Kleine Schriften zur Literatur- und Geistesgeschichte* (Heidelberg, Darmstadt, 1957), 234–235.

[8] Thomas Mann, *Wagner und unsere Zeit: Aufsätze, Betrachtungen, Briefe* (Frankfurt, 1963).

between attraction and repulsion. Certainly, Mann's statements about Wagner were affected by external events and occasions. The most damning remarks on Wagner occur in his open letter to the editor of *Common Sense,* written during the war, in the midst of Mann's anti-Nazi activities. Yet the basic ambivalence is more evident than ever in the following words:

> Dickens, Thackeray, Tolstoy, Dostoievsky, Balzac, Zola— their works, heaped up with the same urge for moralizing grandeur, constitute Europe's 19th century, constitute the world of literary and social criticism. The German contribution, the form which this greatness took in Germany, has no social element nor desires to have anything to do with it. Society is not musical; indeed, not even capable of creative art. The roots of creativeness go down into the pure humanity of the mythical age, into the timeless, nonhistorical proto-poetry of Nature and the heart. That is what the German spirit desired. That was its instinct, long in advance of any conscious decision.

Mann condemns the political implications of this German instinct, but he neither dissociates his own art from it, nor even acknowledges that this is a crude generalization at best. In order to account for certain features of Wagner's art that do not fit in with the generalization, he suggests that "Jewish blood did its share. Certain qualities of this [i.e., Wagner's] art—its sensuousness and intellectualism—speak in favour of the assumption." Even the democratic Mann of 1940, it seems, is a racialist, attributing certain fixed qualities to the Germans and to the Jews—very much the same qualities, incidentally, attributed to both by the Nazi mystagogues. What is far more significant, though, is that Mann is drawing on a purely imaginative, unrealistic complex of associations also evident in his story written some thirty-five years earlier, "Wälsungenblut," in which two Jewish, or half-Jewish, characters commit incest under the influence of Wagner's Siegmund-Sieglinde music. These pampered twins are characterized by the very "sensuousness and intellectualism" attributed in the letter to Wagner's Jewish blood. After the war Mann feels free to praise Wagner once more; and in 1942 he himself sums up the whole matter by writing to a correspondent: "My way of speaking about Wagner has nothing to do with chronology or development. It is and remains 'ambivalent,' and I can write about him in one way today, in another way tomorrow." The same is true of all Mann's attitudes and opinions. What was constant in him was the tension, the duality; and the delicate noncommitment of the artist whose realism —most of the time—saved him from offering fictitious equivalents of his gross antinomies. Where it did not, Mann's characters are caricatures; like the Artist, Spinell, in another Wagnerian study, "Tristan," or his antagonist, the Bourgeois, in the same story. That is where Professor Lukács' case for Mann the great realist breaks down, and his comparison with Shakespeare becomes absurd.

The noncommitment of Thomas Mann differs in one essential from that of the great realists before him. Thomas Mann was not content to present characters and situations without comment or partiality. Just as he used essays in literary criticism as pretexts for indirect self-comment, so in his novels and, less frequently, in his stories he used fictitious characters as mouthpieces for his own ideas—sometimes, as Werner Milch [9] has shown, in a manner that violates the consistency of the characters to whom such passages are attributed. Thomas Mann's celebrated "irony" consists not in the absence of comment, certainly not in a realistic impartiality, but in a profusion of comment that renders his own ambivalent attitudes. The noncommitment arises not from a delight in the interplay of real persons and real things, or from a reverence for their autonomy, but from Mann's awareness that his characters have no reality other than that lent to them by their author's skill in manipulating them. Despite his keen eye for significant detail, Mann lacked the true realist's capacity to lose himself in "otherness." What he played with was not the diversity of human nature—whether observed or imagined and reembodied in fiction—but with a constant dualism that could be variously rendered *through* fiction. In many cases his characters were not even freely imagined, but pieced together out of the disparate

[9] Werner Milch, *loc. cit.*, 231.

features of real persons living or dead. Gerhart Hauptmann and Arnold Schönberg were only two of many acquaintances who recognized parts of themselves in composite caricatures of this kind; and even members of Mann's immediate family were not exempt from such treatment. Its arbitrariness and deliberation distinguishes Mann from the realists proper. Goethe, whose irony should not be confused with Mann's, would have described his would-be successor as a mannerist.

Thomas Mann's irony has been discussed and analyzed *ad nauseam*—not least by Thomas Mann himself. As Professor Erich Heller observed in *The Ironic German,*[10] Mann's *Dr. Faustus* defeats criticism because it is "its own critique, and that in the most thoroughgoing manner imaginable." The phrase is Friedrich Schlegel's, but it accounts for the strange sensation of *déjà vu* or *déjà entendu* aroused by almost anything that can be said about Thomas Mann: as likely as not Thomas Mann himself has already said it. Like his habits of irony and self-parody, this phenomenon is largely due to a self-consciousness so acute as to make one marvel at Professor Lukács' inclusion of Mann among the "naïve" writers.

Professor Heller made no such claim for Mann. If it once seemed that Professor Heller might become the Pascal—if not the Savonarola—of contemporary criticism, his book on Mann suggests that he is more like Pascal's main antagonist, the "Pyrrhonien" of the *Pensées,* or like Bacon's jesting Pilate, "who would not stay for an answer." It is as difficult to summarize the argument of Professor Heller's book on Mann as to summarize the argument of a Mann novel—and for much the same reason. Like Thomas Mann's Aschenbach and his creator, Professor Heller is much given to "antithetical eloquence"; and like Thomas Mann's novels, Professor Heller's study is "its own critique." His thoroughness in anticipating objections to his mainly favorable assessment of Mann has even led him to resort to dialogue form in his chapter on *The Magic Mountain;* there he not only voices some of the most damning strictures to which Mann has been subject—that "everything he does is

[10] London, 1958.

obvious," for instance, or that he is "without mystery"—but mockingly exposes his own peculiarities as a critic, as when one of the speakers says: "You always mean the age; so much so that I have come to think of you as sighing under the burden of a wicked epoch—Atlas with a chip on his shoulder."

No wonder, then, that the book tends to be confusing. To the complexities of Thomas Mann's quarrel with Thomas Mann Professor Heller adds the complexities of Professor Heller's quarrel with Professor Heller—and with Thomas Mann; there are many passages where the reader has to ask himself who is quarreling with whom. Needless to say, this involvement has its positive side. Thomas Mann will never have a more sympathetic interpreter than Professor Heller, though he has had many more flattering and more painstaking, more disposed to gloss over or explain away the blatant self-contradictions to be found in his work. And if Thomas Mann's mind was representative enough to induce a very great number of readers to participate in what Professor Heller rightly calls his "great confession," so, once again, is Professor Heller's. But here one is brought up against the essential difference of medium, and it is this difference that Professor Heller does little to illuminate. If Thomas Mann had not been a writer of fiction—however "philosophical," however ambitiously intent on dealing with the principal issues of the age—no one would have the slightest interest in his ideas.

"Tonio Kröger," for instance, comes as close to being a mere tract on "art" and "life," "life" and *"Geist,"* or whatever we choose to call Thomas Mann's endlessly reiterated and elaborated antinomy, as any work of fiction that still retains its power to fascinate. What, imaginatively, could be a weaker ending than Tonio's letter to his painter friend—a letter addressed to a character who was never more than a means of extracting Tonio's self-confessions? The feeble ending just fails to break the story's impact because we can still see and hear Tonio's experience in the Danish hotel; not because of the shock of discovering that Tonio is a bourgeois after all. Contrary to what most of his interpreters imply, Thomas Mann's main weakness lies in his thinking, or more precisely in the excessive importance he attributed to his vague antitheses—vague, because he felt their power, but lacked the delicacy needed to confine them to their true "objective correlatives."

An open-minded reader may be struck by the recognition that both "Tonio Kröger" and "Death in Venice" would be just as valid and effective if the respective heroes were not writers or artists at all; that it was only Thomas Mann's preoccupation with his personal problems that caused him to formulate the basic antinomy in terms of art and life, artist and citizen—and to send whole generations of students and critics scurrying along the same track. Tonio could be any social misfit of his class with aesthetic leanings; and—as Mann himself came to stress when he identified aestheticism with barbarism—"artist" and "aesthete" are far from being synonyms. Some of the most extreme aesthetes are wholly uncreative, and many creative artists are curiously indifferent to beauty as such. Aschenbach could have been a professor, a politician, a managing director or any professional man accustomed to a regular routine and to minding his p's and q's. The basic conflict is not between life and art, but between conscious will and unconscious impulse. The "vicious circle," which Professor Heller discovers in comparing the two works, is the vicious circle of Thomas Mann's personal and unresolved antinomies. The bourgeois world to which Tonio is drawn is not "artless"—as Professor Heller calls it and Thomas Mann suggests in his inane remark that "society is not musical"—but a product of art; nor is it life that defeats Aschenbach, but the attraction of death for those whose unconscious impulses have been suppressed beyond hope of release. That is one reason why these stories have a much wider appeal than their "problem" would seem to warrant.

How far Thomas Mann himself was misled by his crude and false categories is only too clear in his writings on politics and literature. His reference to "Brother Hitler," mentioned by Professor Heller, is a case in point. Mann was so obsessed with his equations of art with illness as to have blurred the two most relevant considerations: that Hitler was never an artist, but only a neurotic with an "artistic temperament," and that some of the best artists have been rather healthier and less neurotic than the next man. The antithesis between "life" and *"Geist"*—a com-

monplace of German obscurantist thinking, which would also
readily substitute "soul" for "life," opposing it to intellect and
reason—was the worst offender of all. If Mann knew what he
meant by either word at any one moment, his reader can only
guess. "Life" could stand for the civilized bourgeois content
with his environment, or it could denote nature; "Geist" the intellect, the intelligentsia or intellectual life of the country, plain
intelligence, or the numinously spiritual. There is no need to
give many examples of this weakness, which was noted long
ago by Professor Henry Hatfield: [11]

> Convinced that monism is a "boring" philosophy, he divides
> the universe into a glittering series of polar opposites, of
> which the opposition of spirit to life is the most fundamental;
> the antithesis artist-*Bürger* is only a corollary. When one real-
> izes that for spirit one can substitute art, death, illness, or
> love; for "life" nature, the normal, the material, or the naïve,
> a certain looseness in Mann's mode of thought becomes ob-
> vious enough.

Whatever the causes of this looseness, there can be little dis-
agreement about the effects, which can be such as to invalidate
whole passages of the longer novels, as well as many of the critical and autobiographical works. As late as 1945, in a piece included in the Collection *Altes und Neues,* Thomas Mann perpetrated the antinomy of "Geist" and "democracy." So much
for Lukács' phantom of a progressively more democratic Mann!
Conversely, the early study *Friedrich und die grosse Koalition*
(1914), a work of Mann's antidemocratic and nationalistic
phase, shows how precariously his thought was always balanced
between his seemingly irreconcilable extremes. His glorification
of Frederick the Great and the Prussian military tradition was
far from uncritical: one feels that the slightest change of emphasis would have tilted the balance in favor of those humanitarian values that Mann came to uphold with the same ambivalence. When, in 1926, Mann described Germany as the nation
characterized by the *Idee der Mitte* (the idea of the golden
mean), it must have been difficult to know whether he was

---

[11] In *Thomas Mann* (Norfolk, Connecticut, 1951).

being more than usually ironic or confusing true moderation with a balancing act similar to his own. The self-consciousness of a "representative" writer may have been partly to blame for the playful dignity of his manner, elegantly poised between abysses of excess. Certainly it is a relief to turn from Mann's unmistakably public performances to his introduction to Kafka's *The Castle* (1941), in which he simply jots down a series of notes, as if for his own use; but there are few such moments of relaxation, when Mann forgot his self-imposed "responsibilities" toward the public and what with typical, untranslatable mock-pomposity he called his "bürgerliches Menschentum, das sich im Überklassenmässig-Künstlerischem ironisch bewährt." [12]

Mann's intellectual looseness, like his pomposity, did enter into the imaginative works, though only into that stratum of them that was deliberated and willed. It is easy enough to allow for the element of pure play that characterizes Mann's treatment of ideas; and to take them less literally than Mann did when he translated inner tensions into verbal concepts. We can appreciate a character like Peeperkorn without knowing or caring whether he stands for art or life: Gerhart Hauptmann, on whose personal oddities Mann drew for the character, stood for both, as it happens. We can enjoy the adventures of Felix Krull without knowing or caring that Mann described this novel as "in essence the story of an artist"—simply because Krull is an illusionist, an impostor, and a parodist of the bourgeois world —or that the novel is the most intimate of Mann's self-confessions. It is hard to avoid the conclusion, in fact, that the less we know about Mann's motives and intentions, the better for him and for us.

To accept this conclusion, and it will not be readily or widely accepted, is to invalidate a great deal of the philosophical exegesis that has been lavished on Mann's works; and, as Professor Heller's analysis of "Death in Venice" shows, even an inquiry into Mann's use of allegory, symbolism and the leitmotiv is likely to underline the obviousness or tenuousness, rather than reveal the subtlety, of those devices.

[12] Cf. G. C. Lichtenberg's aphorism: "A man always writes absolutely well when he is writing himself"—where "writing" is used transitively. *Gesammelte Werke*, Vol. I (Frankfurt, 1949), 11.

Professor Heller's book, then, will be valued more for its *obiter dicta* on literature and the age than for anything it tells us about Thomas Mann; and, like Professor Fritz Kaufmann's comprehensive and scholarly treatise on the convergence between artistic vision and truth on the one hand, metaphysical vision and truth on the other, in Thomas Mann,[13] Heller's book succeeds admirably in tracing Mann's intellectual ancestry. Once again it was Mann himself who dropped the crucial hints, not so much by his explicit acknowledgments to Schopenhauer, Nietzsche, or Freud, as by his attribution to Aschenbach of a work comparable to Schiller's treatise on "Naïve and Sentimental Literature" and the information that Aschenbach had achieved "the miracle of ingenuousness regained."

Both these statements point to the central concern of German writers since the eighteenth century with the rift caused by Rousseau's playing off of Nature against civilization. It is Hölderlin's dream of restoring the harmony of Nature by means of Art, and Kleist's dream of heightening consciousness to the point where the ravages of the Fall will be undone and men become undivided once more like gods or puppets. Professor Heller writes of Germany as "the country of unquestioning discipline and the undisciplined ecstasies, of soldiers and mystics, of the desire to possess the world and the urge to withdraw from it into lyrical privacy, of engineering and romantic music, of aggressive energy and metaphysical excess." And he suggests that "perhaps there are, after all, only two themes which are new in modern literature, distinguishing the nineteenth and twentieth centuries from all previous epochs: this kind of love" —that is, "the pessimistic ecstasy of love that is no love, but an erotic entanglement impatient of resolution"—"and the tedium of the frustrated spirit." Boredom and vitalism, in short; an excess of knowledge and the escape from it into blind frenzy.

It is Professor Kaufmann who relates Mann's concern with this alternative to other writers of the eighteen-nineties and after. Professor Heller mentions Hofmannsthal, but only in connection with the crisis recorded in the Chandos *Letter,* going on to say that Mann differed from Hofmannsthal "who

[13] Fritz Kaufmann, *Thomas Mann: The World as Will and Representation* (Boston, 1957).

had to support his literary stamina with an extraneous moral resolution." This is the exact reverse of the truth. It is Mann who remained precariously poised between his sense of the amorality of art and his desire to be on the side of the angels; and it is Hofmannsthal whose moral vision was truly and delicately integrated with his poetic gifts, who possessed the "conservative imagination" that Professor Heller attributes to Thomas Mann. The irony of Mann's later works was his way of maintaining the balance, an uneasy truce or cold war between the conflicting claims of reason and impulse; it was the irony of noncommitment, as Professor Heller himself suggests when one of the speakers in his "Conversation on the Magic Mountain" remarks that "beliefs are not held in the ironic sphere."

Thomas Mann, then, did not accomplish "the miracle of ingenuousness regained," any more than his Aschenbach did. It takes a mind at once as supple and as intrepid as Robert Musil's to break the sound barrier of skepticism. Thomas Mann had other virtues: his work, ultimately, will not be judged by its ideas, but by the more conventional criteria of realistic and psychological fiction. Above all, Mann was a magnificent comedian, even in the most humble and histrionic sense of the word; a natural mimic and parodist, fundamentally in earnest like all the best comic writers and clowns, but a specialist in mock solemnities and mock pomposities. This, incidentally, explains his hold over the educated German reading public, whose philosophical pretensions his works both flattered and very cunningly "took off." A German novelist at once ambitious, "representative," and best-selling was bound to be philosophical; but no one who fails to see the tongue in Thomas Mann's cheek can even begin to appreciate his curious and unique talents.

Because of his comic gifts, above all, combined with enough realism to protect him from utter solipsism, Thomas Mann stands out from the lone prophets of his generation. His central concern, as I have suggested, was the same as theirs, but he refrained from offering a visionary panacea or synthesis as they did. The concern itself was familiar to his German readers. In its less extreme manifestations, and stripped of its abstract terminology, it was also universally human. Thomas Mann succeeded in being less parochial than most of his German predecessors, but at the cost of being less prophetic. As Werner Milch was perceptive enough to remark at the time of its appearance, *Dr. Faustus* is a historical novel; it does not point forward into the future.

Pace Lukács, Mann's long and prolific career was distinguished by an extraordinary lack of development, both as an artist and as a thinker. His appropriation of "advanced" ideas or Joycean techniques—as in *The Holy Sinner*—does not conceal his basic incapacity to explore new ground. With the exception of Chekhov, all the subjects of his posthumously collected *Last Essays* had preoccupied him since his youth. Schiller had been the hero of his short story "A Weary Hour," written exactly half a century before the lecture of 1955. Goethe had been the hero of a whole novel, as well as the subject of several earlier essays. Nietzsche had been one of the first and most vital influences on Mann's thought, as well as contributing to the character of Leverkühn in *Dr. Faustus*. A comparison of the early Schiller story with the late essay, delivered as a lecture on the occasion of the one hundred and fiftieth anniversary of the poet's death, shows more clearly still just how constant was Mann's preoccupation not only with these particular writers, but with certain aspects of their personalities and situations which corresponded to his own constant, but variously elaborated, conflict between impulse and conscious will. Not surprisingly, in this very last work of Mann's we read once more about "a second naïveté and unconsciousness. The miracle of ingenuousness regained."

Indeed, the Schiller lecture opens like a short story, with Schiller's funeral; characteristically, it goes on to recapitulate the main and familiar facts of Schiller's life and works. In this piece one is conscious of the public occasion; in his endeavors to be equal to it Mann sheds much of his private skepticism and irony, falling into a sort of lay preacher's rhetoric that merely points to a more radical incongruity in himself. Schiller may have failed at times to practice what he preached; Mann sometimes felt obliged to preach what he could not believe.

The three shorter pieces, happily, are free from this public constraint. Even in the Schiller essay Mann had to exorcise the imps of skepticism and irony by perpetually reminding himself that Goethe had been able to love and admire the man who was his dialectical opposite. In the "Fantasy on Goethe" the self-identification always indispensable to Mann came more easily to him. True, Mann resembled Schiller in creating out of an effort of will and intellect; but for that very reason he admired Goethe's "organic" and effortless growth, as Schiller did, and Goethe was proof against the sharpest pinpricks of Mann's psychological debunking. This allowed him to write about Goethe —and, of course, about himself:

> . . . there was a kind of imperial faithlessness in him, so that it would amuse him to abandon his followers, to confound the partisans of every principle by carrying it to the ultimate— and its opposite as well. He exercised a kind of universal dominion in the form of irony and serene betrayal of mutually exclusive points of view, one to the other. There was in this a profound nihilism; there was also art's—and nature's— objectivistic refusal to analyse and evaluate. There was an ambiguous impishness, an element of equivocation, negation, and all-embracing doubt which led him to make self-contradictory pronouncements.

These words, in fact, are much more true of Mann than of Goethe, who was deeply, instinctively certain about the things that mattered to him.

"Nietzsche's Philosophy in the Light of Recent History" is equally honest and uninhibited. Thomas Mann saw Nietzsche as an ascetic intellectual at war with himself, in love with "life" and with all that he was not. He shows to how great an extent Nietzsche's revolt against reason and morality was conditioned both by his illness and by historical causes, comparing him to a more gentle aesthete and immoralist, Oscar Wilde. He suggests that Nietzsche did not create fascism, "but that fascism created him. That is to say, this nonpolitical and at bottom innocent intellectual was so delicate a recording instrument that he sensed the rise of imperialism and the fascist era of the Occident, in which we are now living and will be living for a long time, in spite of the military victory over fascism." Nietzsche remains important not only as a tragic figure, a great writer, and a great psychologist, but as a prophet of our own age; for one thing, it was Nietzsche who revealed "a close relationship which we have every reason to ponder: that of aestheticism and barbarism."

In the Chekhov essay, Thomas Mann concentrates on a question that he also touched upon in the Goethe and Schiller essays: it is the question of an author's belief in the value of his work to the community. Mann claims that in his last, unfinished tragedy *Demetrius* Schiller "delineated the psychology of a state of ghastly mental stress," and implies that this was a projection of Schiller's own loss of "faith in himself, in his genuineness and sincerity and in his humanitarian mission." The Chekhov essay investigates a case still closer to Mann, a writer in whom such doubts were intrinsic and endemic. Mann speaks of the profound effect upon him of these words of Chekhov: "Am I not fooling the reader, since I cannot answer the most important questions?" Mann, too, could not answer them. Unlike Chekhov, he would not leave them alone, but juggled with them incessantly; yet in this one late essay at least he squarely faced the "profound nihilism" that underlay the performance. Performance is the word; Mann also comments on another affinity with Chekhov, which he describes as "the primitive origin of all art, the inclination to ape, the jester's desire and talent to entertain." It is this urge, and a vast capacity for hard work, that sustained Mann despite all his doubts. "If the truth about life is by nature ironical, then must not art itself be by nature nihilistic? And yet art is so industrious!"

After such reflections, once again more relevant to Mann than to his subject, one can accept his concluding but inconclusive gesture without the discomfort aroused by his call to "beauty, truth and goodness, moral excellence, inner freedom, art, love, peace, and man's saving reverence for himself" at the end of the Schiller essay. This is altogether too much in a tribute not without incidental acerbities and mischievous descents to the ridiculous. The conclusion of "Chekhov" is more modest, more genuine, and more dignified:

It comes to this: One "entertains a forlorn world by telling stories without ever being able to offer it the trace of a saving truth." To poor Katya's question: "What am I to do?" one can but answer: "Upon my honour and conscience, I don't know."

Thomas Mann's works are not only "fragments of a great confession," but variations on a single theme. The public attitudes adopted at different times do not show any true progression. The terms of the dialectic remained constant; and one does not feel moved to argue in terms that have become irrelevant because they have been outgrown. Like a whole succession of Mann characters, the central character of *Dr. Faustus*—the late novel that was designed to be nothing less than "the novel of my era," "big in every sense"—longs for "the miracle of ingenuousness regained"; and most of the flaws in this intricate work have to do with Mann's incapacity to subordinate his intellectual design to the demands of specific characters, specific situations. His constant theme was more important to him than the primary exigencies of fiction. Among the many struggles, self-doubts, and self-criticisms recorded in his *Genesis of a Novel,* Mann made this revealing comment on his failure to give Leverkühn a convincing physical presence: "To depict Adrian's outer appearance was instantly to threaten him with spiritual downfall, to undermine his symbolic dignity, to diminish and render banal his representativeness." No realist could have written those words. Even Hugo von Hofmannsthal, who derived from Symbolist practice, insisted that the depth must be concealed in the surface, that the themes and problems of an imaginative work must be merged in character and situation.

The late long story *Die Betrogene* (*The Black Swan*) is another case in point. Thematically, once again, the story ironizes "the miracle of ingenuousness regained." Like "Tristan," "Tonio Kröger," or "Death in Venice," it is a psychological study in a modern setting; and like these early works, it adds symbolic overtones to a pathological inquiry. No doubt we are expected to read a larger allegory into the love of the middle-aged German widow for a young American, as into the state of emotional and even physical rejuvenation, which is finally shown to be due to an advanced stage of cancer of the womb; and the story could also be read as yet another chapter of disguised autobiography bearing on Thomas Mann's disappointed

American hopes. Whatever the intended overtones, Mann's treatment of the theme offends against the most elementary laws of realistic fiction, namely that its characters and situations must arouse the reader's concern, whether by appealing to his imagination, his sympathy, or his sense of humor. Mann's own ambivalent attitude to his subject, manifested as irony in his treatment of the characters, as self-parody in his style, makes it quite impossible for the reader to take the story seriously, let alone tragically. If the theme were less unpleasant and if the reader were spared the clinically detached account of Frau von Tümmler's illness and death, the exercise might have passed as a *jeu d'esprit*. As it is, the comic effect of her sentimental delusion is neutralized, and one is left with a sensation of irritated indifference or of cold disgust. One cannot believe in her, since she talks like a character in Thomas Mann; and one cannot pity her, since one cannot believe in her. Long before the end of the story one has ceased to care what happens to this lady, to her daughter (an artist, of course, and an unhappy spinster afflicted with a limp), or to Ken Keaton, the American in search of Europe, whose idiosyncracies are just a little too pronounced to make him anything but an agent in the experiment. The irony of this story remains a quality of Mann's own mind; and so does the "deeper" design, since the surface does not engage us.

Yet, fittingly enough, Thomas Mann concluded his imaginative work with a novel that is frankly and exuberantly comic— exuberantly, if that word can be applied to anything written by Mann, because the novel is frank about the basic amoralism that so troubled the conscience of the representative and exemplary writer, the *praeceptor Germaniae*. It was also fitting that both the inception and the setting of *Felix Krull* should go back to the time before World War I; for, in spite of his valiant refusal to withdraw into a hermetic inwardness, Thomas Mann never ceased to belong to the secure and individualistic Europe of that time. Mann's concern with large issues, historical trends, and conflicting philosophical systems had often obscured the essentially comic nature of his art, as well as its essential subjectivity. That is why it was so easy to mistake his fiction for something other than entertainment. Few writers of the interwar and subsequent periods provided entertainments on such a

scale. *Felix Krull,* however, is an exception, for it gives pleasure even on the most superficial level, that of an exciting and
boisterous adventure story.

Felix Krull himself is one of the most endearing and convincing of Mann's comic creations, for the simple reason that
he exists in his own right, not as the embodiment of some satirical or symbolic intention. The same had been true of the characters in the story "Unordnung und frühes Leid" ("Disorder
and Early Sorrow"), which stands out among Mann's shorter
works of fiction by virtue of a realism based not on a skeleton
of ideas but on direct experience and observation of human behavior. That story, too, can be read as autobiography, but it
does not call for such a reading because Mann's intentions are
not superimposed on the autonomous lives of his characters.
Described as a confidence man, Felix Krull could be even more
aptly characterized as an illusionist. It is in his capacity for
creating illusions that young Krull resembles Mann, the "old
magician"—the title of "old pretender," unfortunately, has already been claimed for another novelist; and no one can fail to
notice that there is an exceptional degree of understanding,
sympathy, and complicity between the author and his criminal
hero. Thomas Mann himself said about his last novel that it
was designed to "make people laugh—to make them laugh con-
structively if possible, that is to seduce them into amused self-
recognition." Felix Krull's memoirs are also a highly successful
attempt at self-recognition on the author's part; but for once it
does not matter. Here the *praeceptor Germaniae* let himself go
and allowed himself to be "seduced" into unpretentious farce.
No doubt the moralist would have taken over if Mann had lived
to finish the book, and even Krull would have been denied the
privilege of "ingenuousness regained," but his aptitude for
self-deception and self-delusion brings him as close to it as any
character in Thomas Mann could ever be. The story of Krull's
fall would have been a less appropriate conclusion to Mann's
work.

IX

1912

My introductory remarks under this heading will not be confined to the single year 1912. I have chosen the heading for the sake of brevity; and because 1912 was indeed a kind of *annus mirabilis* in the history of modern German poetry, a year of the most prolific and varied activity and the turning-point which, for better or for worse, established a new kind of poetry and a new conception of what poetry is. This revolution, as far as Germany is concerned, is associated with the movement known as Expressionism; but although the word itself is rarely used in connection with the other principal literatures of Europe, the formal innovations of the German Expressionists have many close parallels to the literatures of England, France, Italy, Spain, Russia and, of course, America.

Toward the end of the first decade of this century a number of young men in various European countries grew aware that Naturalism and Symbolism, the two movements which had been dominating "advanced" literature, no longer met the demands of the age. Marinetti's *Futurist Manifesto,* published in Paris early in 1909, proclaimed that "a roaring motor-car is more beautiful than the Victory of Samothrace." In Germany as elsewhere, this glorification of the "modern" for its own sake and the vague desire for some kind of extreme innovation preceded the positive achievements of the new generation. The German periodicals *Die Aktion* and *Der Sturm* were founded in 1910; and in 1911 a German translation of Marinetti's manifesto appeared in *Der Sturm*. Literary Expressionism began in the same year, with the publication, in *Die Aktion,* of the poem "Weltende" by Jakob van Hoddis, followed soon after by Alfred Lichtenstein's "Dämmerung." At about the same time Guillaume Apollinaire took up some of the main points of the *Futurist Manifesto* and, in June, 1913, published his *L'Antitradition futuriste*. The first Futurist Exhibition was held in Paris in 1912; and a similar exhibition took place a year later in London, where Marinetti himself lectured on Futurism.

In 1913 also, the English *Imagist Manifesto* was published, soon to be followed by Wyndham Lewis' Vorticist movement, whose program and principles he formulated in the first number of *Blast*. Even in the second number of *Blast,* which appeared after the outbreak of war, Wyndham Lewis acknowledged the debt owed by all the modernist movements to Germany.[1] But it is the *Imagist Manifesto* that chiefly concerns me at this point; not because of its decisive influence on the development of poetry in England and America, but because of its clear and concise formulation of a new aesthetic doctrine. I shall therefore quote the six clauses of its program for poetry:

1) To use the language of common speech, but to employ always the exact word, not merely the decorative word.

2) To create new rhythms—as the expression of new moods.

3) To allow absolute freedom in the choice of subject.

4) To present an image. We are not a school of painters, but we believe that poets should render particulars exactly and not deal with vague generalities.

5) To produce poetry that is hard and clear, never blurred and indefinite.

[1] *Blast II* (London, 1915), 5.

6) Finally, most of us believe that concentration is the very essence of poetry.[2]

These formulations apply to much of the best poetry written by the German Expressionists also; but whereas the English and American authors of this manifesto emphasized the formal and stylistic aspects of the revolution in poetry, the German Expressionist manifestos were all too apt to deal only in vague slogans about a "new humanity," a "new community," and a "new intensity." I should therefore like to quote another relevant definition, by Ezra Pound, of the poetic image. "An image," he wrote in *Blast*, "is that which presents an intellectual and emotional complex in an instant of time." [3] It is their relative failure to formulate the aesthetic of their art that makes it so easy to assume that the German Expressionists constituted a movement essentially different from the modernist movements in other literatures. Yet this very unawareness of what they were about aesthetically is interesting enough; and it must be said that, with few exceptions, such as that of T. E. Hulme, their English and American contemporaries tended to be equally unaware of the philosophical implications of the new aesthetic.

But the word movement itself is misleading; for what happened in 1912 affected poets who had no connection with any movement whatever; and poets who had been associated with movements or schools founded long before that time. In 1912 Rilke began, but was unable to complete, his *Duino Elegies;* and, in the next few years, wrote a number of short poems that not only tell us why he was unable to finish the *Elegies,* but show an astonishing change in his style—and in his use of imagery. I cannot deal here with the crisis that Rilke underwent at this time; it has been dealt with at length elsewhere.[4] It was a crisis comparable to that which Hofmannsthal had recorded as

---

[2] In his zealous advocacy of this last clause, Ezra Pound went so far as to imply that the German word "dichten" is related to the adjective "dicht" (dense), and that to write poetry, therefore, is to condense. *ABC of Reading* (1951), 36.

[3] *Blast I* (London, 1914), 154.

[4] In Dieter Bassermann, *Der Späte Rilke* (Munich, 1947).

early as 1902 in his *Letter* of Lord Chandos;[5] and this crisis caused Hofmannsthal to give up lyrical poetry. Donald Davie has already made the connection between the crisis of Lord Chandos and the development of modern poetry, between the "loss of faith in conceptual thought" and the abandonment of logical syntax in poetry, in favor of the dislocated image.[6] He has also related this process to the thought of T. E. Hulme and Bergson, among others; I should like to add the name of Nietzsche, whose shattering effect on almost all the German poets writing in 1912 can hardly be exaggerated. Because he was threatened with a "loss of faith in conceptual thought," Hofmannsthal turned to other media that do not demand the rendering of immediate experience; and refused to contribute to the development of modernist poetry. Rilke, on the other hand, emerged from his crisis with a new philosophy and a new style, a style close to that of the Expressionists and the Imagists. It is no accident that his new philosophy was a kind of existentialism. There is an intimate connection between the existentialist's refusal to accept any a priori explanation of life and the imagistic poet's refusal to evaluate the phenomena that he renders.

A single short extract from one of Rilke's "crisis" poems will have to suffice; it is from the poem "Wendung" of 1914 and deals with the crisis itself, the "turning-point" of the title.

> Tiere traten getrost
> in den offenen Blick, weidende,
> und die gefangenen Löwen
> starrten hinein wie in unbegreifliche Freiheit;
> Vögel durchflogen ihn grad,
> den gemütigen. Blumen
> wiederschauten in ihn,
> gross wie in Kinder.[7]

[5] Hofmannsthal, *Prosa II* (Frankfurt, 1951), 7–22. English version in Hugo von Hofmannsthal, *Selected Prose*, trans. Mary Hottinger and Tania and James Stern (London, 1952), 129–141.

[6] In *Articulate Energy* (London, 1955), 1–5 and *passim*.

[7] Rainer Maria Rilke, *Gedichte 1906 bis 1926,* ed. Ernst Zinn (Wiesbaden, 1953), 116–117.

Animals trustingly stepped
into his open glance, grazing ones,
even the captive lions
stared into it, as at incomprehensible freedom;
birds flew through it unswerving,
it that could feel them; and flowers
met and returned his gaze,
great as in children.

This passage would be wholly imagistic if Rilke had not been concerned to stress the relation between subject and object, the poet's creative eye and the phenomena that enter it so as to be granted their proper significance. He was compelled to stress this relation here, since its disturbance was the subject of his poem. Rilke had not yet completed the philosophical conversion that enabled him to identify subjective and objective processes; but in many of his later poems, especially in the finished *Duino Elegies,* he did, in fact, often suppress the logical link provided by "like" and "as," thus completing the transition to a pure imagism.[8] The metaphor or simile that "illustrates" or "decorates" a statement gives place to the self-sufficient image. Rilke's "Wendung" also satisfies the second demand of the *Imagist Manifesto,* to create new rhythms—as the expression of new moods—with one reservation: his new rhythms show the unmistakable influence of Hölderlin's elegies and hymns.

The powerful influence of Hölderlin's later poetry on the new style coincided with its virtual rediscovery at this period and the first comprehensive edition of his works. The man responsible for both, and for a complete revaluation of Hölderlin's work, was Norbert von Hellingrath, a friend of both Stefan George and Rilke. Not only did Rilke read the volumes of Hellingrath's edition as they appeared, but he went so far as to beg Hellingrath to send him a copy of a volume that he had failed to receive. In doing so, he told Hellingrath that Hölderlin's "influence on me is great and generous, as only that of the richest

[8] The Imagists themselves did not eradicate similes in favor of pure images. The moon, in T. E. Hulme's "Autumn" is "like a red-faced farmer"; and much early Imagist poetry has a naturalistic or realistic component—"objectivist" rather than expressionist.

and inwardly most powerful can be." [9] In the same year, 1914, he wrote his poem in praise of Hölderlin.[10]

At some time between 1799 and December 1803, when he prepared it for publication, Hölderlin wrote a short poem whose imagistic concentration has rarely been equaled, even by deliberate modernists. It is the poem "Hälfte des Lebens" (The Middle of Life):

> Mit gelben Birnen hänget
> Und voll mit wilden Rosen
> Das Land in den See,
> Ihr holden Schwäne,
> Und trunken von Küssen
> Tunkt ihr das Haupt
> Ins heilignüchterne Wasser.
>
> Weh mir, wo nehm' ich, wenn
> Es Winter ist, die Blumen, und wo
> Den Sonnenschein
> Und Schatten der Erde?
> Die Mauern stehn
> Sprachlos und kalt, im Winde
> Klirren die Fahnen.

> With yellow pears the land
> And full of wild roses,
> Hangs down into the lake,
> You lovely swans,
> And drunk with kisses
> You dip your heads
> Into the hallowed, the sober water.
>
> But oh, where shall I find
> When winter comes, the flowers, and where
> The sunshine
> And shade of the earth?
> The walls loom

---

[9] Letter to Hellingrath, July 24, 1914. *Briefe* 1907–1914 (Leipzig, 1933), 372.

[10] *An Hölderlin. Gedichte* 1906–1926 (ed. cit.), 247. English version in *Modern German Poetry 1910–1960,* eds. Michael Hamburger and Christopher Middleton (New York and London, 1962), 29–31.

Speechless and cold, in the wind
Weathercocks clatter.

Except for the adjective "heilignüchtern"—a contraction and
reconciliation of opposites that can only be fully understood
in the light of Hölderlin's conception of "holy pathos" and
"holy drunkenness," as contrasted with the sobriety proper
to modern Germans—this poem is written in the language of
common speech. It creates new rhythms—as the expression of
a mood so new as to be terrifying, had it been rendered without
the beautiful logic that redeems it from mere literalness. It presents an image—or rather two contrasted complexes of images
—in an instant of time that could hardly be more brief. What is
more, it subordinates syntax to imagery and rhythm—another
characteristic of the best Imagist poems not mentioned in the
original Manifesto. The syntax of the opening sentence is a
purely poetic one. The verb "hänget," which should stand at
the end of the third line, is transposed to the first, because the
images of the opening lines are dominated by their relation to
the water into which they hang. The invocation to the swans of
the fourth line has no syntactical connection with the sentence
in which it stands; and it is linked to the symbolic motion of
the next three lines by a use of the conjunction that runs
counter to normal usage. Throughout the poem, alliteration and
assonance support the visual imagery, by making connections
or contrasts. In the first strophe, it is the happy relation between sensuous liquids and spiritual aspirates that predominates; in the second, a war between harsh fricatives and sibi-
lants, ending in the bleak "a" sounds and violent gutturals of
the last three lines.

The dynamic syntax that became typical of the Expressionists was introduced into German poetry as early as the
seventeen-seventies—by Goethe's "Wanderers Sturmlied" and
"Harzreise im Winter." The purest examples of it anywhere occur
in the last two fragmentary versions of Hölderlin's *Patmos,*
written in 1803. Of the following passage, taken from the pen-
ultimate version of *Patmos,*[11] Mr. Edwin Muir has already re-

[11] *Works* (G.S.A.) II (i), 181–182.

marked: "If one did not know who wrote them one would say that these lines were taken from the later poetry of Rilke . . . But the pressure of imagination behind the lines is more solid than Rilke's and the expression more inevitable and less ingenious."

Johannes. Christus. Diesen möcht'
Ich singen, gleich dem Herkules, oder
Der Insel, welche vestgehalten und gerettet, erfrischend
Die benachbarte mit kühlen Meereswassern aus der Wüste
Der Fluth, der weiten, Peleus. Das geht aber
Nicht. Anders ists ein Schiksaal. Wundervoller.
Reicher, zu singen. Unabsehlich
Seit jenem die Fabel. Und jezt
Möcht'ich die Fahrt der Edelleute nach
Jerusalem, und das Leiden irrend in Canossa,
Und den Heinrich singen. Dass aber
Der Muth nicht selber mich aussezze. Begreiffen müssen
Diss wir zuvor. Wie Morgenluft sind nemlich die Nahmen
Seit Christus. Werden Träume. Fallen, wie Irrtum
Auf das Herz und tödtend, wenn nicht einer
Erwäget, was sie sind und begreift.

John. Christ. This latter now I wish
To sing, like Hercules or the island which
Was held and saved, refreshing
The neighbouring one with cool sea waters drawn
From ocean's desert, the vast, Peleus. But that's
Impossible. A fate is different. More marvellous.
More rich to sing. Immeasurable
The fable ever since. And now
I wish to sing the journey of the nobles to
Jerusalem, and anguish wandering at Canossa,
And Heinrich himself. If only
My very courage does not expose me. This first we
Must understand. For like morning air are the names
Since Christ.
Become dreams. Fall on the heart
Like error, and killing, if one does not
Consider well what they are and understand.

The disjointed syntax here is that of a visionary poet no longer conscious of anything but his vision; it is the syntax not of argument, but of thought and feeling in their pre-articulate purity. Yet we need only respond to this passage imaginatively to recognize its peculiar logic. The passage is "difficult" only as long as we try to translate it into the conventional logic of prose argument, which lacks the speed and agility required to follow its daring juxtapositions of thought and imagery. But the syntax of vision is the prerogative of visionary poets; and visionary poets are rare. It is unfortunate, perhaps, that Hölderlin's daring use of syntax and imagery should strike us as so typically "modern." When this freedom itself becomes the dominant convention, as in the later phases of Expressionism, it is bound to be abused by minor poets who would have done better to accept the prosaic limitations of honest minor verse.

The poetic revolution of 1912 was not without precedent in German literature; apart from Goethe and Hölderlin—poets remote from it in time—it was strongly supported by a whole generation of experimental poets older than the first Expressionists themselves. Rilke's new style had little influence on the movement, since he published very few poems during his critical years. Stefan George kept even more aloof; but even his *Stern des Bundes,* written at this time and first published in a limited edition in 1913, responded to the stirring of the new *Zeitgeist,* if only by the cryptic warnings against it contained in poems much more didactic than George's earlier work. Two of the outstanding early Expressionists—Georg Heym and Ernst Stadler—were at one time influenced by George. Three other poets of Rilke's generation were close enough to the movement to be included in several anthologies and miscellanies of Expressionist poetry: Alfred Mombert, who was writing his mythological poem *Äon vor Syrakus;* Else Lasker-Schüler, whose *Hebräische Balladen* were published in 1913; and Theodor Däubler, who was writing *Der Sternhelle Weg.* Both Däubler and Else Lasker-Schüler were among the most enthusiastic apologists and propagators of Expressionism.

To these must be added the Futurist poet August Stramm (1874–1915), whose experiments in diction, syntax, and meter were much more extreme than those of the younger generation, the Expressionists proper. What is most striking about his poems is their complete break with the logic of prose and the total absence in them of those descriptive elements that both Symbolists and Naturalists had found indispensable. I shall quote one of his more conventional pieces, "Schwermut" (Melancholy):

Schreiten Streben	Striding striving
Leben sehnt	living longs
Schauen stehen	shuddering standing
Blicke suchen	glances look for
Sterben wächst	dying grows
das Kommen	the coming
Schreit!	Screams!
Tief	Deeply
stummen	we
wir.	dumb.

These lines contain no visual images at all, no adjectives and only a single adverb. (The word "stummen" in the last line is used neologistically as a verb: "to dumb.") The poem renders nothing but an inward state; but whereas the Expressionist and Imagist poets rendered inward states by projecting them into external scenes, here there is no reference to any recognizable object, person, or symbol.

Stramm reversed the process; he suppressed outward reality so that his poem would express nothing but the dynamism of feeling, an inward gesture. His words are an abstract pattern that corresponds to his inward state; and the pattern is a dynamic one. Hence the importance of verbs and participles in these lines and Stramm's neologistic use of an adjective as a verb. In other poems he invented onomatopoeic and punlike sounds to express emotions that cannot be rendered by existing words.

In drama and prose fiction a similar revolution was taking place. Oskar Kokoschka's little play, *Mörder Hoffnung der Frauen* (*Murder the Women's Hope*), which broke with all the Naturalist and pre-Naturalist conventions, was written as early as 1907, and followed in 1911 by Kokoschka's *Der Brennende*

Dornbusch (*The Burning Bush*). At the same period Carl Stern-
heim was writing his proto-Expressionist social comedies, soon
to be followed by stories in a new, clipped and expressive
prose. R. J. Sorge's tragedy *Der Bettler* (*The Beggar*), the
model for a whole succession of Expressionist plays, appeared
in 1912. In the same year Carl Einstein published his experimental novel *Bebuquin,* Kafka began work on his novel *Amer-
ika* and wrote two of his finest shorter works, *Das Urteil* (*The
Sentence*) and *Die Verwandlung* (*The Metamorphosis*). Robert
Musil's two long stories in the book *Vereinigungen,* which appeared in 1911, were close to Expressionism in style. His novel
Törless had been published in 1906. Together with the three
extant novels of Robert Walser, published between 1907 and
1909, Musil's novel prepared the way for prose works no less
experimental and exploratory than the new poetry. Georg
Heym, Alfred Lichtenstein, and Gottfried Benn wrote prose as
new and individual as their verse, and Georg Trakl's prose
poems have the same visionary intensity that distinguishes his
later poetry. The contribution to imaginative writing of visual
artists like Oskar Kokoschka, Ernst Barlach, Paul Klee, Jean
Arp, Alfred Kubin, and Kurt Schwitters sprang from the same
impatience with academic distinctions between the established
genres and media of art.

Jakob van Hoddis and Alfred Lichtenstein, the authors of
the first Expressionist poems to be hailed as such, were conventional in comparison with Stramm. "Weltende," by Hoddis, was
the first to appear; and Lichtenstein admitted having used it as
a model, though he rightly claimed to have improved on it.[12]
Both poems are rhymed and in regular stanza form. What was
new about them was that they consisted of nothing more than
an arbitrary concatenation of images derived from contemporary life; they presented a picture, but not a realistic one, for
the objects described were not such as can be found together in
the same place and at the same time. They were a kind of *collage;* but *collage* in poetry is a far less drastic device than *collage* in the graphic arts, since poetry has always been free to assemble its imagery without regard to the unity of space and

[12] Introductory note to his posthumous *Gedichte und Geschichten,*
Vol. I (Munich, 1919), 4.

time. Hoddis could not resist giving the show away in the title of his poem—"End of the World"—an exaggeration all the more blatant because so inappropriate to the ironic understatement of the poem itself. (It says that "most people have a cold," relating this observation to others of a more serious kind —for instance, that "the railway trains are falling off the bridges.") Much of the irony is too crude to be effective as satire; but the poem does express a mood that was soon to become endemic.

In Lichtenstein's poem, on the other hand, the images are allowed to speak for themselves. His title—"Twilight"—is ambiguous, though one assumes that his twilight is dusk.

> Ein dicker Junge spielt mit einem Teich.
> Der Wind hat sich in einem Baum verfangen.
> Der Himmel sieht verbummelt aus und bleich,
> Als wäre ihm die Schminke ausgegangen.
>
> Auf lange Krücken schief herabgebückt
> Und schwatzend kriechen auf dem Feld zwei Lahme.
> Ein blonder Dichter wird vielleicht verrückt.
> Ein Pferdchen stolpert über eine Dame.
>
> An einem Fenster klebt ein fetter Mann.
> Ein Jüngling will ein weiches Weib besuchen.
> Ein grauer Clown zieht sich die Stiefel an.
> Ein Kinderwagen schreit und Hunde fluchen.
>
> A flabby boy is playing with a pond.
> The wind has got entangled in a tree.
> The sky looks like the morning after, drained
> And pale as though its make-up had run out.
>
> Athwart long crutches, bowed and chattering
> Across the field a pair of lame men creeps.
> A fair-haired poet may be going mad.
> Over a lady a small horse trips up.
>
> A man's fat face sticks to a window-pane.
> A youngster wants to visit a soft woman.
> A greyish clown is putting on his boots.
> A pram begins to yell and dogs to curse.

If Lichtenstein's dusk (or dawn) is a cosmic one, he neither says nor implies that it is. He makes no attempt to explain or connect the presence in his poem of the fat boy playing with a pond, the two lame men creeping over a field, the clown putting on his boots, the screaming pram or the cursing dogs. His poem is "expressionistic" because its real purpose is to communicate the poet's own sense of the absurd and the ridiculous; yet, by saying that "the sky looks like the morning after," it relates all the disparate images of modern life to a general sense of vanity, as T. S. Eliot was to do with more subtle skill in *The Waste Land*. Lichtenstein's poem is successful not because it expresses a new mood, but because that mood has found its proper "objective correlative"; for all its humor, it is much more disturbing than Hoddis' prognosis of disaster.

Into some of his other poems Lichtenstein introduced a *persona*, Kuno Kohn, as T. S. Eliot was to introduce Prufrock, Burbank, and Bleistein into his early poems. Like Eliot also, Lichtenstein made a point of understatement and of the qualifying "If and Perhaps and But." "A fair-haired poet may be going mad," he says in "Dämmerung." Lichtenstein's irony was a considerable advance on that of earlier poets; though not free from the self-mockery made familiar by Heine and, later, by Corbière and Laforgue, he used the very same ironic effects to mock a whole civilization, without recourse to direct or didactic statement.

The earliest variety of Expressionism, then, was close to caricature, but a kind of caricature that asserted a new freedom of association. The poems of Lichtenstein and Hoddis are distinguished by an irony that has the dual purpose of satirizing contemporary civilization and of expressing a *malaise,* a premonition of doom, which was one of the common premises of all the early Expressionists. That is why the titles of these two early poems were taken up by those who directed the later, more noisy but less significant, activities of the movement. Lichtenstein's "Dämmerung" reappeared in the title of a famous anthology-cum-manifesto of 1920, *Menschheitsdämmerung,* with the difference that his discreet and ambiguous twilight had now become "the dawn of a new humanity." Hoddis' "Weltende" initiated that abuse of the cosmic and chiliastic that led to the gradual inflation of the verbal currency of Expressionism. Soon it ceased to matter greatly whether a poet predicted the end of the world or a new humanity; both became the stock-in-trade of every poetaster.[13]

But the movement, as I have said, is only of incidental relevance here. One of the very best of the early Expressionist poets, Georg Heym, died in a skating accident in January, 1912, when the movement had scarcely begun. Though he died at the age of twenty-four, he left a large number of faultless poems and some interesting experimental prose. Lichtenstein, whose verse and prose are slighter than Heym's but excellent in their way, died in battle soon after the outbreak of war, at the age of twenty-five. By the end of 1914, Ernst Stadler and Georg Trakl were also dead; and August Stramm fell on the Eastern front in the following year. The premature death of all these gifted poets would seem to be one obvious reason why the later developments of Expressionism did not fulfill the promise of 1912. But it is hardly possible to imagine Heym, Trakl, Lichtenstein, or even Stadler as middle-aged men of letters. Expressionism, like the eighteenth-century *Sturm und Drang,* was essentially the product of a crisis; and any poet who survived this crisis was bound to modify his earlier practice or to give up writing poetry.

Georg Heym combined the fastidious elegance of Stefan George with a new range of mood and subject matter; and with that dynamic use of imagery and syntax which is the one stylistic trend common to all the early Expressionists.[14] Many of his poems recall the preoccupations of Baudelaire, rather than those of the Symbolists from whom George largely derived; they are explorations of the modern city, which Heym sees both realistically and apocalyptically, as the scene of material squalor and as the demesne of frightful daemons. Three years

[13] Cf. Robert Musil: "But now circumstances have turned X, who might have been a good writer of stories for the women's magazines, into a bad Expressionist. As such, he exclaims: Man, God, Spirit, Goodness, Chaos, and spurts out sentences formed out of those vocables." *Schwarze Magie,"* in *Nachlass zu Lebzeiten* (Zurich, 1936), 78.

[14] See Karl Ludwig Schneider, *Der bildhafte Ausdruck in den Dichtungen Georg Heyms, Georg Trakls und Ernst Stadlers* (Heidelberg, 1954).

before the outbreak of war he wrote a poem, "Der Krieg,"
which is characteristic both of his vision and his style. I can
quote only the opening stanzas.

Aufgestanden ist er, welcher lange schlief,
Aufgestanden unten aus Gewölben tief.
In der Dämmrung steht er, gross und unbekannt,
Und den Mond zerdrückt er in der schwarzen Hand.

In den Abendlärm der Städte fällt es weit,
Frost und Schatten einer fremden Dunkelheit.
Und der Märkte runder Wirbel stockt zu Eis.
Es wird still. Sie sehn sich um. Und keiner weiss.

In den Abendlärm der Städte fällt es weit,
Eine Frage. Keine Antwort. Ein Gesicht erbleicht.
In der Ferne zittert ein Geläute dünn,
Und die Bärte zittern um ihr spitzes Kinn.

Risen is he that long has been asleep,
Risen below from vaulted caverns deep.
Large and unknown in twilight now he stands,
Gripping the moon to crush it with black hands.

Right through the city's evening bustle loom
The chill and shadows of an alien gloom.
And have reached the markets' whirling round. It froze.
Silence falls. People look round. And no one knows.

In the streets their shoulders gently quail.
It questions them. No answer. A face turns pale.
In the distance bells are quivering, thin.
And a beard quivers on many a pointed chin.

In truly apocalyptic fashion, Heym personifies War, but as a
nameless avenging spirit, not as a mere abstraction or as a
figure taken from some archaic play or picture. The poem begins dynamically, with a verb; and the horror of war is compressed into the image of the last line of the first stanza, that of
War crushing the moon in his black hand. In the second stanza
Heym brings this horror home by introducing familiar images
of city life; its sudden intrusion into the life of ordinary people
is rendered by the three brief sentences of the last line, each a

complete action, but with a cumulative effect. The neutral "fasst es" of the third strophe serves to keep the horror nameless; for at first the victims do not know what it is that takes hold of them. Their bewilderment is rendered in the next line by the asyntactical "Eine Frage. Keine Antwort." a typically Expressionist device. The third line adds a faintly gruesome aural effect to the images and actions presented so far. It is not till the last of the poem's ten stanzas that War receives its full apocalyptic significance, as an agent of divine justice dropping "pitch and fire on Gomorrah." Heym, like Baudelaire and Trakl, was obsessed with evil.

One basic limitation of Heym's poetry was pointed out long ago by Ernst Stadler,[15] who complained that Heym made use of traditional verse forms to render a "modern" vision; but more often than not the very tension between his regular meters and the dynamic force behind them gives his poems an unusual tautness. Stadler admitted as much; and remarked on the peculiarly sinister effect produced by Heym's nonchalant treatment of horrifying subjects—his poems like "a dance of death that observes the polite conventions of courtly ceremonial." In several of his last poems Heym came closer to the "personal rhythm" that Stadler had missed in his work, as in these opening stanzas of a poem from his second posthumous collection:

> Deine Wimpern, die langen,
> Deiner Augen dunkele Wasser,
> Lass mich tauchen darein,
> Lass mich zur Tiefe gehn.
>
> Steigt der Bergmann zum Schacht
> Und schwankt seine trübe Lampe
> Über der Erze Tor,
> Hoch an der Schattenwand,
>
> Sieh, ich steige hinab,
> In deinem Schoss zu vergessen,
> Fern was von oben dröhnt,
> Helle and Qual und Tag.

[15] Ernst Stadler, *Dichtungen,* ed. Karl Ludwig Schneider (Hamburg, 1954) II, 12–13.

Your eye-lashes, long,
Your eyes' dark waters,
Let me dip, let me dive,
Let me go down to the depth.

The miner goes down to the pit,
Waving his lamp's dim light
Over the gate of ore,
High up to the walls of gloom,

Look, I am going down,
In your lap to forget,
Distant the blare above,
Brightness and anguish and day.

The dynamism here is less violent, mitigated by the mood of melancholy tenderness which the almost elegiac meter conveys; but, though the main weight of the poem is carried by its imagery, this imagery is never a static one—as in much Symbolist and Imagist verse—but an imagery of movement. These three stanzas are dominated by the spatial relation between two symbolic planes and by the downward movement from one to the other. Heym breaks up the syntax of the first stanza, so as to be able to present his images before introducing the verb that governs them; he restrains his usual dynamism, so that the static images of long eyelashes and "your eyes' dark waters" may have their full emotive effect before being related to the action. This action or motion is in full progress when he reaches the second stanza; he therefore starts this stanza with the verb—again contrary to normal usage; for what is significant about his metaphor of the miner descending the shaft is the motion of descent itself, rather than any other analogy between the "I" of the poem and the miner's function. The third stanza relates this metaphor to its meaning; not by a logical comparison—the linking "like" and "as" which Rilke, too, discarded when he found his new style—but by an independent action parallel to it. The miner goes down the mine shaft *and* the lover of the poem descends to a dark, subterranean level where noises from above are damped and he is remote from "brightness and anguish and day." The falling cadence of the poem—produced by troches and dactyls—is exactly the right one.

Heym's affinity with Georg Trakl—suggested by the "dying fall" of this poem—becomes more marked in the autumnal imagery of the succeeding stanzas. Ernst Stadler and Franz Werfel represented a different trend of early Expressionism, but one complementary to the other. Their belief in a better future gave their dynamism an ecstatic quality, as opposed to the gloomy forebodings of Heym and Trakl; but both trends arose from the same sense of an imminent cataclysm. Stadler's best-known poem, "Der Aufbruch," has been interpreted too literally as a prophecy and glorification of war. As Karl Ludwig Schneider, the editor of Stadler's works, has observed,[16] its military imagery has little to do with actual warfare, much more with the poet's own personal and literary situation in 1911 and 1912, when he evolved his new style. As a man attached to England, France, and Belgium as well as to Germany, Stadler was bound to loathe the very idea of war; but Stadler was a poet of revolt against prejudice, apathy, and stuffiness. The warlike imagery of "Der Aufbruch" is one of liberation from outworn conventions. The irony of Stadler's fate is not that he welcomed the war that killed him and defeated his hopes for a better Europe, but that the images of regeneration in his poetry corresponded so closely to the catastrophic event. Stadler believed that "it is the future which all true art serves"; [17] even his excursions into squalor, in his poems on the East End of London, poverty, and prostitution, are affirmations of the joy of living and professions of faith in unrealized potentialities. Yet this vitalism is always ambiguous; for the culmination of ecstasy, in Stadler's poems, coincides with a dissolution of consciousness that he usually associates with death. His vitalism—akin to that of Walt Whitman and D. H. Lawrence—gathers momentum in the long, irregular, surging lines of his verse, only to dash itself to pieces in the last.

Der Schnellzug tastet sich und stösst die Dunkelheit entlang.
Kein Stern will vor. Die ganze Welt ist nur ein enger, nacht-
umschienter Minengang,

---

[16] Ernst Stadler, *Dichtungen* (ed. cit.) I, 69–72.
[17] *Ibid.*, II, 10.

Darein zuweilen Förderstellen blauen Lichtes jähe Horizonte
reissen: Feuerkreis
Von Kugellampen, Dächern, Schloten, dampfend, strömend
. . . nur sekundenweis . . .
Und wieder alles schwarz. Als führen wir ins Eingeweid der
Nacht zur Schicht.
Nun taumeln Lichter her . . . verirrt, trostlos vereinsamt . . .
mehr . . . und sammeln sich . . . und werden dicht.
Gerippe grauer Häuserfronten liegen bloss, im Zwielicht
bleichend. tot—etwas muss
kommen . . . o, ich fühl es schwer
Im Hirn. Eine Beklemmung singt im Blut. Dann dröhnt der
Boden plötzlich wie ein Meer:
Wir fliegen, aufgehoben, königlich durch nachtentrissne Luft,
hoch überm Strom. O Biegung
der Millionen Lichter, stumme Wacht,
Vor deren blitzender Parade schwer die Wasser abwärts rol-
len.
Endloses Spalier, zum Gruss gestellt bei Nacht!
Wie Fackeln stürmend! Freudiges! Salut von Schiffen über
blauer
See! Bestirntes Fest!
Wimmelnd, mit hellen Augen hingedrängt! Bis wo die Stadt
mit letzten Häusern ihren Gast entlässt.
Und dann die langen Einsamkeiten. Nackte Ufer. Stille.
Nacht. Besinnung. Einkehr. Kommunion. Und Glut und Drang
Zum Letzten, Segnenden. Zum Zeugungsfest. Zur Wollust. Zum
Gebet. Zum Meer. Zum Untergang.

The express train gropes and thrusts its way through darkness.
Not a star is out.
The whole world's nothing but a mine-road the night has railed
about
In which at times conveyors of blue light tear sudden horizons:
fiery sphere
Of arc-lamps, roofs and chimneys, steaming, streaming—for
seconds only clear,
And all is black again. As though we drove into Night's en-
trails to the seam.
Now lights reel into view . . . astray, disconsolate and lonely
. . . more . . . and gather . . . and densely gleam.
Skeletons of grey housefronts are laid bare, grow pale in the

twilight, dead—something must happen . . . O heavily
I feel it weigh on my brain. An oppression sings in the blood.
          Then all at once the ground resounds like the sea:
And royally upborne we fly through air from darkness wrested,
      high up above the river. O curve of the million lights,
                mute guard at the sight
Of whose flashing parade the waters go roaring down. Endless
              line presenting arms by night!
Surging on like torches! Joyful! Salute of ships over the blue
            sea! Star-jewelled, festive array!
Teeming, bright-eyed urged on! Till where the town with its
           last houses sees its guest away.
And then the long solitudes. Bare banks. And silence. Night.
    Reflection. Self-questioning. Communion. And ardour
                outward-flowing
To the end that blesses. To conception's rite. To pleasure's
    consummation. To prayer. To the sea. To self's undoing.

This poem, "Fahrt über die Kölner Rheinbrücke bei Nacht," is as difficult to elucidate as it is to translate. In spite of its realistic imagery, its organization is a purely subjective one. It renders an actual experience—the crossing of a railway bridge at night—but gives such a vast extension of meaning to the experience that one cannot even be sure that the descriptive details —housefronts, lights, and chimneys, for instance—are that and no more. As in Surrealist poetry and that of Dylan Thomas, one image generates another; but all the disparate images are swept in one direction by the dynamism of feeling. Stadler's poem re-creates an immediate experience; far from being "emotion recollected in tranquillity," it approximates as closely as poetry can to the bewildering moment of sensation. This would be easy enough if the writing of a poem could be synchronized with the experience that occasioned it; but, at its most immediate, poetry is emotion generated in retrospect. Stadler's apparent spontaneity, therefore, was the result of deliberate and skillful application.

In the first few lines of the poem realistic imagery preponderates; one attributes their dynamism to the actual speed of the express train. Yet they prepare the reader for the larger symbolism that emerges more clearly later; for the journey is one into the "entrails of night"; and, as in Heym's poem, there is an allusion to a descent into the subconscious, symbolized by the mine gallery. It is only the connection between the river of the poem, the Rhine at Cologne, and the sea that establishes a primarily symbolic significance. When the poet writes of "Salut von Schiffen über blauer See," we are suddenly aware that these ships are not part of the actual setting of the poem; his imagination has traveled with the river to the sea. And it is the extraneous image of the sea that dominates the whole poem; for the whole poem is a glorification of the flux of life itself; and the sea is the destination of that flux.

On its realistic level, Stadler's poem is comparable to Hart Crane's *The Bridge;* both poems are affirmations of the new age and attempts to mythologize—or at least to generalize—its specific achievements. Symbolically, Stadler's poem affirms only life itself—and death. The poem ends with the word "Untergang," submergence or extinction; it does so because the utmost intensity of feeling burns itself out. Just as the river's motion comes to rest in the sea, Stadler's ecstatic awareness of being alive culminates in the extinction of consciousness. The last line makes the connection, frequent in Stadler's love poems also, between the total fulfillment of individuality and its total dissolution.

Stadler goes further than Heym in the breaking up of regular syntax, for his vitalism was more impatient of conventional restrictions. For the same reason he was much more apt to coin new combinations of words. Examples in this poem are "nachtumschient" ("railed round with night") and "nachtentrissene Luft" ("air snatched away from night"). Because of their extreme dynamism, his poems have a rhetorical effect; but it is private rhetoric, as it were, not aimed at the reader in the manner of Werfel and many of the later Expressionists. Only his excellent craftsmanship saved Stadler from other dangers. Few poets would have got away with the long succession of asyntactic words—most of them abstract and general—in the last two lines; one would expect them to read like a parody of the new style, quite apart from the inclusion of prayer in the list, between the ecstasy of procreation and self-extinction in the sea.

Stadler brings off these verbal and mental leaps, just as he manages to keep his long line from spilling over into prose, and
makes his rhymes all the more effective for being delayed.

These varieties of Expressionist poetry—and there are many
others—will have to suffice here. All of them go back to before
World War I—a fact that must be stressed only because Expressionism was long regarded as a phenomenon of the interwar years. Even so acute an observer of contemporary life and
literature as Robert Musil noted in his diary that when he returned to civilian life "there was Expressionism," contrasting it
with the poetry of "intellectual intuition" that had existed before the war. He also noted that "the nature of Expressionism
is that of a synthetic method as opposed to the analytical. Expressionism refrains from analysis . . . That is why it tends towards dogmatism. That is why it tries to discover a new cosmic
sense as a chemist tries to discover synthetic rubber. Its limitation: that there is no such thing as a purely synthetic process." [18] Both of Musil's observations are perfectly just if we
remember that Expressionism was a style before it was a movement; and Musil was writing about the movement rather than
the style. Musil's own novel *Die Verwirrungen des Zöglings
Törless,* published in 1912, has been treated as an example of
early Expressionist prose. It was the movement that tended toward dogmatism, a political dogmatism, which Musil rightly
deplored; but most of the prewar Expressionists were so far
from being dogmatic about either religion or politics that one
has the greatest difficulty in deducing their beliefs and opinions
from their poetry. Musil's observation that Expressionism was a
synthetic method, on the other hand, applies to the style as well
as to the movement. The Expressionist style, from the very
start, was synthetic; and this is where the danger lay.

"Skepticism," Stadler wrote in a book review, "can only lead
to the end of all creative power, to decadence. The truly creative man, on the other hand, is he who can create the world
anew, who opposes his new and different idea of the world to
the created world as it is; the man with a teleological direction,

[18] Robert Musil, *Tagebücher, Aphorismen, Essays und Reden,* ed.
Adolf Frisé (Hamburg, 1955), 206–207.

not the one who merely counts up (existing phenomena) on his fingers." [19] Musil's antinomy between the synthetic and analytical processes in literature is the old quarrel—already touched upon frequently in this book—between head and heart, Reason and Energy, Logos and Imagination; but the quarrel had become more violent and more extreme. Stadler was aware of the extreme implications of his statement; for he proceeded to qualify it by writing that "this was not to justify the blind destructive impulses, as certain radical revolutionaries do"; and that "the new artist should rely on his intellect in the first place, no blind creature of instincts, not a person orientated only by feeling." In theory, this is unobjectionable; and Stadler himself, as it happened, was well balanced, being a critic and a scholar as well as a poet; but I have already observed that the vitalism of his poetry was essentially self-destructive. Musil's analytical subtlety, on the other hand, proved no less dangerous to him. His extreme skepticism, directed against his own impulses, prevented him from finishing most of the imaginative works which he began or continued in later life, including his masterpiece. Musil's difficulty was that he could not arrive at a synthesis; the more he knew, the more difficult he found it to reduce the complexity of his knowledge to its bare, imaginative essence. Because extremes meet, his skepticism finally turned a somersault and became a kind of mysticism; but a kind of mysticism no less difficult to reconcile with the novelist's primary task.

After 1914, then, Reason and Energy tended to go their separate ways. The finest critical minds of the age, those of Hofmannsthal and Musil, for instance, refused all contact with the dominant generation; and the dominant generation accepted no critical guidance. Hofmannsthal was despised as an "uncreative" traditionalist—because he did not believe that it is the writer's business "to create the world anew"; and, like Musil, Hofmannsthal was indeed inhibited from writing all he might have written by his horror of what was happening in his time. A peculiar melancholy attaches to those writers of the German-speaking nations—both Hofmannsthal and Musil, of

[19] Stadler, *Works* (ed. cit.) II, 28. The review was written in 1913.

course, were Austrians—who were conscious of working within a humanistic tradition; it is the melancholy of Grillparzer, who prophesied that modern civilization would move "from humanity through nationalism to bestiality"—a prophecy not unlike that which emerges from Hofmannsthal's tragedy *Der Turm*. It is the melancholy of Jakob Burckhardt, who refused Ranke's chair of History in Berlin and left it to Treitschke—the most antitraditional of nationalists. And the melancholy of Hofmannsthal himself, a liberal conservative living at a time when all spontaneous energy tended toward revolt, violence, and anarchy.

"Expressionism was dead at the moment when it became a deliberate style," an excellent critic [20] of the style has written; and it is certainly true that—judged by their poetry alone—the initiators of this style seem less conscious of their innovations than their numerous successors and imitators. Yet, in a different sense, the art of Heym and Trakl was more deliberate than that of the later Expressionists, whose manner strikes us as self-conscious only because it had become a mannerism. In Stadler too intellect and energy were at war; but he was skillful enough to maintain the balance in his poetry. Much of the verse of the later Expressionists is not more, but less, vitalistic than Stadler's; it is the incongruity between their dynamic style and their flabbiness of feeling that makes their rhetoric more offensive than Stadler's.

As for the death of Expressionism, Schneider's remark is apt enough; but one must add that no corpse has ever raised such a hullabaloo. By 1918 Expressionism was the most influential and the most prolific movement in German, if not in European, literature. (In 1922, 35,859 books were published in Germany —nearly three times as many as in Great Britain.[21] It would be interesting to know just how many of these would have qualified as Expressionist.) Many of the Expressionist poets thought nothing of publishing three collections of verse in a year; [22] and each of these volumes would be highly "original"—if one did not analyze it or compare its "originality" with that of dozens

[20] K. L. Schneider, *Der Bildhafte Ausdruck, op. cit.*, 158.
[21] I take these figures from Robert Musil's diary (ed. cit.), 273.
[22] Johannes R. Becher published five in 1919.

of others—highly topical and bursting with vitality. Those of the innovators who had died before or during the war were post-humously recruited into the movement; to march with it willy-nilly in the columns of such anthologies as *Menschheitsdäm-merung*. Gradually the style turned into a weapon of revolu-tionary dogmatism, pacifist at first, but pugnaciously so.

The hysterical note characteristic of later Expressionism was first sounded by Franz Werfel before the war; but Werfel was not primarily a political poet. He wrote out of the sincere con-viction that "we must love one another or die"; and even his rhetoric had the charm of ingenuity, an elegance reminiscent of the Baroque. For a time, Werfel became the spiritual leader of the movement; but after 1920 his poetry ceased to develop. He was succeeded by Johannes R. Becher, the most prolific and the most widely read of the political Expressionist poets. Here is the opening of his "Hymne auf Rosa Luxemburg," written in 1919:

> Auffüllend dich rings mit Strophen aus Oliven.
> Tränen Mäander umwandere dich!
> Stern-Genächte dir schlagend als Mantel um,
> Durchwachsen von Astbahnen hymnischen Scharlachbluts . . .
> O Würze du der paradiesischen Auen:
> Du Einzige! Du Heilige! O Weib!—
>
> Durch die Welten rase ich—:
> Einmal noch deine Hand, diese Hand zu fassen:
> Zauberisches Gezweig an Gottes Rosen-Öl-Baum . . .

> Filling you up all around with strophes of olives.
> May the meander of tears wander about you!
> Wrapping star-nights around you as a cloak,
> Interlaced with branch tracks of hymnic scarlet blood . . .
> O you the spice of paradisean fields:
> Unique one! Saint! O woman!—
>
> Through the worlds I roar—:
> Once more to grasp your hand, this hand:
> Magical boughs on God's attar of roses tree . . .

The dynamism, the asyntactic, exclamatory phrases, the unex-pected images and new combinations of words—all the ingredi-

ents of early Expressionism are there; but they have degener-
ated into rhetorical devices, determined neither by inward nor
outward necessity. The revolutionary heroine of the poem is
addressed as a saint—a confusion of terms typical of the diction as a whole, its imprecision and impurity; and after the
false sublimity of "Saint!" there follows the bathos of
"Woman!" All the imagery is arbitrary; one cannot even call it
decorative, for there is nothing to decorate. It is a rank growth
that covers up a void; a booby trap for the reader foolish
enough to be drawn to these "strophes of olives," only to be
caught and bludgeoned into false admiration for the unfortunate
and truly admirable subject of the poem. The poem goes on for
another sixty lines at this pace; and there is no reason why it
shouldn't go on for six hundred, or end with the sixth line.
Becher creates an illusion of energy by starting the poem with
the present participle of a verb; but whereas the early Expressionists used such devices to render the logic of feeling or of
imagination, Becher uses it to wind up the mechanism of his
rhetoric. Yet the effect of such verse was to undermine the
judgment and coarsen the sensibility of its readers.

This was not a purely German phenomenon; but no public
was less critical of it than the German. Hence, in part, the
events of 1933, possible only in a country that had been sys-
tematically demoralized and brutalized. The later developments
of Expressionism are inseparable from politics; for the new
style, as I have said, had been turned into a political weapon.
A poet of complete integrity, Oskar Loerke, entered the following note in his diary on February 19, 1933: "I stand between
the terrorists of the Right and the Left. Perhaps I shall be destroyed. My nerves won't stand any more. The anguish of being
confronted with terrible consequences, without having done, or
even known the least thing." [23]

Since my subject here is the Expressionist style, not the
movement or the events that led to its suppression, I shall end
the survey at this point. Gottfried Benn has divided the Expressionist era into two periods, which he calls Phase I and Phase
II: Phase I being the period before 1933, Phase II the period

[23] Oskar Loerke, *Tagebücher 1903–1939*, ed. H. Kasack (Heidelberg/
Darmstadt, 1955), 261.

after 1933, represented almost exclusively by Benn himself. A better division would be that into three phases: Phase I, then, would cover the years between 1911 and 1914; Phase II the years between 1914 and 1933; Phase III from 1933 to the present time. Of the few Expressionist poets who survived both wars and continued to write, only Gottfried Benn and Yvan Goll can be said to have even attempted to develop the style. J. R. Becher, another survivor, changed his style beyond recognition; his later rhetoric was not avant-garde but subliterary. Unlike such French Communist poets as Aragon, whose prewar poetry resembled Becher's in combining political propaganda with an "advanced" technique, Becher was no longer obliged to write for an unconverted bourgeoisie or to compete with "bourgeois" writers. Aragon's verse of the war years is considerably better than Becher's verse of the same period, though both are deliberate reversions to popular modes.

Yvan Goll, a bilingual poet who had been active both in France and in Germany, lived to write a worthy epilogue to his German verse of the interwar years. During the long illness of which he died in 1950, he wrote a series of poems on the traditional themes of love and death, posthumously collected and published as *Traumkraut*.[24] Unlike the rhetorical verse of his earlier years, they are concentrated and astonishingly lucid; but their simplicity is that of reduction. They are the essence left in the retort after all the diverse experiments that began before World War I. They neither break with Goll's past—as Becher's later poetry did with his—nor initiate a new style; they make use of everything that Goll had learned in his association with the modernist movements in Germany, France, and America, but in a curiously chastened and transmuted form. These poems are imagistic, but their imagery is clearly symbolic; their syntax is the dynamic syntax of Expressionism and Surrealism, but the dynamism is controlled by an obvious logic. In a short poem called "Morgue," [25] Goll could combine such modernist metaphors as "the ice of sleep" with another that recalls the conven-

[24] Yvan Goll, *Traumkraut: Gedichte aus dem Nachlass* (Wiesbaden, 1951).
[25] *Ibid.*, 22. "Morgue" is a title reminiscent of 1912, when Georg Heym and Gottfried Benn published poems on that subject.

tional imagery of medieval verse, "the inn of Earth." This juxtaposition could be called eclectic or naïve, and it is the difficulty of distinguishing between true and false naïveté that laid the new style open to abuse. The style was fashioned by the "innocent eye" of true poets; but it was exploited by those who deliberately violated reason, so as to release energy. Innocence can be renewed, and does, in fact, continually renew itself; but in its own good time. To force the process is to fall into crudity and barbarism.

X

GEORG TRAKL

Of all the early Expressionists, Trakl was the least rhetorical
and the least dogmatic; and he was an Expressionist poet only
insofar as he was a modernist poet who wrote in German. Expressionism happened to be the name attached to modernist poetry written in German; but Trakl would not have written differently if there had been no movement of that name. Nor did
he have any contact with the initiators of the movement, all of
whom were active in Berlin; whatever he had in common with
Hoddis, Lichtenstein, Heym, and Benn, he owed to the *Zeitgeist,* not to any program or theory. If Trakl had written in
English—but, of course, it is inconceivable that he should have
done—he would have been called an Imagist, though it is most
unlikely that he ever heard or read this word. Neither label is
very useful, but Imagist would at least have the virtue of indi-
cating the most distinctive characteristic of Trakl's art; all poets
express themselves, but Trakl expressed himself in images. To
treat Trakl's poems as self-expression, that is to say, as frag-

ments of an autobiography, is to misunderstand them; for Trakl's dominant aspiration was to lose himself.

Trakl has also been called an Existentialist; and I have already alluded to the intimate, though obscure, connection between an existential mode of thought and imagist practices. Just as Existentialists tend to leap straight from the bare condition of existence to the absolute—God, if they believe in Him, Nothing if they do not—so imagist poets deal with bare phenomena in the form of images, not as an ornament added to what they have to say, or as a means of illustrating a metaphysical statement, but as an end in itself. The mere existence of phenomena is their justification; and to understand their Being is to understand their significance. The poetic image, then, becomes autonomous and "autotelic," or as nearly so as the medium of words permits. It follows that the pure imagist technique is likely to break down as soon as a poet wishes to convey truths of a different order than the ontological; and that is one reason that nearly all the poets who once practiced a purely imagist technique have either modified or abandoned their practice. Poetic statements bearing on religious dogma, on ethics, history, and social institutions require such a modification, since the pure image is unrelated to all these spheres.

Every interpretation of Trakl's works hinges on the difficulty of deciding to what extent his images should be treated as symbols—to what extent they may be related to the spheres enumerated above. This, of course, raises the question of his beliefs, for belief comes into play as soon as we attempt to "interpret" an image at all; a purely existential image has no meaning other than itself. Since Trakl undoubtedly lent a symbolic significance to his images—or to some of them at least—these two basic questions are bound to be raised. Trakl's poetry is so essentially ambiguous—so "laconic," as one of his interpreters has observed [1]—that many different interpretations of its symbolism are possible. The most one can hope to do is to avoid too heavy a personal bias toward one symbolism or another; and to allow each reader to make his own choice.

[1] Professor Eduard Lachmann, "Eine Interpretation der Dichtungen Georg Trakls," *Kreuz und Abend* (Salzburg, 1954).

Georg Trakl was born at Salzburg on February 3, 1887. His mother, née Halik, was the second wife of Tobias Trakl, a prosperous ironmonger who belonged to a Protestant family long established in this Roman Catholic city. Both the Trakl and Halik families were of Slav descent; the Trakls had originally come from Hungary, the Haliks—much more recently—from Bohemia. The family house at Salzburg, with its old furniture, paintings and statuary, as well as the family garden in a different part of the city contributed images to many of Trakl's poems, especially to the sequence *Sebastian im Traum*. The whole of Salzburg—or Trakl's vision of it—is present in much of his work; it is the "beautiful city" of his earlier poems, a city in decay because its present does not live up to its past.

It is difficult to say whether Trakl's childhood was as melancholy and as lonely as his retrospective poems suggest. From accounts of him by his school friends it appears that he showed no signs of extreme introversion until his late adolescence; and the first part of *Sebastian im Traum* is a vision of childhood that can no more be reduced to factual narrative than any other poem of Trakl's, for all its references to identifiable objects:

Mutter trug das Kindlein im weissen Mond,
Im Schatten des Nussbaums, uralten Holunders,
Trunken vom Safte des Mohns, der Klage der Drossel;
Und stille
Neigte in Mitleid sich über jene ein bärtiges Antlitz,

Leise im Dunkel des Fensters; und altes Hausgerät
Der Väter
Lag im Verfall; Liebe und herbstliche Träumerei.

Also dunkel der Tag des Jahrs, traurige Kindheit,
Da der Knabe leise zu kühlen Wassern, silbernen Fischen hin-
                                                    abstieg,
Ruh und Antlitz;
Da er steinern sich vor rasende Rappen warf,
In grauer Nacht sein Stern über ihn kam;

Oder wenn er an der frierenden Hand der Mutter
Abends über Sankt Peters herbstlichen Friedhof ging,
Ein zarter Leichnam stille im Dunkel der Kammer lag
Und jener die kalten Lider über ihn aufhob.

Er aber war ein kleiner Vogel im kahlen Geäst,
Die Glocke lang im Abendnovember,
Des Vaters Stille, da er im Schlafe die dämmernde Wendel-
                                    treppe hinabstieg.

Mother bore this infant in the white moon,
In the nut-tree's shade, in the ancient elder's,
Drunk with the poppy's juice, the thrush's lament;
And mute
With compassion a bearded face bowed down to that woman,

Quiet in the window's darkness; and ancestral heirlooms,
Old household goods
Lay rotting there; love and autumnal reverie.

So dark was the day of the year, desolate childhood,
When softly the boy to cool waters, to silvery fishes walked
                                    down,
Calm and countenance;
When stony he cast himself down where black horses raced,
In the grey of the night his star possessed him.

Or holding his mother's icy hand
He walked at nightfall across St. Peter's autumnal churchyard
While a delicate corpse lay still in the bedroom's gloom
And he raised cold eyelids towards it.

But he was a little bird in leafless boughs,
The churchbell long in dusking November,
His father's stillness, when asleep he descended the dark of the
                                    winding stair.

On the evidence of these lines it has been suggested that Trakl's
mother must have been a drug addict, like her son! But narcot-
ics and intoxicants, in Trakl's poetry, are associated with original sin. Drunkenness, traditionally, began after the Flood, when
men were so far removed from their first state that life became
unbearable without this means of escape. For the same reason
it is with compassion that the father's bearded face looks down
at the mother of this poem.

Trakl seems to have been fond of both his parents and at
least one of his five brothers and sisters, Margarete, who became a concert pianist and settled in Berlin. Much has been

made of Trakl's attachment to this sister, for critics of the literal persuasion insist on identifying her with the sister who appears in his poems; but neither the references to incest in Trakl's early work nor the personage of the sister in his later poems permit any biographical deductions. Incest is one of many forms of evil that occur in Trakl's work; and the personage of the sister is a kind of spiritual alter ego, an anima figure, so that in certain poems a brother-sister relationship symbolizes an integration of the self. Trakl used many other legendary or archetypal personages in his poetry; not to write his autobiography, but to compose visionary poems of an unprecedented kind.

As a boy, Trakl shared Margarete's love of music and played the piano with some skill. At school, on the other hand, he proved less than mediocre. When he failed his examinations in the seventh form, he was unwilling to sit for them again and decided that he was unfit for the professional or academic career originally planned for him. For a time he received private tuition at home. An Alsatian governess taught him French; and he took this opportunity to read the French poets, especially Baudelaire, Verlaine, and Rimbaud. Other influences on his poetry are those of Hölderlin, Mörike, and Lenau; and his thought was decisively influenced by Kierkegaard, Dostoievsky, and Nietzsche. When, toward the end of his life, he decided to do without books, it was the works of Dostoievsky with which he found it hardest to part. Already at school Trakl belonged to a literary club. Toward the end of his school years he grew taciturn, moody, and unsociable; he began to speak of suicide, drank immoderately and drugged himself with chloroform. The career he now chose, that of a dispensing chemist, gave him easy access to more effective drugs for the rest of his life.

From 1905 to 1908 Trakl was trained for this career in his native town. During this time, two of his juvenile plays were publicly performed; *Totentag,* acted in 1906, was something of a *succès de scandale; Fata Morgana,* a one-act play put on later that year, was an unqualified failure. In the same year Trakl began to contribute short dramatic sketches and book reviews to a local paper. He left Salzburg in October, 1908, to complete his training at the University of Vienna, where he took a two-year course in pharmacy. His hatred of large cities dates from this period. At this time he worked at a tragedy, *Don Juan,* of which only a fragment remains, and at an extant puppet play on the Bluebeard theme. After his second year in Vienna, during which his father died, Trakl entered on one year's military service as a dispensing chemist attached to the medical corps; he was posted to Innsbruck, then back to Vienna, but took the earliest opportunity of being transferred to the Reserve.

In 1912 he considered emigrating to Borneo; but in the same year he began to write his best work and met his patron, Ludwig von Ficker, in whose periodical *Der Brenner* most of Trakl's later poems first appeared. It was mainly owing to Ficker's friendship and support that Trakl was able to devote the remaining years of his life to the writing of poetry. In January, 1913, he accepted a clerical post in Vienna, but returned to Innsbruck after three days' work. Except for a number of other journeys—to Venice, Lake Garda, various parts of Austria, and Berlin, where he visited his sister Margarete and met the poetess Else Lasker-Schüler—and three more abortive attempts to work for his living in Vienna, Trakl moved between Innsbruck and Salzburg till the outbreak of war. In 1913 Trakl's first book, a selection of his poems made by Franz Werfel, was published by Kurt Wolff; a second collection appeared in the following year.[2]

By 1913 Trakl had become a confirmed drug addict. In December of that year he nearly died of an overdose of veronal; but in spite of this and his alcoholic excesses, his physical strength remained prodigious, as various anecdotes testify. A prose poem, "Winternacht," derives from one of Trakl's own experiences: after drinking wine near Innsbruck, he collapsed on his way home and spent the remainder of the night asleep in the snow—without suffering any ill effects. In July, 1914, Ludwig von Ficker received a considerable sum of money— 100,000 Austrian crowns—with the request to distribute it as he thought fit among the contributors to *Der Brenner*. Trakl and Rilke were the first beneficiaries; but when Herr von Ficker took Trakl to the bank to draw part of the grant, Trakl's

---

[2] Georg Trakl, *Gedichte* (1913); and *Sebastian im Traum* (1914).

good fortune so nauseated him that he had to leave the bank before the formalities had been completed.[3] Long after the event Ficker revealed the identity of Trakl's and Rilke's patron;[4] he was the philosopher Ludwig Wittgenstein, who gave away most of his inheritance at this time. Later, Wittgenstein wrote to Ficker about Trakl's poetry: "I don't understand it; but its *tone* delights me. It is the *tone* of true genius."

Late in August, 1914, Trakl left Innsbruck for Galicia as a lieutenant attached to the Medical Corps of the Austrian army. After the battle of Grodek Trakl was put in charge of ninety serious casualties whom—as a mere dispensing chemist hampered by the shortage of medical supplies—he could do almost nothing to help. One of the wounded shot himself through the head in Trakl's presence. Outside the barn where these casualties were housed a number of deserters had been hanged on trees. It was more than Trakl could bear. He either threatened or attempted suicide, with the result that he was removed to Cracow for observation as a mental case. His last poems, "Klage" and "Grodek," were written at this time.

Trakl now feared that he, too, would be executed as a deserter. According to the medical authorities at Cracow he was under treatment for dementia praecox (schizophrenia); but his treatment consisted in being locked up in a cell together with another officer suffering from delirium tremens. During this confinement Ludwig von Ficker visited Trakl and asked Wittgenstein, who was also serving in Poland, to look after Trakl; but Wittgenstein arrived too late. After a few weeks of anguish, Trakl took an overdose of cocaine, of which he died on November 3, or 4, 1914. It has been suggested that he may have misjudged the dose in his state of acute distress; this was the opinion of his batman, the last person to whom Trakl spoke.

Apart from his juvenilia—poems, plays, and book reviews—Trakl's work consists of some hundred poems and prose poems written between 1912 and 1914, the year of his death at the age of twenty-seven. The horizontal range of these poems is

---

[3] Both these incidents from Erwin Mahrholdt; cited in Georg Trakl, *Dichtungen*, ed. Horwitz (Zurich, 1946), 200–204.

[4] In *Der Brenner* XVIII. Folge, 1954 (Innsbruck), 234–248.

not wide; it is limited by Trakl's extreme introversion and by his peculiar habit of using the same operative words and images throughout his later work. But Trakl's introversion must not be mistaken for egocentricity. "Believe me," he wrote to a friend, "it isn't always easy for me, and never will be easy for me, to subordinate myself unconditionally to that which my poems render; and I shall have to correct myself again and again, so as to give to truth those things that belong to truth." [5] Trakl's inner experience is "objectified" in images and in the symbolic extension of those images; his concern, as he says, was with general truths and with the rendering of general truths in a purely poetic manner. For that reason, the melancholy that pervades his work was only a premise, not the substance, of what he wished to convey; it is as important, but no more important, than the key of a musical composition. It was certainly a limitation of Trakl's that he could compose only in minor keys; but the same could be said of Leopardi and of other lyrical poets whose poetry conveys a distinct mood. Nor should Trakl be assessed in terms of optimism and pessimism, categories that are largely irrelevant to his vision. As Rilke was one of the first to point out, Trakl's work is essentially affirmative; but what it affirms is a spiritual order that may not be immediately perceptible in his poems, filled as they are with images pertaining to the temporal order that he negated.

"Trakl's poetry," Rilke wrote, "is to me an object of sublime existence . . . it occurs to me that this whole work has a parallel in the aspiration of a Li-Tai-Pe: in both, falling is the pretext for the most continuous ascension. In the history of the poem Trakl's books are important contributions to the liberation of the poetic image. They seem to me to have mapped out a new dimension of the spirit and to have disproved that prejudice which judges all poetry only in terms of feeling and content, as if in the direction of lament there were only lament— but here too there is world again." [6] This tribute is especially important for two reasons; because of Trakl's influence on

[5] Letter to Erhard Buschbeck. Georg Trakl, *Nachlass und Biographie Works,* Vol. III (Salzburg, 1949), 26.

[6] R. M. Rilke, Letter to Erhard Buschbeck of February 22, 1917. *Briefe* 1914–1921 (Leipzig, 1937), 126.

Rilke's own work, and because Rilke interpreted Trakl's poetry existentially when other critics, less close to Trakl's way of thought, read it as a record of Trakl's morbid states of mind. As late as 1923, in a letter to Ludwig von Ficker, Rilke reaffirmed his admiration for Trakl's poetry.[7] What Rilke meant by "world" in the letter cited is what professional Existentialists would call "being"; and he believed that it is the poet's business to affirm whatever aspect of being is manifested to him, whether it be bright or dark. The mood is incidental; what matters is the intensity of the poet's response to the world and his ability to render his perceptions in words and images. Rilke always insisted that praise and lament are not mutually exclusive, but complementary functions; for lament, too, is a kind of affirmation, a way of praising what is lost or unattainable, a way of accepting the limitations of human life or even—in a sense different from that intended by Blake—of "catching a joy as it flies." That is why dirges and laments are a traditional form of poetry, though poetry, by the same tradition, is always affirmative. Within the bounds of a Christian orthodoxy that has very little in common with Rilke's private existential creed—but rather more with Trakl's beliefs—the poet's dual function in an imperfect world emerges from George Herbert's lines:

> I will complain, yet praise,
> I will bewail, approve;
> And all my sowre-sweet dayes
> I will lament, and love.

It was Rilke's insight, then, which directed the attention of Trakl's readers away from the categories of optimism and pessimism and toward that "truth" which Trakl himself thought more important than his own predicament. As the work of so many of Trakl's contemporaries shows, optimism can be just as morbid a symptom as pessimism, because there is a kind of optimism that is a hysterical perversion of the truth; its premises give it the lie. Trakl, on the other hand, wrote of what he knew; he was true to his premises, and these premises were positive enough.

[7] Quoted by Ficker in *Rilke und der unbekannte Freund; Der Brenner*, 1954, 234.

The temporal order that Trakl's poems negate was that of materialism in decay. That is the significance of the decaying household utensils in the first part of *Sebastian im Traum*. To this order, Trakl opposed an existential Christian faith akin to Kierkegaard's and an unreserved compassion akin to that of certain characters in Dostoievsky. All this is implicit in Trakl's poetry, since he rarely stated or defined his beliefs, but translated them into images. Yet all the external evidence supports this interpretation of his beliefs; and, shortly before his death, Trakl handed the following short note to Ludwig von Ficker: "(Your) feeling at moments of deathlike existence: all human beings are worthy of love. Awakening, you feel the bitterness of the world: in that you know all your unabsolved guilt; your poems an imperfect penance." [8] Because poetry is an imperfect penance, Trakl castigated himself to the point of self-destruction.

What Trakl lamented was not the fact or the condition of death, but the difficulty of living in an age of cultural decline and spiritual corruption. The immediate background of Salzburg, an ancient and beautiful city unable to live up to its past, was one element in his melancholy, though it does not account for his own obsession with guilt and death. "No," he wrote as early as 1909, "my own affairs no longer interest me"; and in 1914—after his breakdown on active service—"already I feel very nearly beyond this world." [9] The dead who people his poems—the mythical Elis, for instance—are more vivid, more full of life, than the living. In the poem "An einen Frühverstorbenen" ("To One who Died Young"), the surviving friend is haunted by the other who

> . . . ging die steinernen Stufen des Mönchbergs hinab,
> Ein blaues Lächeln im Antlitz und seltsam verpuppt
> In seine stillere Kindheit und starb;

---

[8] *Der Brenner, ibid.*, 251. It is interesting to note that a German poet who has much in common with Trakl, Johannes Bobrowski, also regarded his work as an art of expiation. Cf. my Introduction to *Johannes Bobrowski: Shadow Land* (London, 1967), 8.

[9] Letter to Buschbeck. *Works* III, 19.

Und im Garten blieb das silberne Antlitz des Freundes zurück
Lauschend im Laub oder im alten Gestein.

Seele sang den Tod, die grüne Verwesung des Fleisches . . .

. . . walked down the stone steps of the Mönchsberg,
A blue smile on his face and strangely cocooned
In his quieter childhood, and died;
And the silvery face of this friend remained in the garden,
Listening in leaves or in ancient stone.

Soul sang of death, the green putrefaction of flesh . . .

It is the dying friend who smiles, the survivor who becomes obsessed with death and decay. The reason, it appears from other
poems, is that those who die young preserve "the image of
man" intact; wherever they appear in Trakl's poems they are
associated with righteousness and with images of the good life;
and this, in turn, is associated with an earlier stage of civilization, opposed to modern life in the large cities. One thinks of
Rilke's cult of those who died young; but Trakl's dead are symbolic of a state of innocence that cannot be identified with
youth or childhood, or even with a rustic and pastoral stage of
civilization. It is an innocence that precedes original sin. That
is why, in his poem on the Kaspar Hauser legend, Trakl describes the murdered boy as "unborn." Kaspar Hauser is murdered as soon as he reaches the city, after living in the woods
in a wild state. The whole poem is an allegory of the relation
between innocence and death, not, as one might easily think, a
glorification of a "noble savage" murdered by the corrupt inhabitants of the city.

Trakl, of course, can be criticized for his inability to bear the
guilt of being alive. Shortly before his death he said of himself
that as yet he was "only half born"; and he did not want his
birth to be completed.

Most of Trakl's later poems are written in a form of free
verse that owes much to the elegies and hymns of Hölderlin.
Without in fact imitating the classical hexameter, Trakl suggests
its movement by the frequent use of dactyls and spondees (as in

the long lines of *Sebastian im Traum*); but in many of his last poems he uses a short line which is also irregular, though more frequently iambic than his longer lines. These last poems are closer to Hölderlin's hymns than to his elegies; and the landscape in these poems is the grand alpine landscape of Innsbruck, as distinct from the more gentle, elegiac landscape of Salzburg and its surroundings. Trakl's long lines do not translate well into English because the language lacks the inflections that makes German so satisfactory a medium for the imitation of classical meters and cadences. Another obstacle to translation is that Trakl's adjectives carry much more weight than English usage allows; but though part of this weight might have been transferred to verbs and nouns in the English version, the result of this process would have been something altogether different from what Trakl wrote. Trakl's adjectives—and especially his color adjectives—have a function that is partly pictorial, partly emotive (often by means of synesthesia), and partly symbolic. Like all his favorite devices, the color epithets recur throughout his mature work with a persistency reminiscent of the Wagnerian leitmotiv (and Trakl is known to have gone through a youthful phase of enthusiasm for Wagner's music).

In spite of a few innocent plagiarisms, Trakl's debt to Hölderlin should not be exaggerated. Trakl also borrowed a few devices and images from Rimbaud, but very much less has been made of this debt or of his no less obvious debt to Baudelaire. It was Emil Barth,[10] in 1937, who first treated Trakl's work as a kind of continuation of Hölderlin's, by drawing attention to the affinity between Trakl's early rhymed poems and the very last poems of Hölderlin, the rhymed poems written in his madness. The theme was developed by Eduard Lachmann; [11] and Martin Heidegger has developed it further—to its ultralogical conclusion.[12]

The mere fact that Heidegger has thought Trakl worthy of

[10] Emil Barth, *Georg Trakl* (Krefeld, 1948).

[11] *Trakl und Hölderlin: Eine Deutung.* Appended to Trakl, *Works* III, 163–212.

[12] Martin Heidegger, "Georg Trakl," *Merkur,* Vol. VII, No. 3 (Stuttgart, March, 1953), 226–258.

his particular form of exegesis, which combines what seems like close textual analysis with the most far-reaching philosophical deductions, implies one kind of affinity between Trakl and the other German poets—Hölderlin and Rilke—to whom Heidegger has devoted similar studies; this affinity, of course, is one of perception, and it undoubtedly exists. But only a poet who uses words with the utmost precision, and with the utmost consistency as well, can be expected to bear the weight of Heidegger's exegesis; and Trakl's use of imagery, on which every interpretation of his poems must rest, was not consistent.

A comparison with Hölderlin is also implied by Heidegger's premises; for it is from Hölderlin that he derived many of his ideas about the function of poetry, and it is in the light of these ideas that he examines Trakl's work, inevitably linking it to Hölderlin's. Heidegger believes that the function of poets is "to name what is holy"; but this naming, he writes,[13] "does not consist in merely giving a name to something already known, but only when the poet speaks the significant word is the existent nominated into what it is. Poetry is the institution in words of being." This view is not very different from Rilke's conception of poetry as affirmation and praise of the visible world, and its transformation in the poet's "inwardness" into pure significance. Heidegger goes further than Rilke only in clearly stating that poets "institute being," rather than merely affirming it in words. Hölderlin, however, had a more modest end in mind when he wrote—at the end of *Patmos*—that the function of poets is to see that "the existing be well construed." The difference, once more, is that between a religion of the *logos* and a religion of the heart. If the *logos* was at the beginning, there is no need for poets to create the world all over again by endowing it with meaning. The question, in Trakl's case, is whether his poems were intended to "institute being" or merely to construe it.

Heidegger sees Trakl as the poet of the transitional age of which Hölderlin wrote in *Brod und Wein,* an era of Night in which there is no divine revelation, but only waiting and preparation for a new epiphany. It is certainly true that, in a very

[13] Martin Heidegger, *Erläuterungen zu Hölderlins Dichtung* (Frankfurt am Main, 1951), 38.

different sense from the later Expressionists, Trakl wrote of a "new humanity" or at least of a humanity different from that of the present day; but he did so in the form of images and of those mythical personages who inhabit his poems, not in the form of statements that one can easily quote in support of an argument. It is also true that his images of decay, his nocturnes, autumnal landscapes, and visions of doom are often relieved by images of regeneration, which point to a reality quite distinct from his immediate circumstances. These images Heidegger interprets as intimations of a regenerate Occident.

Trakl wrote poems that refer explicitly to the Occident. These are "Abendländisches Lied" and "Abendland." The first, which is the earlier poem, begins with images of a past, feudal and pastoral, way of life; it is difficult to place these images historically, for there are allusions to shepherds, to "blood blossoming beside the sacrificial stone," to the Crusades, and "glowing martyrdom of the flesh," to the "pious disciples" now turned into warriors, to "peaceful monks who pressed the purple grape," to hunting and to castles. The general impression is that the poem moves from a remote pastoral age to New Testament times, then to the early and later Middle Ages. In the last stanza Trakl turns to the present:

> O, die bittere Stunde des Untergangs,
> Da wir ein steinernes Antlitz in schwarzen Wassern beschaun.
> Aber strahlend heben die silbernen Lider die Liebenden:
> *Ein* Geschlecht. Weihrauch strömt von rosigen Kissen
> Und der süsse Gesang der Auferstandenen.

The ambiguity of these lines is such that they are untranslatable. All one can say with certainty is that Trakl sees the present as "the bitter hour of decline, when in black waters we gaze at a stony face"—images that suggest a narcissistic isolation and the guilt which, as in other poems of Trakl's, petrifies every faculty; and that the next three lines express a hope of regeneration. It is the nature of that regeneration which is obscure; for "die Liebenden" could be lovers "lifting up silvery eyelids" to look at each other; they could be Christian worshipers raising their eyes after prayer toward the altar. The ambiguity is maintained in the next line; for *"ein* Geschlecht" could mean *"one* sex," *"one* kind," or *"one* generation." And the "rosy cushions" from which incense wafts could conceivably be hassocks, if one takes the color epithet to be symbolical. Perhaps Trakl intended both meanings: the fusion into one of the sexes, which symbolizes an integration of the psyche—so that the individual is redeemed from narcissistic solitude; and the fusion of Christian worshipers into one community by the act of worship and their redemption by Christian love. The concluding line—"and the sweet song of the resurrected"—accords with both interpretations.

Neither interpretation, however, accords with Heidegger's argument; for the regeneration of which he speaks is one peculiar to his own philosophy. As for the latter of the two poems, "Abendland," it ends with a vision of unrelieved gloom:

> Ihr grossen Städte
> steinern aufgebaut
> in der Ebene!
> So sprachlos folgt
> der Heimatlose
> mit dunkler Stirne dem Wind,
> kahlen Bäumen am Hügel.
> Ihr weithin dämmernden Ströme!
> Gewaltig ängstet
> schaurige Abendröte
> im Sturmgewölk.
> Ihr sterbenden Völker!
> Bleiche Woge
> zerschellend am Strande der Nacht,
> fallende Sterne.

> You mighty cities
> stone on stone raised up
> in the plain!
> So quietly
> with darkened forehead
> the outcast follows the wind,
> bare trees on the hillside.
> You rivers distantly fading!
> Gruesome sunset red

is breeding fear
in the thunder clouds.
You dying peoples!
Pallid billow
that breaks on the beach of Night,
stars that are falling.

Heidegger argues that the second part of this poem, which is more peaceful in mood but filled with images of decay, cancels out the apocalyptic third part (quoted above). If this were so, the development of Trakl's poem would be strange indeed; it would mean that the poem proceeds from a valid vision to one that has been invalidated by the preceding vision. Heidegger admits the ambiguity of Trakl's poetry—indeed, he writes that "it speaks out of an ambiguous ambiguity!"—but his awareness of the ambiguity does not prevent him from interpreting the whole of Trakl's work in the most general terms.

The main obstacle to such a sweeping interpretation is that Trakl used the same images and epithets for different purposes, sometimes descriptively, sometimes symbolically. This applies even to his favorite color epithets—"golden coolness," "purple stars," "black pillow," "blue animal," "rosy sighs," and even "the white night"; but "brown tree," "yellow corn," "red flowers," "blueish pond," "green boughs." After deciding in every instance whether a color epithet is to be taken literally or not, one has to go on to the much more difficult question of whether the nonrealistic epithets are strictly symbolic or whether they amount to nothing more than an emotive synesthesia.

Certain painters and poets of the Expressionist era were greatly interested in the symbolism of colors; [14] but Trakl's color symbolism was certainly not traditional and most probably not even conscious. His critics and interpreters, too, disagree over this vital point. Heidegger and Emil Barth believe that his colors are symbolic, but Barth does not say what they symbolize and confuses symbolism with synesthesia. Heidegger sees all Trakl's colors as symbolic—even where they conform

[14] E.g., Theodor Däubler, "Expressionismus," *Insel Almanach* (1918), 177–186.

to the conventions of realism—but believes that this symbolism is ambiguous. He cites the instance of "golden" in Trakl's line from "Winkel im Wald": "Auch zeigt sich sanftem Wahnsinn oft das Goldne, Wahre." (Often to gentle madness the golden, true, is revealed") in which "golden" is explicitly identified with "true," whereas in a different poem Trakl speaks of "das grässliche Lachen des Golds" ("the horrible laughter of gold"). Heidegger infers that Trakl's "golden" has two antithetical but complementary meanings, both of them symbolic. He does not mention that in all Trakl's poems there is only one instance where gold has unpleasant associations; and that this is one of the few poems in which Trakl forsakes his symbolic landscapes to write about a large city which—like his contemporary Georg Heym—he sees as demonically possessed. The poem in question, "An die Verstummten," is more didactic than visionary:

O, der Wahnsinn der Grossen Stadt, da am Abend
An schwarzer Mauer verkrüppelte Bäume starren,
Aus silberner Maske der Geist des Bösen schaut;
Licht mit magnetischer Geissel die steinerne Nacht verdrängt.
O, das versunkene Läuten der Abendglocken.

Hure, die in eisigen Schauern ein totes Kindlein gebärt.
Rasend peitscht Gottes Zorn die Stirn der Besessenen,
Purpurne Seuche, Hunger, der grüne Augen zerbricht.
O, das grässliche Lachen des Golds.

Aber stille blutet in dunkler Höhle stummere Menschheit,
Fügt aus harten Metallen das erlösende Haupt.

Oh, the great city's madness when at nightfall
The crippled trees gape by the blackened wall,
The spirit of evil peers from a silver mask;
Lights with magnetic scourge drive off the stony night.
Oh, the sunken pealing of evening bells.

Whore who in her icy spasms gives birth to a dead child.
With raving whip God's fury punishes the brows possessed.
Purple pestilence, hunger that breaks green eyes.
Oh, the horrible laughter of gold.

But silent in dark caves a stiller humanity bleeds,
Out of hard metals moulds the redeeming head.

The "gold" here has nothing to do with the adjective "golden" that Trakl uses symbolically elsewhere; it stands for nothing more esoteric than material wealth. Its function in this poem is neither antithetical nor complementary to its function in other poems; it is simply different.

The "silver mask" of the third line could also be interpreted in terms of Heidegger's ambiguous symbolism. The epithet "silver," he points out, "is the pallor of death and the twinkling of stars." The inference is that Trakl's symbols and symbolic epithets are ambiguous because of his simultaneous perception of two orders of reality, of the present and the timeless (or future) aspect of any scene. This Heidegger attributed to Trakl's belief in a homecoming ("Heimkunft") after the transition (Übergang") of this life and the departure ("Abschied") of death. This homecoming Heidegger interprets as that of a new generation or race ("Geschlecht") that will eventually succeed the "degenerate" one of the present. "Trakl," Heidegger writes, "is the poet of the still hidden Occident."

Very few, if any, of Trakl's poems bear out this interpretation, which simply ignores the contradictions in Trakl's work. One of these contradictions appertains to his use of color epithets.[15] The "silver mask" in the above poem, for instance, has no primary connection with either death or the stars, but an obvious one with the artificial lights that "drive off the night" and prevent the city dwellers from facing their guilt and seeking redemption. In other cases, Trakl's color epithets serve to induce that "systematic derangement of the senses" which Rimbaud prescribed. Nor does his color symbolism—where it is a symbolism—always agree with the traditional one preserved by the alchemists; to them, the metal silver corresponded not with the stars, but with the moon, and its color was gray.

It is the last lines of the poem, with their allusion to "the redeeming head," that may seem to support Heidegger's thesis of

[15] Trakl's lack of a conscious design or system, his openness and even his uncertainty in the composition of his poems have been confirmed by the textual researches of Walther Killy. Trakl frequently replaced a word in early drafts of his poems with the semantic opposite. e.g., "decline" with "perfection" or "completion," "prepared" with "closed" or "concluded." See Walther Killy, *Bestand und Bewegung in Gedichten Georg Trakls,* in Festschrift für Bernhard Blume (Göttingen, 1967), 246–257.

a future regeneration; but these lines raise the question of Trakl's own beliefs. From the evidence of his poetry alone, his precise beliefs remain doubtful. Much of his imagery derives from Roman Catholic rites, though Trakl was a Lutheran; he went so far as to call one sequence of poems *Rosenkranzlieder* ("Rosary Songs"). The question of his orthodoxy must remain open here; but there can be no doubt at all that Trakl was a Christian. According to an account by Hans Limbach [16] of a conversation between Trakl and Carl Dallago, which took place at Innsbruck in 1914, Trakl professed beliefs very different from Heidegger's interpretation:

"By the way, do you know Walt Whitman's work?" he [Dallago] asked him suddenly.

Trakl said he did, but added that he thought Whitman pernicious.

"How so?"—D. exclaimed—"How do you mean, pernicious. Don't you admire his work? Surely your manner has a good deal in common with his."

F. [Ficker] observed that the two poets were really radically opposed, since Whitman simply affirmed life in all its manifestations, whereas Trakl was thoroughly pessimistic. Didn't life give him any pleasure, then?—D. continued his inquisition. Didn't his creative work, for instance, satisfy him at all?

"Yes," Trakl admitted, "but one should be suspicious of that satisfaction."

D. leant back in his chair in his boundless astonishment.

"Well, in that case, why don't you go into a monastery?" he asked after a short silence.

"I am a Protestant," Trakl replied.

"Pro-te-stant?"—D. asked again. "I must say, I should never have thought so.—Well, at least you shouldn't live in town, but move to the country, where you'd be far from the madding crowd and nearer to nature."

"I have no right to remove myself from Hell," Trakl replied.

"But Christ did so," the other retorted.

"Christ is the Son of God."

D. was almost speechless.

[16] Appended to Trakl, *Dichtungen* (Zurich), 208–213.

"So you believe too that all salvation comes from Him? You take those words, 'the Son of God,' quite literally?"

"I'm a Christian," Trakl answered.

"Well, then, how would you explain such un-Christian phenomena as Buddha or the Chinese sages?"

"They too received their light from Christ."

We fell silent, pondering on the profundity of this paradox. But D. could not let the matter rest.

"And the Greeks? Don't you agree that men have sunk much lower since their time?"

"Never have men sunk so low as now, after the appearance of Christ," Trakl replied. "They *could* not sink so low," he added after a pause . . .

One can question the accuracy of this report and its relevance to Trakl's poetry; but any interpretation of his symbolism must take Trakl's Christian faith into account, allowing for the influence of Kierkegaard and the wholly undogmatic nature of Trakl's poetry. Like Rimbaud, Trakl was "an alchemist of the word"; but even alchemists could be orthodox in their acceptance of dogma, as Paracelsus protested that he was. The real issue is whether Trakl's poetry can be interpreted as a whole or whether the seeming consistency of his later work—due to his use of recurrent images and epithets—is deceptive.

Heidegger evades this issue by assuming that Trakl is a great poet and that his practice was consistent. "Every great poet creates his poetry out of a single poem," he claims; and adds that "this poem remains unspoken." I doubt that this is true of all great poets, at least on a level that permits discussion; but since the archetypal poem remains "unspoken," it is almost useless to object that some great poets may well have more than one of these archetypal poems to draw on. Even if one succeeded in showing that certain great poets derived from two or more of such archetypes, these, in turn, could be traced back to an archetype even more archetypal; but here we leave the domain of literary criticism, which is not qualified to deal in the unspeakable.

In certain of his poems, Trakl applied the epithets "silver" and "golden" in a sense that is undoubtedly symbolic. Thus in a short poem, "Untergang" ("Decline"), addressed to a friend:

Über den weissen Weiher
Sind die wilden Vögel fortgezogen.
Am Abend weht von unseren Sternen ein eisiger Wind.

Über unsere Gräber
Beugt sich die zerbrochene Stirne der Nacht.
Unter Eichen schaukeln wir auf einem silbernen Kahn.

Immer klingen die weissen Mauern der Stadt.
Unter Dornenbogen
O mein Bruder klimmen wir blinde Zeiger gen Mitternacht.

Over the white pond
The wild birds have travelled on.
In the evening an icy wind blows from our stars.

Over our graves
The broken brow of the night inclines.
Under oak-trees we sway in a silver boat.

Always the town's white walls resound.
Under arches of thorns
O my brother, blind minute-hands
We climb towards midnight.

In this poem, Trakl sees both the friend and himself as transitional figures passing though death-in-life to spiritual regeneration. The whole meaning of the poem is in the images and the symbolic epithets, the "white" and "silver," which Trakl associates with death. There are only three brief references to the two persons of the poem, at the end of each strophe. The first strophe begins with an image suggesting transience, but without direct reference to the human personages of the poem. This reference is withheld till the third line; and even this reference is indirect. The second strophe connects the malignant influence of the stars with death; but death, to Trakl, is itself a state of transition. Boats, as in Hölderlin and Nietzsche, symbolize existence; this boat is a silver one because the lives of the two friends are overshadowed by death. The concluding strophe introduces another image that symbolizes existence here and now, the temporal order; the town's white walls are white because that temporal order itself wears the color of death, because it is doomed. In an age such as the one they live in the two friends can only suffer and wait for death. The "arch of thorns" suggests both suffering in general and the Passion.

A special significance attaches to the "silver boat" of this poem, because elsewhere Trakl has a "golden boat," which is in complete contrast with this one. The golden boat occurs in one of Trakl's poems about Elis, a mythical boy who is either dead or "unborn"—in Trakl's peculiar sense of that word. We might not know that he is not of this life, but for a different poem, "An den Knaben Elis" ("To the Boy Elis"):

> . . . Ein Dornenbusch tönt
> Wo deine mondenen Augen sind.
> O, wie lange bist, Elis, du verstorben.
>
> Dein Leib ist eine Hyazinthe,
> In die ein Mönch die wächsernen Finger taucht.
> Ein schwarze Höhle ist unser Schweigen,
>
> Daraus bisweilen ein sanftes Tier tritt
> Und langsam die schweren Lider senkt.
> Auf deine Schläfen tropft schwarzer Tau,
>
> Das letzte Gold verfallner Sterne.

> A thorn-bush sounds
> Where your lunar eyes are.
> O Elis, how long since you died.
>
> Your body is a hyacinth
> Into which a monk dips his waxen fingers.
> Our silence is a black cavern
>
> From which at times a gentle animal
> Steps out and lowers heavy lids.
> Upon your temples black dew drips,
>
> The last gold of perished stars.

Because Elis is dead or "unborn," he is introduced by images of an innocent mode of life in the poem called "Elis":

> . . . Am Abend zog der Fischer die schweren Netze ein.
> Ein guter Hirt

Führt seine Herde am Waldsaum hin.
O! wie gerecht sind, Elis alle deine Tage.

Leise sinkt
An kahlen Mauern des Ölbaums blaue Stille,
Erstirbt eines Greisen dunkler Gesang.

Ein goldener Kahn
Schaukelt, Elis, dein Herz am einsamen Himmel.

. . . At nightfall the fisherman hauled in his heavy nets.
A good shepherd
Leads his flock along the forest's edge.
Oh, how righteous, Elis, are all your days.

Softly sinks
The olive tree's blue stillness on bare walls,
An old man's dark song subsides.

A golden boat
Sways, Elis, your heart against a lonely sky.

The significance of the "golden boat" here is indicated by its connection with Elis' righteousness and with the images of the good life that precede it. Both the fisherman and the shepherd stand for an order opposed to that of modern life, but what is important about them is their obvious connection with Christ; they are not righteous because they are primitive, but their primitiveness symbolizes righteousness. The golden boat, in this context, symbolizes a mode of existence unthreatened by death or decay. "Golden," here, may well be symbolic of truth, for Trakl identified truth with innocence and righteousness.

Yet the very same poem begins with a line in which "golden" has a function that is primarily visual or emotive: "Vollkommen ist die Stille dieses goldenen Tags . . ." ("Perfect is the stillness of this golden day . . ."). The noun "gold" occurs again in one of Trakl's late poems of the Innsbruck period, "Das Herz" ("The Heart"), an angry and despairing poem closely related to the apocalyptic "Abendland." In this poem death, for once, is terrible; and it is the word "gold"—used in a purely symbolic sense—that tells us why. I shall quote the whole poem:

Das wilde Herz ward weiss am Wald;
O dunkle Angst
Des Todes, so das Gold
In grauer Wolke starb.
Novemberabend.
Am kahlen Tor am Schlachthaus stand
Der armen Frauen Schar;
In jeden Korb
Fiel faules Fleisch und Eingeweid;
Verfluchte Kost!

Des Abends blaue Taube
Brachte nicht Versöhnung.
Dunkler Trompetenruf
Durchfuhr der Ulmen
Nasses Goldlaub,
Eine zerfetzte Fahne
Vom Blute rauchend,
Dass in wilder Schwermut
Hinlauscht ein Mann.
O! ihr ehernen Zeiten
Begraben dort im Abendrot.

Aus dunklen Hausflur trat
Die goldene Gestalt
Der Jünglingin
Umgeben von bleichen Monden,
Herbstlicher Hofstaat,
Zerknickten schwarzen Tannen
Im Nachtsturm,
Die steile Festung.
O Herz
Hinüberschimmernd in schneeige Kühle.

The wild heart turned white in the wood;
O the dark fear
Of death, when the gold
Died in a grey cloud.
November evening.
By the bare gate of the slaughterhouse there stood
The crowd of poor women.
Into every basket
Rank flesh and entrails fell;
Accursed fare!

The blue dove of nightfall
Brought no atonement.
Dark trumpet call
Rang through the elm-trees'
Damp golden leaves,
A tattered banner
Steaming with blood,
So that wild in his sadness
A man gives heed.
O brazen ages
Buried there in the sunset red.

From the house's dark hall there stepped
The golden shape
Of the maiden-youth
Surrounded with pale moons
Of autumnal courtliness,
Black pine-trees snapped
In the night gale,
The steep-walled fortress.
O heart
Glistening away into snowy coolness.

Death is terrible in this poem because "the gold died in a grey cloud"; that is to say, the true, spiritual order has been momentarily obscured, so that the poet is at the mercy of that materialism to which death is simply the cessation of life—an event more fearful than any. The harsh realism of the images that follow—the poor women who are fobbed off with putrid meat and entrails—belongs to the same materialistic order; one might almost take these images as an indictment of the social order, if it weren't for their unrealistic context. The "dove of nightfall" is blue not only because certain night skies are deep blue, but because blue stands for the spiritual in Trakl's poetry: the spiritual, at present, is powerless.

The "maiden-youth" of the third strophe is "golden" because this hermaphrodite stands for a mode of being exempt from original sin; Trakl also has a personage called "die Mönchin" (female form of "monk"), who belongs to the same order. The "sister" of other late poems has the same significance; although not hermaphrodite in herself, she is the feminine complement of the poet's masculine spirit. The absurdity of identifying this sister with Trakl's sister Margarete is evident from his last poem, in which it is the sister's shade that appears; and Trakl's sister was neither dead at the time (although she later committed suicide also) nor actually present on the battlefield. In "Das Herz," it is the appearance of the "Jünglingin" that reconciles the poet to death; for "snowy" coolness denotes the whiteness both of innocence and of death.

Heidegger cites Trakl's two last poems, "Klage" and "Grodek," as evidence that Trakl was not a Christian poet. He asks why Trakl does not invoke God or Christ in the extremity of his despair, a despair which, Heidegger claims, "is not even Christian despair." The answer is that poetry is not prayer, or a substitute for prayer; Trakl himself said that it was an "imperfect penance." Direct references to the deity are rare even in the earlier poems of Trakl, which contain unmistakable allusions to Christian sacraments—unmistakable, that is, to all but Heidegger. In the second part of *Sebastian im Traum,* for instance, Christ is quite clearly invoked, but Trakl leaves the name "unspoken":

> . . . Oder wenn er an der harten Hand des Vaters
> Stille den finstern Kalvarienberg hinanstieg
> Und in dämmernden Felsennischen
> Die blaue Gestalt des Menschen durch seine Legende ging,
> Aus der Wunde unter dem Herzen purpurn das Blut rann.
> O wie leise stand in dunkler Seele das Kreuz auf . . .

> . . . Or holding his father's horny hand
> In silence he walked up Calvary Hill
> And in dusky rock recesses
> The blue shape of Man would pass through his legend,
> Blood run purple from the wound beneath his heart.
> O how softly the cross rose up in the dark of his soul . . .

Christ is referred to as "der Mensch," which could mean either "Man" or "the man." In the same way, few would doubt that Trakl alludes to Christ in his poem "An die Verstummten," since the "redeeming head" of the last line has a more explicit counterpart in "Abendländisches Lied":

. . . Ruh des Abends,
Da in seiner Kammer der Mensch Gerechtes sann,
In stummem Gebet um Gottes lebendiges Haupt rang.

. . . Quiet of evening,
When in his room a man gave thought to righteousness
And for God's living head grappled in silent prayer.

It is very strange that Heidegger, who looks only for Trakl's
"unspoken" poem throughout the greater part of his essay, persistently ignoring such literal evidence as the line cited above,
should suddenly require literal proof of Trakl's Christian faith
where it isn't provided. But Heidegger despises logic as much
as he despises "values." [17] His philosophy reduces the world to
its primal chaos and then proceeds to re-create it in the shape
of Heidegger's mind. Since his literary criticism is an extension
of his philosophizing, one must not expect it to balk at mere
facts; but it is illuminating in its own right, as pretextual rather
than contextual criticism.

Of Trakl's last two poems, the earlier, "Klage," does render
a vision of unmitigated despair; unmitigated, that is, except for
a grammatical qualification that often escapes notice. The verb
in the fourth line, "verschlänge," does not render an event that
has occurred but an event that is to be feared. Here is the poem
"Klage" ("Lament"):

Schlaf und Tod, die düstern Adler
Umrauschen nachtlang dieses Haupt:
Des Menschen goldnes Bildnis
Verschlänge die eisige Woge
Der Ewigkeit. An schaurigen Riffen
Zerschellt der purpurne Leib.
Und es klagt die dunkle Stimme
Über dem Meer.
Schwester stürmischer Schwermut
Sieh ein ängstlicher Kahn versinkt
Unter Sternen,
Dem schweigenden Antlitz der Nacht.

[17] See his "Über den 'Humanismus,' " in *Platons Lehre von der Wahr-
heit* (Berne, 1954), 55, 58, 99–100.

> Sleep and death, the dark eagles
> Around this head swoop all night long:
> Eternity's icy wave
> Would swallow the golden image
> Of man; on horrible reefs
> His purple body is shattered.
> And the dark voice laments
> Over the sea.
> Sister of stormy sadness,
> Look, a timorous boat goes down
> Under stars,
> The silent face of the night.

What is important is that the poem deals with two different disasters. The first, which has not occurred but which the poet fears, is that "eternity's icy wave would or may swallow" the "golden image of man"; that is to say, that men will be untrue to their Creator beyond all possibility of redemption. Heidegger rightly points out that "eternity's icy wave" is not a Christian concept; but Trakl, after all, had read Nietzsche, to whom Heidegger owes so much, and his despair was bound to be colored by the current modes of unbelief. That is why he grew angry when Dallago mentioned Nietzsche to him, saying that Nietzsche was a madman suffering "from the same disease as Maupassant." [18] In order to express his despair—a conditional despair—he had to resort to the language of unbelief; and in other late poems too, as we have seen, Trakl was overwhelmed by his foreboding of doom.

The "purple body" of man—as distinct from his "golden *image*"—*is* being shattered, for the poem alludes to the war. Since boats symbolize existence, the sinking boat of the tenth line has the effect of a final disaster: this disaster is the senseless destruction of war, a death that is mere carnage and not the expiation of guilt that Trakl welcomes in other poems. Since the sister is invoked at the end, as a witness to the sinking boat, the extinction that Trakl fears is not the physical annihilation of mankind. One would be inclined to read a reference to Trakl's own death into these lines, if the tone of the poem were not so impersonal.

[18] Limbach's account, *loc. cit.*, 211.

Trakl's last poem, "Grodek," is more hopeful; but it is no less difficult to interpret. The "unborn grandsons" of the last line have been taken too literally as a later generation who will profit by the sacrifice of war. In an earlier poem, "Der Abend," Trakl writes of "the white grandsons whose dark future is being prepared by the decaying generation (or kind) which, cold and evil, inhabits the city":

> Mit toten Heldengestalten
> Erfüllst du Mond
> Die schweigenden Wälder,
> Sichelmond—
> Mit der sanften Umarmung
> Der Liebenden,
> Den Schatten berühmter Zeiten
> Die modernden Felsen rings
> So bläulich erstrahlt es
> Gegen die Stadt hin,
> Wo kalt und böse
> Ein verwesend Geschlecht wohnt,
> Der weissen Enkel
> Dunkle Zukunft bereitet.
> Ihr mondverschlungnen Schatten
> Aufseufzend im leeren Kristall
> Des Bergsees.

> With dead figures of heroes
> The moon is filling
> The silent forests,
> O sickle-moon!
> And the mouldering rocks all round
> With the soft embraces
> Of lovers,
> The phantoms of famous ages;
> This blue light shines
> Towards the city
> Where a decaying race
> Lives coldly and evilly,
> Preparing the dark future
> Of their white descendants.
> O moon-wrapped shadows

Sighing in the empty crystal
Of the mountain lake.[19]

In another poem, "Das Gewitter," Trakl has "the boy's golden war-cry and the unborn sighing from blind eyes." Both these poems are relevant to the "prophecy" that ends "Grodek"; and so is the despair of "Klage," for the two poems are complementary. In "Grodek," too, the sister appears; but she does not appear to the poet and is explicitly described as a "shadow." (In German usage "die Schwester" means both "the sister" and "*my* sister"; hence the biographical deductions. But in "Grodek" there is no question of any "I.")

Am Abend tönen die herbstlichen Wälder
Von tödlichen Waffen, die goldenen Ebenen
Und blauen Seen, darüber die Sonne
Düstrer hinrollt; umfängt die Nacht
Sterbende Krieger, die wilde Klage
Ihrer zerbrochenen Münder.
Doch stille sammelt im Weidengrund
Rotes Gewölk, darin ein zürnender Gott wohnt,
Das vergossne Blut sich, mondne Kühle;
Alle Strassen münden in schwarze Verwesung.
Unter goldnem Gezweig der Nacht und Sternen
Es schwankt der Schwester Schatten durch den schweigenden
                                                    Hain,
Zu grüssen die Geister der Helden, die blutenden Häupter;
Und leise tönen im Rohr die dunkeln Flöten des Herbstes.
O stolzere Trauer! ihr ehernen Altäre,
Die heisse Flamme des Geistes nährt heute ein gewaltiger
                                                    Schmerz,
Die ungebornen Enkel.

At nightfall the autumn woods cry out
With deadly weapons and the golden plains,
The deep blue lakes, above which more darkly
Rolls the sun; the night embraces
Dying warriors, the wild lament
Of their broken mouths.

[19] Georg Trakl, *Selected Poems,* trans. David Luke (London, 1968; New York, 1969), 109.

But quietly there in the pasture land
Red clouds in which an angry God resides,
The shed blood gathers, lunar coolness.
All the roads lead to blackest carrion.
Under golden twigs of the night and stars
The sister's shade now sways through the silent copse
To greet the ghosts of the heroes, the bleeding heads;
And softly the dark flutes of autumn sound in the reeds.
O prouder grief! You brazen altars,
This day a great pain feeds the hot flame of the spirit,
The yet unborn grandsons.

In this poem death in battle has the significance that Trakl's despair denies to it in "Klage"; it is a sacrifice and an expiation.
But "unborn grandsons" does not denote a specific generation
as yet unborn; there is no conceivable reason that the third generation, rather than the second or the fourth, should be redeemed by the death of these soldiers. "Unborn," as I have
pointed out, has another sense besides the literal one in Trakl's
poetry; it denotes a state of innocence more complete than the
innocence of childhood. It is possible that the grandsons of
"Grodek" are not a future generation at all, but the very same
generation whose "dark future" was prepared by the cold and
evil city dwellers in "Der Abend." In that case they would be
the soldiers themselves, whose expiatory death grants them a
return to innocence. If we take "unborn" literally—and Trakl
uses the word literally in the passage quoted from "Das
Gewitter"—the last lines of "Grodek" are indeed a prophecy,[20]
but a prophecy which it is wisest to leave alone at this stage.
To fix a date for its fulfillment or to specify the exact nature of
the regeneration in which Trakl believed is to put too great a
strain on his poetry.

If it is frustrating not to be able to end this study with a clarion call, it is also a tribute to Trakl's art. Expressionist poetry
yields opportunities for any number of clarion calls, as loud
and as rousing as anyone could wish. But the difficulty of sum-

[20] Eduard Lachmann identifies the "grandsons" of "Der Abend" with
those who will meet their fate in World War II, *Kreuz und Abend,* 74.
Lachmann does not discuss the identity of the "grandsons" in "Grodek."

ming up Trakl's work as a whole, and the much greater difficulty of interpreting it as a whole, are two reasons that his work stands out from the German poetry of his time. Trakl's plagiarisms—and especially his self-plagiarisms—lend a deceptive consistency to his work—deceptive, because his poems are essentially ambiguous. His ambiguities derive from the tension between image and symbol, the phenomenon and the Idea. Sometimes this tension remains unresolved, so that one cannot tell whether an image is to be taken descriptively or symbolically, an epithet synesthetically or qualitatively. It is true that each of Trakl's poems offers some kind of clue to the next; but it is a clue that can be very misleading.

Trakl's ambiguities are not deliberate or cerebral; he was an imaginative poet, not a fanciful one. That is why his plagiarisms are never disturbing or offensive. His debt to Hölderlin alone was such that, by all the usual criteria, his work should be very nearly worthless. He appropriated Hölderlin's imagery, rhythms, and syntax; yet Trakl's originality is beyond doubt. Any group of three lines detached from one of his later poems is immediately recognizable as his own. Trakl carried plagiarism further by continually quoting himself, repeating, varying, and adding to his earlier poems. But there is no reason that a poet should not steal his own property in order to rearrange it; and this very habit points to the harmlessness of Trakl's borrowings from other poets. The laws of property do apply to literature, insofar as no writer can deliberately steal what he lacks himself and get away with the swag; but they do not apply to the imagination. The imagination can only borrow, never steal; and, by its very nature, it can only borrow those things to which it has a right.

Trakl's debt to Hölderlin is a curiosity of literature; it does not mean that his symbolism can be interpreted in terms of Hölderlin's or that his vision begins where Hölderlin's left off. Heidegger not only presupposes such a tradition of vision and prophecy, but reads his own philosophy into Hölderlin and applies this reading to Trakl. The result is a fascinating, but ruthless, gesture, which sweeps away all evidence of Trakl's own thought in order to turn him into the prophet of an Occident regenerated by the philosophy of pure being. It is true that existential creeds tend to look alike, especially if they have been expressed in poetry alone; and Trakl's Christian faith was an existential one. But this faith is essential to his poetry, as most of his critics agree.[21] Heidegger's exegesis would not have been possible at all but for Trakl's imagist practice; because of the noncommittal character of imagism, it would also be possible to argue that Trakl was an alchemist (as his astrological metaphors confirm!) or a Marxist (because of his vision of capitalism in decay!).

In an age of conflicting creeds and sects, such openness is an advantage. Horizontally, Trakl's range is that of a minor poet, but his vertical range is out of all proportion to it. By "vertical" here I mean neither profundity nor sublimity, but a dimension related to harmony in music. Trakl's poetry is a series of microcosmic variations, poor in melodic invention, rich in harmonic correspondences. Another way of putting it is to say that his work is valid on many "levels" of meaning. It depends as little as possible on the poet's person, opinions, and circumstances. One reason is that Trakl was conscious neither of himself nor of his reader; all his poems had his undivided attention. Of T. S. Eliot's "three voices of poetry," Trakl had only the first; but because it never even occurred to him to cultivate the others, his monologue was strangely quiet and pure.

[21] See Irene Morris, "Georg Trakl," *German Life & Letters,* Vol. II, No. 2 (January, 1949), and the same author's "Georg Trakls Weltanschauung," *Trivium,* Vol. VI, No. 2. Also Egon Vietta, *Georg Trakl. Eine Interpretation seines Werkes* (Hamburg, 1947).

GOTTFRIED BENN

At the time when Georg Trakl feared for the "golden image of man," Gottfried Benn had already given it up for lost. His concern was with the "purple body" of man in hospital beds or on the dissecting table. The two poets could hardly have less in common. Gottfried Benn too was a solitary poet, but his awareness of being so prevented most of his work from being pure monologue. He was like a man talking to himself in a room full of silly people, trying hard to ignore them but always irritated by their insolent scrutiny; his attitude toward them was one of aggressive self-defense. The trouble, of course, was his own self-consciousness; but since monologue is the only kind of communication that Benn thought valid, and since he knew his self-consciousness to be incurable, he reconciled himself to his paradoxical function, that of an *enfant terrible* as much in demand for his terrible outbursts of scorn and anger as for the aura of his self-absorption.

This *enfant terrible,* meanwhile, turned into "one of the grand old men of literary Europe," as a younger poet and critic, Hans Egon Holthusen, called him; adding that Benn "represents the melancholy" of these grand old men. Much of the interest that attaches to Benn's last writings and utterances is the interest aroused by the sole survivor from a great shipwreck. But though Benn has much to say of his generation and of Expressionism, Benn's later development was strongly influenced by a reaction against the excesses of the later Expressionists, and especially against that desperate optimism which took the form of political agitation: and, from the start, Benn's poetic practice differed essentially from that of all his contemporaries.

Gottfried Benn was born at Mansfeld, Brandenburg, in 1886, the son of a Lutheran clergyman. After attending school at Frankfort on the Oder, he studied theology and German at the University of Marburg, but abandoned these subjects in favor of medicine. He was trained to be a military doctor. After a few months' service in 1912, he was invalided out of the Army and settled in Berlin. Except for war service from 1914 to 1918 and again from 1939 to 1944, Benn practiced in Berlin as a specialist in skin and venereal diseases. Although never a party man, Benn's reaction against the dominant ideology of the interwar years, that of the Left, caused him to welcome the extremists of the Right in two essays of 1932 and 1933; [1] but he did not change his style, and Expressionism was soon condemned as "degenerate art." In 1937 Gottfried Benn was forbidden to publish his works and took refuge from his persecutors in the Party by reentering the Medical Corps. His description of the Army as "the aristocratic form of emigration" became famous in the war years.

Benn's premises go back to two definitions by Nietzsche which he is fond of quoting: "The world as an aesthetic phenomenon" and "Art as the last metaphysical activity within European nihilism." Gottfried Benn accepts this nihilism as one accepts the weather. In an article of 1949,[2] set out in the form of answers to questions put to him in an interview, he wrote:

[1] "Nach dem Nihilismus" and "Der neue Staat und die Intellektuellen."

[2] "Phase II," *Merkur,* Vol. IV, No. 1 (January, 1950), 24.

"When you announced your visit, you promised not to ask me whether I'm a nihilist. And indeed the question is just as meaningless as to ask me whether I'm a skater or a stamp collector. For the important thing is what one makes of one's nihilism." Benn believes that nihilism is the inevitable frame of mind of every contemporary European whose intellect is highly developed; but, in later years especially, he also speaks of "transcending nihilism," and this is done by setting up new values to take the place of those no longer tenable—much as Nietzsche spoke of the "transvaluation of all values." At one time, the particular mode of "transcendence" that Benn recommended was a brutal vitalism; since he identified nihilism with a highly developed intellect, sometimes even with consciousness itself, the only way to "transcend" it was to glorify crude energy, to drug the conscious mind and release subconscious impulses. That is why Benn was drawn to National Socialism for a time. In an address delivered in the Prussian *Akademie der Künste* in 1932, Benn made this pronouncement: "For if there is still any kind of transcendence, it must be a bestial one, if there is still any place for a link with the superindividual, only organic matter provides such a place." [3] The aestheticism that Benn advocated in place of that bestial transcendence is also an escape from the "affliction of thinking"; but it is one that has become so familiar as to be respectable.

What is least clear about Benn's thought is his grounds for assuming the inevitability of nihilism in our time. The reasons he gives for this assumption have varied greatly, according to Benn's momentary preoccupations; and they are neither consistent nor convincing. At times he based his belief on biological factors, at other times on psychological ones—though he tended to treat psychology as a subcategory of biology— sometimes historical, in the large sense of the word lent to it by Vico, Herder, and Hegel; and he was decisively influenced by Spengler's prognosis of Europe's decline, a prognosis based on a vast and dubious compilation of symptoms. Whatever his reasons, Benn was convinced that "the white peoples are at the stage of egress, no matter whether the theories about

[3] *Frühe Prosa und Reden* (1950), 231. Benn's pronouncement is based on a remark by Thomas Mann.

their decline are considered valid to-day or not . . . The race has become immobile, it remains fixed around its kernel, and this kernel is intellect, that is to say, nihilism." [4] The truth may well be that Benn's belief in nihilism amounted to a blind faith. Artistically, this faith enabled him to travel light; to be as inconsistent as he pleased, to abandon himself to the moment, to experiment freely with words and ideas.

Benn goes one stage further than Nietzsche, who also praised the delights of nihilism, but suffered agonies of contrition. "What distinguishes the situation of the man of 1940—the man concerned with intellectual questions and deductions—from Nietzsche's situation is, above all, that he has broken off relations with the public and with that pedagogic-cum-political sphere which Nietzsche's works, especially those of the eighteen-eighties, passionately cultivated." [5] But, as already implied, Benn's isolation was an ambiguous one; a writer who has "broken off relations with the public" does not take part in the transactions of a national academy of the arts—as Benn did with notorious zest in the early nineteen-thirties—nor does he lend his name to the publication of an interview concerning his books. For all his concern with ethics and morality, one cannot imagine Nietzsche doing either of these things. In a section of his *Ausdruckswelt* headed "Pessimism," Benn elaborates on this theme of intellectual isolation: "Men are not lonely, but thinking is lonely. It is true that men are closely surrounded with mournful things, but many take part in this mourning and it is popular with everyone. But thinking is ego-bound and solitary." This, of course, depends on how one thinks; but for Benn there is no question of the kind of thought that enlarges consciousness beyond the bounds of selfhood. It is feeling that does so, intoxication and vital impulse. All his theories, aesthetic, metaphysical, and political, derive from his sense of the disharmony between the part and the whole, inward and outward reality. "That which lives is something other than that which thinks," is how he formulates this basic dichotomy.

It is significant that Benn's first poems were concerned with an aspect of outward reality that repelled him. The bitterness of

[4] *Weinhaus Wolf* (1937), in *Der Ptolemäer* (1949), 30.
[5] *Ausdruckswelt* (1949), 40.

his first collection, *Morgue,* published in 1912, was in its realism. With one exception, all these poems are a direct reaction to Benn's professional duties. The diction is coarsely colloquial, with compassionate or sentimental undertones which Benn is reluctant to admit. In most of these clinical poems he employs a loose free verse, deliberately empty of tension; so in "Schöne Jugend" ("Lovely Childhood"). The poem contains no symbolism, though perhaps an ironic comparison with a poetic subject, the death of Ophelia:

Der Mund eines Mädchens, das lange in Schilf gelegen hatte,
sah so angeknabbert aus.
Als man die Brust aufbrach, war die Speiseröhre so löcherig.
Schliesslich in einer Laube unter dem Zwerchfell
fand man ein Nest von jungen Ratten.
Ein kleines Schwesterchen lag tot.
Die andern lebten von Leber und Niere,
tranken das kalte Blut und hatten
hier eine schöne Jugend verlebt.
Und schön und schnell kam auch ihr Tod:
Man warf sie allesamt ins Wasser.
Ach, wie die kleinen Schnauzen quietschten!

The mouth of a girl who had long lain among the reeds looked
          gnawed away.
As the breast was cut open, the gullet showed full of holes.
Finally in a cavity below the diaphragm
a nest of young rats was discovered.
One little sister lay dead.
The others thrived on liver and kidneys,
drank the cold blood and
enjoyed a lovely childhood here.
And sweet and swift came their death also:
They were all thrown into the water together.
Oh, how the little muzzles squeaked! [6]

Artistically, this poem is without interest; its shocking impact could have been produced just as easily in prose. Its relation to early Expressionism is a purely superficial one; it expresses the

[6] *Contemporary German Poetry,* trans. Babette Deutsch and A. Yarmolinsky (London, 1923).

spiritual *malaise* common to all the early Expressionists, but, of all the new freedoms, it makes use of only one, and the least essential at that: freedom in the choice of subject matter. Benn had not yet found his characteristic style. Another poem from the same collection comes closer to it; in "Negerbraut" ("Negro's Bride"), Benn is less inhibited by his self-imposed bedside (or bier-side) manner:

> Dann lag auf Kissen dunklen Bluts gebettet
> der blonde Nacken einer weissen Frau.
> Die Sonne wütete in ihren Haar
> und leckte ihr die hellen Schenkel lang
> und kniete um die bräunlicheren Brüste,
> noch unentstellt durch Laster und Geburt.
> Ein Nigger neben ihr: durch Pferdehufschlag
> Augen und Stirn zerfetzt. Der bohrte
> zwei Zehen seines schmutzigen linken Fusses
> ins Innre ihres kleinen weissen Ohrs.
> Sie aber lag und schlief wie eine Braut:
> am Saume ihres Glücks der ersten Liebe
> und wie vorm Aufbruch vieler Himmelfahrten
> des jungen warmen Blutes.
>   Bis man ihr
> das Messer in die weisse Kehle senkte
> und einen Purpurschurz aus totem Blut
> ihr um die Hüften warf.

> Then there lay bedded on cushions of dark blood
> the very fair neck of a white woman.
> The sun was furious with her hair
> and slobbered here the length of her thighs
> and knelt around her somewhat darker breasts,
> undisfigured yet by vice and birth.
> A nigger next to her: his eyes and forehead
> mangled by a horse's hoof. He bored
> two toes of his filthy left foot
> into the inside of her small white ear.
> She, however, lay and slept like a bride:
> on the verge of her happiness, her first love,
> and just as though on her way to many ascensions
> of her youthful warm blood.
>   Until in her,

Deep in her white throat, they sank the blade
and a rich purple apron of dead blood
was thrown around her hips.[7]

The realism here is deceptive, for it serves to render an emotion not at all intrinsic to the phenomenon described. This poem about two corpses manages to convey something of the vitalism that was Benn's reaction to his daily contact with the sick and the dead. The syntax is still that of prose logic; but the rhythms are stronger than in "Schöne Jugend," the irony and cynicism less emphatic. The same vitalism comes out more strongly in the most widely praised poem from this first collection, "Mann und Frau gehn durch die Krebsbaracke"—an uneven poem, but one in which Benn escapes from physical decay to the "superindividuality" of the organic, of the life force:

> . . . Hier schwillt der Acker schon um jedes Bett.
> Fleisch ebnet sich zu Land. Glut gibt sich fort.
> Saft schickt sich an zu rinnen. Erde ruft.—

> . . . Around each bed already ploughed fields swell.
> Flesh levels into land. Heat passes on.
> Juices prepare to flow again. Earth calls.—

Disintegrating bodies, then, were the given reality, because Benn had chosen to be a doctor; but of course there was no more need for him to write about corpses than for Trakl to write about medicine bottles or T. S. Eliot about bank balances. It is not a question of what we know, but of how we place the things we know; whether, nihilistically, we see the phenomenon as isolated or, positively, as part of a larger reality that includes our own consciousness. Benn's compulsion to make poetry out of his immediate experience was an ambivalent one. It was a compulsion to relate the whole of himself to an extreme reality which is usually reserved for the partial attention of specialists, who deal with it by switching off all but their practical faculties; and, since Benn was unable to bear the full weight of this contemplation, it was also a compulsion to detach himself from

[7] From *Wake 12*, trans. Edgar Lohner and Cid Corman (New York, 1953).

the reality more effectively than his practical duties allowed. Hence the occasional sentimentality of these poems—due to a self-identification never complete—and the somewhat gloating cynicism elsewhere.

Benn's next collection, *Söhne,* is dominated by the theme of revolt that became a commonplace of the Expressionist drama: the conflict of generations, or rather the young man's complaint against the parents who stand for smugness, deceit, and corruption. These poems, on the whole, are still somewhat imitative, except where Benn's vitalistic frenzy breaks through. The pathos of such poems as "Mutter" is derivative; Rilke's *Buch der Bilder* seems to have provided the model:

> Ich trage dich wie eine Wunde
> auf meiner Stirn, die sich nicht schliesst.
> Sie schmerzt nicht immer. Und es fliesst
> das Herz sich nicht draus tot.
> Nur manchmal plötzlich bin ich blind und spüre
> Blut im Munde.

> I bear you like a wound
> in my forehead, that will not close.
> It doesn't always hurt. And my heart
> itself does not flow dead from it.
> Only at times I am suddenly blind and find
> Blood in my mouth.[8]

The three poems on cafés are interesting genre pieces, related to the caricatures of George Grosz, who in fact called one of them "Dr. Benn's Café." The diction of these poems takes realism further than in *Morgue;* it brutalizes reality into caricature, as in "Nachtcafé":

> . . . Grüne Zähne, Pickel im Gesicht
> winkt einer Lidrandentzündung.

> Fett im Haar
> spricht zu offnen Mund mit Rachenmandel
> Glaube Liebe Hoffnung um den Hals.

[8] Lohner and Corman, *op. cit.*

Junger Kropf ist Sattelnase gut.
Er bezahlt für sie drei Biere . . .

. . . Green teeth, pimples on his face
waves to conjunctivitis.

Grease in his hair
talks to open mouth with swollen tonsils
faith hope and charity round his neck.

Young goitre is sweet on saddle-nose.
He stands her three half-pints . . .

Most of the poems in the collections that followed *Söhne*—up
to the early nineteen-twenties—were in this vein; they are
much more disgusting than Benn's studies of the dead, because
the dead are less vulnerable to this pseudoscientific mode of vision. In the collection called *Fleisch,* Benn sees human beings
as so much meat which, while alive, also has the misfortune to
be invested with a substance that he calls not "mind" but
"brain." Since "thinking is lonely," there is no bond between
one human being and another; only one's own ego is real, other
people's, at best, are an abstract hypothesis.

   Söhne contains one poem that points to Benn's later style
and thought, his release from the dilemma of realism. The dynamic syntax of "D–Zug" ("Express Train") relates this poem
to Stadler's vitalism, though Benn's is interrupted by a cynicism
that derives from self-division; his poem, therefore, is not all of
a piece. The joints show:

Braun wie Kognak. Braun wie Laub. Rotbraun. Malaiengelb.
D–Zug Berlin—Trelleborg und die Ostseebäder.—

Fleisch, das nackt ging.
Bis in den Mund gebräunt vom Meer.
Reif gesenkt. Zu griechischem Glück.
In Sichel-Sehnsucht: wie weit der Sommer ist!
Vorletzter Tag des neunten Monats schon!—

Stoppel und letzte Mandel lechzt in uns.
Entfaltungen, das Blut, die Müdigkeiten,
Die Georginennähe macht uns wirr.—

Männerbraun stürzt sich auf Frauenbraun:

Eine Frau ist etwas für eine Nacht.
Und wenn es schön war, noch für die nächste!
O! Und dann wieder dies Bei-sich-selbst-sein!
Diese Stummheiten! Dies Getriebenwerden!

Eine Frau ist etwas mit Geruch.
Unsägliches. Stirb hin. Resede.
Darin ist Süden, Hirt und Meer.
An jedem Abhang lehnt ein Glück.——

Frauenhellbraun taumelt an Männerdunkelbraun:

Halte mich! Du, ich falle!
Ich bin im Nacken so müde.
O dieser fiebernde süsse
Letzte Geruch aus den Gärten.——

Brown as cognac. Brown as leaves. Red-brown. Malayan yellow.
Express train Berlin-Trelleborg and the Baltic Sea resorts.

Flesh, that went naked.
Tanned to the very lips by the sea.
Deeply ripe, for Grecian pleasure.
And yearning for the scythe: how far the summer seems!
Almost the end of the ninth month already!

Stubble and the last almond thirst in us.
Unfoldings, the blood, the weariness,
The nearness of dahlias confuses us.

Man-brown hurls itself upon woman-brown:

A woman is something for a night.
And if it was good, for the next night too!
O! And then again this being by oneself!
These silences! This letting oneself drift!

A woman is something with fragrance.
Unspeakable. Dissolve. Reseda.
In her the south, shepherd and sea.
On every slope a pleasure lies.

Woman-light-brown reels towards man-dark-brown:

Hold me, dear; I'm falling.
I'm so weary at the neck.
O, this feverish sweet
Last fragrance blown from the gardens.[9]

Only part of this poem is rendered in imaginative terms; and since the generalizations in the twelfth and thirteenth lines are hardly of universal validity, it was all the more necessary not to make them explicit. Metrically, the poem is too lax to convey the orgiastic impulse behind it; and the realism of the last lines produces a harsh incongruity. But the poem marks Benn's peculiar way of escape out of cerebral isolation. Whether this way deserves the name of "transcendence" is another matter. It is a hedonism of the imagination as much as of the senses. Indeed, the distinction was soon to become irrelevant to Benn's work. Only transitional poems like "D–Zug" and "Untergrundbahn," with their realistic settings, relate Benn's fantasies to their occasion. "Untergrundbahn" ("Underground Train"), from the same early collection, sums up Benn's dilemma and his drastic solution:

> . . . Ein armer Hirnhund, schwer mit Gott behangen.
> Ich bin der Stirn so satt. Oh, ein Gerüste
> Von Blütenkolben löste sanft sie ab
> Und schwölle mit und schauerte und triefte.
>
> So losgelöst. So müde. Ich will wandern.
> Blutlos die Wege. Lieder aus den Gärten.
> Schatten und Sintflut. Fernes Glück: ein Sterben
> hin in des Meeres erlösend tiefes Blut.
>
> . . . A wretched braindog, laden down with God.
> My forehead wearies me. Oh, that a frame
> Of clustered blooms would gently take its place,
> To swell in unison and stream and shudder.
>
> So lax, adrift. So tired. I long to wander.
> The ways all bloodless. Songs that blow from gardens.
> Shadows and Flood. Far joys: a languid dying
> down into ocean's deep redeeming blue.

[9] Adapted from Lohner and Corman, *op. cit.*

Benn's "bestial" or organic "transcendence" and the aesthetic are one and the same. Images of sexual union, from now on, are inextricably mingled with images of a return to the primal source of life, images of tropical or Mediterranean vegetation, images of the sea, images of remote or mythical cultures, the scent of flowers and colors (especially blue, the tropical color that is like an "open Sesame" to Benn's store of associations).

This transcendence is still hampered by a compulsion to incongruous realism in this early collection of poems; but a few years later, in the prose of *Gehirne* (1916), Benn had found a medium that could reconcile his scornful and cynical realism with excursions into pure fantasy. *Gehirne* is a collection of short stories, or rather of autobiographical sketches, which record Benn's release from "reality." Since the hero, Rönne, is a doctor, his "reality" is akin to that of Benn's first poems; he performs his medical duties like a somnambulist, always on the verge of escaping into a more congenial trance, erotic and aesthetic fantasies divorced from his own situation, daydreams of exotic landscapes and tropical flowers. Having dismissed the realities of science as one form of delusion, he turns to a different ambition, "to look for forms and bequeath himself."

In an autobiographical sketch of 1934,[10] Benn admits that the character of Rönne is based on his own—an admission that is almost unnecessary, since Benn rarely wrote with any degree of sympathy about anyone but himself. This is how he describes Rönne in retrospect: "The year 1914/15 in Brussels was enormous, it was then that Rönne was created, the doctor, the flagellant of individual phenomena, the bare vacuum of facts, Rönne who could not bear any reality, nor take any in, who knew only the rhythmic opening and shutting of the ego, the personality." In the same sketch Benn wrote of himself that "he was never free from this trance that there is no such thing as reality."

This trance, as we have seen, has a long history in German literature. Heinrich von Kleist experienced something very much like it after his crisis of 1801, when his reading of Kant convinced him that there was no such thing as absolute truth.

[10] Published in *Doppelleben* (1951); reprinted in *Works IV* (1961), 30.

Kleist too, abandoned science at this time, but continued to be divided between trancelike fantasies and the fascination of bare facts; he became a playwright and storyteller of genius, but also a journalist powerfully attracted to any real event on which he could report with scientific detachment. Benn's experience of this fragmentation of reality was very much more acute. His development after 1914 was a perpetual struggle between his ego and the external world. Total reality had been disposed of; all that remained was the isolated fact and the autonomous fantasy, the two components of his later poetry and prose. *"Disintegration of reality,"* he noted in 1932: "A new phase of cerebralization seems to be approaching, a more frigid, colder phase: one's own existence, history, the universe, only to be grasped in two categories: the abstract concept and hallucination." And again, in his excellent and unusually sober essay on Goethe [11] of the same year: "Progressive cerebralization—seen phylogenetically, conceived in precise historical terms: ever more compulsive the distance between instinct and periphery, between perception and concept, between colour and number, ever more dangerous the tension, ever more destructive the spark: odour of annihilation and burnt flesh throughout the century: Nietzsche . . ."

The following passage from *Gehirne* describes how Rönne succumbs to the fascination of facts:

> Now, there was a picture on the wall: a cow in a meadow. A cow in a meadow, he thought, a round, brown cow, the sky and a field. Ah, what ineffable bliss that picture gave him. There it stands on four legs, one, two, three four legs in a meadow of grass, looking at three sheep, one, two, three sheep —the number! How I love numbers, they're so hard, they're so inviolable from every side, they bristle with unassailability, they're quite unambiguous, it would be ludicrous to find fault with them in any way . . .[12]

This passage, of course, combines the fascination of facts with its complement, hallucination; for these animals appear on a

[11] "Goethe und die Naturwissenschaften," *Die Neue Rundschau*, Vol. XLIII, No. 4 (April, 1932), 488. Reprinted in *Works I* (1959), 162–200.
[12] *Gehirne* (1916), 12.

painting, so that their function is mainly formal. And numbers, in any case, are symbols. Rönne's perversity may be "phenotypal"—one of Benn's favorite words—but it remains perverse. To describe a woman as "a heap of secondary sexual characteristics, grouped in anthropoid fashion"—as Rönne does in his mind—is not more factual or more scientific than to describe her in terms of the popular novelette; and it tells us rather less about her. But it does convey Rönne's state of mind; and *Gehirne* remains a most interesting psychological study, as well as a new intensification of German prose.

Rönne is obsessed by the unreality of other people because he is obsessed by the unreality of his own life: "We have come to the end, he felt, we have outgrown our very last organ. I shall walk along the corridor, and my footfall will resound. For must not a footfall resound in a corridor? Yes, it must, that is life; and what about a little jocular word in passing to the lady official? Yes, indeed, that also!" From this nightmare of convention Rönne escapes to the freedom of fantasy: "Still abandoned to the satisfaction of being able to associate so extensively, he was struck by a glass plate with the inscription: Cigarettes Maita, lit up by a sunbeam. And now via Maita—Malta—beaches—shining—ferry—harbour—guzzling mussels—depravities—the bright ringing tone of a soft dispersal began, and Rönne swayed in an access of joy." From this disparity between his environment and his imagination, Rönne concludes: "What had been the way of humanity hitherto? It had tried to impose order on something that ought to have remained a game. But in the end it had remained a game nonetheless, for nothing was real. Was he real? No; only all things were possible, that was he."

Among other things, Rönne is engaged in trying to "create the new syntax . . . To eliminate the you-character of grammar seemed to him to be required by honesty, for this form of address had become mythical." Strangely enough, Benn was unable to do without the second person in his poetry. In his later poems he commonly addressed a "you" that is purely functional and therefore even more "mythical" than the form he tried to eliminate; this later "you" is a part of Benn's own mind, the poetry a kind of divided soliloquy addressed to himself. This, again, points to the psychopathological aspect of Rönne's withdrawal into solitude, an aspect to which Benn has never drawn attention, convinced, as he is, that Rönne is a "phenotype," the representative of a new stage of "cerebralization." Psychologically, Rönne is a case of "inflated consciousness," which C. G. Jung characterizes as follows: "An inflated consciousness is always egocentric and conscious of nothing but its own presence. It is incapable of learning from the past, incapable of understanding contemporary events, and incapable of drawing right conclusions about the future. It is hypnotized by itself and therefore cannot be argued with. It inevitably dooms itself to calamities that must strike it dead. Paradoxically enough, inflation is a regression of consciousness into unconsciousness." [13] Benn is well aware of the regressive nature of the "transcendence" he advocates; but he justifies it as a biological and metaphysical necessity.

A little poem of this period, one of the two "Gesänge" ("Songs"),[14] renders the regressive urge with classical simplicity:

> O dass wir unsere Ururahnen wären.
> Ein Klümpchen Schleim in einem warmen Moor.
> Leben und Tod, Befruchten und Gebären
> Glitte aus unseren stummen Säften vor.
>
> Ein Algenblatt oder ein Dünenhügel,
> Vom Wind Geformtes und nach unten schwer.
> Schon ein Libellenkopf, ein Möwenflügel
> Wäre zu weit und litte schon zu sehr.

> Oh that we were our primal ancestors,
> A little lump of slime in tepid swamps.
> Our life and death, mating and giving birth
> A gliding forth out of our silent sap.
>
> An alga leaf or hillock on the dunes,
> Shaped by the wind and weighted towards earth.
> A dragonfly's small head, a seagull's wing
> Would be too far advanced in suffering.

[13] C. G. Jung, *Psychology and Alchemy* (London, 1954), 461.
[14] Reprinted in *Trunkene Flut* (1952), 33.

The same urge is present in "Icarus," [15] the most ambitious of
Benn's poems written before the nineteen-twenties. If the two
"Gesänge" are classical, "Icarus" is their romantic counterpart.
The neologisms and the free verse only partly obscure its affin-
ity with the Tennyson of "The Lotos-Eaters" and "Tithonus,"
the romanticism of extreme languor:

1
O Mittag, der mit heissem Heu mein Hirn
zu Wiese, flachem Land und Hirten schwächt,
dass ich hinrinne und, den Arm im Bach,
den Mohn an meine Schläfe ziehe—
o du Weithingewölbter, enthirne doch
stillflügelnd über Fluch und Gram
des Werdens und Geschehns
mein Auge.
Noch durch Geröll der Halde, noch durch Land-aas,
verstaubendes, durch bettelhaft Gezack
der Felsen—überall
das tiefe Mutterblut, die strömende
entstirnte
matte
Getragenheit.

Das Tier lebt Tag um Tag
und hat an seinem Euter kein Erinnern,
der Hang schweigt seine Blume in das Licht
und wird zerstört.

Nur ich, mit Wächter zwischen Blut und Pranke,
ein hirnzerfressenes Aas, mit Flüchen
im Nichts zergellend, bespien mit Worten,
veräfft vom Licht—
o du Weithingewölbter,
träuf meinen Augen eine Stunde
des guten frühen Voraugenlichts—
schmilz hin den Trug der Farben, schwinge
die kotbedrängten Höhlen in das Rauschen
gebäumter Sonnen, Sturz der Sonnen-sonnen,
o aller Sonnen ewiges Gefälle—

[15] *Ibid.*, 29–31.

2

Das Hirn frisst Staub. Die Füsse fressen Staub.
Wäre das Auge rund und abgeschlossen,
dann bräche durch die Lider süsse Nacht,
Gebüsch und Liebe.
Aus dir, du süsses Tierisches,
aus euern Schatten, Schlaf und Haar,
muss ich mein Hirn besteigen,
alle Windungen,
das letzte Zwiegespräch—

3

So sehr am Strand, so sehr schon in der Barke,
im krokosfarbenen Kleide der Geweihten
und um die Glieder schon den leichten Flaum—
ausrauscht du aus den Falten, Sonne,
allnächtlich Welten in den Raum—
o eine der vergesslich hingesprühten
mit junger Glut die Schläfe mir zerschmelzend,
auftrinkend das entstirnte Blut.

1

O noon that with hot hay reduce
my brain to meadow, shepherds and flat land,
so that I flow away, my arm immersed
in the stream's water, and to my brow
draw down the poppies—noon that's vaulted wide,
now mutely winging above the curse and grief
of all that is and will be,
unbrain my eye.
Still through the hillside boulders, still through land-carrion,
turning to dust, through beggarly sharp shapes
of rocks—still everywhere
deep mother-blood, this streaming
deforeheaded
weary
drifting away.

The animal lives only for the day
and in its udder has no memory,
the slope in silence brings its flower to light
and is destroyed.

I only, with a sentry between blood and claw,
mere brain-devoured carrion, shrieking and cursing plunged
into annihilation, bespat with words,
guyed by the light—
O noon that's vaulted wide,
but for one hour infuse my eyes
with that good light which was before eyes were—
melt down the lie of colours, hurl
these cavities pressed by filth into the roar
of rearing suns, whirl of the suns of suns,
o everlasting fall of all the suns—

2

The brain eats dust. Our feet devour the dust.
If but the eye were round and self-contained
then through the lids sweet night would enter in,
brushwood and love.
From you, the sweetly bestial,
from out your shadows, sleep and hair,
I must bestride my brain,
all loops and turns,
the ultimate duologue—

3

So near the beach, so much embarked already,
dressed in the victim's crocus-coloured garment,
and round your limbs the light and delicate down—
O sun, you rustle forth from out your folds
each night new universes into space—
oh, one of these, obliviously scattered here
with its young glow is melting down my temples,
drinks my deforeheaded blood.

"Icarus" may seem more modernist than romantic; but its diction, imagery, and syntax still do not answer all the requirements of the Imagist Manifesto. To begin with, it is a rhetorical poem; though, in parts, it borrows the dynamic syntax of Expressionism, its dynamism is more deliberate, more exclamatory, than that of Heym or Trakl. Much of its imagery could be altered without any loss of significance or effectiveness. It is also romantic in the sense of being a culmination of the European trend that began with Rousseau. Benn's Icarus is the last of a line of poetic *personae* which includes Goethe's Ganymede and Hölderlin's Empedocles; but his sacrifice is a bitter reversal of theirs. Benn's Icarus, too, returns to Nature, but in order to separate himself from the divine; for his God is immanent not in Nature, but in the consciousness that he seeks to destroy. Benn's poem expresses a pantheism in reverse, a suicidal and retrogressive solipsism.

Benn's revival of the doctrine of Art for Art's sake—which he calls *"Artistik"*—is simply another aspect of his denial of "reality," of moral and political institutions, of the importance of history, of all that men achieve by conscious endeavor. "Works of art," he has written,[16] "are phenomena, historically ineffective, without practical consequences. That is their greatness"; and *"Artistik* is the attempt of Art to experience itself as a meaning within the general decay of all meaning, and to form a new style out of this experience; it is the attempt of Art to oppose the general nihilism of values with a new kind of transcendence, the transcendence of creative pleasure. Seen in this way, the concept embraces all the problems of Expressionism, of abstract art, of anti-humanism, atheism, anti-historicism, of cyclicism, of the 'hollow man'—in short, all the problems of the world of expression." [17]

The doctrine itself is not new; it goes back to Nietzsche and, without its conscious connection with nihilism, to the German Romantics and the French Parnassians, Symbolists and Naturalists. Mallarmé and Villiers de L'Isle-Adam went as far as Benn in their disparagement of "reality." In his Oxford lecture on music and literature, Mallarmé said: "Oui, que la Littérature existe, et, si l'on veut, seule, à l'exclusion de tout." Benn has not done better than that; but Mallarmé was a devout Platonist and only denied reality in favor of the Idea. Art, therefore, was truly transcendental, not "autotelic," like a kitten chasing its tail. Mallarmé's disparagement of "reality" was a gesture of sublime scorn that makes Benn's pronouncement sound like the crudest of simplifications; the difference is in the diction. Mal-

[16] *Können Dichter die Welt "ändern,"* in Fazit der Perspektioen, 1930. *Works* V, 215.

[17] *Probleme der Lyrik. Works* I, 500.

larmé's words, too, occur in a lecture, but that was no reason for making them any clearer or any more direct; to do so, would have been a shameful concession to the very "reality" that they scorn: *"Un grand dommage a été causé a l'association terrestre séculairement, de lui indiquer le mirage brutal, la cité, ses gouvernements, le code, autrement que comme emblèmes ou, quant à notre état, ce que des nécropoles sont au paradis qu'elles évaporent: un terreplein, presque pas vil."* One may disagree with that statement, one may even smile at it, but one must respect it in spite of oneself; other men may dismiss human institutions as a brutal mirage, but no one, ever again, will have the courage and the composure to pronounce the "presque pas vil" that qualifies the condemnation.

It is always the qualifications that one misses in Benn's pronouncements. Paul Valéry, too, believed that the outstanding characteristics of true works of art are their uselessness and their arbitrariness; he speaks of the artist's "useless sensations" and "arbitrary acts." But he continues: "The invention of Art has consisted in trying to confer on the former a kind of usefulness; on the latter, a kind of necessity." [18] Because it lacks the necessary qualifications, Benn's statement about the nature of works of art invites contradiction. It is simply untrue to say that works of art are historically ineffective; they have proved to be most effective in modern times, and nowhere more so than in Germany. If Benn meant to say that they ought to be historically ineffective, his statement would be provocative, but valid as a definition of their nature, as opposed to their function; and the same qualification applies to his statement that they have no practical consequences. As for his definition of *Artistik,* it is the definition of a vicious circle; for the "general nihilism of values," which he wants Art to transcend, has been largely brought about by those who—like himself—are out for the destruction of these values. It is only Benn's wholly specious determinism that allows him to regard nihilism as a biological, historical or otherwise general predicament. Nor has Benn been true to his own premises; for he has persistently advocated nihilism as an attitude to life, in terms no less didactic

[18] Paul Valéry, "Notion Génerale de l'art," *Nouvelle Revue Française,* No. 266 (November, 1935), 684–686.

than those of any preacher or humanist. The very word transcendence in that context is meaningless. All that Benn's definition conveys is the fact that human nature abhors a vacuum; for, after denying the seriousness of every human pursuit, he insists that the game which is his own substitute for these pursuits is not only serious, but "transcendent." *Artistik* is a pathetic attempt on Benn's part to climb out of the nihilistic pit that he has dug for others. But reality is indivisible. Art may be a fungus that thrives on the decay of other values, as Benn would have it, but even decay presupposes growth; and Benn would have his fungus grow in the dry dust of organisms which, according to him, were dead even before he began to write.

Perhaps one ought not to take Benn's theories and critical pronouncements too seriously; but though he believes in "absolute prose" and "the absolute poem, the poem without faith, the poem without hope, the poem addressed to no one, the poem made of words which you assemble in a fascinating way," [19] he is also what Valéry called a *poète de la connaissance,* a poet who deals in ideas as much as in words and images. And Valéry also said that "every true poet must necessarily be a critic of the first order." [20] If Benn's "absolute poem" were possible in practice, one could leave his theories alone and confine one's attention to the way he assembles words. But words have a habit of conveying meaning; and when these words are made public, they also have the "practical consequence" of being a means of communication, as well as their essential function of merely existing as "Significant Form" (and even form is *significant,* even where we prefer not to say of what). If Benn had not wished to communicate anything, he would have kept his work to himself; and he would certainly not have troubled to explain the creative process to others, or to defend his own premises with such stubborn persistence. It is therefore necessary to point out a few of the basic inconsistencies that result from Benn's false premises and his egocentric habits of thought.

What Benn means by "absolute prose" is a kind of prose whose primary function is expressive, rather than logical. For that reason, his critical essays may suddenly modulate from

[19] *Works* I, 592.
[20] *Poésie et Pensée Abstraite* (Oxford, 1939), 24.

sober exposition to prose poetry, or even to verse thinly disguised as prose. The following is a passage of this type from an early essay: [21]

> Vier Jahrtausende Menschheit sind gewesen, und Glück und Unglück war immer gleich: Wende dich ab von deinem Nächsten, wird die Lehre sein, wenn jetzt die Memnonsäule klingt.

> Four thousand years of human kind have passed, their fortune and misfortune still the same: to turn your back upon your neighbour, will be the doctrine now, when next old Memnon's statue sounds.

This is a new departure in prose, and an admirable one; it relieves the tedium of prose rhythms and the stale vocabulary of criticism. But even if this passage is addressed to no one, or to Benn himself, it is undoubtedly didactic: it proclaims a philosophy of cyclic recurrence—borrowed from Nietzsche—that is "anti-historical" and "anti-humanistic"; and it specifically invites the (nonexistent?) addressee to turn his back upon his neighbor—in explicitly anti-Christian terms. Benn has done his best to dissociate himself from the commandment, by attributing it to Memnon's oracular statue; but he would need a more subtle device to be able to disclaim responsibility for the doctrine.

Another passage of "absolute prose," from his essay "Das moderne Ich" of 1920, renders the isolation and introversion of the modern poet: [22]

> Erloschenes Auge, Pupille steht nach hinten, nirgends mehr Personen, sondern immer nur das Ich; Ohren verwachsen, lauschend in die Schnecke, doch kein Geschehnis, immer nur das Sein.

> Extinguished eye, the pupil turned about, no persons anywhere, but always only the Ego; ears closed to sound, listening into the helix, but no event, always only being.

[21] "Das moderne Ich," in *Frühe Prosa und Reden,* 165.
[22] *Ibid.,* 171.

It is with amazement, therefore, that one reads Benn's dictum of 1928 [23] that "poets are the tears of the nation," words quite incomprehensible in the context of Benn's work; but they occur in a tribute to a dead writer and friend, on one of the few occasions where Benn leaves the prison of his own ego not in order to sneer, but to praise. One has to make similar allowances for many of Benn's critical utterances, first ascertaining whether they refer to himself or to others. When he says that "God is a bad stylistic principle," he is criticizing others; when he says that "God is form," he is justifying himself, on the same grounds on which he has asserted that "style is superior to truth." Style, however, is not superior to truth, but inseparable from it; that is why Benn is capable of stylistic lapses no less offensive than his half-truths.

On page 53 of his *Ausdruckswelt* (1949), Benn argues that the State has no right to complain of the damage done by artists as long as it wages wars that kill off three million men in the space of three years; on page 107 he writes: "In my opinion, the West is not being destroyed by the totalitarian systems or the crimes of the S.S., nor by its material impoverishment or its Gottwalds and Molotovs, but by the dog-like grovelling of its intellectuals before the political concepts." The blatant contradiction between these two statements can only be understood by allowing for Benn's extraordinary dialectic: in the first instance Benn is referring to intellectuals like himself under a regime hostile to them, in the second to intellectuals hostile to him under a different regime. The real question, of course, is whether or not writers are responsible for what they write; but this is not a question that Benn cares to answer in either context, since he wants one law for himself, another for those whom he dislikes.

Benn's "antihistoricism" is another case in point. His whole view of life and art is based on the assumption that nihilism is a *fait accompli* and that the destructive trends in contemporary Europe are a biological phenomenon. Such a view cannot possibly be called "antihistorical," though it substitutes a biological determinism for both the religious and the humanistic

---

[23] "Totenrede für Klabund," *ibid.*, 206.

conceptions of history. His "antihistoricism" is really an aesthetic doctrine and, more particularly, an excuse for his own addiction to exotic fantasies. This becomes clear from a remark in his "Roman des Phänotyp": [24] "Remote things are much nearer to one than things that are near; indeed, the things that are present are strangeness itself." What Benn is against is not the historical view, but the encroachment of the present on his consciousness. It suits Benn to see himself as a link in that process of "progressive cerebralization" which he associates with the "odour of annihilation and burnt flesh pervading the century" and, ultimately, with the end of the "cycle" known as Western civilization. He has made it clear enough that he finds this odor stimulating artistically; and that his "transcendental" pleasure in art is none other than the pleasure of fiddling while Rome burns. Benn himself describes his method of composition as a "prismatic infantilism. It probably reminds everyone of children's games: we ran about with small pocket mirrors and caught the sun, to cast its reflection on shopkeepers on the other side of the road, arousing anger and ill feeling, but we ourselves kept in the shade." [25]

As a method of composition, this game is beyond criticism; it has led to delightful color effects in prose and verse. One only wishes that Benn had really "kept in the shade"; but he continually drew attention to himself, now to show off his naughtiness, now to protest his innocence. This is the disadvantage of a childish attitude to society: however resourceful and inventive, a child's naughtiness remains dependent on adult standards, and on the adults' capacity to be annoyed. Benn's lapses of style and taste are due to a childish egocentricity, a childish lack of tact. His attitude to society has not changed since the nineteen-twenties, when he wrote:

> . . . die Massenglücke
> sind schon tränennah,
> bald ist die Lücke
> für die Trance da . . .

[24] 1944, published in *Der Ptolemäer* (1949), 47.
[25] *Ibid.*, 137–138.

. . . mass pleasures mass joy
are closer to tears
already a gap clears
for trance to break through . . .

Trance certainly did break through about a decade later; but
when Benn discovered that this general trance was not conducive to his private one, it never seems to have occurred to him
that his attitude called for revision. Writing of Berlin in 1947,[26]
he describes the ruined city, its starving population, and the
luxuries imported by the occupation forces; and continues:
"The population looks on greedily through the windows: culture is advancing again, little murder, more song and rhythm.
Inwardly too the defeated are well provided for: a transatlantic
bishop arrives and murmurs: my brethren;—a humanist appears and chants: the West;—a tenor wheedles: O lovely Art,
—the reconstruction of Europe is in progress."

The bad taste of that observation is especially offensive because "O lovely Art" is also a summary of Benn's own creed;
and since he regards art as a drug, he has no grounds at all for
thinking his own variety superior to any other. The value of a
drug is measured by its effectiveness. The same moral obtuse-
ness has permitted him to enumerate the misfortunes of his own
family in the Preface to his *Ausdruckswelt,* a work in which he
elaborates his antihumanism and criticizes the Nazi regime on
no other grounds than its lack of "style" and its lack of understanding for the independent artist. If the reader accepts Benn's
standards, he must reject this account of Benn's family as irrelevant; if he sympathizes with Benn or with Benn's family, he
must reject Benn's standards. This question of sympathy arises
frequently over Benn's prose works, strange mixture of fact and
fantasy, statistics and self-confession that they are. It is peculiarly irritating to be asked for sympathy on one page, only to
have it violently rejected on the next, when the pervading mood
of cynical or stoical toughness takes over from a passing mawk-
ish one.

Benn is Baudelaire's "dandy" up to date, *au fait* with all the
sciences and even with the newspapers; Benn too "ne sort ja-

[26] *Ibid.,* 107.

mais de soi-même." But the dandy was only one of Baudelaire's *personae;* Baudelaire was also the "homme des foules," who could lose himself in others and complete himself. Like every great poet, he contained a moralist. Benn's chief limitation as a poet and critic is that nearly all his thinking is determined by a reaction against one thing or another—against literary or ideological fashions, against a bourgeoisie already hard pressed from other directions, or against his own better nature; but reaction is only a different sort of dependence. Always to be sneering at the vulgar is a sort of vulgarity.

With very few exceptions—the essay on Goethe and the natural sciences is an outstanding one—Benn's prose writings are not an exploration of other minds, but comments on his own practice and justifications of his own attitude. He has even found it necessary to assure his readers that he is human by writing an account of his "double life" (*Doppelleben*); here the difficulty of reconciling his two selves—the conscientious doctor and the amoral artist—has proved insuperable and involved him in arguments too silly and too casuistic to bear repetition. The sharp self-awareness that results from self-division has enabled him to write brilliantly about the creative process, as experienced by himself; particularly in *Probleme der Lyrik*. His belief in "absolute" prose and poetry—that is, in prose and poetry written for their own sake, without a primarily didactic purpose—has had the very salutary effect of opposing the tendency, still very wide-spread in Germany at the time, to think that poetry is only a matter of expressing sublime sentiments in regular stanzas. He has made up for the early Expressionists' indifference to questions of form and diction; but he has done so with an exclusive emphasis on art as self-expression—or rather as self-indulgence—which may well have repelled readers more squeamish than he.

Benn's writings are highly exhilarating and abysmally depressing in turn, as befits an intoxicant. They can induce a euphoria of infinite possibilities, which results from the total release of energy from the bonds of reason; and a corresponding hangover, when Benn returns to himself and reminds us that despair is the mother of all his inventions. Self-pity is the chink in Benn's armor, as in Nietzsche's, who also dramatized his solitude, though with more justification than Benn; for in spite of his claim to the contrary, Benn's solitude is less extreme than Nietzsche's, if only because Nietzsche had already charted the place. Benn himself has summed up his dilemma; but for "we," read "I": "We lived something different from what we were, we wrote something different from what we thought, we thought something different from what we expected and what remains is something different from what we intended." [27]

It is probably too early to say what will remain of Benn's work; generally, one is inclined to agree with him, that which was furthest from his intentions, furthest from the tedious dialectic of nihilism. In view of his professed aestheticism, one might expect his poetry to have the consistent quality of—say —Valéry's, Stefan George's or, of his own generation, Trakl's; but even Benn's aesthetic standards are curiously unreliable. Almost every one of his collections contain pieces that are not only grossly inferior to his best work, but simply unformed— cerebral jottings in loose free verse or mechanical rhyme that all too clearly communicate something—Benn's concern with his own ego or with ideas not realized poetically. Again it is Benn who has indicated the reason, in one of the few passages of a late work that qualify his earlier views: [28] "Nihilism as the negation of history, actuality, affirmation of life, is a great quality; but as the negation of reality itself, it means a diminution of the ego."

But, as his last collections show, Benn continued to diminish his ego by perpetuating the quarrel between subject and object which—however fruitful a field for metaphysicians—is full of dangers for modern poetry. I have already said that all poetry, whatever its theme, affirms life; it does so because form itself is the progeny of the marriage of mind and matter. Only the unformed poem, the bad poem, can be negative. That is why Benn's "subjectivity" is depressing: subjectivity did not become odious until the first ego asserted its independence from the external world; Pascal's *moi haïssable* was the direct consequence of the *cogito ergo sum* of Descartes. The ego has been

[27] *Drei Alte Männer* (1949), 22.
[28] Preface to *Ausdruckswelt*, 8.

growing more and more odious since, because more and more interested in its own reflection in the mirror. Benn's nihilism and Winckler's "affliction of thinking" are the recoil of consciousness from a mirror that has lost its mercury and become a blank prison wall. Very little of Benn's work breaks down this prison wall; but what little of it does so derives a special importance from the point where this breach is made. *Ex nihilo nihil fit;* if Benn's best poems seem to contradict this maxim, it is because they affirm life despite their author's intention. (And of course it is nonsense to affirm "reality" without affirming life, as Benn claims to have done, unless by life he means only some particular mode or manifestation of life, an environment he dislikes.) The poems of Benn's best period, the early nineteen-twenties, are almost consistently remarkable; but only two or three of them are faultless. The difference has to do with truth as much as with style; for the fault is always due to the intrusion of irrelevant ideas and inessential phenomena into a poem that ought to have been purely imaginative; and these ideas and phenomena always appertain to Benn's immediate environment. The most blatant of these faults is the introduction of abstract neologisms and scientific terms—witty, and therefore self-conscious—where they have no business to occur. I refer to such new compound words as *Bewusstseinsträger* (consciousness-bearer), *Satzbordell* (sentence brothel) and *Tierschutzmäzene* (Maecenases of the R. S. P. C. A.) and of scientific terms like *Selbsterreger* (auto-exciter), used in the manner of clever journalism. These words—and many more of the same kind—appear in Benn's most outstanding collection of poems, his *Spaltung* of 1925. Of the twenty-eight poems in this book, only one is wholly free from such satirical irrelevances; and one or two more are successful in spite of them, because the tension between myth and modernity is essential to them.

These poems, unfortunately, are the least translatable, precisely because they are the nearest possible approximation to Benn's ideal of "absolute poetry." As an example of the fruitful tension between myth and modernity—and of a single line that is "absolute" in the sense of being pure music—I shall quote the opening stanza of "Die Dänin":

Charon oder die Hermen
oder der Daimlerflug
was aus den Weltenschwärmen
tief dich im Atem trug,
war deine Mutter im Haine
südlich, Thalassa, o lau—
trug deine Mutter alleine
dich, den nördlichen Tau—

Benn has never written with greater mastery than at this time and in this medium—poems in trochaic or sprung rhythms, in short lines with alternating feminine and masculine rhymes. The poem quoted, as it happens, is one positive even in theme, a poem in praise of a Danish girl, which affirms the present as well as the mythical past, Greece and Scandinavia; because of this affirmation, there is no incongruity in the "Daimlerflug" of the second line. The line of "absolute poetry" to which I alluded—"südlich, Thalassa, o lau"—is an elliptical rendering of the whole Mediterranean and tropical complex so rich in associations for Benn; he is particularly addicted to the "au" sound in southern contexts, probably because it rhymes with "blau" and therefore evokes a vision of blue skies and seas. And indeed the color itself presents itself without fail in the next stanza:

meerisch lagernde Stunde,
Bläue, mythischer Flor . . .

In the later stanzas, unfortunately, the tension between past and present is heightened almost to breaking point, again out of a self-conscious ingenuity, a virtuosity bordering on the specious:

Philosophia perennis
Hegels schauender Akt:—
Biologie und Tennis
über Verrat geflaggt.

Benn's tendency to be distracted into the merely topical or into abstract slogans would not matter so much if it were confined to separate poems like the jazzy, polyglot, and obscene "Banane-," though even this poem detracts from the others by parodying them. Benn summed up his purpose at the time in the phrase *trunken cerebral,* (drunkenly cerebral); his poems break down where they become cerebral without being drunken. This is always due to his basic self-division, which assumes the guise of a conflict between inward and outward reality. When this conflict becomes too acute, the mind cries out for its own dissolution or for the destruction of the world. Most of his poems of this period dwell on the second possibility; but where they do so with sufficient intensity, the conflict itself is reconciled and Benn's very nihilism becomes an affirmation of life. So in "Namenlos," "Spuk," and—most flawlessly of all—in "Palau." True, what "Palau" affirms is a biological life force, "bestial" and indestructible; but its philosophical implications are suspended, because it never lapses into cerebral abstractions:

"Rot ist der Abend auf der Insel von Palau
und die Schatten sinken—"
singe, auch aus den Kelchen der Frau
lässt es sich trinken,
Totenvögel schrein
und die Totenuhren
pochen, bald wird es sein
Nacht und Lemuren.

Heisse Riffe. Aus Eukalypten geht
Tropik und Palmung,
was sich noch hält und steht,
will auch Zermalmung
bis in das Gliederlos,
bis in die Leere,
tief in den Schöpfungsschoss
dämmernder Meere.

Rot ist der Abend auf der Insel von Palau
und im Schattenschimmer
hebt sich steigend aus Dämmer und Tau:
"Niemals und Immer"
alle Tode der Welt
sind Fähren und Furten,

und von Fremden umstellt
auch deine Geburten—

einmal mit Opferfett
auf dem Piniengerüste
trägt sich dein Flammenbett
wie Wein zur Küste,
Megalithen zuhauf
und die Gräber und Hallen,
Hammer des Thor im Lauf
zu den Asen zerfallen—

wie die Götter vergehn
und die grossen Cäsaren,
von der Wange des Zeus
emporgefahren—
singe, wandert die Welt
schon in fremdestem Schwunge
schmeckt uns das Charonsgeld
längst unter der Zunge—

Paarung. Dein Meer belebt
Sepien, Korallen,
was sich noch hält und schwebt,
will auch zerfallen,
rot ist der Abend auf der Insel von Palau,
Eukalyptenschimmer
hebt in Runen aus Dämmer und Tau:
Niemals und Immer.

"Evening is red on the island of Palau
and the shadows sink—"
sing, from woman's chalices too
it is good to drink,
deathly the little owls cry
and the death-watch ticks out
very soon it will be
Lemures and night.

Hot these reefs. From eucalypti there flows
a tropical palm concoction,
all that still holds and stays
also longs for destruction
down to the limbless stage,

down to the vacuum,
back to the primal age,
dark ocean's womb.

Evening is red on the island of Palau
in the gleam of these shadows
there issues rising from twilight and dew:
"Never and Always";
all the deaths of the earth
are fords and ferries,
what to you owes its birth
surrounded with strangeness—

once with sacrificial
fat on the pine-wood floor
your bed of flames would travel
like wine to the shore,
megaliths heaped around
and the graves and the halls,
hammer of Thor that's bound
for the Aesir, crumbled, falls—

as the gods surcease,
the great Caesars decline,
from the cheek of Zeus
once raised up to reign—
sing, already the world
to the strangest rhythm is swung,
Charon's coin if not curled
long tasted under the tongue—

Coupling. Sepias your seas
and coral animate,
all that still holds and sways
also longs to disintegrate,
evening is red on the island of Palau,
eucalyptus glaze
raises in runes from twilight and dew:
Never and Always.

"Palau" transcends nihilism not because it is "absolute" in any
sense invented by Benn, but rather because in it Benn has
found the precise "objective correlative" for his state of mind.
The poem, therefore, is positive, even if the state of mind is

not; it is a poem of tragic affirmation and, as such, requires no reference to the author's intentions or beliefs. Benn's best poems succeed in spite of his theories, because he could not keep reality out of them. He could be indifferent to the meaning of his poetry and to its effect on others; he could disclaim responsibility for it on the grounds that he had no other purpose than to express or please himself; but he could not prevent the isolated fact and the autonomous fantasy from returning to the indivisible reality of which they are parts. He could banish his mind to an island, but he could not make that island disappear from the universe.

Gottfried Benn is one of the very few Expressionist poets who did their best work during Phase II, the interwar years. It was not till his incantatory poems of the nineteen-twenties that he learned to avail himself of the new freedoms and to combine them with a discipline peculiar to his work. "Palau" makes good use of the dynamic syntax of Expressionism, but its form is much closer to that of the choric poems in Goethe's *Faust* than to any verse form cultivated by the other Expressionists.

With Benn's later work—that of the period which he called Phase II and I have called Phase III of Expressionism—I can deal only very briefly here. Already his *Statische Gedichte,* a collection of poems written mainly between 1937 and 1947, contains poems in at least three distinct styles: the incantatory style of "Palau," a more sober neoclassical style—sometimes clearly derivative from Goethe's later lyrics, as in the poem "Ach, der Erhabene"—and a self-consciously "modern" style mainly confined to poems in loose free verse. These three styles recur in Benn's last collections.

But for his prose works of the same period, which remained as provocative as his earlier ones, it would be clear to everyone that what Benn calls "Phase II" is no more than an "aprèslude" [29] to Expressionism. Indeed, even his late prose works are not quite as belligerent as the earlier, though one has to read between the lines—or skip a good many—to arrive at the truth about a development that Benn has done his best to

---

[29] *Aprèslude* (1955) was Gottfried Benn's last collection of poems.

resist. His *Drei Alte Männer,* published in 1949, belongs to a genre especially dear to Benn, being a peculiar mixture of fact and fantasy, prose lyricism and polemical journalism. The three old men of the title meet at the house of one of them to reflect on their experiences of the past, discuss their attitude to the present, and prove their superiority to the future—in the shape of a young man whose main function is to prompt the main speakers. These speakers are not sufficiently differentiated to qualify as distinct characters; their dialectic is that of Benn's own mind; and their preoccupations those which we know to be his own. Many of their utterances are mere reiterations of the nihilistic or aesthetic commonplaces familiar enough from the earlier works. "God is a drug," for instance; "the only thing that really belongs to us is what we drink"; or "we only live when we forget." But there is also a new note, a mood of melancholy resignation and hopeless courage. "We were a great generation," one of them says: "sorrow and light, verses and weapons, sorrow and light, and when night comes, we shall endure it." The nihilism is unchanged, but it has lost its dynamism, its ecstasy, and its aggressiveness. These old men too speak of the "occidental finale: to believe that something exists," but instead of mocking this belief—as Benn did a decade earlier, in his *Weinhaus Wolf*—they attribute the greatness of Western man to its recurrence after every possible kind of breakdown. The main trend of *Drei Alte Männer* is toward a stoical acceptance of the worst: "To err, and yet to be compelled to renew his belief in his own inner motives, that is man; and beyond both victory and defeat his fame begins."

Die Stimme hinter dem Vorhang (The Voice Behind the Curtain), a later work by three years, is also a conversation piece. The voice is that of the Father; and "the programme is: what does the progenitor say to his sons and daughters— nowadays." A number of "examples"—presumably meant to be representative of these sons and daughters—give accounts of themselves. There is a man of sixty whose chief aim in life is to commit adultery with young women; an old-age pensioner who is content to let the government provide for him and hopes that "the others will die" before his turn comes; a woman who keeps a brothel that caters for all tastes; and a landlord who is obsessed with different ways of exploiting and cheating his tenants without infringing the law. When they first appear, these characters profess the belief that "what is holy is manifested in all things." In the second part, various sons and daughters confront the Father with a Sunday paper, which provides them with opportunities to poke fun at such institutions as modern democracy, psychoanalysis, and the P.E.N. Club. Their taunts and complaints culminate in more serious accusations, but mainly that of cruelty and indifference to their well-being. To every charge the Father replies: "Well, what do you expect," but finally loses patience and roars out a string of coarse insults that put an end to the discussion. The third conversation takes place two months later, when the "examples" reappear with a Chorus; they accept the fact that "the Old Man too has left us in the lurch" and decide to make do without him. Once again, resignation is their last resort: "To live in the dark, in the dark to do what we can."

In *Monologische Kunst*—? (1953)—an exchange of letters between Gottfried Benn and the Austrian poet Alexander Lernet-Holenia—Benn answers his correspondent's objections to this unorthodox morality play. He argues that faith is a gift which has not been granted to him; that he does not deny the existence of a Creator, but that a "distant" relationship to Him is preferable to one that "exploits God" by too immediate a dependence. "To gape at Him continually with eyes and lips, in my view, is a great offence, for it presupposes that we mean something to Him, while my veneration assumes that He only passes through us with some force, with very limited force, and that it then passes on to something other than ourselves." Lernet-Holenia also tells Benn that "it is time you began to speak to the Nation," proposing the example of Hofmannsthal and warning Benn that it was solitude that brought about Nietzsche's ruin. Benn defends both Nietzsche's solitude and his own; but after rightly distinguishing between Nietzsche's solitary habits and his mental isolation from the community, he proceeds to confuse the issue by a discussion of his own personal habits. Benn affirms that he will not try to emulate the cultural rôle of Hofmannsthal, a rôle for which he was wholly unfitted; but he does qualify his earlier insistence on the totally isolated ego. He admits a certain invisible link between one ego and another, as he must after professing belief in the Creator. "Express your I," he concludes, "and you will be passing on your life to the Thou, passing on your loneliness to the community and the distance."

Both in *Monologische Kunst*—? and another late prose work, "Altern als Problem für Künstler" (1954), Benn still insists on the antinomy between truth and style. The last fifty years, he claims in the essay on Nietzsche appended to the former work, were marked by strange movements, "above all, by those that have done away with truth and laid the foundations of style." In the later work, an interesting investigation of the effect of old age on artistic production,[30] he repeats that "art, of course, isn't concerned with truth at all, only with expression." But "style," one of his old men says, "is exaggeration; expression is arrogance and suppression: by such foul methods the mind proceeds." Literature, to Gottfried Benn, remained a form of self-indulgence, the most effective of the drugs that make life bearable. It is therefore of the same order as any other stimulant or narcotic, such as crime, which one of his characters recommends for similar reasons: "And indeed only crime gets us any further." [31]

There is something admirable as well as pathetic about these attempts of Benn's to cheer himself up and startle his readers with squibs kept in storage for thirty years or more; but the poem knows better than the poet, and much of Benn's later poetry contradicts this obstinate clinging to his function of *enfant terrible* and *fort esprit*. Of Benn's three styles in his collections of the nineteen-fifties the neoclassical was a neutral, impersonal style almost free from the more drastically expressive syntax of his modernist phase. Many of the best poems in *Fragmente, Destillationen,* and *Aprèslude* are of this kind, regardless of theories that Benn continued to expound. "Blaue Stunde," for instance, is a love poem, clearly addressed to someone, and someone other than Benn himself. All of them

---

[30] Translated as "Artists and Old Age" in *Partisan Review,* Vol. XXII, No. 3 (Summer, 1955); reprinted in Gottfried Benn, *Primal Vision* (New York and London, 1958).

[31] *Die Stimme hinter dem Vorhang,* 33.

communicate something that would be valid even if translated into prose. The lessons of recent history are implicit everywhere behind the stoical despair—tinged with remorse in "Die Gitter" or even with compassion in "Denk der Vergeblichen." The informal free-verse poems, on the other hand, may look like a reversion to Benn's earliest mode, to the manner of *Morgue, Söhne,* and *Fleisch.* Yet Benn's unacknowledged change of heart is even more striking in these informal pieces than in the best of the neoclassical poems, such as "Der Dunkle," "Jener," and "Eingeengt." The informal, less general and less abstract diction of the free-verse poems admits not only direct personal experience but the historical consciousness that Benn had done his best to oppose and exclude in the interwar years. Indeed, the deliberate prosiness of his late free verse is at the opposite pole to "absolute poetry," as defined by Benn or by his French predecessors. It is close to the practice of Brecht and to that of younger poets writing after World War II. Part of the poem "Spät" (in *Destillationen*) corresponds word for word with a passage in the prose dialogue *Die Stimme hinter dem Vorhang.* Whereas in the earlier phase Benn's prose had tended to erupt into lyricism, in the later phase quite a number of his poems tended toward the rhythms, diction, and syntax of prose. So in "Ideelles Weiterleben?" ("Ideal Survival?"):

Bald
ein abgesägter, überholter
früh oder auch spät verstorbener Mann,
von dem man spricht wie von einer Sängerin
mit ausgesungenem Sopran
oder vom kleinen Hölty mit seinen paar Versen—
noch weniger: Durchschnitt,
nie geflogen,
keinen Borgward gefahren—
Zehnpfennigstücke für die Tram,
im Höchstfall Umsteiger.

Dabei ging täglich soviel bei dir durch
introvertiert, extrovertiert,
Nahrungssorgen, Ehewidrigkeit, Steuermoral—
mit allem musstest du dich befassen,
ein gerüttelt Mass von Leben in mancherlei Gestalt.

Auf einer Karte aus Antibes,
die ich heute erhielt,
ragt eine Burg in die Méditerranée,
eine fanatische Sache:
südlich, meerisch, schneeig, am Rande hochgebirgig—
Jahrhunderte, dramatisiert,
ragen, ruhen, glänzen, firnen, strotzen
sich in die Aufnahme—
Nichts von alledem bei dir,
keine Ingredienzien zu einer Ansichtskarte—
Zehnpfennigstücke für die Tram,
Umsteiger,
und schnell die obenerwähnte Wortprägung:
überholt.

Soon
a sawed-off, out-of-date
man who died early or maybe late,
of whom one speaks as of a singer
whose soprano is worn out
or of poor little Todhunter and his handful of verses—
even less: average,
never flew in a plane,
never drove a Borgward—
pennies paid out on the tram
a return fare at the most.

Yet daily so much passed through you
introverted, extroverted,
money troubles, marriage vexations, tax morality—
with all these you had to concern yourself,
a full measure of life in many a shape.

On a postcard from Antibes
which I received today
a castle looms over la Méditerranée,
a fanatical object, that:
southerly, snowy, marine, alpine at the edges—
centuries, dramatized,
loom, rest, gleam, glaze, swell
into the photograph—
Nothing of all this about you,
no ingredients at all for a picture postcard—

pennies paid out on the tram
return fares,
and quickly then the above-named caption:
out of date.

The person, as well as the subject, of that poem is the man whom Benn had once relegated to a life separate and distinct from that of the "absolute" poet. Although Benn retains his habit of addressing himself in the second person, the autobiographical character of the poem is as unmistakable as its concern with an order of reality, the empirical and worldly, which Benn's ecstatic poem of the nineteen-twenties had negated or dissolved in an inward flux. The relaxation of this poem's gesture is carried to the point of slackness, as in the placing of the word "man" (line 4) so close to the "Mann" of line 3.

Another reversal of Benn's premises and assumptions occurs in the late poem "Menschen Getroffen" ("People Met"), which not only admits but celebrates the "neighbour" so consistently banished from his earlier works. But for those premises and assumptions Benn's belated recognition here that other people exist might seem so naïve or perverse as to make the reader wonder not at those people but at the poet's wonderment:

Ich habe Menschen getroffen, die,
Wenn man sie nach ihrem Namen fragte,
Schüchtern—als ob sie garnicht beanspruchen könnten,
Auch noch eine Benennung zu haben—
"Fräulein Christian" antworteten und dann:
"Wie der Vorname," sie wollten einem die Erfassung erleicht-
                                                      ern,
Kein schwieriger Name wie "Popiol" oder "Babendererde"—
"Wie der Vorname"—bitte, belasten Sie Ihr Erinnerungs-
                                            vermögen nicht!

Ich habe Menschen getroffen, die
Mit Eltern und vier Geschwistern in einer Stube
Aufwuchsen, nachts, die Finger in den Ohren,
Am Küchenherde lernten,
Hochkamen, äusserlich schön und ladylike wie Gräfinen—
Und innerlich sanft und fleissig wie Nausikaa,
Die reine Stirn der Engel trugen.

Ich habe mich oft gefragt und keine Antwort gefunden,
Woher das Sanfte und das Gute kommt,
Weiss es auch heute nicht und muss nun gehn.

I have met people who, when asked what their names were,
Apologetically, as if they had no right to claim one's attention
Even with an appellation, would answer,
"Miss Vivian," then add, "Just like the Christian name";
They wanted to make things easier, no complicated names
Like Popkiss or Umpleby-Dunball—
"Just like the Christian name"—so please do not burden your
                                                                                memory!

I have met people who grew up in a single room together with
Parents and four brothers and sisters; they studied by night,
Their fingers in their ears, beside the kitchen range;
They became eminent,
Outwardly beautiful, veritable *grandes dames,* and
Inwardly gentle and active as Nausicaa,
With brows clear as angels' brows.

Often I have asked myself, but found no answer,
Where gentleness and goodness can possibly come from;
Even today I can't tell, and it's time to be gone.[32]

What matters is that Benn continued to develop as a poet until his death at the age of seventy—even while denying the change of heart which made that development possible. Benn's "Phase III" of Expressionism may strike us as a reluctant retreat from a position that history had made untenable, but the retreat did carry his poetry over into the postwar, post-Expressionist and post-modernist era, as well as enabling others to bridge the same gap; and as Benn wrote in his *Epilogue* (1949) to his early and late work:

> Leben ist Brückenschlagen
> über Ströme die vergehn.
>
> Life is the building of bridges
> over rivers that seep away.

32 *Primal Vision,* trans. Christopher Middleton, 289.

In a different and more crucial sense, it is Benn's earlier, exclusively and frenziedly expressive work that is regressive, because its intensity was attained at the cost of reason and consciousness, the emotional drive channeled as narrowly as possible to produce the more energy. Unlike the singing voice of Benn's more ecstatic poems—those written in the nineteentwenties—the speaking voice of the late free-verse poems is that of a civilized man, aware of history, of society, of the little realities that make up our outward lives. Whether he acknowledged it or not, Benn had seen or sensed the connection between absolute art and absolute politics, alike in their total rejection and elimination of all that is not grist to their mill, and the poet had learned the lesson, even if the essayist and public speaker had not. Seen as a whole, Benn's poetry has the full range and tension of those perennial contraries Reason and Energy, realism and imagination, phenomenon and idea; and he produced rather more than the "six or eight consummate poems," which he claimed to be all that a poet of his time could achieve.

Selected Bibliography

Only texts and translations are listed here. Secondary sources drawn upon are named in the text or notes.

BENN, GOTTFRIED. *Gesammelte Werke,* ed. Dieter Wellershoff. 4 vols. Wiesbaden: Limes Verlag, 1958–1961.
————. *Primal Vision,* ed. E. B. Ashton. New York: New Directions; London: The Bodley Head, 1958.
BÜCHNER, GEORG. *Werke und Briefe,* ed. Fritz Bergemann. Leipzig: Insel-Verlag, 1949; Frankfurt: Insel-Verlag, 1958.
————. *The Plays of Georg Büchner.* Translated by Geoffrey Dunlop. London: Vision Press; New York, 1928.
————. *Lenz.* Translated by Michael Hamburger, in *Three German Classics.* London: Calder & Boyars, 1966.
HEINE, HEINRICH. *Sämtliche Werke,* eds. Rudolf Fürst, Julius Zeitler, and Rudolf Unger. 10 vols. Leipzig: Tempel-Verlag, n.d. Paperback edition by Hans Kaufmann, 14 vols. Munich: Kindler, 1964.
————. *Der Salon.* 4 vols. Hamburg: Hoffmann und Campe, 1852–1861.

————. *The North Sea.* Translated by Vernon Watkins. London: Faber & Faber; New York: New Directions, 1955.

HEYM, GEORG. *Dichtungen und Schriften,* ed. K. L. Schneider. 4 vols. Hamburg: Heinrich Ellermann, 1960–1968.

HÖLDERLIN, J. C. F. *Sämtliche Werke. Grosser Stuttgarter Ausgabe,* eds. Friedrich Beissner and Adolf Beck. Stuttgart: Kohlhammer, Vols. I to VII(i), 1943–1968 (not yet complete). Several of the volumes are in two parts, referred to as (i) or (ii), the second of which contains variant readings and notes.

————. *Sämtliche Werke und Briefe,* ed. Franz Zinkernagel. 5 vols. Leipzig: Insel-Verlag, 1914–1926.

————. *Poems and Fragments.* Translated by Michael Hamburger. London: Routledge & Kegan Paul, 1966; Ann Arbor, Michigan: The University of Michigan Press, 1967.

KLEIST, HEINRICH. *Sämtliche Werke und Briefe,* ed. Helmut Sembdner. 2 vols. Munich: Carl Hanser Verlag, 1953. One-volume edition, 1966. Paperback edition, 7 vols., 1964.

————. *The Marquise of O.—and Other Stories.* Translated by Martin Greenberg. New York: Criterion Books, 1960; London: Faber & Faber, 1962.

————. *Penthesilea,* translated by Humphry Trevelyan, and *The Prince of Homburg,* translated by James Kirkup, in *The Classic Theater,* ed. Eric Bentley. New York: Doubleday Anchor Books, 1959.

LICHTENSTEIN, ALFRED. *Gedichte und Geschichten.* 2 vols. Munich: Georg Müller, 1919.

MANN, THOMAS. *Werke.* 20 vols. Frankfurt: S. Fischer, 1967 and 1968.

Modern German Poetry 1910–1960. Bilingual anthology, eds. Michael Hamburger and Christopher Middleton. London: MacGibbon & Kee; New York: Grove Press, 1963.

NIETZSCHE, FRIEDRICH. *Werke,* ed. Karl Schlechta. 3 vols. and Index volume. Munich: Carl Hanser, 1954–1965.

————. *Friedrich Nietzsches Werke des Zusammenbruchs,* ed. Erich F. Podach. Heidelberg: Rothe, 1961.

————. *The Complete Works of Friedrich Nietzsche,* ed. Oscar Levy. 18 vols. Edinburgh; London: T. N. Foulis, 1909–1913; New York.

————. *The Portable Nietzsche.* Selected and translated by Walter Kaufmann. New York: Viking Press, n.d.

————. *Thus Spoke Zarathustra.* Translated by R. J. Hollingdale. Harmondsworth, Middlesex: Penguin Books, 1961.

Novalis. *Schriften*, ed. J. Minor. 5 vols. Jena: Eugen Diederichs, 1923.

————. *Schriften*, eds. Paul Kluckhohn and Richard Samuel. 4 vols. Leipzig: Bibliographisches Institut, 1929.

————. *Schriften*, eds. Ludwig Tieck and Friedrich Schlegel. Paris: Tétot Frères, 1837.

Stadler, Ernst. *Dichtungen*, ed. K. L. Schneider. 2 vols. Hamburg: Heinrich Ellermann, 1954.

Stramm, August. *Die Gesammelten Dichtungen*. 3 vols. Berlin: Verlag "Der Sturm," 1919.

Trakl, Georg. *Die Dichtungen*, ed. Kurt Horwitz. Zurich: Die Arche, 1946.

————. *Gesamtausgabe*, ed. Wolfgang Schneditz. 3 vols. Salzburg: Otto Müller, 1939–1949. New critical edition by Walther Killy in preparation.

————. *Erinnerungen an Georg Trakl*. Salzburg: Otto Müller, 1959.

————. *Selected Poems*, ed. Christopher Middleton. London: Jonathan Cape, 1968; New York: Grossman, 1969.

Van Hoddis, Jacob. *Weltende*. Berlin: Verlag "Aktion," 1918.

THE AUTHOR

Michael Hamburger was born in 1924 and educated in Berlin, Edinburgh, London, and Oxford. After four years in the army and four years of writing, he became a university lecturer. Until 1964 he was Reader in German at the University of Reading. Since then he has devoted most of his time to writing, although recently he served as a visiting professor at the State University of New York, Buffalo.

Among Mr. Hamburger's translations are: *Twenty Prose Poems of Baudelaire, Beethoven: Letters, Journals and Conversations, Hugo von Hofmannsthal: Selected Plays and Libretti,* and *Hölderlin: Poems and Fragments.* For these and other works Mr. Hamburger has been awarded a number of international translation prizes, including that of the Deutsche Akademie für Sprache und Dichtung.

Flowering Cactus, The Dual Site, Weather and Season, and *Travelling: Poems 1963–1968* are among Mr. Hamburger's volumes of poetry. And as a critic he has also published *Reason and Energy, From Prophecy to Exorcism,* and, most recently, *The Truth of Poetry.*

Mr. Hamburger lives and works in London.